A HERO OF OUR OWN

A HERO OF OUR OWN

||||||||||||||||||||||||||

The Story of Varian Fry

SHEILA ISENBERG

 RANDOM HOUSE   NEW YORK

RANDOM HOUSE and colophon are registered trademarks
of Random House, Inc.

Library of Congress Cataloging-in-Publication Data
Isenberg, Sheila.
A hero of our own: The story of Varian Fry / Sheila Isenberg.
    p.   cm.
Includes bibliographical references and index.
ISBN 0-375-50221-1
1. Fry, Varian. 2. Righteous Gentiles in the Holocaust—United States.
3. World War, 1939–1945—Jews—Rescue—France. 4. Holocaust, Jewish
(1939–1945)—France. 5. Refugees, Jewish—France—Biography.
6. Refugees, Jewish—United States—Biography. I. Title.
D804.66.F79 I84 2001   940.53'18—dc21   2001019283

Printed in the United States of America on acid-free paper

Random House website address: www.randomhouse.com

98765432

FIRST EDITION

Book design by Carole Lowenstein

In memory of those who did not escape

Whoever saves a single life
Is as one who has saved an entire world.

Mishnah Sanhedrin 4:5

Preface

▌▌▌▌▌▌▌▌▌▌▌▌▌▌▌▌▌▌▌▌▌▌▌▌▌▌▌

Varian Fry, an editor, journalist, and teacher, was raised in New Jersey, educated at Harvard, and lived in New York City and Connecticut. Without training or experience, and not at all certain that he possessed any courage, during thirteen months in 1940 and 1941, this American hero led the most successful private rescue mission of World War II.

Fry saved the lives of more than a thousand refugees from Hitler, most of them Jewish, including creative men and women whose legacy to the world is abiding: Marc Chagall, Max Ernst, Jacques Lipchitz, Marcel Duchamp, Hannah Arendt, André Breton, André Masson, Hertha Pauli, Franz Werfel, and Lion Feuchtwanger. A Protestant, Varian Fry is the only American honored at Yad Vashem, Israel's Holocaust memorial.

What made Fry offer to go to France? Why did he endanger himself to save strangers?

In the old epics a character is occasionally inhabited by a god, and then he acts beyond himself.

During one extraordinary year, Fry experienced this divine inspiration. The intersection of his moral beliefs, political ideology, and desire to help the Jews and other refugees of Europe motivated him. Using his disdain for authority, restless intelligence, and quirky personality, he improvised—with the aid of a small band of loyal colleagues—intricate and illegal methods for smuggling refugees across borders.

Fry saved not only well-known intellectuals and artists but also ordinary men, women, and children. Most emigrated to America where they profoundly affected this nation and changed its culture immeasurably. "Varian, who had rescued a whole culture from Surrender on Demand," said writer Hertha Pauli, "will always remain the hero to whom we owe our lives."

Contents

PART ONE

||||||||||||||||||||

NEW YORK
TO MARSEILLE

CHAPTER ONE

||||||||||||||||||||||||||

THE
DIXIE CLIPPER

Dear Eileen,
We have left the Azores far behind and are now nearing Lisbon . . .
there are some Don Quixote windmills on the brow of the hill be-
hind the town, turning just as they must have been when he tilted at
them. The Azores would be a delightful place to have a villa—at the
end of one's days.

Varian

EARLY IN THE AFTERNOON of August 4, 1940, Varian Fry crossed the ramp at La Guardia Airport to board a Pan American Airways Boeing B-314 to Europe for what would turn out to be the greatest adventure of his life. His wife and a small group of friends were there to see him off. As he walked toward the water where the seaplane was docked, sunlight danced off Fry's glasses, mirroring the delight in his eyes. A slender man, above-average height, with dark brown hair and green eyes, he sparkled, pressed and immaculate, eager to be on his way. Over the gangplank, onto the Clipper, and belted in, Fry sank back finally to wave farewell to his wife and friends through the tiny window.

His destination was Marseille, a large, dirty port city near the south-ernmost tip of France that had become the last stop for many thousands of refugees from Hitler. From there, they hoped to embark to the United States, Britain, Canada, Mexico, Cuba—any country without a Nazi presence. By the time of Fry's trip, Marseille was jammed with penniless, bedraggled exiles from all over Europe struggling to emigrate. Long before he left New York, he was aware that most were failing at these attempts, that some were already interned in French concentration camps under primitive and inhumane conditions. His mission, once he arrived, was to assist in any way he could, a handful of people, the intellectual elite of Europe, whose names had been given him by various leaders in American arts and sciences.

Fry left behind his wife of nine years, Eileen Hughes Fry, who had expressed a hope that he would return with a French child for them to adopt. He had taken a four-week leave of absence from his job as an editor at the Foreign Policy Association's Headline Books. Naively thinking his mission to save the refugees could be accomplished in that short time, he had purchased a return Clipper ticket for August 29. Just before he left New York, worried whether he had the correct clothing, Fry went on a last-minute shopping spree, buying items that he imagined necessary for a month on the Continent.

Taped to his leg were a list of two hundred names, the most endangered refugees, and three thousand dollars in cash. As European representative for the Emergency Rescue Committee (ERC), an ad hoc group organized days after the fall of France, his mandate was to help German and Eastern European refugees obtain the visas and other documents they needed to escape from France.

Just before he left, Fry's conversations with his wife revealed how little he understood public opinion in America regarding the European war and its refugees. He did not realize that it would be nearly impossible to mobilize Americans to support both refugee rescue and the liberalization of U.S. immigration policy. Eileen tried to explain the state of mind of the American people, but he never got it. Fry, who cared deeply about the well-being of all people, could not comprehend the narrow, selfish isolationist viewpoint of a majority of Americans who wanted neither to fight in the war nor to help its victims. This inability to understand American attitudes would hurt and hinder him during his year in Marseille as he came up against them repeatedly while he was dealing with American officials.

In some ways, Varian Fry was a likely candidate for the job he had undertaken. He spoke good French and some German, was Harvard-educated, and had a liberal Protestant background with a strong family emphasis on helping others. His paternal grandfather, Charles Reuben Fry, had been a prominent social worker and "child saver."

Varian Fry was also a passionate antifascist who would now be able to act on his beliefs. Despite his political predilection for this work, however, his personality did not lend itself to his becoming a foreign emissary. He was outspoken and undiplomatic, and often anxious and moody. In addition, the leadership of the ERC, and Fry himself, had doubts about sending him to Europe because of his lack of experience in this type of political work. In the end, however, he was the only volunteer, and therefore the one to go.

His antifascism had been reinforced on a visit to Europe five years earlier, during the summer of 1935, when he witnessed Nazi storm troopers beating Jews on the streets of Berlin. His memory of this incident, of a victim's "hand nailed to the table beside the beer mug," influenced his decision to volunteer for the mission to Marseille.

Haunted by what he had seen in Berlin, Fry wrote about it. Working at a series of editorial positions from 1935 on, he tried desperately but unsuccessfully to bring public attention to the coming Holocaust. Even front-page articles he wrote for *The New York Times* about the storm troopers' brutality and its aftermath did not bring condemnation of Nazi actions. The majority of Americans were not interested. With isolationists dominant in American society, Fry and others with like views were generally ignored.

Since September 1939, Germany had vanquished the nations of Europe, including, during the April, May, and June 1940 "Blitzkrieg," Belgium, Holland, Denmark, Norway, and Luxembourg. "The enemy is aiming for the heart of France," wrote Russian émigré Victor Serge, "and Paris is threatened." In New York, as they waited for the inevitable invasion of France, Fry and other politically concerned people were frantically trying to figure out how to help their European friends.

Fry became involved in a number of different groups that were forming. He lunched often at Child's restaurant on Fortieth Street in Manhattan with the dashing and mysterious Karl Frank (aka Paul Hagen) and his second wife, activist-heiress Anna Caples. (It was at these meetings that the groundwork was laid for the formation of the Emergency Rescue Committee.) He joined the American Friends of German Freedom, which Frank had created along with the progressive theologian Dr. Reinhold Niebuhr. When Frank first arrived in New York in 1935, he had read Fry's *New York Times* article about the Nazis beating Jews in Berlin and sought out the young journalist. A psychoanalyst and "professional revolutionary," Frank had been a communist militant in Austria during the twenties, then head of the German Socialist Party in Prague. Niebuhr, formerly a pacifist, was now urging "Christians to support the war against Hitler." Fry also met the daring and glamorous Buttingers. From 1934 to 1938, Joseph Buttinger led the underground Austrian Socialist Movement, then emigrated to the United States with his wife, Muriel Gardiner, the scion of a wealthy American family.* As other bright politically concerned young people gathered around the locus of the Franks and the Buttingers—including Ingrid Warburg, of the influential banking family, and Eileen Hughes Fry—Fry became involved in yet a third group, the International Relief Association (IRA). Founded in 1934 by Albert Einstein to aid refugees from Hitler, this group operated independently in Europe for a time.

On June 14, 1940, German forces, which had been bombing on the outskirts of Paris, entered the city and marched triumphantly down the Champs Elysées to the Arc de Triomphe. As French citizens cried tears of "heartbroken rage," Fry and his circle across the Atlantic were also grief-stricken. France fell days later, on June 22. Article Nineteen of the Franco-German Armistice called for France to "surrender on demand" to the Nazis all Germans who sought asylum "in France as well as in French possessions, colonies, protectorate territories, and mandates."

" 'Germans' included Austrians, Czechs, and, in practice, any others whom the Nazis chose to terrorize . . . no one doubted that the Gestapo would soon start tracking down these old enemies." At that time, how the French would respond to Article Nineteen was unclear, and as a result all refugees in France felt at risk because the Nazis *could* demand they be surrendered.

When Germany conquered France, the country was divided into "unoccupied" and "occupied" zones, with the unoccupied sector under a nominal French government headquartered in Vichy. This government, led by Marshal Henri-Philippe Pétain, immediately forbade expressions of French nationalism, such as the national anthem, "La Marseillaise," and substituted "Work, Family, Fatherland" for the French motto of "Liberty, Equality, Fraternity."

---

*Gardiner has claimed to be the model for the underground hero "Julia," described by Lillian Hellman in her memoir *Pentimento*.

In New York, Fry and his friends, horrified that refugees in France might have to be handed over to the Germans, were appalled by Vichy's plans to rid France of its foreigners, particularly Jews. Germans and other European exiles who had fled Hitler were now outcasts in the country where they had sought refuge. They had chosen France for asylum over Belgium and Switzerland. Refugees in Belgium were often pushed back and forth over the French-Belgian border, nor was the Swiss government much better; it was stingy with permits allowing refugees to remain. Although it was difficult for refugees to gain entry into France, once inside, it was easier for them to remain.

Unfortunately, after the fall of France, the Vichy government passed legislation preventing refugees from leaving the country. Vichy, if it so decided, could then surrender them on demand to the Germans. As a result, antifascists, writers, "degenerate" artists, scientists, labor leaders—most of them Jewish—were trapped in France, waiting for the Germans to pounce.

Since, from the spring of 1940 on, there were fewer and fewer passenger ships sailing from Europe until "points of departure . . . narrowed almost to Lisbon and the British ports," the refugees' dilemma was how to get from France to Lisbon, and then to a free nation. This was one of the chief questions considered by Fry and his friends in New York as they held meeting after meeting. But there was no resolution, no plan of action. On June 24, the American Friends of German Freedom wrote to Eleanor Roosevelt asking for her support, which she gave. A day later, the group held a fund-raising luncheon at the Hotel Commodore in Manhattan. Radio commentator Raymond Gram Swing spoke on the plight of the European refugees. Fry, an organizer of the luncheon, was moved by Swing's eloquence. Reinhold Niebuhr asked the two hundred guests to donate money, then led a discussion about resolving the problems of the refugees. Many spoke out, including Erika Mann, Thomas Mann's daughter. Everyone agreed that a new organization was needed, an amalgam of Einstein's IRA and the American Friends of German Freedom, whose sole purpose would be to help the European refugees. Finally, Fry thought, some action. The Emergency Rescue Committee was born that day. Although most of its members were journalists, religious leaders, and activists from the traditional American left, Fry's background was more intellectual and humanitarian. His instincts were the same as the other founders of the ERC, but his political agenda was always second to his strong desire to help people.

The leaders of the ERC, including Fry, met again a few days after the luncheon, at Ingrid Warburg's apartment on West Fifty-fourth Street, to discuss the desperate need to send someone to France to see what was actually going on. Fry said he would consider volunteering if no one else could be found.

The ERC took shape with an office at 122 East Forty-second Street and several new members: Methodist minister and University of Newark president Dr. Frank Kingdon; New School for Social Research president Dr. Alvin Johnson; perennial presidential candidate and socialist Norman Thomas; and other leaders in the arts, education, religion, labor, and the media. Kingdon became the committee's chairman, David F. Seiferheld was its treasurer, and Mildred Adams its secretary. Harold Oram, a socialist militant who had raised funds for Spanish Civil War refugees in the thirties, would oversee fund-raising, and Ingrid Warburg volunteered to be Kingdon's assistant. A national committee to boost the fledgling organization's profile included writers John Dos Passos and Upton Sinclair; the presidents of Yale University, Smith College, and the University of Chicago; and journalist Dorothy Thompson.

In late June, Fry wrote to the president and received an answer from Eleanor Roosevelt: "The President has seen your letter of June 27," she wrote. "He will try to get the cooperation of the South American countries in giving asylum to the political refugees." By early July, lists were being compiled of endangered refugees, including not only Jews but communists, leftist political activists, religious war objectors, and other outsiders.

The ERC was still seeking a representative to send to France. "In the end," Fry wrote, "I volunteered myself." He had no "experience in the underground" and made his offer "out of impatience at delay," as well as his real desire to do some good. "I believed in freedom," he wrote later. "I remembered what I had seen in Germany. I knew what would happen to the refugees if the Gestapo got hold of them. . . . It was my duty to help them. . . ." Despite Kingdon's conservative tendency toward safety first, action later, the ERC moved ahead and appointed Fry, an unknown quantity, as its European representative. He would travel to France and meet with as many endangered refugees as possible, helping them acquire visas and other necessary documents so they could escape Europe before they were arrested and turned over to the Nazis.

Fry prepared for his departure while the ERC raised money, calling an emergency fund-raising luncheon for Tuesday, July 30, 1940. Asking for help for the "1,000 German anti-Nazi[s] . . . in peril," the ERC focused on the plight of the refugees and on the war, trying to make Americans more sensitive to the situation and more willing to help. Fry and several members of the committee maintained contact with Eleanor Roosevelt with many letters passing back and forth. Fry hoped she could influence U.S. visa policy through the president and through her friendship with leaders in the State Department.

A restrictive U.S. visa policy had been in place for years, reflecting attitudes central to American society, such as anti-Semitism, "nativistic nationalism [or] America for Americans," isolationism, and "fear of the alien as a threat to American culture." The U.S. Immigration Act of 1917 had been reinterpreted to exclude "persons likely to become public charges, a method . . . by which entry of aliens could be almost completely ended." The Immigration Act of 1924 specified how many people from each country could immigrate to the United States, setting entry quotas of "2 percent of each Caucasian nationality represented in the 1890 U.S. census." Economic hardship and unemployment caused by the Depression led President Hoover in 1930, through the State Department, to further limit immigration.

Although the number of Europeans allowed into the United States was less than those seeking entry, "the solidity of the national origins quota system" was based on the feelings of most Americans. They did not want refugees, even children, allowed into the United States, even though they faced being murdered by the Nazis. A 1938 survey in *Fortune* magazine revealed that two-thirds of Americans had negative attitudes about European refugees and wanted to keep them out of the United States. Anti-Semitism and fear of spies also played a part in American public opinion.

> Of the roughly half a million German-speaking emigrants who fled Germany and Austria during Hitler's reign of terror . . . about 132,000 eventually made their way to the United States.

The quotas were more than twice this number but the United States was reluctant to allow in too many Jews. While Great Britain took in "10,000 Jewish children and [a] large number of Social Democrats," the U.S. Congress chose "not to admit 20,000 Jewish children from Germany."

President Roosevelt had made some early attempts to assist the desperate, clamoring refugees, and in 1938 he formed the President's Advisory Committee on Political Refugees as a liaison between private refugee agencies and the government. When events around the world heated up and pressure increased within his own administration, however, he did not act to help the refugees. And he did nothing when, in June 1940, the State Department cut the flow of refugees coming in from Germany and central and Eastern Europe by one-half. (Later, the rigid quota system was not modified, despite the genocide that was taking place in Europe.) "The half-filled quotas of mid-1940 to mid-1941, when refugee rescue remained entirely feasible, symbolize 20,000 to 25,000 lives lost." It may seem a small number relative to the millions murdered by the Germans, "[b]ut the value of one life cannot be discounted because it is only one."*

Since neither the Roosevelt administration nor the Congress did anything to modify restrictive immigration policies, they remained in place during the years leading up to and including World War II. This was the face shown to the world by the great democracy, America, as thousands upon thousands of Europeans came knocking on its locked doors during the 1930s and, in 1940, when Varian Fry went to Marseille. "On the eve of the war, France probably had 40,000 refugees from Germany, although some estimates put the figure at 60,000."

Clearly the only hope for the people Fry was sent to help was special permits to enter the United States called emergency visitors' visas.†
They were first issued on July 2, 1940, when American Federation of Labor (AF of L) president William Green presented the State Department with a list of "endangered European labor leaders and intellectuals" who needed these special permits.

Fry knew that European refugees had one friend in Washington,

*After 1941, quotas from Germany and other Eastern European countries were filled even less than they had been earlier. This "was not the result of any abatement in Nazi oppression. Indeed, in late 1941 the policy of extermination was initiated."

†During 1940 and 1941, according to historian David Wyman, an estimated two thousand political and intellectual refugees actually escaped to America through the emergency visa program, most of them saved by Fry.

Eleanor Roosevelt, who sent numerous memos to the State Department, particularly to her friend, Undersecretary of State Sumner Welles, about the refugee situation. Much later, when the problems involved in helping refugees to emigrate were clarified, she asked: "Is there no way of getting our consul in Marseille to help a few of these people out?" Because of her persistence, the State Department did issue emergency visas, and Karl Frank, who had initially involved Fry in the American Friends of German Freedom, thanked Mrs. Roosevelt: "It is due to your interest that many hundreds of people have been saved."

Fry realized that despite her good intentions, however, there was little Mrs. Roosevelt could to do to significantly influence the visa business. These were private organizations sending representatives to Europe to help the refugees, including Fry's ERC, and none had connections with the U.S. government. The government's lack of concern with European refugees merely reflected the state of mind of most Americans. In addition, the fall of France unfortunately coincided with the transfer of immigration services from the Department of Labor under Frances Perkins to Assistant Secretary of State Breckinridge Long.

Long, who headed the Special War Problems Division of which the Visa Division was a part, instituted measures "to delay and effectively stop" efforts to aid immigration, lest these efforts take away from the U.S. war effort. He worked to "keep America for Americans" and rejected aiding the European refugees. The State Department had "been very generous in offering hospitality" to certain labor leaders and intellectuals, and others from "Germany, Poland, and near-by territories." But U.S. immigration laws had to be followed and "the President's Committee [must] be curbed in its activities so that the laws again can operate in their normal course." Long wrote that he was "very careful to limit the authorization of visas to the end that the law be observed."

Long had been misguided for years; early in his career, he erred famously when he wrote about the "[i]mpossibility" of India revolting against British rule. As U.S. ambassador to Italy in 1933, he had expressed approval of fascism. As late as 1939, he stated that Hitler would never go so far as to attack Western Europe. His views of refugees, which were shared by many others in the State Department, supported severe and cruel limitations on immigration during the critical years leading up to and including the war.

Private arrangements had to be made, then, to help the refugees, and, in addition to Fry, other men were being prepared for travel to Europe. A coalition formed by the Jewish Labor Committee (JLC), the AF of L's William Green, and the president of the International Ladies' Garment Workers' Union, David Dubinsky, planned to send a representative to France. This coalition asked Long and Secretary of State Cordell Hull to issue four hundred U.S. emergency visas for its representative to take with him to Europe. When Long and Hull agreed, a list was assembled of Germans, Austrians, and others in danger of being arrested by the Nazis—as well as Bundists, Mensheviks, and Labor Zionists wanted by the Stalinists—and was submitted to the State Department. The JLC's European representative, Dr. Frank Bohn, a former militant turned journalist, would deliver the four hundred visas and assist a handful of refugees to emigrate. Arriving in Marseille only days before Fry, and also carrying three thousand dollars, Bohn met with U.S. consuls and located some refugees from his list, providing them with living expenses and helping a few to escape. Bohn did not admit his JLC affiliation, likely because of the danger of being aligned with a Jewish organization. He claimed to represent the AF of L's Green.

Meanwhile, in New York, Fry was packing and saying his farewells. One day before his departure, he signed a contract with the ERC, which stated that his "personal judgment must, under the circumstances existing, play a large part in the success or failure" of his mission. The contract gave Fry "reasonable latitude" in satisfying his mandate. He was to figure out how to transport the refugees out of France and how to finance their travel. He was also to observe and report on the attitudes of American and foreign officials in France toward the refugees. Above all, his main objective was to get the people on his list to Lisbon or Casablanca, the first stops on the way to freedom.

Fry landed in Lisbon on August 5, 1940, exhausted from the long flight. The whalelike Dixie Clipper, traveling at 190 miles an hour, had taken thirty-six hours to make the Atlantic crossing, including two long refueling stops. His list and cash remained securely strapped to his leg, and he went through customs without a problem, passing himself off as a representative from the American YMCA. Fry recuperated from the flight in the Portuguese capital, spending a week meeting with consuls from various countries to find out their positions on the refugees and the war. To learn what was being done for the refugees, he met with representatives from religious and other aid groups who were in Europe on missions similar to his. They told him of the gloomy conditions in France.

Just before he left Lisbon, he wrote to Eileen, relating what he had heard: "France is in a very sad plight indeed . . . wherever you go you see men sitting with their heads in their hands, just sitting. . . . Children are already dying for lack of milk, and many more will die when winter comes." Always able to joke, however, he added that he was leaving Lisbon that day, Monday, August 12, for Spain and wished himself "*bonne chance.* It's a Spanish plane!" In Spain, he took a series of trains from Barcelona to his final destination, arriving at Marseille's Gare St.-Charles on Thursday, August 15. He quickly found a porter and marched briskly down the steps to the boulevard d'Athenes, followed by the man bearing his suitcase, inflatable mattress, and sleeping bag.

Fry intended to stay at the Hôtel Splendide, which had been recommended to him back in New York, but it was full, so he followed his porter across the street to the Hôtel Suisse. His room there was small, on the street, and smelled "of drains and garlic," but at least he had a place to sleep. He washed and change his shirt, then went out in search of the U.S. consulate's Visa Division to find out if any refugees on his list had been issued U.S. visas since he'd left New York.

At the consulate,* the receptionist, a "hard-looking, peroxide blonde" named Mme. Delapré, told Fry the Visa Division was a quarter of an hour out of town and reachable by trolley. He rode the trolley, along with a tired-looking, dusty crowd, and disembarked when they did. While the others formed a straggly line in front of the building, Fry, not a patient man, entered through the front door. A guard yelled at him but he quickly said, "I am an American." He was allowed to wait in the hall, but after ten minutes another guard chased him out. In the street, Fry waited for a while among the crush of refugees.

---

*Sixty years later, in October 2000, place St. Ferreol, the location of the consulate, was renamed place Varian Fry.

Finally, unaccustomed to the heat and sun, he returned to town in late afternoon without ever seeing the U.S. counsel. He was dismayed at this first glimpse of his country's attitude toward the ragtag foreigners. The guards had been arrogant, shouting and chasing him out—and he was an American! He could only imagine how they treated refugees.

That night, Fry called on Czech writer Franz Werfel and his wife, Alma, two people on his list, at the Hôtel du Louvre et de la Paix and they had dinner together. He had been given their address by Werfel's sister in Lisbon. Werfel's popular novels, sold and read all over the world, were expressionistic statements of his belief that "the world is meaningful . . . a spiritual world." An early and outspoken critic of Hitler's murderous regime, the writer fled Germany when Hitler banned his work and as a result was in mortal danger from the Nazis. "When the last vestige of the world's meaning is obliterated in a soul," Werfel had written, ". . . madness assumes mastery."

While Werfel appeared helpless and frightened to Fry, Alma was spirited and fiercely protective of her husband. In this "time of great dread," the writer was haunted by an erroneous British radio announcement telling of his murder by the Nazis, a fate that Werfel was convinced would be his if he could not escape quickly. Alma was more optimistic. The former great beauty had "made a career of collecting famous husbands" and lovers. She had been married to composer Gustav Mahler, then to architect Walter Gropius. One of her many lovers, artist Oskar Kokoschka, lived for two years with a life-size replica of his beloved Alma.

At the time of the Anschluss, Germany's takeover of Austria, the Werfels were living in relative comfort in Paris. Now, however, the seductive muse and the aging, overweight novelist, unprepared for the difficult circumstances in which they found themselves, needed Fry's protection and help to emigrate. Although Werfel carried with him a letter from the Catholic foreign secretary describing him as "one of the leading Catholic writers," he was Jewish. In addition to this letter, the couple had Czech passports and an affidavit from Thomas Mann in support of their applications for U.S. emergency visas.

During dinner, Franz Werfel told Fry of a critical stop they had made on their journey south from Paris. Having heard about the "wondrous history of the girl Bernadette Soubirous" who had seen, a century earlier, a vision of the Virgin Mary in a grotto in the small town of Lourdes, they had spent a few weeks there. In the grotto, the writer had offered a prayer in the form of a bargain: If he and Alma were spared death at the hands of the Nazis, he would tell the world about Bernadette Soubirous. In Marseille, Werfel begged Fry: "You must save us." New to his job and nervous about his mission, Fry had little idea how to save anyone, including the couple across the table, and could only promise to do his best.

The next morning, Fry's second day in Marseille, Fry discovered that Frank Bohn was at the Hôtel Splendide, where he had tried to stay, and went to see him. Bohn's list was filled with political activists and labor leaders, while Fry's was mainly writers, painters, and intellectuals. Talking with Bohn, Fry found out the extent of documentation needed by refugees to travel from city to city, country to country. First, they needed "safe-conduct" passes to travel within France, from one city or town to another; a refugee from Montredon, for example, traveling to Marseille to see the U.S. consul, had to have a safe-conduct pass in his possession. Second, any refugee trying to leave France required a French exit visa. At the moment, Bohn told Fry, because Vichy was not issuing any exit visas, even though Bohn had brought with him U.S. emergency visitors' visas for a number of refugees, they could not legally leave the country. Third, Spanish and Portuguese transit visas were required for legal travel through those countries. Finally, an overseas travel visa was needed, with one from the United States the most prized. All documents had to be in order and unexpired. On the positive side, Bohn told Fry that Vichy was too disorganized to check for safe-conduct passes and that any refugee possessing a valid overseas visa was generally able to get Spanish and Portuguese transit visas. Even without a French exit visa, then, it was possible for a refugee to cross the French border into Spain. It would, of course, be an illegal passage.

Neutral Spain and Portugal were at that time still readily handing out transit visas, even to Jews and anti-Nazis. Fry understood that if a refugee could not obtain all the papers required for legal emigration, he would have to emigrate illegally. Typically, visas were continuously expiring and, as a result, it was nearly impossible to have a full set of documents in order.

There were also, Fry learned, some refugees who had no papers at all. These *apatrides,* stateless persons without passports, could not obtain any legal papers, including visas. Most were Jews and antifascists who had fled Germany or Austria. A small number of *apatrides* managed to obtain "affidavits in lieu of support," which took the place of, and were as valid as, passports. There were also those whose names and faces were well known to the Nazis; because of this, even if they had papers, they still could not travel without fear of arrest.

Bohn informed Fry that Vichy had been interning people for some time; hundreds were imprisoned, starving and filthy, in French concentration camps all over the south of France.

As little as Fry knew about visas and passports, when he left New York he was well aware of the Jewish flight from Germany that had begun in 1933, when Hitler came to power. He also understood that there had been "two emigrations from Germany, a political and a 'racial' immigration." The political movement included activists,* writers, artists, and politicians who opposed Hitler. The "racial" immigration occurred after the German government defined Jews as "aliens" or "undesirables" on a racial basis and began forbidding their participation in German life. Under the September 1935 Nuremberg Laws, both "part-Jews" and Jews lost their German citizenship. German Jews were excluded from working as doctors, lawyers, professors, and teachers; their books were outlawed, then burned. They could not hold public office or do public service. Cutting-edge art, most of it by Jewish painters, sculptors, and composers, was classified as degenerate and was confiscated and destroyed.

Sitting in their shirtsleeves in Bohn's tiny room, heads close together, the two young Americans talked about the contradictory legislation on refugee emigration that had been passed by Germany and France, and the United States' administrative measures regarding immigration. At that time, despite the "surrender on demand" clause in the armistice, the German occupying forces were not yet organized enough to round up the "criminals" on their wanted lists. The new Vichy government was similarly disordered. Fry and Bohn decided to take advantage of the chaos by helping refugees escape through the bureaucratic cracks. They confirmed a division of refugee cases: Bohn would handle the trade unionists, labor leaders, and older socialists,

---

*"Of the refugees who fled from the Nazis between 1933 and 1940, perhaps 5 percent emigrated because of political opposition to the Hitler regime."

while Fry would help writers, artists, and other intellectuals, and younger left-wing political types.

After their talk, Fry returned to his hotel room to figure out how to carry out his mandate. What Bohn told him had disillusioned him about the French. They were isolationist, xenophobic, and anti-Jewish. Unemployment and a large refugee population encouraged these attitudes, according to Bohn, and during the two years *before* Germany smashed through France, twenty thousand refugees seeking political asylum had been interned by the French government. Fry, a Francophile, had difficulty reconciling his own humanitarian and liberal views with the deeply rooted anti-Semitism in the French national character. This anti-Semitism was not "vicious" or "premeditated," according to Tony Judt, writing in 1996. "It was ordinary, quotidian French anti-Semitism of the kind that had been rampant in the Thirties and before."

Maybe the only good thing that happened that day was that Fry succeeded in getting a room at the Splendide. He checked out of the Hôtel Suisse, and, sitting quietly in his new room, his determination grew: He would succeed. He would find "his" refugees and save every single one.

Within a day of Fry's arrival, the word went out through the refugee population and "spread all over France that an American had arrived, like an angel from heaven, with his pocket full of passports, and a direct connection with the State Department enabling him to get anybody any kind of visa desired at a moment's notice." Rumors circulated in Montauban and Toulouse, nearby towns with large refugee populations, about "an American in Marseille who carries money in his pocket." Young Karel Sternberg, a refugee working for Einstein's International Relief Association helping fellow refugees in Montauban, heard about Fry. In Toulouse, an American art student, Miriam Davenport, heard the news, too.

The gregarious Davenport had many friends in the refugee community, including Alsatian journalist and musicologist Charles Wolff and German writer Konrad Heiden. Both were wanted by the Nazis, Heiden especially, for his censorious biography of Hitler. After hearing about Fry, Davenport decided to go to Marseille and see for herself. Heiden emerged from his shelter in an abandoned movie theater and, with Wolff, threw her a farewell party and asked for her help: "When you get to Marseilles, you must find some American who is interested in . . . political refugees who will wrap us in the American flag," they told her. "That is the only way we can be saved from the Gestapo." Davenport left Toulouse for Marseille.

On Fry's third day in France, in his hotel room, he began writing to the people on his list, some of whose addresses he had been given in New York. But before he had time to write a single word, he heard a knock at the door. The deluge had begun, a never-ending stream of European émigrés seeking help, and some Americans, such as Davenport, who wanted to work with him. German poet and novelist Hans Sahl* was among the first to arrive at Fry's doorstep. Born in Dresden, Sahl emigrated to Czechoslovakia in 1933, then to France, where he worked with Fry for a time before he made his escape. Sahl never forgot his first meeting with Fry.

> [W]ho should open his door but a friendly young man in shirt sleeves who welcomed me in, put his arm around my shoulders. . . . Imagine the situation: the borders closed; you're caught in a trap, might be arrested again at any moment; life is as good as over—and suddenly a young American in shirt sleeves is stuffing your pockets full of money . . . and whispering with the conspiratorial expression of a ham actor: "Oh, there are ways to get you out of here," while, damn it all, the tears were streaming down my face . . . and that pleasant fellow . . . takes a silk handkerchief from his jacket and says: "Here, have this. Sorry it isn't cleaner."

Compared to many of the refugees, Fry, at five-feet-ten, was relatively tall. He was also handsome, well dressed, and maintained a relaxed, easy manner at all times. Despite some initial suspicions about his true motives, it took only days for Fry to establish himself with the refugees as someone who cared. He consoled, cajoled, and listened. He was always reassuring and managed to calm even the most frightened men and women.

Now that he was actually meeting some of the people on his list, Fry grew more comfortable with his responsibility toward them; but other than handing out money for food and shelter, he still did not know

---

*Sahl was number 1155 on Liste Complète des Clients du Centre Américain de Secours, an imperfect list of refugees who sought Fry's help. It was compiled by Fry and others after the Marseille operation ended.

how to help them escape. Negotiating red tape to obtain visas and other documents, methods of illegal emigration—these remained a mystery to him.

Nevertheless, he cheered and encouraged the refugees, most of whom had emigrated more than once from their homelands to Paris, then from Paris to the south of France. Most had no possessions, with the Germans the poorest of all, since their country had taken everything. That first week, Fry hid his own confusion and feelings of being overwhelmed, and opened his heart to the people who converged on him. Modeling himself after his activist, humanitarian grandfather, and acting on his own contempt for fascism, he tried to give the refugees what they really wanted: hope, and ultimately escape.

Initially, he studied the differences between refugees, noting that well-known politicians, Social Democrats, and antifascists from Germany and Austria, such as Rudolf Breitscheid and Rudolf Hilferding, former leading statesmen of Germany's Weimar Republic, were at the greatest risk. Then there were nonpolitical Jewish refugees who had been hounded from country to country for years and were completely demoralized. Some refugees had denied reality for so long that now they were in shock at their dislocation. Certain intellectuals, such as Werfel, Heiden, and Heinrich Mann, were wanted by the Gestapo for their political views (and, in some cases, for being Jewish) rather than for their writings.

There were a handful of refugees who had no interest in emigrating and preferred to die where they had lived. For some older people, the idea of crossing the ocean to a new continent was out of the question. In his autobiography, Austrian writer Carl Zuckmayer,* who had emigrated earlier and lived in Vermont, described what it meant to abandon one's roots for a new and unknown place. "The most difficult thing to bear," he wrote, "was parting from those graves."

> There is much from which we had to part in the Old World. People, things, graves. Many died whom we did not believe we could spare . . . we now can say they were fortunate to have died at the right time. . . . Many others, too, have had to go but left behind to us the image of their personalities, like so many helping angels.

*Carl Zuckmayer married Karl Frank's first wife, Alice von Herdan, and became stepfather to the Franks' daughter, Michaela.

"We must take one step at a time, as one does in new, unexplored territory," wrote Zuckmayer. "Then we shall begin to feel . . . that exile is not a flight and a curse but a destiny." Fry quickly found out that it was easier to work with people who viewed emigration as "destiny" than those who felt they were being ripped from their roots.

On his fourth morning in Marseille, Fry answered a knock at his door to find a group of Austrians standing in the hallway, members of Neu Beginnen, a Social Democratic group that had been led by Karl Frank before he emigrated to the United States. They were strong and independent; one even had a map of the border and a plan for crossing it. When Fry spoke with these brave young people whose names were not on his list, he began to wonder about the list's relevance. More and more, he was learning that Marseille was brimming over with thousands of people in danger who were completely unknown in the United States.

Fry's list included artists, writers, and other intellectuals supplied to him by well-established individuals and institutions in New York. But he saw that another category, a much larger group, consisted of political activists and antifascists who had opposed Hitler. "I am afraid that I have allowed myself to forget how little everyone in the U.S. really knows about the situation here," Fry wrote to his wife, Eileen. After only days in France, Fry recognized that his list was incomplete. For the time being, some of the people on it were safe. Either they had already emigrated, or they were in the French Army as *prestataire,* paramilitaries who worked alongside the soldiers. Others had been rounded up and were interned in French camps. A few were dead. Some of the "great" ones, such as the artist Henri Matisse, had no intention of leaving France.

Since a majority of the refugees he saw were not on the list, did that mean he was not supposed to help them? But he had met them and had seen their hunger and exhaustion and terror of arrest. In Marseille only a short time, faced with a job he doubted he could handle, Fry came to an understanding and a decision. No one in New York had yet grasped the situation, and he would have to invent methods and strategies for doing his job as he went along.

After those first few days, Fry forged his own way, enlarging his mandate to include political refugees, Social Democrats, and some "farther to the left" who were former communists. He expanded his list to include those refugees whom he considered most at risk, including intellectuals as well as leaders of the Social Democratic and Labor movements. "The people who were in danger, they were the people we helped."

Fry decided to create a refugee center as a cover, pretending to be concerned only with providing the refugees with food, clothing, and money. He would keep quiet about the emigration business, "which was not strictly kosher. . . . We said we were giving advice and living allowances." Although his center would not be operative for a while, Fry had his own cover, as an aid worker, in place within days after his arrival.

Since his real goal was to help the refugees escape, he would need assistance and cooperation from the U.S. consul in handing over visas. But his early run-in at the Visa Division had left him with little faith in American officials. For the duration of his stay in Marseille, American consular and embassy representatives would be as hostile and dismissive to Fry as were the guards that first day. With only two exceptions, American officials showed no sympathy for the refugees, and evidenced "neither humanity nor sense in their immigration policies."

"Visas were granted in the merest trickle," wrote Victor Serge, "in a manner so criminally stingy that thousands upon thousands of real victims, all fine human beings, were left to the mercies of the Nazis."

By the beginning of his second week, Fry was setting up his organization, which he named the Centre Américain de Secours. As he intended, it would over time become the refugees' lifeline and salvation.

|||||||||

Two Deserted People: The Ullmanns

Fry's operation sustained a large number of people for quite a while. They were all kinds of refugees, some of whom had sought help from Americans long before Fry arrived in Marseille. He provided support for many of them, including those who never escaped and others who suffered for months, even years, before they got out. One couple, Ludwig and Irene Ullmann,* were hiding in Montauban when they wrote to the Emergency Rescue Committee, the same day that Fry took off

---

*The Ullmanns were numbers 1382 and 1383.

from New York. The Ullmanns had heard from friends that U.S. emergency visitors' visas were available for certain people.

In his letter, Ludwig, a native of Vienna, explained that he and his wife urgently needed to emigrate to the United States because for years he had been an anti-Nazi editor, critic, and author and was now wanted by the Gestapo. Ludwig and his prodemocracy newspaper, *Wiener Allgemeine Zeitung,* "were among the first enemies of Nazidom in Austria," and after he became editor in chief his paper was the "only one . . . which led the public campaign against Hitlerism and Fascism."

When Hitler annexed Austria on March 13, 1938, Ludwig left the country, crossing "the Hungarian border on foot at midnight." He arrived sometime later in Paris, where, from 1938 on, he was correspondent for a Czech newspaper as well as the secretary of the Federation of Austrian Immigrants. After France fell, Ludwig, now married, and his wife, Irene, went to the unoccupied zone in the south, along with thousands of other refugees.

In his letter of August 1940, Ludwig wrote that writers Franz Werfel and Stefan Zweig, Hollywood producer Max Reinhardt, and journalist Dorothy Thompson would "vouch" for him, and that he would surely find work once he was in the United States. The Emergency Rescue Committee tried to help by getting affidavits of support (attesting that he would not become a financial burden to the U.S. government) and of moral sponsorship (testifying that he was of upstanding character) for Ullmann and his wife from their friends in America. Since emergency visas were only for refugees "who would be in grave danger if apprehended by the Nazis," the ERC also secured a biography of Ludwig Ullmann, telling of the work he had done during his lifetime that put him in great danger of arrest.

Two months later, Ludwig and Irene were still trapped in France. "[A]s of today, the whole situation has changed," he wrote now, less polite and more desperate. They could not even obtain Portuguese transit visas without a U.S. visa.

Ten months after the Ullmanns' original plea for help, the ERC learned that the Visa Department and the American consul in Marseille could not locate them. The ERC sent the Ullmanns' address to the consul but heard nothing for six months. An American friend of Ludwig's, who wanted to pay for the couple's passage to the United States and was forty-five dollars short, asked the committee to pay the difference and to "continue to help these two deserted people." In Marseille, Fry supported the Ullmanns during this period as they waited for their visas, providing them with money for food, shelter, and other necessities.

Typically, refugee cases went on for months, even years, and this one was no different. In May 1942, the President's Advisory Committee on Political Refugees reported that the names of Ludwig and Irene Ullmann had been cabled to "the appropriate American official for consideration of visa applications." Six days later, ERC chairman Frank Kingdon sent a message to the Marseille office that "United States visas [for] Ludwig Ullmann [had been] cabled."

The Ullmanns finally escaped, according to a U.S. State Department report. They somehow got to Lisbon, then sailed to America on the *Serpa Pinto* during the summer of 1942. It had been two years since Ludwig first wrote that his "case is currently an urgent one."

CHAPTER TWO

|||||||||||||||||||||||||

AUGUST: ARRIVAL

The only thing to be cheerful about was the arrival of Varian Fry in Marseille.

Albert Hirschman

F RANCE IS NOW not only subject to the law of the conqueror, but is also going through a period of political reaction," wrote Daniel Bénédite, who later became a close ally of Fry's. "[I]ts rules therefore are not friendly to the democratic refugees who, until now, have enjoyed protection as exiles."

Hitler had his moment of triumph a short time before Fry arrived, in a clearing in the woods in northeast France. There, in the same railroad car in which Germany had surrendered at the end of World War I twenty-two years earlier, representatives of the French government were forced to sign an armistice agreement with the German High Command of the Armed Forces on June 22, 1940.

Two months later, Fry began his first full week in Marseille, on Monday, August 19, with the city's residents in "about the worst mood of any collective group" that one young refugee had ever seen. Fry rolled up his shirtsleeves and at nine A.M. opened the door to his room at the Hôtel Splendide, ready to greet the refugees who already lined the stairs and hallway. Fry interviewed each person, asking his name, then whether he had a passport, identity papers, or visas. He listened to stories of fear and terror with understanding and compassion. He related well to these people, and his reassuring manner gave them confidence. While some individuals felt "the old sort of European skepticism" about the young American, most believed in him. He was naive, even innocent, but he learned quickly and he clearly "meant business [and] was well intentioned."

He was initially burdened by his desire to help everyone, then by trying to decide whom to help first. All night he thought about his daytime interviews and the "special" refugees who were in the most danger. Each day, he found new people at risk of arrest and added their names to his original list. In the evening, he cabled their names to the Committee in New York. These people, who had "particular merit because of intellectual, artistic accomplishments . . . or political accomplishments," were the "anti-Nazi refugees who had spoken out freely throughout the previous seven years" and "were now largely helpless." They became Fry's priority. He also knew he had to help Jews, all of whom were in danger.

Although Fry "tried to save all," recalled Albert Hirschman, who would become Fry's assistant, "we knew precisely who the Germans were after . . . even though they were not on the ordinary lists." For those people he could not rescue, Fry would provide money and referrals to other relief groups.

Ironically, both the German occupiers and the vanquished French had a similar goal when it came to foreign Jews: They wanted them out of Europe. The Germans expressed a "lack of interest in non-aryans south of the Demarcation Line. The French could do as they liked with these 'undesirables,' and their departure from Europe was obviously welcomed." Although the Germans "continued at least until April 1941 to push more Jewish refugees into unoccupied France," this was a direct contradiction to Vichy's own stated policy of ridding itself of Jews, foreigners, and other "undesirables."

Three organizations that helped refugees were then in operation: the New York–based HIAS (Hebrew Sheltering and Immigrant Aid Society); the Lisbon-based HICEM; and the American Jewish Joint Distribution Committee, known as "the Joint," which dispensed money collected by American Jewish groups to the refugees. In addition, the Quakers and the Unitarians had sent representatives to Europe with whom Fry would work closely. These groups, helpful as they were, provided aid alone. Fry's was the only operation whose goal was to help refugees escape.

Fry categorized refugees according to the visas they held. First, he checked to determine if a refugee already had a U.S. emergency visitor's visa. Although emergency visas stipulated that "the immigrant agreed to depart from the United States as soon as possible and would start immediately to make efforts to do so," these refugees "did not have homes . . . to which they could return without facing death," so the United States ignored the usual six-month limit. However, the organizations recommending the refugees, such as Fry's ERC, "had to assure the State Department that they would do all they could to move the immigrants rapidly to other countries."

By 1940, the President's Advisory Committee had taken over "coordinating efforts to obtain emergency visitors' visas for endangered political and intellectual refugees," but soon became another obstruction preventing these people from obtaining visas in a timely manner. After an applicant was reviewed by this committee, if he was validated he was then referred first to the Justice Department, then to the State Department. If approved, he would then receive an emergency visa from the consulate nearest his residence in Europe—*if* the consul was willing to hand out the precious document.

Many consuls were not. As individuals, they were generally opposed to allowing refugees into the United States, and the State Department also discouraged them from issuing these visas. Between August 1 and September 10, 1940, for example, 567 names were submitted for emergency visas, but only forty had been issued by late September. On September 19, consuls in Europe received instructions from the State Department "to check carefully . . . and require . . . clearer evidence" from refugees seeking emergency visas.

However, if a refugee was fortunate enough to possess either a U.S. or another country's overseas visa, Fry helped him secure Spanish and Portuguese transit visas, which were necessary for travel through those countries. At this time, Spain readily issued transit visas to refugees who were on their way to Portugal. And Portugal's transit policy was also liberal, with refugees receiving transit visas "on the basis of almost any evidence that they could proceed to another country."

No one, however, had a French exit visa. They were not issued, in general, and "certainly were not given to Jews." On August 12, 1940, the French government completely stopped exit visas and would not issue them again until the spring of 1941. As a result, no refugee could leave the country legally. France had two reasons for this. First, government officials wanted to prevent French citizens from fleeing the country for Britain, where they might join Charles de Gaulle and what would become the Free French forces. Second, Vichy believed this policy would "facilitate the Gestapo's work of capturing persons wanted by the German government." Many Frenchmen, citizens and officials alike, obeyed their German conquerors, caring only for the future of their nation and nothing for the foreign refugees.

Because of this situation, Fry, a proper Harvard-educated Protestant American, came to accept that he would have to find illegal methods and underground routes. In addition, after refugees who had fought with the Republicans in Spain told him they dared not use their own names for travel through Spain, he realized he would also have to go into the forgery business and create documents for them under phony names. Just as he improvised to enlarge his mission from the original two hundred names, Fry grew comfortable with "secret sailings, passage of frontiers without necessary papers, use of false identification papers, transformation and alteration of passports, purchase of visas." In his youth, he had broken rules and defied authority, but this was quite different. Now he had to break the laws of a foreign country that was under fascist control, with serious, perhaps fatal consequences if he were discovered.

Looking for illegal escape routes, Fry wondered if the maps of an underground route across the Pyrenees into Spain, which young members of Neu Beginnen had given him during his first days in France, were viable. They had told him that crossing the foothills of the Pyrenees was not that dangerous, because of chaos at the French-Spanish border and administrative disorganization within the Vichy government. Slipping across the border was possible, since "guards on the French side were generally well-disposed and kindly" to refugees.

Then Fry met Heinrich and Claire Ehrmann, anti-Hitler activists who were on his original list, and because of their background and youth thought they might be the ones to try out the route and report back to him.

Claire, whose Jewish father was killed by the Nazis because he was a Social Democrat, had been a member of a German Social Democratic youth organization before she emigrated, first to Holland, then to France. Heinrich, a German Jewish lawyer who lost his job with the state, had been imprisoned and tortured by the Nazis for his anti-Nazi work as a member of Neu Beginnen. After escaping, he skied over the mountains to Czechoslovakia, then emigrated to France. Claire and Heinrich were married in Paris, then went south after the fall of France. Both of them were on "the famous Gestapo lists," which came into Fry's possession much later, lists "of people to whom the Germans forbade the French to give exit visas," Fry wrote. "Many of these people were subsequently arrested and extradited."

American friends had arranged U.S. emergency visitors' visas for the Ehrmanns, and, when they met, Fry and the Ehrmanns "hit it off very well," recalled Heinrich. "[I]f anybody should try out where these visas lead . . . namely, out of France and through Spain," Fry said it should be this young couple, who spoke French well and were expert hikers. "As soon as you are ready, in two or three days, you try," said Fry. He suggested they use his Neu Beginnen maps, and they agreed.

The Ehrmanns left Marseille, intending to try out the Neu Beginnen routes into Spain; they would return via the same routes and tell Fry what they had learned. Their initial attempts were unsuccessful. First, they were arrested by Vichy customs officials and "forced . . . off a train at the border town, Cerbère." Their second failed attempt occurred after police caught them walking on a road near the border. Finally, realizing they had to find a safer place to cross the border, they asked for help from Vincent Azéma, the mayor of another border town, Banyuls-sur-Mer. Azéma, who was friendly and helpful to the refugees, "pointed out . . . a trail which was quite visible to the naked eye," according to Heinrich, an old "hiking trail that the Republican fighters had used to cross the Pyrenees between France and Spain during the Spanish Civil War."

The Ehrmanns set off for the third time, hiking on Azéma's trail across the foothills of the Pyrenees all afternoon and evening, careful to avoid French border guards. Through the night, they "continued up the mountain, fairly high," waiting in the dark for hours, until two in the morning. "We saw the lights and very slowly and rather hesitantly we made our way down and went into . . . the Spanish border station," said Heinrich. The two or three guards in the station were "completely astonished" to see a man and a woman walking out of the woods in the middle of the night. "Why are you coming here at this hour?" they asked. "We said we like to hike at night," recalled Claire. Guaranteeing their safety with a bribe of American cigarettes for the guards, the Ehrmanns continued on into Spain, and through to Portugal. They sent Fry the map of the route they had taken; then, in Lisbon, they boarded the *Nea Hellas* for New York.*

During the early months of Fry's operation, the Ehrmanns' route was followed by dozens of refugees until, later on, better passages were found. Fry oversaw at least one expedition himself and hired guides to lead others. He had to decide whether refugees were capable of walking across the mountains, based on their age and health, and whether they had young children or aged parents with them.

Just before the Ehrmanns left for the last time, Fry had requested them to find him an associate who spoke German and understood the political situation. "With whom am I going to deal?" Fry asked the Ehrmanns. "I don't know anybody here." Heinrich introduced him to an old friend of his from Germany, Albert Otto Hirschman. Hirschman was "in French uniform . . . and was highly suited for the liaison Varian Fry needed," said Heinrich. When they met, Fry could see that Hirschman was what the French called *débrouillard*, "someone who knew how to slip through the net, evade controls and generally take care of himself." After leaving his homeland at seventeen, Hirschman fought on the Republican side in the Spanish Civil War and later joined the French Army. When he was demobilized and his French commanding officer allowed him to choose a new name and birthplace, he reinvented himself and became Albert Hermant from Philadelphia.

A tall man "with large, innocent-looking gray eyes," Hirschman, now twenty-five, was smart and politically sophisticated. Fry immediately nicknamed him "Beamish" because of his "sweet, boyish smile." To Hirschman, Fry was "very likable, very very pleasant, amusing, intelligent, a little bit flippant," and an "adventurist to come to Europe at that particular moment." He appreciated Fry's "optimism and hope

---

*The Ehrmanns made it to the United States, where Heinrich changed his name to Henry. A year later, the announcement of their son's birth included this exuberant note: "We sincerely hope the State Department will at least recognize what Varian Fry did for the American birth rate!"

and activism," while Fry found the young German's political savvy invaluable. During Fry's first five months in France, Hirschman's ability to network and make deals was critical. Because of his experiences, Hirschman had the sophistication of a much older person, allowing him to grasp undercurrents among the refugee population and to understand the political atmosphere. One of his many gifts was that he radiated optimism, expressing certainty that no matter how terrible "this evil thing" was, "nothing like that could win." Fry loved and relied on his assistant, as he later wrote: "He was the best of them all, and I got to be very fond of him and very dependent on him."

With his new assistant at his side, Fry divided the work into manageable parts. First, he would hire an international staff to deal with the different languages spoken by the refugees. Second, he would establish a routine for interviewing people, because routine had a calming effect. In addition, since his three thousand dollars would not last long, he had to somehow acquire more money. And finally, he had to help the refugees to obtain the documents they needed to escape.

Fry wanted to hire Europeans who understood the anti-Nazi groups and movements, and borders and conditions in Europe, as well as Americans whose presence would connect his operation with the United States' authoritative and safe image. He hired a secretary, Lena Fischman, "an ebullient Polish girl who could take dictation in a dozen languages," who had previously worked for "the Joint." His bookkeeper was Heinz Ernst Oppenheimer, "Oppie," a German refugee with "a talent for keeping books that would pass a police inspection." Oppie covered up illegal expenses with a complex system of false names and other subterfuge, "organized the office," took care of details, "and made frequent extremely shrewd suggestions of policy."

Bedrich "Fritz" Heine, a former executive with the German Social Democratic Party, was Fry's expert on Social Democrats. Franz von Hildebrand, "an Austrian Catholic aristocrat who had picked up a saving touch of vulgarity [and perfect English] at Williams College," was hired both for his expertise and his Polish. "Franzi" knew about the nonsocialists, and had the distinction of being listed in "both the *Almanach de Gotha* [the almanac of Europe's reigning families] and the wanted list of the Gestapo." Two refugees, Hans Sahl and Walter Mehring, both writers, helped Fry weed out communists, as did Hirschman, for his organization did not aid communists.

Within a short time, Fry had assembled an effective group of associates who knew the politics of the war and the refugee situation. Many had already been active "in underground operations trying to smuggle anti-Nazi documents back to Germany or antifascist literature . . . into Italy." While he searched for a few Americans to hire, Fry used his hotel room as an office, with a couple of desks and a typewriter jammed alongside his bed. Fischman and the others worked there with him while Hirschman went out into the streets of Marseille to make contacts. Despite the tiny room, Fry and the others managed to interview a good number of refugees each day, so many that the Vichy police grew suspicious of the activity centering around his room. They came to the Splendide, unnerving refugees waiting in the corridor to see Fry by questioning them as to why they were there.

One morning, Fry was in his room conducting an interview when the police showed up with a police wagon, referred to as a *panier à salade,* or salad basket. After they "rounded up a number of [refugees] . . . and took them off to the Préfecture [police headquarters]," Fry rushed downstairs in search of a lawyer. He knew he had to quickly formalize some sort of legal cover operation so the police would not bother "his" refugees again. He found a lawyer and asked him to file papers establishing the Centre Américain de Secours (American Relief Center). The lawyer agreed but advised Fry to also seek permission from the *préfecture* to operate such an organization.

Fry went back to his room and was preparing to visit the *préfecture* when he heard a loud knock, quite unlike the tentative taps of the refugees: The police had come to him. A commissioner entered and interrogated Fry. Why was he in Marseille? What was he doing in this room? Why were refugees lining up to see him? Fry said he was in Marseille as "the representative of an American committee interested in bringing relief to the refugees." To determine the needs of the refugees, he told the officer, it was necessary to conduct interviews. The official seemed satisfied and left, but Fry knew he still must visit the *préfecture* to get official permission to operate the Centre.

Vichy police remained in shock and disarray over France's capitulation to Germany, the "tremendous catastrophe" that had "befallen this very proud country," in Hirschman's words. Among the police, there were differing opinions: Some were fascists and supported the Germans, while others were antifascists. Many cared only about upholding the honor of France. But there was at least one police officer who was sympathetic to Fry and helped him from time to time, Captain Dubois. On his first visit to the *préfecture,* however, Fry was received as an interfering American who was pushing his way in where he had no business. He told the officer that he was in Marseille only to aid "refugees in distress and asked for permission to found a small committee for the purpose." He received authorization to operate the Centre but was warned not to do anything illegal. Outside of the police barracks, within the city of Marseille itself, Fry found that a number of ordinary citizens were sympathetic toward any efforts that resisted the Germans. They opposed their country's surrender to Germany and refused to cooperate in surrendering refugees to the Nazis.

By the end of August, Fry's hotel room was too small for his growing refugee business and he rented an office on the rue Grignan. Inside the dimly lit building, one flight of stairs led up to the office; inside, large floor-to-ceiling windows opening onto the street flooded the room with light. Fry furnished the office with cast-off desks purchased from the previous tenant and placed "two stiff, wooden chairs" next to each desk. On one wall, he hung a large American flag because "in those days, the American flag was held in great regard" and lent credibility to the operation.

Two Americans were about to enter Fry's life and play important roles in what he was trying to do. The first, tall, good-looking Charlie Fawcett, arrived at rue Grignan one day asking for the man in charge. The young American had heard about an American with "visas to give and money to help people." Wearing a ragged but still identifiable ambulance-driver uniform and coat, Fawcett impressed Fry with his semimilitary appearance and height and brawn, and was hired on the spot. "You are certainly needed to keep order . . . in case we have trouble here," Fry told him.

Fry learned Fawcett's story over the next few days. Only twenty-one, the former college wrestler from Virginia had arrived in Paris in 1938 to study sculpture. When Paris fell, Fawcett found himself as horrified at the Germans' treatment of Jews as Fry had been in Berlin in 1935. Fawcett told his understanding fellow-American how he had been awakened one day to the truth about German anti-Semitism. It was a tale less violent but as dramatic as Fry's own epiphany in Berlin. "Usually Jews would get up and leave when any German military person came in the [café]," said Fawcett. "But this time, after a Jewish group got up and left, I saw the disdain with which these two German officers . . . pointed to their coffee cups and said, 'Take these away and sterilize them.' "

Fawcett and a German-speaking friend, William Holland, had left jobs with the American Volunteer Ambulance Corps in Paris, intending to join the Free French, when they had a daring idea: They would rescue people from the Nazis. Pretending to be Gestapo officers, the two young men, dressed in military-style ambulance-driver uniforms, bluffed their way into a hospital, Holland screaming in German at the staff to hand over their patients. Fawcett and Holland liberated "twenty-three of the walking wounded," including British soldiers and a few refugees, "and packed them one on top of the other into [a stolen] ambulance."

"One little Scottish soldier was sitting on the lap of one of these big tough soldiers," recalled Fawcett. "He patted the guy's hair. 'Am I hurting your legs, darling?' Everybody was scared to death, you know, but suddenly everybody started laughing. From that moment on, we had a pretty good time." When they ran low on gas, they bribed a railroad worker to let them ride a freight train to Marseille. At the Gare St.-Charles, police were checking the papers of everyone who tried to exit, so Fawcett was temporarily stymied. Then he met a waiter in the station restaurant who showed him the private door used by the staff of the connecting hotel when they slipped into the station café for their morning coffee. (Fawcett told Fry of the location of this private exit and it proved invaluable, as refugees used it to slip in and out of the train station.)

After he maneuvered his charges outside, Fawcett drove them in a stolen fruit truck to the Montredon estate of Countess Lily Pastré, an heiress who sheltered refugees, including, for a time, cellist Pablo Casals and entertainer Josephine Baker. (Pastré sponsored performances at the estate under the direction of a "radical theater director," Sylvain Itkine, whom Fry would meet months later.) After the countess agreed to hide Fawcett's human cargo, he returned the truck and went in search of Fry.

Fawcett was Fry's "doorman and bouncer" for months. Once, someone planted an incriminating paper in the office, and after that Fawcett was responsible for being the last one out at night after burning all the papers that were lying around. He did that well, he recalled, but had more difficulty as a doorman. He was effective only as long as no one appealed to his soft heart; if he noticed a particularly exhausted refugee, he escorted him right past the line and into the office. "I felt awful when I couldn't help people," said Fawcett. As doorman, "I couldn't give them anything and had to let them go in one at a time."

A short time after Fawcett began working for Fry, another American who would play a key role in the operation arrived on the scene. Miriam Davenport was a petite "dishwater blonde," as she described herself, who wore her Phi Beta Kappa key "as a kind of dogtag." Twenty-five and a graduate of Smith College, she had been studying art in Paris when she fell in love with a Yugoslavian exile. They were separated during their migration south after the invasion of France, and Davenport had spent time in Toulouse before traveling to Marseille.

When she first got to Marseille, she ran into an American she knew slightly, Mary Jayne Gold, at a popular watering hole, the Café Pelikan. The two young women confided to each other that they wanted to help the refugees but did not know how to get involved. One day, Walter Mehring, a Toulouse acquaintance of Davenport's, told her that he had been to see "the savior Varian Fry." Because he had been arrested immediately afterward, however, he was afraid to go back to see Fry. Would she go for him? Davenport readily agreed, hoping it was her chance to play a part in refugee work.

That first day, she stood in line with the refugees, waiting to see Fry. Her first impression was of "a young man with curly, dark hair, a high domed forehead, and horn-rimmed eyeglasses," who appeared "committed, self-righteous, and publicly imperturbable." She noted his clothing: He was "correctly got-up in a well-tailored . . . pin-striped suit, Finchley shirts with detachable collars, good cufflinks, good shoes, a Patek Philippe watch, and a Homburg hat." He had the "bearing" of a Harvard man and a "direct, unblinking regard and cordial, impersonal smile [that] spoke louder than words." Fry's impression of Davenport was less detailed; he saw a bright young woman who talked a lot.

Davenport told Fry about Mehring's problem, and they discussed other refugees, including one person on Fry's list, the writer Konrad Heiden, whom Davenport had known in Toulouse. She also described her own disillusioning experience at the U.S. consulate's Visa Division. After checking in at the American consulate, the same "hard-looking, peroxide blonde" who had sent Fry to the Visa Division also directed Davenport to the out-of-the-way location. Davenport, too, had "observed the consulate's doorman being offensively rude to [the refugees]" and noted the "strong odor of xenophobia and anti-Semitism [that] permeated the premises." She concluded from this encounter that "the business of my government was business. . . . Americans with jobs or investments overseas had no passport problems; those with moral obligations or family ties were a nuisance."

Fry, hearing her story and opinion of attitudes expressed at the Visa Division, decided that Davenport had the right politics. Not long after their meeting, he sent her a note: "Do you do typewriting? If you can, will you stop up at my hotel tomorrow? I very badly need help." Thrilled to finally be of some use—and to have a job, since she was nearly destitute—Davenport showed up promptly and Fry hired her as an interviewer at a salary of twenty-seven dollars a month. It was the beginning of a lifelong friendship: "Varian and I recognized each other. . . . We came from the same kind of schools."

Fry and Davenport, more than the others, referred to the operation as "Emerescue"—short for Emergency Rescue Committee—after its New York cable address. Each morning, Fry was at the office by eight. He and his staff conducted interviews until noon, and again from two until seven, taking time out for the "sacred" two-hour lunch. They interviewed about 100 to 120 refugees daily.

At night, after dinner, the staff would retire to Fry's hotel room to conduct the Centre's real business. Fry presided over these critical meetings wearing undershirts and "Black Watch or Royal Stuart plaid boxer shorts," which appeared dressier, according to Davenport, than ordinary underwear. Although these nighttime meetings were "playful, sometimes ribald, sometimes raucous," Fry and his colleagues figured out who to help and how to get them out of France. Despite the seriousness of these decisions, this was when the group released their tension. "[T]he atmosphere was far from conspiratorial or dreary. Occasionally the occupants of neighboring rooms would complain about our loud 'parties,' " wrote Davenport. Nevertheless, by the end of the meeting, sometime during the middle of the night, Fry had a new clandestine route mapped out or a list of refugees who needed forged documents.

As the crew trooped noisily down the stairs to catch a few hours' sleep in their own hotels, they would talk about their favorite subject, Varian Fry. Always trying to decipher the enigma that was their boss, they spent endless hours analyzing everything he did and trying to figure out why he did it. But they never understood him, in part because he behaved differently according to each situation. Fry could be meticulous, precise, and demanding, but he could also be kind, tender, and gentle. They were mystified by his insistence on factual accuracy. "He wanted very, very precise facts. He was always interested in getting things down right." Hirschman thought it was a quirk of his personality. Others believed it was due to his background as a journalist. The greatest puzzle to his staff was the reason behind his devotion to the refugees. "We always wondered what made him do it." They often discussed his motives for being, in Davenport's words, "an unlikely hero." She thought it a miracle that "a white, Anglo-Saxon Protestant from a Presbyterian family" would risk his life for a population that was almost entirely Jewish.

Fry, whose accomplishments were a degree in classics from Harvard and a background as an editor and journalist, had previously shown no tendency toward risk-taking. No one on his staff knew about Fry's youth spent opposing authority and enjoying many unconventional adventures. To Davenport, Fry "wasn't the sort who did daring things." She and the others were also confused by Fry's two distinct sides, the bohemian and the proper Protestant. The rebel led evening conferences in his underwear, but the Harvard man donned a bowler hat when appropriate.

Despite the dangerous work, it sometimes seemed as if Fry was hosting a giant party. He and his staff chose not to "whine or weep" and found ways to joke, even at their nightly meetings, where the subject matter was quite grim. "By the end of the day, [Varian] was usually well lubricated with one—or several—of the grand crus of claret or Burgundy, topped off by some old Armagnac with his coffee." Being in France contributed to a bright atmosphere despite the desperation of war around them. One night Fry, Davenport, and Hirschman walked into the Cintra, a favorite bar, to get a drink. As soon as they sat down, Dubois came over and warned Fry that "there was going to be a visit," meaning a call on him by Vichy police. After that, they really wanted a drink and Davenport asked for Armagnac. The waiter said, "No, mademoiselle, this is a day without alcohol." This was one of France's periodic days when bars and cafés were forbidden to serve distilled spirits. She said, "My God, what am I going to drink?" When he said, "May I suggest champagne?" Davenport thought, "God bless the French." Champagne was not considered to be alcohol.

Everyone on the staff had nicknames. Fry was "Buster," although it is not clear why. The tiny, talkative Davenport was called "Mickey Mouse" and Hirschman was "Beamish." Fry carried a gun, as did Fawcett, because his job required him to carry messages to refugees in hiding. Fry took responsibility for everything, keeping most of the critical information to himself; the less the staff knew, the safer they were. He never acted fearful, although "there was always a danger," recalled Hirschman.

One day, Fry met Fawcett in a café to hand him some papers to deliver. When the younger man asked his boss if he was ever afraid, Fry looked him in the eye and answered, "All the time." Fawcett was impressed: "He was the one who inspired us all. We would do anything for him and we were ashamed to let him down even though most of us were scared to death." No matter what he felt, Fry always maintained an even façade; his behavior was composed and diplomat-like, his demeanor understated. He believed composure would instill confidence in the refugees and in his staff. It would also convince the police that he had nothing to hide.

His greatest fear was not of discovery and arrest, but of failure. As Fry gave up on getting his refugees away from France by legal methods, realizing "the only way to engage in this illegal passage was by way of the frontier," he became even more insecure. Since he had no idea how to proceed, he put Hirschman, who knew better than anyone how to live underground, in charge of all clandestine operations. Hirschman bought forged passports and other faked papers, worked out escape routes for smuggling refugees over borders, and changed dollars to francs on the black market. He was indispensable to Fry.

Fry needed dozens of foreign visas because refugees had to show them in order to obtain Spanish and Portuguese transit visas. Hirschman found foreign consulates from Panama, Cuba, Chile, and China willing to sell overseas visas for emigrations that would never take place. Once the refugees had these visas, Fry helped them apply for their transit visas. Hirschman also located sources for false passports.

Once he got the knack, Fry, too, became adept at the underground work. With Hirschman's help, he learned to smuggle refugees, hire forgers, and lie to the police. Despite the danger, theirs "was a very loose operation—Fry took care of some people and I took care of some others," recalled Hirschman. Although Fry and Hirschman dealt with men who were "probably part of the underworld," at the time, they viewed the connections they made as "sort of a little bit hit and miss" rather than associations with serious criminals.

Fry contacted other refugee aid workers, and one, Donald Lowrie, the YMCA's representative in France, introduced him and Hirschman to the Czech consul, Vladimir Vochoč. In the past, Lowrie had worked with Vochoč to help refugees escape from Czechosolvakia. Vochoč "was willing to hand over authentic Czech passports to anyone who would be useful in fighting the common enemy," and for a time he supplied Fry and Hirschman with phony passports.

In late August, Fry sent Hirschman to the office of the Lithuanian consul to purchase passports for a refugee couple. Whereas the United States placed career diplomats in its consular offices, many other countries appointed ordinary businessmen as their consular representatives. At some point, some of these businessmen—who, of course, had the power to issue visas and other documents—realized how much extra money they could earn by selling papers marked with their country's official stamp. The Lithuanian consul, who was particularly "commercially active," sold the passports to Hirschman for one hundred dollars. "I had to give him [the couple's] real names and I had to have some sort of document, such as an identity card, to start with." Hirschman had the cash in his pocket, the consul had his official stamp, and the transaction took place on the spot.

But Fry soon found that he could not purchase every document he needed, and as a result he hired a forger. Fortunately, he found a candidate in his office, being interviewed by Davenport. Young Bill Freier (his real name was Wilhelm "Bil" Spira), a cartoonist, told Davenport, "I want to be saved." She introduced him to Fry. "He was very gentle," Freier said. "I was not on his list. He wanted to do something for me, but he didn't know what." The cartoonist was brave and daring. He had been caught and arrested in France after he fled his native Austria but had returned again to France "the black way," through the underground, and had changed his name there to Bill Freier. (*Frei* means "free" in German, and he joked later that he was "more free than Fry.") Within a day, Fry called the Austrian at his hotel on the rue de Musée, saying he "had something" for him. When they met again, Fry asked Freier to forge documents, but the young man hesitated, saying he only knew how to draw cartoons.

Fry suggested Freier meet Frédéric Drach, who had worked for the intelligence service of the French Army and was involved in everything illegal then going on in Marseille. Drach, an invaluable source of Danish and Dutch passports, was, in Fry's words, *louche*, "squint-eyed, dubious, doubtful," someone he needed rather than trusted. He "had a double personality," Freier recalled. Freier finally agreed to do the forgeries for Fry and called on Drach at his villa just outside the city. Drach answered the door in his slippers, then showed his visitor a closet filled with new and used passports from all over, and special stamps from France and other countries. He taught the young cartoonist how to forge, and Freier was soon invaluable to Fry. To make it safer for Freier, Fry contacted him through Drach. "We would try not to see each other," recalled Freier.

Fry knew that even with the documents forged by Freier, the refugees still could not get out, and that he had to find the safest place to smuggle refugees over the border, not necessarily the path used earlier by Neu Beginnen youth or Claire and Heinrich Ehrmann. He needed a spot where the French frontier station was far enough from the Spanish station so that an individual crossing illegally "could make a kind of arc around the French" patrol and end up in Spain. Hirschman refined the Ehrmanns' route between Banyuls-sur-Mer, on the French side, and Portbou, on the Spanish side. Refugees would take a train to Banyuls-sur-Mer, then, pretending to be "French vineyard workers," they would meet their guide. The guide would escort them through the foothills, then up the mountain for two or three hours and down into Spain. The trip took one day but was not for everyone. Some were unable to meet its physical demands. Others, whose lives "had been spent being upright citizens . . . simply refused to engage in this maneuver" because it was illegal.

Fry and Hirschman organized the border crossings and hired guides. Le'on "Dick" Ball, a friend of Fawcett's from the Ambulance Corps, became one of the best guides. An American who had lived in France for many years, running a lard factory, he "had a heart of gold and a villa in which he used to hide people," said Fawcett. Ball worked for Fry for months, until one day he suddenly and mysteriously disappeared. No one ever heard from him again.

In late August, money was becoming scarce. The three thousand dollars Fry had brought with him to Marseille was nearly gone, so he cabled New York for more. The Committee sent him a small sum, but the exchange rate at that time was unfavorable, and later it became worse. Because of this, Fry had Hirschman change dollars into francs on "the parallel market." Refugees emigrating to America wanted to change their francs into dollars and Hirschman, at Fry's direction, made these exchanges also. The "parallel of the black market" gave the best rates and since Hirschman could get "more francs per dollar" than if he made the exchange legally, he had no choice but to use this risky method, he recalled. "Otherwise our money would just not have gone anywhere." The penalty if he had been caught was a lengthy prison term.

Despite the unfriendly reception he had received from various officials, Fry continued to make regular visits to the American consulate and to the Vichy police. He was also constantly in touch with the Quakers and the Unitarians, and called on refugee "clients who were too endangered to come to the office." Because of the feverish nature and urgency of his work, he had no time to reflect on the danger around him. His manner gave the refugees hope. Many who were "distraught . . . by the collapse of everything around them," took heart, "seeing this young and enterprising and undaunted kind of American."

Each day, however, he repeatedly faced his most challenging problem. He had to sort through the dozens of people who begged for his help and decide who should receive it. "One of my major problems has been to find a clear-cut definition of an 'intellectual,' " he wrote his mother. "There were innumerable problems of policy (to assist or not to assist scientists . . . just which 'friends' to help, and which not)."

Each night, he agonized over what he knew were the life-and-death decisions he had to make. All political refugees were at risk: If a particular person "had a very clear anti-Nazi attitude, then he could not stay in France." He found many people who fit into this category and cabled their names to New York in hopes that friends and relatives would submit affidavits for them. To his great sadness, he had to turn away "ordinary refugees . . . who hadn't done anything to put themselves in danger"—except that they were Jewish. Fry, filled with guilt, referred these people to the American Friends Service Committee and to HICEM.

Everyone who came to the Centre was seen by either Fry or a staff member. Since there was always the risk of an enemy agent infiltrating the operation by posing as a refugee, each person was interviewed carefully and his claims verified. Fry had help from several "old Mensheviks [who were] socialists, but they were not communists," recalled Davenport. (When Russia's Social Democratic Labor Party split in 1903, Mensheviks were the minority and Bolsheviks the majority.) On Fry's staff, Bedrich Heine was familiar with Socialists, as were refugee-writers Mehring and Sahl. If a refugee was not known by others from his homeland, he usually was not helped.

By the end of August, the Centre was fully functional. Fry had a solid staff and a much better understanding of the work. He relished its clandestine aspects and enjoyed working undercover. He kept many secrets in his head, including the locations of hotels and rooming houses in which the refugees lived. Many times, their very names remained secret.

Unfortunately, the refugees themselves often gossiped about who was living where and about the details of escape attempts. Fry tried to discourage this talk but had little success. Not infrequently, after he and Hirschman had made a complicated underground arrangement, everyone talked about it, even the political émigrés, who should have known better. "[R]are indeed were those who did not communicate to a dozen or so of their friends . . . the news of their secret departure and the plans pertaining thereto." Refugees of all nationalities "clung [and] sat together, talked together. There was a great need to communicate, to tell each other what their plans were for escape and for future life." This was "not without its dangers," since Gestapo agents were always in their midst. The Vichy police were also undercover in the cafés, trying to find out more about the refugees, and the American and his Centre.

Fry turned out to be perfect at underground work because he was always cool and collected. No one could have guessed at the dimensions of the illegal actions taken by him, Hirschman, and the others, in order to smuggle the refugees out. Years later, author Herman Wouk asked Fry to comment on the authenticity of a character, Mike Eden, in his new novel, *Marjorie Morningstar.* Eden was doing "secret rescue work," as Wouk put it, smuggling refugees across borders just before the start of World War II. Fry loved the character, probably because he embodied Fry's own attitudes. "Eden is admirable," he wrote to Wouk, "even down to the unconscious motivations." Eden's explanation of his motivations provides insight into Fry's own psyche:

> I'll tell you something . . . there's a hell of a lot of fun—though that's not quite the word—in rescue work. . . . It's stimulating to be outside the law. It makes you look sharp, it simplifies the day's job. Above all it makes every hour you stay uncaught very pleasant. And as for depression, anxiety—all that pattern simply vanishes.

In addition to enjoying life on the edge, Fry was motivated by a desire to save lives and a belief that he could. In *Marjorie Morningstar,* Eden says, "For three years I've had the unshakable conviction that my remaining destiny in life was to save one child . . . from destruction by Hitler. . . . Hitler's going into the wholesale skeleton-manufacturing business . . . Jewish skeletons. Nothing can stop it. At least I'm cutting down on the number of skeletons." Like Eden, Fry was convinced of Hitler's murderous intentions toward the Jews and had been since 1935. Now he could finally do something about it.

IIIIIIIII

From Marseille to Hoboken:
Bruno and Klara

In August 1940, a young German couple, Bruno and Klara Barth (not their real names) made their way to Marseille. The couple had first met in Berlin in 1931 after a decade spent as members of the socialist youth movement there. When Bruno was arrested in June 1933 along with other party members, he was held as a political prisoner.

After his release from prison, Bruno left Germany. Klara remained behind, working as a secretary and also doing underground work, using a pseudonym, for a small socialist group. "I stayed in Germany and I was still in an underground movement of the Social Democratic Youth Movement. We were in groups of five people. Nobody knew where the other groups were," recalled Klara. As "Marelena Krauss," she noted "how people reacted toward the Nazi regime" and sent reports to Bruno, who was then in Switzerland. He forwarded the reports to leaders of their movement outside Germany. He was a member of an organization called "ORG," which would later become Karl Frank's Neu Beginnen. At this time, ORG was an underground group of young intellectuals, former communists, all Jewish except for Bruno.

In 1935, Klara was arrested by the Gestapo and spent fifteen months in a Nazi prison. When her sentence ended, she left for Switzerland, and she and Bruno were reunited in Bern in January 1937. A short time later, they went to Paris. Klara had a passport and was able to travel legally, but Bruno "had to cross illegally." In August, they were married at the Hôtel de Paris.

Sometime after war broke out in Europe in September 1939, Klara was interned at Gurs, a French concentration camp mainly for women. "Gurs was terrible . . . these were barracks like you see in Auschwitz. . . . We were ten people in a separate barracks which was three times surrounded by barbed wire." When France and Germany signed the armistice, Klara was released. "They said everybody can leave," she recalled. At about the same time, she received "two steamship tickets from America, from Neu Beginnen. They were mailed to me."

Meanwhile, Bruno, who had been in a French camp, was now *prestataire* in the French Army. "The French [intended to hand us to] the British Expeditionary Force," he said. "Then came Dunkirk . . . and the British had to leave France at once. . . . We made a demand, wrote a letter to the British leadership to take us along because we were all in danger. We were Jewish and political prisoners. They heard nothing from their homeland and so they couldn't make that decision."

The British departed without taking Bruno or the other refugees. Left behind along with a few French officers who "didn't know what to do with themselves [because] they had no orders; we suggested we go as far south in France as we possibly can. . . . They, of course, had the power to get gasoline and food for us. We took off and . . . wound up in Toulouse." There, Bruno was given a legal document stating that he had been relieved of all military duties. This established a legal identity for him for the first time in years. He used the document to secure a safe-conduct pass so he could travel further, to find Klara.

After Gurs, Klara was headed to Montauban, a community where many refugees sought shelter. But she experienced hardships along the way and ended up in another town in the south of France. Her goal was to find Bruno. "The first thing was I wrote to my friend in Montauban," she recalled. "I asked her, 'Where is Bruno? Tell him I am here.' A couple of days later, a [friend] who knew Bruno—I was just cleaning the boxcar when she said, 'Klara, come out. Bruno is walking here.' I said, 'You are kidding.' When I came out, Bruno was there. He had gotten my letter that I wrote to my friend. . . ."

Reunited, the couple's next hurdle was to acquire U.S. visas; for this, they had to go to the American consulate in Marseille. This terrified them because "Marseilles was then a very hot place" for certain refugees. "Frequent inspections, hotels all filled, too many refugees, and spies from everywhere" made the city dangerous. "There were arrests day and night. There were raids," recalled Bruno. "We spent our lives in cinemas, hiding."

But they could not leave Marseille until they obtained visas; Bruno, they knew, was wanted by the Germans. They tried at the U.S. consulate but were told there were no visas waiting for them. After a while, they gave up waiting in Marseille and hid in Avignon, a smaller town and one they believed to be safer.

After three weeks, they received a note: "A man from America has arrived with visas and money." They returned to Marseille. "When we came out in Marseilles, we had the good information which side of the station to leave, otherwise we would face arrest," said Bruno. "So we knew the safe way out of the railway station." Klara waited at a hotel while Bruno went to see Fry. Their meeting was either at the Hôtel Suisse or the Hôtel Splendide; Bruno is not certain. Since Bruno spoke no English, "it wasn't easy to make contact, but we both knew what it was all about." They were both sure that "he had the right person and I had the right person." Fry offered Bruno a whiskey, his first ever. Fry was "a convincing-looking personality that we needed and that we had expected from America. And so I was overjoyed to be in contact with him."

Fry supported the couple for some time while they waited for U.S. emergency visitors' visas. The papers finally arrived, and Fry sent the Barths to the frontier. They took a train to Banyuls-sur-Mer, where they received instructions for crossing the border from Mayor Azéma. "The mayor of the village gave us a route how to pass through the Pyrenees. But we left as fast as we arrived. We left at night and went into the mountains. . . . It was windy out." They traveled quickly because they had heard that vehicles of the German Wehrmacht would soon be on the road.

But it took them eight hours to traverse the mountainous path, four more than normal because Klara was wearing the wrong shoes. "The path was all stone, and no trails and anything and just straight into the mountain, up and down again." Small pebbles slowed them down, but eventually they arrived at the border and crossed into Spain, using cigarettes to bribe the Spanish soldiers. "Anybody in uniform you could buy for cigarettes. You never used money." One officer gave them a hard time, asking, "Why did you come over the mountains?"

"Because they are there," Bruno replied, and the officer waved them on.

In Spain, they traveled to Madrid, then on to Lisbon, where they waited two or three weeks for a ship. On September 3, they sailed for America on the *Nea Hellas*. As the ship crossed the ocean, dozens of rumors circulated among its passengers, including one that German submarines would torpedo them, even though it was a Greek ship and Greece was still neutral. "It was an anxious time. Nobody quite knew what would happen," recalled another passenger on the ship. The *Nea Hellas* encountered no problems, however, until it reached New York Harbor, where it collided with a Norwegian tanker. There was little damage, so the *Nea Hellas* docked in Hoboken, New Jersey, on September 12, 1940. Bruno and Klara Barth had arrived in the New World.

CHAPTER THREE

||||||||||||||||||||||||||

EARLY DAYS

. . . for us it was kind of a miracle that it went on day after day. But then one gets used to miracles as to anything else.

Albert Hirschman

FRY CAME to the business of saving lives after a lifetime as an outsider, opposed to authority, but also believing that he had a responsibility to help others, especially those less fortunate. His early years were exceptional; there was never anything average or usual about Fry or his circumstances. An adored and pampered only child reared in a houseful of adults—mother and father, two maiden aunts—he was the center of their energy, love, and attention. When he was old enough to venture outside and make friends, Fry, needing to stand out, was somewhat prickly and disagreeable. Those friendships he had were short-lived, since no one was able to put up with his refusal to compromise or participate in group decisions. This pattern of behavior and outsider status continued throughout his life.

However, his bright, inquisitive intelligence won him considerable admiration, and as a result some people liked and respected him; others, however, found him cold and disdainful. Throughout his youth, Fry never found his right place—he chafed at the world.

It all began with his parents, who were themselves singular. His mother, Lilian Mackey, an educator, had schooling far beyond what was usual for her time and she possessed interests that were uncommon as well. She graduated from Hunter College and worked as a schoolteacher for years before marrying. A bookish woman of Scotch Presbyterian background and quite undomestic, Lilian passed on her love of books, reading, and writing to her son.

Fry's father, Arthur, was born on Christmas Day 1871 into a religious family. His parents were Charles Reuben Fry, a carpenter and social worker, and Anna Duncan Fry, daughter of a Scots stonemason. Christian practice and Christian charity were the themes in the Fry home, and Arthur grew up with a strong conviction that, as a "good Christian," one must be kind and do charitable acts, a belief system he later passed on to his son.

Fry's paternal grandfather, Charles, whom he adored without reservation all his life, played a great role in shaping him. "He would have these sentimental moods [and] tears would come to his eyes describing his beloved grandfather," recalled Annette Fry, Fry's second wife. Charles was born in Washington, D.C., to a family so poor that upon finishing elementary school he went immediately to work, training as a carpenter and cabinetmaker. He taught manual training at the Children's Aid Society, which was founded in 1857 by a Protestant clergyman to help orphaned, abandoned, and mistreated children; this was the beginning of his lifelong affiliation with the organization. He became an early leader of the society's "orphan trains," which transported more than fifty thousand children from New York City to live on farms and in small towns in the Midwest. This "migration of children unique in human history" lasted for more than seventy-five years.

Later, Fry wrote that his grandfather's "whole life was devoted to children. They knew and loved him so well that when he walked through the poorer sections of the city they came running to him from all directions, calling out his name, catching onto his sleeves and coattails, asking to be picked up and hugged, giving, and receiving love." That image, of a savior reaching out to those less fortunate, inspired Fry throughout his life.

Fry's mother, Lilian, a delicate, high-strung woman, argued often with the quiet Arthur Fry. He spoke with a pronounced Brooklyn accent, which was in reality "a Scottish guttural," saying " 'bahttle' instead of 'bottle' and 'boid' instead of 'bird.' " Despite "a long and sometimes stormy courtship," Lilian and Arthur married, optimistic that their differences would fade in time. The ceremony took place on October 7, 1902, at the Holy Trinity Episcopal Church on Manhattan's Upper West Side.

Whether it was because Lilian did not want to be alone with her new husband or that she felt sorry for her two unmarried sisters is unclear, but those sisters, Laura and Florence Mackey, lived with the couple from the first day of their marriage.

Five years later, on October 15, 1907, a son, Varian, was born at home, at 408 West 150th Street. Lilian was thirty, then considered an advanced age for a first-time mother. In 1909, the family moved to a small house in Ridgewood, New Jersey, where they lived for many years.

Although the Frys were solidly middle-class with a comfortable standard of living, events occurred during Fry's boyhood, nevertheless, that left him feeling vulnerable and insecure. This was due primarily to his mother's emotional illness, symptoms of which manifested themselves shortly after his birth. Her disorder was so severe that she was often incapacitated. Although Fry's aunts, Laura and Florence, replaced his mother as his primary caregivers and provided a comfortable home for him and his father, he suffered as his mother became more and more inaccessible emotionally. She had a series of breakdowns and had to be institutionalized. Now she was physically as well as emotionally absent. "She had 'nervous breakdown' after 'nervous breakdown,' " Fry later said, "necessitating long years in sanitariums and lengthy treatments in between the sanitariums." The sensitive, bright Fry saw his mother taken away, time after time, and felt her absence for the weeks or months that she was in a sanitarium. When she was home, however, perhaps to make up for lost time with her son, she "fussed over him frightfully."

The contrast between the fragile, ill Lilian and the responsible Arthur was something Fry thought about often. Over time, the disparity between his parents caused him to become angry at his mother. He felt sorry for his weary father, who often had to carry the burden of the family alone. Over the years, Fry polished Arthur's image until Arthur became the perfect parent—strong, dependable, always there for his son.

In business, Arthur worked hard and eventually became the office manager and a partner in a stock brokerage firm on Wall Street. When

Fry was young, his father often worked late and saw his son rarely; Varian went "to bed and to sleep before [his father] got home." His mother, or his aunts, saw to his daily needs, and his father's role remained minimal.

Arthur's fortunes changed after the stock market crash of 1929, and, although he remained comfortable financially, he was far from wealthy. Despite the business problems and the difficulties at home, Arthur never lost his upbeat, cheerful spirit. His son greatly admired that his father could work hard and accept whatever life handed him, without complaint. Fry always kept a copy of a saying that his father had treasured: "I haven't met tomorrow's woes;/And yesterday's have gone away—/So why excite myself about/The ones I'll leave behind today?" On it, Fry wrote his own commentary: "[B]anal though the verse is, it sums up the philosophy by which my father always lived . . . he was a realist. He lost no time crying about the past, and little worrying about the distant future. His eyes were on today."

Fry's grandfather, Charles, was the second most important influence on the boy, after his father, compensating somewhat for the love and guidance his ill mother could not provide. After Charles was promoted to superintendent of the Children's Aid Society's Summer Home in Brooklyn, Fry visited twice a year, in spring and fall. The Summer Home was in rural Bath Beach, near Coney Island, where Charles, to his grandson's delight, kept cows. Watching his grandfather overseeing "children from the city's steaming slums for one week vacations in the country," Fry learned lessons that remained with him. From his grandfather and father he developed a belief system that rested firmly on the conviction that humans are connected and thus responsible for one another. Years after the orphan trains, Fry facilitated a different sort of migration in Marseille, an effort based on this ethic he had internalized as a child. It was important to Fry that his grandfather never bragged about his own rescue work, and as a result, years later, when he returned from France, Fry also did not talk about what he had done. He tried to live up to his grandfather's credo: "I try to be to the weak, strength; to the discouraged and disheartened, encouragement; and to all, a defence and protection."

Arthur Fry was also an exemplar of kindness. "He called every one of his more than four hundred clerks by first name," Fry said. "More than that, he defended them with a passion. . . . My father was intuitively following one of the basic principles of modern-day personnel management: show genuine interest in your men as the individual human beings they are, and they will work hard and long for you." Arthur's goodness was evident after Charles retired from the Children's Aid Society. He received no pension or Social Security (that legislation had not yet been passed), but Arthur made certain his parents' bank account always had enough in it to support them. "My father never told them what he was doing," Fry remembered. "Instead, he wove tales of the clever ways he had invested their capital for them." (Fry tried to emulate this when, later on, his father experienced business failures and had barely enough money to support himself and Fry's mother.)

To the same degree that he admired his father and grandfather, Fry blamed his mother for being ill and for the trouble she had caused the family. "I have sometimes ruefully wondered what quality it was in my father's nature that induced him to make my mother his life's companion," Fry said in 1958. "She was a very intelligent woman, and in her youth she was a very pretty woman. But she was also a very sick woman. . . . Yet . . . he always spoke of [his marriage] as though it were idyllic."

As a child, Fry stayed home from school often, perhaps modeling after his mother. He was a hypochondriac as well as a faker, often pretending to be ill to miss school, according to a cousin, Elizabeth Richardson, who lived with the Frys for a year when Fry was in fifth grade. Fry's solace came from books and nature, and he became a dedicated bird-watcher at a young age, an interest he cultivated for the rest of his life. Once, the "tender-hearted" boy saved an injured cedar waxwing by snatching it from the jaws of a cat, and brought it for nursing to a member of Arthur Fry's garden club, Ernest Keller. Keller later invited "Master Frye" to visit the cedar waxwing after it was healed, but, as it happened, the bird flew away just before the child arrived to see it. Fry, twelve at the time, "looked somewhat disappointed," wrote Keller, "but . . . thanked me and with a smile of satisfaction said, 'I am glad he got well.' "

Fry's beloved grandfather died when he was thirteen. A year later, he went off to boarding school. At the Hotchkiss School, in Lakeville, Connecticut, he soon changed from a quiet, gentle boy into an outspoken one. During his two and a half years at Hotchkiss, Fry acted out and often disobeyed school officials. He pulled schoolboy pranks occasionally, such as during his second year, when he and others threw oranges, got into a fracas, and flashed "sunshine into a classroom with a mirror." Fry ended his letters home, "Love, Tommie," because at this stage of his development he desperately wanted to fit in and Tommie seemed a much more normal name. Despite efforts to get his parents and classmates to call him by this name, it did not stick, and he remained Varian to everyone.

A few serious outbursts occurred at Hotchkiss during which Fry revealed an uncontrollable rage. Once, "he had to be pulled off another boy whom he was trying to throttle." (When he was younger, he had "almost killed a little playmate when he tried to hit him over the head with a soup tureen.") He was also, at this time, developing a disdain for authority, a real inability to follow rules and dictates set up by others.

Each time he got into trouble, Fry wrote guilt-filled letters to his father in which he expressed "depths of melancholy and despair." He complained to Arthur that he was always unfairly singled out in school as the "aggressive party" and claimed that none of his behavior was unusual or awful. "I tell you this not to make my foolish act seem less foolish, but to ease your poor mind," Fry wrote to his father. "I can't tell you how I suffer when I think of the worry I have caused you. The Lord knows that you have enough to think about." As an adolescent, Fry's double-sided personality, both sensitive and confrontational, made it difficult for school administrators and teachers to understand and deal with him. As Annette Fry later said, "That was the enigma of the man because he had this tremendous sentimental streak and then he also had this very pugnacious, confrontational side."

At Hotchkiss, because Fry was part of a student group working to overturn a ban on the publication of *Ulysses* in the United States, he managed to obtain a copy from its publisher in Paris. He enjoyed reading the book both on his own and aloud to a small group of friends, as he told his wife many years later. (Before a 1933 court decision allowed the book's publication in America, "reading it was considered subversive, dangerous and threatening to western democracy.") Fry loved *Ulysses* so much that he made it the subject of his college-board English essay.

In December 1924, Fry expressed his opposition to a time-honored

Hotchkiss hazing tradition by refusing to climb hand-over-hand on scalding-hot steam pipes, something that upperclassmen forced juniors to do every year. Hazing was sanctioned by the school, according to the Student Handbook of 1922–23: "The fundamental principle of Hotchkiss life is the seniority of the graduating class." Fry's refusal to participate threatened order and organization and, therefore, the administration insisted he comply. As a result, Fry decided to leave school. The headmaster wrote Arthur that his son was "unalterably opposed to some features of the traditions and customs of the school" and had decided to resign.* Fry's righteous indignation and moral superiority when he resigned from school stands as his first principled flouting of rules and regulations; it would not be the last. This "defiance of power and authority" first conceived at Hotchkiss would flower and bear fruit two decades later in Marseille.

Although he had acted on strong principles, Fry still needed the approval and acceptance of his father and, as usual, Arthur did not let him down. He drove to Hotchkiss immediately. "The headmaster explained [to my father] that a tradition of forty or fifty years' standing cannot be changed," Fry recalled. His father responded sharply, "If it's that old, it's high time it was changed." Then he and Fry left.

Living up to Fry's image of him as a saint, Arthur immediately and calmly applied for his son's admission to another good prep school, Taft, in Watertown, Connecticut. Fry began attending classes there in the spring of 1925. During the semester, Fry learned that he had earned an almost unheard of score of 99 on the college-board exam he had taken at Hotchkiss, which included his essay on *Ulysses*. Fry loved playing up this episode. His retelling of it included the declaring of a school holiday in his honor, though Taft seems to have no record of such an event.

At Taft, Fry excelled in English and showed "an appreciation of the beautiful . . . far beyond the ordinary boy," according to the head-

---

*Although it is common knowledge that violent, sometimes fatal hazing incidents occur in prep schools and colleges, nearly seventy years after Fry resigned to protest hazing, the Hotchkiss archivist wrote: "It seems very unlikely that the headmaster would have taken the side of the hazers had such a painful incident been reported to him." According to Fry's own account of this incident, however, it was indeed with the headmaster's knowledge that he was urged to climb the steam pipes.

master. But he still had "difficulty . . . on the human side" and could not get along with his schoolmates. Arthur, pained by his son's solitariness, advised him to stop having "fixed ideas as to a standard to which a [friend] must measure up." But Fry could not relax his ideals and spent a friendless half year at Taft. Arthur asked Taft administrators not to inform Lilian about his son's social difficulties. "Mrs. Fry has recently been in a very nervous condition," he wrote. "I believe it might be better for us to talk . . . not in her presence."

Because Fry was once again unhappy, his father enrolled him for his senior year in a third school, the Riverdale Country School, just north of New York City. This allowed Fry to live with his parents and commute to classes in the brand-new four-door Packard convertible that his father purchased for him. Perhaps because he was living at home and felt more secure, or maybe because he was older, nearly eighteen when the school year began, Fry managed this time to make a few friends and, as a result, seemed more content at Riverdale than he had been at Hotchkiss or Taft. Some of his friends were interested in music while others, surprisingly, were involved in sports, something to which Fry had always "frankly confesse[d] an aversion." *Ulysses* again made him a bit of an attraction. Ferdinand Thun, a Riverdale classmate, recalled how "the more sophisticated boys congregated in Fry's room to read various portions of it out loud."

Inevitably, however, an unpleasant incident occurred, although school records do not provide specifics, and Fry ended up, once again, an outsider. As a result of what the headmaster described as a "loss of control and unpardonable impertinence," Fry was suspended. His friends dropped him also. "He had become a prig," wrote the headmaster, "much disliked by his fellows" and, as a result, had an "unhappy year."

His first sexual encounter occurred during this period, however. Typically continuing his behavior of defiance, his liaison was with the wife of a faculty member. Later in life, he romanticized the encounter: "It was like 'Tea and Sympathy'—lonely wife and a nice-looking youth comes along."

During the spring of 1926, he applied to Harvard and was accepted. He had excelled academically throughout prep school, especially in English and Latin, and had varied interests, including music, literature, and drama; in June, he received high scores on his Scholastic Aptitude

Tests. Harvard took him, ignoring comments about his personality that were included in his application: "Here is a strange boy," wrote Riverdale's headmaster, Frank Hackett. "His mother an invalid and his father working intensely to pay this cost." The headmaster mentioned the incident that had caused Fry's suspension but added that this "jolt" had "brought him to his senses. He is now doing far better. . . . His mind in many respects is brilliant."

Fry entered Harvard in the fall of 1926, a "thoughtful, scholarly, shy, introspective" young man with a love of books and learning, and a tendency both to withdraw from society and to bitterly criticize it. Fry had "a kink somewhere in his makeup," according to a note received by the dean of Harvard, but no one seemed able to name it. Fry was difficult, holding everyone to impossibly high measures, idealizing his father and grandfather, and harboring resentment toward his mother. His insecurities likely came from his mother's inability to parent for a good part of his childhood, and also from the shifting from school to school during his formative adolescent years. He had made no lasting friendships during these years and only in literature and in scholarship did he find pleasure, security, even companionship. He entered Harvard very much alone.

He did not remain this way for long, however, and his Harvard years were marked by distinguished achievement, intense socializing, and an ongoing series of confrontations with authority. During his freshman year, the precocious, literary, and artistic loner met a soul mate, Lincoln Kirstein,* who lived one floor away from him in the freshman dormitory, Gore Hall. "These two kids . . . felt left out by the elite, the proper Bostonian types at Harvard. They weren't invited to be in the right clubs. . . . Kirstein was a Jew and Fry was from a middle-class family in New Jersey with no social pretensions." The friendship between Fry and Kirstein grew, as they shared not only a penchant for wild parties but a desire to make an intellectual contribution to Harvard.

During the winter of freshman year, Kirstein unsuccessfully attempted to win a seat on *The Harvard Advocate*'s editorial board in

*With others Kirstein founded Harvard's Society for Contemporary Art, a precursor of New York's Museum of Modern Art. With George Balanchine, Kirstein established the seminal School of American Ballet, which later became the New York City Ballet.

order to have a say in its content and style. According to Fry, the two young men "thought the Advocate was very, very bad indeed. It was so schoolboyish, and we were so self-consciously aware of Not Being Schoolboys Any Longer." Eventually, they gave up that effort as "Varian's tart antagonism and my own strict 'modernism' made it plain that we'd never win the Advocate," according to Kirstein. There was only one thing to do in response to the *Advocate*'s rejection: Start their own magazine and "make a sensation."

That winter, they created *Hound & Horn*, "A Harvard Miscellany," taking its name from "The White Stag," by Ezra Pound: " 'Tis the white stag Fame we're hunting;/Bid the world's hounds come to horn!" In addition, Fry "snatched a tag from Plato as well, enjoining 'excellence . . . ,' " which was printed in *Hound & Horn* in the original Greek. Underneath it, in "musical notation [was] a theme from Brahms's 'hunting-horn' trio. . . ."

They set to work on their magazine, and it turned out to have unexpected dimension and breadth, lasting as an influential literary journal for seven years. The magazine was "funded, in large part," by Kirstein's father, Louis, the owner of Boston's Filene's department store. As they began putting together the first issue, T. S. Eliot's "The Waste Land" was their inspiration: "The poem became our breviary," wrote Kirstein. "Put to memory, our shavings, showerings, eating, drinking, sleeping, and waking were studded with quotes from its quotations, each one cosmically apt."

Through the modernist *Hound & Horn*, Fry and Kirstein intended to introduce contemporary artists, writers, and composers, such as Joyce, Eliot, Picasso, Gertrude Stein, and Stravinsky, to Harvard. "[W]e felt that Harvard undergraduates ought to know more about them than they did," wrote Fry. (Seven years before Fry's rescue operation in Marseille, the magazine published a review of Hitler's *Mein Kampf*. "Such a man," wrote reviewer M. R. Werner, "will probably push Germany and Europe to destruction, for Hitler . . . lacks creative imagination and can only wish to destroy.")

At Fry's suggestion, they decided to make the first issue a half-size "trial" and published it in the spring of 1927. From the beginning, according to Kirstein, "Varian established the tone and style" of *Hound & Horn*. After the first issue, during summer vacation, Fry worked as "assistant, curator, treasure room [at] Harvard College Library," while

Kirstein visited Eliot in England. That fall, at the beginning of their sophomore year, the two young men urged the university to appoint Eliot to a distinguished professorship.*

In September, they published the first full-size edition of *Hound & Horn.* It included an editorial by Fry "to hail the new and glittering world . . . and to bid farewell to the stodgy in the nineteenth century and its heavy hand on the twentieth. . . ." He also contributed a bibliography of Eliot's works and edited several articles.

Because of their connection with *Hound & Horn,* Fry and Kirstein were suddenly coveted as party guests and celebrities by Boston society. Despite the fact that Kirstein was Jewish and "it wasn't a good deal to be a Jew [in Boston] at that point," the two young men were the "hot intellectuals for the Harvard and Boston Brahmin community [and its] intellectual and academic world."

But a rift had occurred between the two young publisher/editors. Kirstein, pragmatically seeking to attract a wider readership, insisted on including in the first issue a football memoir written by a Harvard alumnus. This angered Fry, who viewed it as an intellectual compromise. At the time, Fry was a "fair classical scholar with working knowledge of Greek and Latin, a good pianist, with old-fashioned courtly manners of a sardonic twist." It was during this period that he began to behave in a manner that would continue to the end of his life, acting as if he were smarter than everyone else, correct when all others were wrong. His righteousness was difficult to take. "He felt his cerebration superior to that of his classmates," wrote Kirstein. "Of this I was less certain, but I found him sympathetic, although I was wary of his covert disdain."

Their next disagreement was Kirstein's desire to add two new staff members, Richard Blackmur and future psychoanalyst Bernard Bandler. Bandler espoused the philosophy of humanism, which assumed, among other things, "that there is a dualism of man and nature, and that man's will is free." Fry rejected this ideology, which found its "ultimate ethical principle in restraint . . . turning to the Hellenic doctrine of reason, and away from romanticism. . . ." He objected strongly to Blackmur and Bandler, but Kirstein prevailed.

Not long after, the staff had a real "family quarrel," and Fry re-

---

*Ten years later, Harvard appointed Eliot the Norton Professor of Poetry.

signed. Once again, he had been unable to compromise his opinions or accede, for the sake of a larger goal, to the will of others. Nor could he participate in group discussions. As a result, he was out of *Hound & Horn,* but his founding of the magazine always remained a defining moment in which, for the first time, he felt himself to be powerful and important, a player in the intellectual arena.* After he left, he was once again the outsider and felt bitter, frustrated, and dejected; he had lost—or relinquished—something wonderful, and he knew it.

Although he was no longer part of the magazine, his social life with Kirstein and other friends continued. They were "an extraordinarily brilliant, inventive, imaginative, bubblingly creative set of young men," recalled Katherine Durand, who was then the wife of a young Harvard instructor. Their "set" alternated between intense intellectual debates and drunken brawls, with Fry a leader in both. At Harvard, his defiance of and disdain toward authority took over as his rowdiness escalated at the raucous parties he hosted and attended until he was arrested several times for disorderly conduct. His twin strains of rebelliousness and gifted intelligence were never more evident than during his Harvard years.

Katherine Durand recalled one midnight when she heard "a sharp knock" at her door. Fry burst in, crying, "Get up quickly and we'll all go to Linc's! There's a party!" When his hastily dressed friends joined him, Durand, a Quaker, said to her husband, still in his red pajamas, "Mind thy fly!" Fry found this hysterically funny and shouted out at intervals throughout the night, "Mind thy fly!" He drove the exuberant young people to Kirstein's in his large Packard. When a chain across the road blocked his way, he "revved up the motor and crashed into the chain." When it held, he backed up and gunned the motor again, crashing into it with even more force, with "a muttered vow that he was bound not to let [anything] restrain his efforts—his definitely reasonable efforts!" Eventually, he was forced to give up and find a different route. (Durand suggested that a plaque be erected at Harvard in honor of Fry: "To one who dared to defy Authority and Attempts at restraining the human impulses for good.")

---

* *Hound & Horn,* an influential literary and critical journal well into the thirties, went far beyond the goals of its founders. "It was to have been an attempt," Fry wrote, "to provide a great university with a medium of expression worthy of the most imaginative, creative work that university fosters or influences."

During Fry's years at Harvard, repeating his prep-school pattern, he first acted out and brought the authorities down on him. Then, contrite, he begged forgiveness from the school and from his father. Harvard dean C. N. Greenough wrote to Fry's former headmasters at Taft and Riverdale to find out more about his troubling and troubled student. He learned that Fry's current behavior was nothing new, that he had "great power" but "little sense . . . and . . . [is] intensely selfish," according to the headmaster of Riverdale.

After too many late-night wild parties, Harvard placed Fry on probation, while Arthur Fry, of course, immediately forgave his son. In April of his sophomore year, Fry appealed to Harvard's administration to change his probationary status, blaming his many absences, including three missed midterms, on "unusually poor health." He overplayed his illnesses but somehow convinced the university of his sincerity, for at the end of his second year at Harvard he was "promoted to the Junior Class in good standing."

That summer, Fry traveled to Greece on the SS *Sinaia*. When he returned from studying at the American School of Classical Studies to begin his junior year, there was a tragic incident, in which Fry, while driving his Packard, hit a boy, James Carroll, who had darted out between two parked cars. Fry appeared in court on November 25, 1928, to testify about Carroll's death. It was ruled an accident and Fry "was found not guilty of the boy's death."

During his junior year, he cut classes often, claiming recurrent malaria, which he had caught in Greece. When he petitioned the authorities in February to exempt him from Harvard's rules about absences and missed exams, a physician backed up his complaint. Fry "was incapacitated somewhat by the malaria throughout the earlier part of the year," wrote the doctor, and should have a limited schedule so he could survive "the year without any fatigue."

Fry was robust enough during this period, however, to get a "girl in trouble." Fearful that his father's "stern Scotch Presbyterian upbringing" would at last force him to reject his son, Fry nevertheless confided his troubles to Arthur. Arthur had never discussed sex with Fry, except the time "when he . . . warned me to keep away from bad women." Now, Fry remembered, "he put his big, strong, protecting arm around my shoulder, and with not so much as a single word of censure, he stood by me . . . until my ordeal and my girl's was over." With Arthur's support and financial backing, the young woman had an abortion.

Still the rebel, Fry was arrested at the end of the year. In June, after final exams, he had stolen a FOR SALE sign and planted it on the lawn of the Harvard president, Abbott Lawrence Lowell. When questioned by the police, Fry and a cohort, Allan R. Rosenberg, lied: "One told the policeman that he was shooting pigeons and the other said that he was waiting for a street car." In court, Rosenberg's charges were dropped, but Fry was convicted.

This was too much for Harvard, and the administration informed Fry he was to be expelled. Although guilty of serious misconduct in the past, he had escaped consequences because "of the state of [his] mother's health," officials said, but now it was too late for excuses. They did, however, leave the door slightly open, informing Fry that he would not be "cut . . . off forever from Harvard." They would permit him to apply for readmission after a year if he could prove that he had "developed a proper sense of responsibility and . . . would not bring disgrace" to the college.

Although Fry's actions may have been caused in part by factors beyond his control—both Riverdale and Harvard blamed his problems on his mother's illness—Harvard was firm in its decision to expel him. Fry asked two friends, Eileen Avery Hughes (whom he had met during the year and would later marry) and a Harvard professor, William C. Greene, to petition the university on his behalf. Fry was an "able" student, wrote Greene, with "literary gifts" and "a real determination to become a physician." (At this time Fry, who often changed his major, was pre-med.) The professor asked the dean to find "some other penalty, the effects of which might prove less disastrous."

Hughes, six years older than Fry, presented herself as a mature, responsible editor and teacher, giving no indication that she was passionately in love with the young man whose case she was pleading. Taking the dean into her confidence, she shared private information, explaining that Fry had been on his own for years because of his mother's illness. All he needed was the guidance of "older and wiser people who will take an interest in him and at the same time regard him as a person not yet thoroughly mature." His work on *Hound & Horn,* she added, proved his talent as well as his determination to succeed.

Harvard softened a bit after hearing from Hughes and Greene and informed Fry that if he took an "industrial" job, and kept it for some time, the university would consider readmitting him. Fry, of course, welcomed this news, but because of his contentious nature could not adhere to Harvard's stipulations. He had lined up summer work for himself as companion to the son of a Dr. Friedman, he told Harvard, insisting that this job was more suitable for him than "industrial" work; he was physically weak as the result of colitis, gastritis, bronchitis, and several other ailments, and could not handle a strenuous job. In addition, he wanted to be self-supporting while he was not in school, and could earn more as a companion. But Fry lost this round and took a job at Moth Aircraft in Lowell, Massachusetts; it was not physical labor, though, but a position as an accountant.

In the fall, he was readmitted to Harvard. Instead of being a senior, however, he had to repeat his junior year, and he would be on probation for at least six months. If he did well, his status might change by March, the university informed him. For those six months, Fry followed the rules, attended classes, and heeded Eileen. But he could not completely curb his tendency to rebel and on November 24 hosted a midnight soiree for fifty in his apartment at 427 Broadway in Cambridge. At one in the morning, a caterer delivered orange noisette, café parfait, bombe glacé, "fancy cake," and coffee for fifty guests, plus china, silver, linen, a table, punch bowl and glasses, ladles, twelve gold chairs—and a waiter. The expense was likely borne by Arthur Fry, who seemed unable to refuse his son anything.

Fry kept the party secret and by February was off probation; his grades were excellent and he even made Dean's List. But just two months later, while visiting friends at Princeton University, he was arrested after a drunken brawl in a Trenton, New Jersey, restaurant. When he contacted Eileen after his arrest, he asked "wistfully whether two can marry without a wedding and still charge Father for a new cutaway."

A New Jersey court found Fry "guilty of malicious mischief" and ordered him to pay five dollars in damages. Eileen had contacted Arthur Fry and the two, united in their love for Fry, discussed how to keep their boy out of trouble. Fry met with his father, on orders from Eileen, and promised he would "go straight [back] to Cambridge." He sent a cable detailing this meeting to Eileen, signing it, "Obedient Puss."

Eileen loved her young boyfriend and was eager to marry him. To her, he was handsome, charming, bright, and fun. To him, she was an irresistible combination of stunning intellect and warmth. From the time they met, until much later when circumstances intervened to force a role reversal, Fry was Eileen's lad and she gave the orders. She also cared for and protected him, and defended him when necessary.

Eileen Avery Hughes was born on August 3, 1901, in San Diego, California, but attended school in England: the prestigious Roedean School; then Somerville, Oxford University's first women's college. When she returned to the United States, she taught at Smith and was an editor at *The Atlantic Monthly.* (Much later, she was the secretary and treasurer of Harold Oram's fund-raising firm, and for two years she worked with Albert Einstein as the financial manager for the Emergency Committee of Atomic Scientists at Princeton.) She and Fry met when he was twenty-two and she was twenty-eight, and they soon fell in love. It was a relationship of like minds, both brilliant, literary, and witty. But they fought often, as she "bossed him around and treated him like a little boy." During his last years at Harvard, it was Eileen who kept him on course.

He finally began his senior year in the fall of 1930, with the stipulation that he earn at least a C in each of his five courses. Even under Eileen's supervision, he still cut too many classes and again received a warning from the administration. Since it had worked previously, Fry once again submitted a medical excuse backed up by a physician, who informed the university that his patient had "stomach ulcers." Somehow, Fry managed to pass all his courses and graduated in May 1931 with a bachelor of arts degree.

Just before graduation, he had filled out a questionnaire on which he listed "foreign trade, European representative" as the occupation in which he was most interested. Other fields he considered were "archaeology, law, medicine, farming, teaching, etc., in fact almost everything." The position he really wanted, however, was "European representative, preferably in France, Spain, Italy, or Greece," an idealistic goal for a penniless young man whose country was in a depression.

Several months earlier, in November, Fry and Eileen became engaged and applied for a wedding license at Cambridge City Hall. On June 2, after he had graduated, they were married by a justice of the peace at the home of Eileen's sister, Kate, at 7 Marlboro Street in Boston. Fry moved into Eileen's apartment at 35 Fayette Street in Boston for the summer; she worked but he was unemployed.

That fall they moved to upstate New York and spent their first winter as a married couple in a house lent to them by writer and literary critic Granville Hicks, in Grafton, three hours north of New York City. They "lived in freezing poverty" and often did not have enough to eat. They were "so poor they were reduced at one time to eating fried dough as there was nothing in the house but flour and lard."

Then Fry got a real job, as a part-time staff writer for *Consumers' Research,* and he and Eileen moved to East Eleventh Street in New York City. Their financial situation improved because Fry also taught English and Latin part-time, two of his favorite subjects. He found himself a leader again for the first time since *Hound & Horn* when he joined the Association of Unemployed College Alumni and worked to improve the job market for college graduates. He and Joseph P. Lash, who would become a confidante and biographer of Eleanor Roosevelt, led the association's march on Washington in May 1933. Fry and Lash met with the president, an occasion Fry later described as one of the few times in his life he "felt shy." They asked Roosevelt to "appropriate money to bolster tottering State educational systems" and reminded him that their hard-earned diplomas were virtually worthless. The Washington march and the meeting with Roosevelt gave Fry a forum in which to express his concern about social issues, something he had ignored for years, perhaps since his objection to hazing at Hotchkiss. In Washington, he spoke convincingly and eloquently about his concerns regarding adequate funding for education.

Fry's next job, as assistant editor at *Scholastic Magazine,* was the first in a series of editorial positions he would hold during the thirties. At the same time, as evidence of his continued interest in "foreign trade, European representative," he registered at Columbia University's School of Graduate Faculties and over the next six years took thirty graduate credits as a political science major. (Still uncertain about what he really wanted to do, in 1935 he applied to Harvard graduate school to study fine arts, but he never pursued this interest.)

In his work, Fry was focused and determined to succeed, according to writer and editor Quincy Howe, who hired Fry to replace him as editor in chief of *The Living Age* in 1935. He had met Fry earlier, in connection with *Hound & Horn.* When Fry became its editor, *The Living Age* had been publishing "material from the foreign press" for nearly a hundred years. Howe always remained sure of Fry's talents and abilities. "Nothing so became me on *The Living Age* as my leaving of it," he said later. "My final editorial inspiration was surely my finest. I saw to it that Fry took over. . . . Fry's politics were more discriminating, more subtle than most—based as they were on sound aesthetics—a commodity then in short supply."

As the editor of a journal that published foreign-affairs news, Fry's first undertaking was a three-month trip to Europe in order to witness foreign politics firsthand. He left for Germany in May 1935, several months before that country's passage of the Nuremberg Laws, which denied German Jews basic civil rights.

Fry traveled third class on the *Bremen,* a fast German ship, where he ran into Alfred Barr, the Museum of Modern Art director since 1929, and his wife, Margaret Scolari Barr, whom Fry knew slightly from the *Hound & Horn* days. He told the Barrs that "he [was] going to Berlin to look into the treatment of the Jews. . . ." In Berlin, Fry stayed at the fifty-room Hotel-Pension Stern, Kurfurstendamm, located in a pleasant part of the city. There, he became acquainted with Bernard Apfel, a defense attorney, whom he would meet years later in Marseille and whose tragic and untimely death he would witness.

On the evening of July 15, Fry ventured out of his hotel, planning to head to the nearby Café Hessler. On the street, he stopped short as he witnessed a scene he could scarcely believe. He "saw the S.A. men . . . throwing chairs and tables through the plate-glass windows of Jewish-owned cafés, dragging Jewish men and women out of buses and chasing them up the streets, or knocking them down and kicking them in the face and belly as they lay prostrate on the sidewalk." He heard their awful chant: *"Wenn Judenblut vom Messer spritzt, Dann geht es nochmal so gut!"* ("When Jewish blood spurts from the knife, then everything will be doubly fine.") Fry watched a soldier stab a man's hand, impaling it to a sidewalk café table. Moments later, the soldiers walked away laughing and singing. The man who had been stabbed remained in his seat crying, his hand held fast by the knife. Fry was in shock but returned to his room and quickly put pen to paper. Believing this to be one of the first pogroms in Berlin, he wrote an eyewitness account and sent it to *The New York Times,* which published it on July 17, 1935. The next day, a Dr. M. Kleinfeld, one of the Jews who had been attacked, died as the result of his injuries.

Fry immediately went to see Ernst "Putzi" Hanfstaengl, a German

American who had graduated from Harvard a decade before him.* Hanfstaengl, now Hitler's chief of the Foreign Press Division at the Propaganda Ministry, gave Fry an inside look at Nazi depravity. Hanfstaengl told him that while the moderates wanted to solve "the Jewish question" by emigration, the extremists, led by Joseph Goebbels and Hitler, preferred annihilation. "Hanfstaengl told me, in his cultured Harvard accent, that the 'radicals' among the Nazy Party leaders intended to 'solve' the 'Jewish problem' by the physical extermination of the Jews," Fry later wrote. "I only half believed him.

"Extermination was, I am almost certain, the exact word he used. (We spoke English, having both gone to Harvard)," Fry wrote. "[T]hat there were men in positions of power and authority in western Europe in the twentieth century who could seriously entertain such a monstrous idea" was something Fry, like so many others, found difficult to believe. Nevertheless, he wrote an article based on his interview with Hanfstaengl, and *The New York Times* published that, too, on the front page. Fry's reportage established a very early date—1935—for the "emergence of the idea of exterminating the Jews of Europe."†

By the time he returned to the United States in August, he had shed his last bit of naïveté and was convinced that the Nazis intended to murder the Jews. He wrote article after article denouncing the Nazi regime, urging America to condemn and challenge Hitler and support the initial U.S. boycott of the 1936 Olympic Games in Germany. Hitler's fascism, propaganda, and censorship, and his brutal anti-Semitism must be checked before it was too late, Fry warned. "German people are afraid to talk of the government," he said in a

---

*Upon his graduation from Harvard, Ernst Franz Sedwick "Putzi" Hanfstaengl traveled to his father's country, Germany. He met Hitler and, enthralled with fascism, grew close to the dictator and worked for him for years. In 1942, he and Hitler fell out. In a strange twist, Hanfstaengl was saved by the U.S. government from certain death and, at great cost and effort, was brought to America to work as a spy for the Roosevelt administration. He had no difficulty getting a U.S. visa.

†Fry proclaimed years later that he was "historically . . . the first person to reveal that the National Socialist Party was already planning to exterminate the Jews in the summer of 1935." In the years since World War II, debate has raged over what the United States knew in the late thirties and early forties. In July 1999, the Simon Wiesenthal Center in Los Angeles concluded, based on newly declassified government documents, that information about the planned extermination of the Jews was definitely in the hands of State Department officials during 1940 and 1941, the years that Fry was in Marseille.

radio talk. "Even neighbors may report to the government. When any-one discussed politics with me they closed the doors and shades before they even mentioned Hitler." Fry's voice was one of many raised about the Germans as Americans traveled to Europe and came home bearing tales of horrors witnessed and horrors to come. But even those, such as Fry, who had a forum for their views, were basically ignored by both the public and America's political leaders.

During the remaining years of the decade, while always conscious of the imminent European nightmare, Fry edited his magazines, took graduate courses, and moved with Eileen to Irving Place, near Gram-ercy Park. Fry was a "sweet, shy young man . . . and we all loved him," recalled one woman with whom the young couple socialized. The other, edgy Fry, was passionate about politics and never let up on his campaign against the Nazis.

In 1937, Fry became editor in chief of the Foreign Policy Associa-tion's Headline Books. He wrote and edited a number of books pub-lished by this research and educational nonprofit foundation, books that were designed to explain complex foreign-policy issues to a wide audience. This position gave him an opportunity to write about the political situation in the world as he saw it. He authored several Head-line books, including *The Peace That Failed, War in China, Bricks Without Mortar, The Story of International Cooperation,* and *The Good Neighbors.* Remaining true to his political ideology and demonstrating his prescience in many areas, these books "alerted young readers . . . [to] the perils of war and dictatorships. . . ."

In 1937, at the height of the Spanish Civil War, Fry worked part-time for the Committee to Aid Spanish Democracy, where he met Norman Thomas. During the last three years of the decade, Fry was as stable in terms of work and marriage as he had ever been. But he still "got a kick out of riling people," and loved confrontation, argument, and being right.

As the thirties drew to a close, however, a storm was brewing that would end the relative tranquillity of these years, drawing Fry into it, far more intensely than he could ever imagine.

||||||||

All Is Okay:
Paul and Elena Krantz

The routes that brought refugees to Fry were as various as their backgrounds. At the beginning of his year in Marseille, Charles Joy, the European representative of Boston's Unitarian Service Committee, passed along several "special cases," people who were being "hidden in order to avoid extradition." One was Paul Krantz, pen name Ernst Erich Noth,* a German Catholic writer. His wife, Elena Krantz,* who was Jewish, was also in danger.

A best-selling author in Germany and France whose subject was the ideology of antifascists, Krantz was forced to leave Frankfurt in 1934 because his works "were displeasing to the Nazi regime." He continued to write, explaining why the defeat of Germany was necessary for the survival of Europe. He lived in Aix-en-Provence for years, creating denunciations of Hitler's regime for the French Propaganda Ministry. There, he fell in love with and married an Italian Jewish opera singer, Elena Fels; they had two children, Pierre and Jean. After the fall of France, the Germans placed Krantz on its wanted list and he was forced to hide. "If the German government orders the French government to give up [Krantz], he will be . . . put to death or interned in a concentration camp."

Krantz was known in the United States; Thomas Mann had supplied his name for Fry's original list and several people had contacted the ERC about him. After Mildred Adams told Krantz's American friends that the Krantzes could obtain U.S. emergency visitors' visas if it could be proven that he was in "grave danger of [being] apprehended by the Nazis," his sponsors filed affidavits of support for him.

Elena Krantz contacted Fry in November 1940. Would he help them get visas? she asked. She wrote to Fry repeatedly from November through January, but he was not able to secure the visas. In January, when Fry invited Elena to the Centre to discuss the situation, she rebuked him: "[For] almost three months I don't have any news from your office. I am waiting to get some news from you."

*The Krantzes were numbers 952 and 953.

By this time, the Krantzes had separated. Fry, still unable to get their visas, intended, however, to support them. "I think we should help her and the kids," he wrote in a memo. At issue was how long a family could live on the largesse of the Centre, with its limited funds. Certain refugees, such as Elena Krantz, were demanding and complained if their weekly allowance was late. Fry and a colleague at the Centre differed, a rare occurrence, when the other man suggested that Fry end his support of the Krantzes. Other refugees were getting nothing "because their place is taken by an old regular customer," he wrote, adding that Elena Krantz was Fry's "pet." Fry was adamant, however, and the Krantzes continued to receive a weekly stipend.

By April, Fry had managed to secure the family's U.S. visas and had purchased their passages. While they waited for Portuguese transit visas, Fry intended to "continue to carry them unless we know they don't need our help." Finally, the Portuguese visas were granted and they left for Lisbon on June 20. On the Fourth of July, the Krantz family departed Lisbon for the United States, arriving a month later. After nearly a year of anguish, the endangered writer, his Jewish ex-wife, and their children were finally safe. In typical understatement, a member of Fry's staff summed it up: "All is okay."

CHAPTER FOUR

||||||||||||||||||||||||||

OVER THE MOUNTAINS

Nothing that's human is strange to me.

Marta Feuchtwanger

B Y SEPTEMBER, more than thirty thousand German-speaking refugees were hiding in the south, and Vichy was interning increasing numbers of them. At this point, it was unknown if any of the feared extraditions under the terms of Article Nineteen had taken place, but each day brought new people to the doors of Fry's Centre. Despite the stumbling block of no French exit visa, many of the Centre's clients had successfully escaped over the French-Spanish border during that first month.

"We had no premonition of the horrible things that were to come at that point," recalled Albert Hirschman. Compared to the Europeans around him who "were all steeped in the dangers of this moment . . . and what was threatening," recalled Hirschman, Fry sometimes "spoke too openly in the cafés" and displayed a certain casualness. On the other hand, his relaxed attitude was useful in "maintaining the energy and . . . being able to continue the work under this terrific [pressure]."

On September 2, the Vichy government issued a statement that it planned to arrest any foreigner considered dangerous. Although Marseille was in the unoccupied zone, Fry heard rumors of Gestapo agents in the city and felt an ominous Nazi presence. He found out much later that, during this period, he had been under "close surveillance by the Gestapo." Then he heard from M. Barellet, the *préfecture* in Marseille, that the Gestapo, becoming more active, was beginning to close in on the refugees and had even instructed him to arrest three of the most important German refugees: Rudolf Breitscheid,* Rudolf Hilferding, and Georg Bernhard. Breitscheid had been Prussian minister of the interior and then a leader of the German Social Democratic Party in the Reichstag. Hilferding had been finance minister of the Reich, a member of the Reichstag until 1933, and the most important financial expert among the Social Democrats. Bernhard was former minister of economics in the Weimar Republic, editor of Germany's leading newspaper, and editor in chief of Germany's largest publishing house. In Marseille, these men had done nothing to protect themselves and walked about the city as if they were free and safe, rather than refugees wanted by the Gestapo. Breitscheid and Hilferding sat and talked openly in the cafés. Bernhard, too, frequented the cafés, attracting attention with his curly white hair and great height. Despite warnings from his family to sit down and be quiet, he would take his time, look around, and say, "I want to see if I see anybody I know."

Fry was continuing to expand his own organization. Miriam Davenport told him of two people she believed would be helpful, Justus Rosenberg, a teenage boy whom she knew from Toulouse, and her friend Mary Jayne Gold. Rosenberg was now in Marseille, needing a place to sleep and trying to emigrate. Fry appointed "Gussie," as he was called, as the office boy. He slept at the rue Grignan office and kept watch after Fry and the others had left for the night. Gussie had a well-developed sense of responsibility as a result of being on his own; he and a school friend had ridden their bicycles from Paris to Marseille. Gussie was "the son of Danzig Jews" who sent him to Paris figuring he would be safe, said Davenport. "Both kids had only the clothes on their backs and a change of underwear, but they were madly cheerful and prone to clowning." Once, Gussie was in a café with Davenport and the writer Hans Sahl. "I'm so envious," said Sahl. "You have your whole life ahead of you." When Davenport responded, "Gussie is a

*Breitscheid was number 164.

refugee Jew from Danzig. He's only fourteen and doesn't know a soul here. He could be picked up at any time and sent to a concentration camp," Sahl realized they were all in the same boat and stopped envying Gussie's youth.

Mary Jayne Gold, an American heiress and a member of café society, had a pilot's license and had flown around Europe in her own Vega Gull, a "low-winged monoplane," before donating it to the French government. "Big, beautiful, and blonde," Gold was wearing a pink linen suit, ankle socks, and sandals, recalled Davenport, when the two young women met in Toulouse. They became friends and remained close. Davenport told Fry that Gold had a proposition for him. Gold's funds, which were considerable, had been delayed, so she was temporarily broke. If Fry agreed to lend her "sufficient money for her personal needs," when her money arrived she would donate several thousand dollars to his Centre and he could use the money to help refugees who were not on his original list. Fry was irate at this suggestion. "I know nothing about that woman!" he shouted at Davenport. "How do I know she's trustworthy? She's just another rich playgirl, probably one with a passion for dukes and duchesses and whose friends are ultrareactionary."

Hirschman, always on the lookout for money, overheard this interchange and suggested to Davenport that he, rather than Fry, deal with Gold. "[I]n a very short time, the Centre Américain de Secours was some 330,000 francs [about seven thousand American dollars] richer," wrote Davenport. "The money was specifically earmarked for those not on the New York lists," thus creating what became known as the Gold List to help those who would not otherwise have been supported. (Karel Sternberg, future head of the International Rescue Committee, was one of the first to gain his freedom thanks to Gold's generosity.)

Even after Hirschman made the deal with Gold, Fry still hesitated in hiring her; he had difficulty with lavish, spirited women. Fry finally got over his discomfort and asked Gold to join his staff, but in a sense he was right about her. She struck up an affair, which Fry found disturbing to his operation. In a short time, though, just a few weeks, her personality and appearance turned out to be exactly what were needed to carry out an important and dangerous assignment. Gold's regular duties on Fry's staff were delivering messages and conducting interviews. She often met with refugees in her room at the Continental Hotel when they were too endangered to go to the office. They were "rank-

and-file militants . . . tired and half beaten." Their determination was obvious, she wrote. "[T]hey would have done it all over again despite the failure of their efforts and the bleakness of their present prospects."

During her time in Marseille, Gold may have enjoyed "herself a little bit too much perhaps" after she became involved in a romance with Jacques Danois, known as "Killer," a former French Foreign Legionnaire. "If we had taken Mary Jayne into the Committee more actively from the beginning," Fry later wrote, "I think she would not have got involved in that silly business of hers. I think she would have given us even more than she did." Spirited and conscientious, as well as charitable, Gold donated generously to Fry's operation, and she and Fry soon became good friends.

Despite their intelligence and courage, however, Davenport and Gold remained outside the inner circle of Fry's closest associates. The Centre was a man's world, where men took the risks and enjoyed the excitement while the women generally conducted interviews, ran errands, typed, and took shorthand. "I was not made privy to the undercover stuff although I knew it was going on," said Davenport. Fry refused to accept opposition from her or any other woman. Although she "loved him dearly," they got "into terrible shouting matches" because he "brooked no superiority from a woman. He just could not believe she was right." Nevertheless, Fry's entire staff, including Gold and Davenport, remained loyal and devoted. Their protégés, as Fry now referred to the refugees, were well protected by his diligence, Hirschman's underground connections with gangsters from competing Corsican organizations, and the dedication of the entire staff.

Hirschman, who was irresistible to women (he even had "a little bit of a relationship" with Davenport) and a charmer with men, continued broadening his network of associates, many in the Marseille underworld. He met Malandri, "a Corsican businessman," through the receptionist Mme. Delapré at the American consulate, with whom he had a brief fling. Malandri introduced him to Jacques, a Corsican gangster and restaurant owner. Hirschman attempted to change money on the black market through Jacques, who did not like Americans, so instead introduced Hirschman to Dimitru.* Although Dim-

---

*"Malandri," "Jacques," and "Dimitru," were pseudonyms created by Fry for his 1945 memoir *Surrender on Demand.*

itru "turned out to be all spy," in September Fry hailed him as an unsavory savior because he changed dollars sent by the ERC in New York into francs.

Very early in September 1940, Fry received word that the first ship carrying refugees had made it across the Atlantic to America. The *Nea Hellas,* which had sailed on Tuesday, September 3, from Lisbon, the jumping-off point for ships from Europe, had docked safely in New York. The ship carried a large group of German and Austrian socialists and labor leaders, including Claire and Henry Ehrmann. It was a great moment for Fry, for it proved that his methods worked, that the kinds of people he wanted to help could be helped. Everything he had been trying to do, from securing visas to smuggling refugees out of France, had succeeded. He had saved lives, as he had come to France to do.

Muriel Gardiner Buttinger, whom Fry had known in New York, had sponsored the U.S. emergency visitors' visas for many of the *Nea Hellas* passengers, including the Ehrmanns, and the prominent Austrian Social Democrat Otto Leichter and his young sons, Franz and Henry. Claire Ehrmann recalled that during the voyage Otto Leichter "asked me to help the boys wash some socks." The boys' mother, Käthe Leichter, an Austrian sociologist and leading Social Democrat, had been arrested by the Gestapo, imprisoned, and transported to Ravensbrück, where she died in 1942. Her arrest, and her death, "happened early, at a time when they weren't killing people," recalled Peter Berczeller,* who knew the Leichter family.

Kurt Sonnenfeld, a passenger on the *Nea Hellas* and a member of Neu Beginnen, recalled the irony of having to exit France illegally, since only a short time earlier he and his family had slipped *into* the country illegally. After the Anschluss, the Sonnenfelds, who were Jewish, had left Austria for Switzerland but found they were not welcome there. Just before the Swiss sent them back, they crossed the Alps into France. In France, they managed to secure U.S. visas.

In a "joint venture," Fry and the Jewish Labor Committee arranged the Sonnenfelds' escape from France, and they began the trek across the Pyrenees. The family made several unsuccessful attempts to cross into Spain, but were always turned back by French border guards. On

---

*Berczeller was a boy of nine when he and his father, Richard, number 90 on Liste Complète, and his mother, Frances, were helped to freedom by Fry in the summer of 1941.

their third day in Cerbère, only one guard was on duty, instead of the usual two or three. This officer turned to young Kurt, who spoke and understood French perfectly, and said, "Look, I'm going to turn my head now, and I am not seeing you." Kurt quickly realized that they were being given a chance to escape, but his mother, whose French was poor, was about to give up and turn back. Kurt tugged on her arm, shouting, "No!" He pulled her in the direction of the border and, as the guard looked away, Kurt led his parents the short distance to the Spanish side. After traveling without difficulty through Spain and Portugal, since they had both Spanish and Portuguese transit visas, they reached Lisbon and boarded the *Nea Hellas*.

"During these six blessed weeks [in August and September] nearly 250 clients of the Committee . . . were able to cross [into Spain] without incident." Fry developed several routes across the Pyrenees, ranging from easy to difficult. The steepest route was the fastest, but only the fittest, youngest refugees could manage this trail. The easiest path, used by those who were older or ill, posed a greater threat of capture and imprisonment, so Fry and the others learned tricks to ensure the refugees' safety, such as putting "pepper in the cuffs of our trousers to ward off police dogs who might follow," according to one guide.

Also in September, Fry met Austrian writer Karl Frucht. Frucht, along with writer Hertha Pauli,* had founded Koires Pouding, a literary agency that marketed German and Austrian authors to foreign news agencies. In 1938, Pauli and Frucht left Austria for Paris, where Pauli became involved romantically with the poet Walter Mehring. (He never quite got over her.) Frucht was interned by the Vichy government but escaped to Marseille, where he worked for Fry as a guide and further developed the land routes. Every three weeks, he made the climb over the Pyrenees, taking groups of Fry's protégés from Banyuls-sur-Mer to Spain, resting in between expeditions. Frucht made detailed maps of the routes and added sarcastic comments, such as, "Early autumn tour in the Pyrenees recommended to illegal tourists." He suggested that when "crossing [the] frontier on foot, choose siesta time; French guards will be asleep." Frucht added directions to the maps: "Leaving Banyuls; go up dry riverbed, leaving it at a well, climbing through yards, aiming at a Norman tower from where Cerbère on

---

*Fry helped Pauli escape during his first weeks in Marseille.

the Spanish side [can be] seen. Descend and surrender to Spanish frontier guards."

After crossing the Spanish border, Fry's protégés traveled by train through Spain, then continued on to Portugal. In the great port of Lisbon, the Portuguese Jewish Committee gave a number of refugees money for ship passages. "Some of them stayed a week, some of them a month, and some forever. Others left immediately on the boat." Although luck played a role, much depended on a refugee's status and the influence of his American friends.

Not every refugee was the same. Some, like Breitscheid, Hilferding, and Bernhard, were foolhardy and acted as if they had nothing to fear. Others were terrified; Franz Werfel, despite his worldwide fame as a poet, dramatist, and novelist, was among the most frightened refugees. For this reason, Fry decided to include Werfel when he made plans to travel to Spain. Fry wanted to see what it was like to cross the border. He also had another reason for going to Madrid: He wanted to discuss with British embassy personnel there the possibility of escape by sea for his refugees.

Because crossing the Pyrenees was difficult for older or infirm refugees, or those traveling with children, Fry and Frank Bohn had fantasized for weeks about getting them out on ships from the port of Marseille. There were enormous problems with this idea, since vessels sailing from Marseille were strictly regulated by Vichy and would certainly not be allowed to travel with a cargo of refugees. Also, the open seas during wartime were dangerous. Despite these obstacles, escape by sea "remained a haunting mirage" to both Fry and Bohn. Fry thought the British might help and intended to bring with him to the British embassy in Madrid a coded map, created by an Italian refugee and anti-Mussolini activist, Emilio Lussu, that described a sailing route from the port of Marseille.

Fry organized his expedition to Spain with Werfel and several others: famed German novelist Lion Feuchtwanger and his wife, Marta; Golo Mann, Thomas Mann's son; Heinrich Mann, a "widely read" writer in whose work "critics found . . . beauty of style and a deep earnestness of feeling," and brother of Thomas; Heinrich's wife, Nellie; and graphic artist Egon Adler and his wife, Bertha Maria Adler.*

---

*Egon and Bertha Maria Adler were numbers 13 and 14.

Feuchtwanger was a popular and widely read historical novelist and dramatist whose first anti-Hitler novel, *Success,* had been published in 1930. "As he became known to the world for his novels, he also became a target of the Nazis." Feuchtwanger escaped from Germany in 1933 and lived with his wife in Sanary-sur-Mer, in the south of France, until he was arrested by Vichy in the summer of 1940. He was interned in Les Milles, an experience he described in *The Devil in France.* Many of his works concerned German émigrés who "had to flee because of their political beliefs," who were "forced into leaving their homeland only because they or their parents were listed as Jews." He also wrote of non-Jews who left Germany "voluntarily because they simply couldn't breathe the air of the Third Reich any longer."

In July, a month before Fry arrived in France, President Roosevelt himself had helped secure U.S. emergency visitors' visas for Feuchtwanger and his wife. But the writer was still imprisoned. From Les Milles, he had been moved to St. Nicola, "the health resort of concentration camps," where he was not heavily guarded and was allowed by the camp commandant to take outings and swim in the river. One day in August, Feuchtwanger and some friends from the camp were walking along the road toward the river, unguarded. A woman he recognized as a friend of his wife's walked up to him and handed him a note. Amazed, he opened it and saw that it was from his wife. "Do exactly as you are told," Marta Feuchtwanger had written. "Do not stop to consider. It is all straightforward and perfectly safe." A man wearing a white suit and knit gloves emerged from a car waiting nearby and beckoned to Feuchtwanger. The writer said good-bye to his friends, donned the dark glasses and woman's coat and shawl handed to him by this mysterious man, and climbed into the car, which sped away.

His rescue, he soon learned, had been organized by U.S. vice consul Hiram "Harry" Bingham, one of only two American consular officials who went "out of his way" and took "a personal risk and a personal initiative" to help refugees. The scion of a prominent American family, Bingham felt a sense of personal obligation toward others, perhaps because of his privileged background. His great-grandfather was a founder of Tiffany & Co., his father was a U.S. senator, and his brother was editor of the magazine *Common Sense.* "Bingham was a great guy," said Mary Jayne Gold. "He was the only man in the consulate who was sort of for us." The other helpful American vice consul was Myles Standish, the man in the white suit who came to get Feucht-wanger that day.

After Standish whisked Feuchtwanger from the camp, Bingham hid him at his villa while the writer recovered from dysentery, which he had contracted in the camp. Fry visited Feuchtwanger and told him of his plan to organize an escape for Werfel and several others. He invited the writer along, and for weeks Feuchtwanger waited for the plan to take shape.

But just before they were to leave, Fry received word that Spain was no longer admitting stateless refugees from Germany, Austria, or other vanquished countries whose citizenship had been stripped from them either because they were Jewish or because they were anti-Nazis, or both. This was bad news for the Feuchtwangers, German Jews who fell into this category. Fry told them that they must remain behind, but promised to find another way to get them out. He would send word, addressing them in code as "Harry's friends," when he found out more about Spain's new regulations.

In addition to the Feuchtwangers, Bingham was sheltering Golo, Heinrich, and Nellie Mann. Golo, described as the "most solidly grounded of Thomas's six gifted children," was only two years older than Fry, and the two men grew close as the escape expedition was planned and executed. Even as a young boy, Golo had hated Hitler. He loved Europe, however, so when his father emigrated to the United States, he chose to remain behind. He lived in Switzerland, then in France. When Golo volunteered for the French Army, he was immedi-ately arrested as an enemy alien and spent "some not very pleasant months in these internment camps."

Although he was overshadowed by his younger brother, Thomas, Heinrich Mann was a leading liberal intellectual during the twenties, belonged to Berlin's Academy of Fine Arts, and was the author of *Pro-fessor Unrat,* the novel upon which the film *The Blue Angel* was based, as well as other novels, plays, and short stories. Shortly after the Nazi minister of education ordered him to resign from the Academy of Fine Arts, Heinrich also lost his German citizenship and his property. He emigrated to France, where he continued to write about "the Nazi menace."

In Fry's own account of this expedition, Egon and Bertha Maria Adler, who were part of it, are left out. "As Fry rather sheepishly told me years later," recalled Karel Sternberg, "he had cut [Adler] out of the story because nobody knew him." Adler, born in Czechoslovakia, emigrated in 1938 to Paris, where he designed posters and created publicity for Fox Films. He and Sternberg worked together until the Germans entered Paris. Adler, who was Jewish, was lucky enough to obtain American visas for himself and his wife. From Marseille, he wrote to Sternberg, who was living in Montauban: "What you doing in Montauban anyhow? If you want to get out, you have to be in Marseilles." Sternberg took the advice, arrived in Marseille just as Adler was set to leave with Fry, and took over Adler's hotel room. Sternberg had already heard of Fry: "Everything in Marseille centered around the *Centre Américain.*"

Within the group Fry had assembled, Adler's matter-of-fact attitude—"He was not one of the hysterics"—offset Werfel's anxiety. "There wasn't that much to fear then," said Sternberg. "When you lived it, it was not a matter of constant apprehension." Some refugees would not have agreed with him.

On the morning of Thursday, September 12, Fry left his hotel before dawn to walk the short distance to the Gare St.-Charles, his collar turned up against the wind. He was to meet Werfel and the others at 5:00 A.M. The taxi bearing the Werfels from their hotel, the Normandie, to the train station was crowded with twelve suitcases and their dog. Heinrich, and Nellie and Golo Mann also went to the station, as did the Adlers and Dick Ball, who helped Fry on this trip.

When he saw the Werfels, Fry hid his emotions, trying to control his own anxiety in order to keep the group calm. But he was horrified that they had brought along a dog and a dozen suitcases. Then, when he heard at the train station that Vichy was enforcing its visa regulations more strictly than usual, Fry despaired. Should he advise the group to return to town and go back into hiding? No one wanted to do that. Ball remained optimistic, and Fry decided to push on. They climbed aboard the train for Perpignan, beginning what Golo Mann described as "the romantic excursion that the young American . . . was worried about."

From Perpignan, Fry intended to take all the luggage by train over the Spanish border, while the others, guided by Ball, hiked the path. He arranged to rendezvous with them in Portbou, on the Spanish side of the border. From there, he would accompany them to Lisbon.

Everyone in the group, except for Golo Mann, was hesitant and fearful; Werfel, noting that it was Friday the thirteenth, was nervous that he could not make the steep climb, especially in the hot sun. Fear of the Nazis won out, and despite their liabilities—Werfel was overweight and out of shape, Mann was seventy, the women were not used to physical exertion—they pushed on.

Fry reviewed the refugees' documents before he left them to board his train. Golo had an American affidavit in lieu of passport,* the Werfels used their Czech passports, and the Adlers had U.S. emergency visas. Heinrich Mann and his wife would be all right, he thought, despite the closing of the Spanish border to Germans, because they had American passports in false names: "Mr. and Mrs. Heinrich Ludwig." They also had honorary Czech passports in their real names, which they destroyed as Fry watched. Just before they parted, Fry handed the refugees French cigarettes for bribing the Spanish border patrols.

Burdened by the suitcases, Fry headed toward the train station while the others, guided by Ball, straggled out of town. None of them was dressed appropriately for a climb over mountains. Alma Werfel wore a white dress and sandals and clutched a large satchel that she never let go of for a second. Later, Fry discovered she had carried out of Europe the first draft of Werfel's *The Song of Bernadette,* original manuscripts by her former husband, Gustav Mahler, and "the original score" of Anton Bruckner's Third Symphony. Fry had been concerned with Mrs. Werfel's stamina, but she surprised everyone: "[S]he was always ahead of us," recalled Golo Mann. The only one who had real difficulty was Heinrich Mann, who was carried much of the way by his nephew and Ball. After several hours of strenuous climbing, they crossed the French-Spanish border and entered Spain.

That evening, after they were reunited with Fry in Portbou, the group celebrated their adventure with great relief. They talked and drank and laughed late into the night until Fry felt a tap on his shoulder. He looked up into the sharp eyes of a British official whom he had met on his way to France a month earlier. Outside, where they could

---

*An affidavit in lieu of passport was a document signed by an official of the American consulate and used like a passport. It attested to the identity of a refugee and included name, address, physical description, date of birth, and this statement: "That he is of German nationality but is unable to obtain a German passport on account of conditions prevailing in France at the present time."

speak privately, the Englishman told Fry that the uniformed man sitting at the opposite end of the room from Werfel and company was "the head of the Spanish secret police of this region" and "not a very pleasant chap." Fry should be "careful," he added. Heeding this warning, Fry broke up the party. After the others went to bed, Fry and Golo Mann relaxed by swimming in the harbor. By Monday, September 16, they were all in Madrid, and Fry saw the Manns and Werfels off on flights to Lisbon.

The next day, Fry went to the British embassy, where he saw Major Torr, an operative in MI6 (British Secret Intelligence Service). Torr was not impressed with Fry's idea or his map and said that escapes by ship were destined to fail. In fact, said Torr, the British had not figured out how to use ships to evacuate their own stranded servicemen, the remainder of the British Expeditionary Force in France, many of whom were languishing in Marseille's Fort St.-Jean. Torr told Fry these men would most likely escape by first crossing the foothills of the Pyrenees. Once in Spain, the police would arrest them, but then the British government "would get them out" and send them on to Gibraltar, and freedom.

The next morning, Fry left for Lisbon to meet with the Unitarians' Charles Joy. When Fry arrived at Joy's office, a cable from Fry's secretary, Lena Fischman, was waiting for him. Vichy police had come for several of his most endangered refugees: Breitscheid, Hilferding, Arthur Wolff, a criminal defense attorney, and Mehring. Three of the men had been apprehended, wrote Fischman, but Mehring was safe for the moment.

Even though Fry was upset at the arrests, there was also some good news. Spain had suddenly opened its borders to Germans and people from German-occupied countries, another example of the arbitrariness of border regulations. Fry cabled Fischman that it was now safe for "Harry's friends"—the Feuchtwangers—to cross the border into Spain.

It was essential that he hurry back to Marseille, but Fry went by way of Madrid to see Torr again. In a surprise move, however, Torr turned the tables and asked for Fry's help. Would he sign on as an agent for MI6? The British who were then in France had no money or friends among the French people, so they needed the neutral Americans to help them. Would Fry work with them? Fry was ushered into the office of Sir Samuel Hoare, the British ambassador to Spain, who offered Fry a deal if he agreed to smuggle British soldiers out of France into Spain. "The problem for the English at the time was that they had no money in France, and probably also not enough connections with the French people," wrote Hirschman. As a quid pro quo, Hoare agreed to provide money for ships to transport refugees and British soldiers out of France, but Fry had to find the ships and make the nearly impossible arrangements. Hoare would give Fry ten thousand dollars if he agreed to help evacuate British soldiers into Spain and also try to arrange escapes by boat.

Fry needed no convincing. Not only could this arrangement benefit his refugees, but he welcomed the chance to be a British agent, no matter how briefly. Fry had only one caveat: The British must be the ones to find and hire Spanish fishing boats to sail from Barcelona up the coast to Marseille. Hoare agreed, but he added a condition: Fry "should never involve English soldiers and Italians at the same time, as this would unnecessarily compromise the English."

Fry had faith in the British government and believed, as a result of his deal with Hoare, that his dream of refugee rescue by ship would happen. Although Hoare offered to give him the money on the spot, Fry asked him to send it to the Emergency Rescue Committee in New York. Fry's records indicate that he kept separate accounts, never mixing funds from regular sources earmarked for refugees with his stipend from British intelligence.

Before he left the embassy, British intelligence agents from MI6 urged Fry to tell Hugh Fullerton, the American consul in Marseille, to fire the receptionist, Mme. Delapré, who they knew was supplying information to the secret police in Vichy, who were, in turn, supplying it to the Nazis.

Fry returned to Marseille the next day, not knowing where to direct his attention first. While he worked on the ship plan and contacted the British soldiers, he asked Hirschman to try to get some of the soldiers out across the Pyrenees. A senior British captain named Mills discussed with Hirschman a plan to go to the town of Bourg-Madame, at the frontier, and then cross the Pyrenees along a route that would be shown them "by some Catalan smugglers working on both sides of the frontier." Hirschman went to see for himself.

At this time, the first extradition under the terms of the surrender-on-demand clause had taken place. On September 16, a former German finance minister named Dussenpack was arrested by Vichy, turned over to the Nazis, and sent back to Germany.*

The Feuchtwangers had left France, but of the refugees who had been arrested—Breitscheid, Hilferding, Wolff, and Mehring—only Mehring continued to elude the police. The others were living in *résidence forcée* (house arrest) in Arles. Wolff had been invaluable to Fry and Hirschman, providing them with leads into the Marseille underworld. Breitscheid and Hilferding were symbols of courage and resistance in the refugee population; their arrests "spread panic . . . everybody was sure it was the beginning of the end," wrote Gold. Fry had to remind himself that Breitscheid and Hilferding had stubbornly refused to accept their situation and would not be intimidated in any way. "Nobody refused on . . . principle [to hide his identity] except these two rather exceptional individuals," said Hirschman.

Fry faced his first real failures. Two major political figures were under house arrest, vulnerable to being turned over to the Nazis under the surrender-on-demand clause. He blamed himself forever for what ultimately happened to these men, but at the time he was furious at their stubbornness. Both men had U.S. emergency visitors' visas and had obtained from Bohn and Fry Czech passports and Spanish and Portuguese transit visas under false names. They refused, however, to leave France illegally (without French exit visas).

Hirschman said that Breitscheid and Hilferding's intransigence "was particularly poignant" because their party, the Social Democrats, once the largest in Germany, had been defeated the same way, "by its insistence on . . . never doing anything that in the slightest way could be interpreted as going against the Constitution."

Fry could directly help only one person, Mehring, who had evaded arrest and was now safely hidden in Fry's bed at the Splendide. The tiny, unprepossessing man, dressed always in the same ragged clothing, was "thin as a comma with a delicate face and a nose sharpened to a very fine point." His fear made him conspicuous, but on paper he was ferocious: "He looked rather timid but when he wrote, he wasn't timid

*Although by the end of Fry's year in Marseille, there had been only twenty-one such extraditions, at the time, the refugees experienced the threat as a real terror and lived in excruciating uncertainty from day to day, not knowing if, when, or how they would be captured by Vichy and turned over to the Nazis.

at all," recalled Karel Sternberg. The Germans "would have killed" Mehring because he "was a Jew and an anti-Nazi poet . . . they would have beaten him to death. They would have been merciless because he also had provoked them with his poems." Mehring was not the easiest person to get along with, and Fry had his difficulties with the man Karel Sternberg called "a miserable little fellow" and Egon Adler referred to as "the Mickey Rat." Mehring demanded rather than requested Fry's help; his bossy attitude and sense of entitlement made him repugnant to Fry.

Two weeks earlier, Fry had arranged for Mehring to escape because the little poet "felt his star had risen, and . . . [he] did not want to be part of one of Dick Ball's convoys." Fry set it up so that Mehring took a train to the border, then walked across the foothills into Spain. He had an American affidavit in lieu of passport but was afraid to travel through Spain with it and insisted that Fry get him a Czech passport, which he did. Mehring also had a U.S. emergency visitor's visa. After Fry gave Mehring traveling money and said good-bye, the poet went off with Sternberg, who had volunteered to accompany him to the train because Mehring was so terrified. On the way to the station, Mehring took out his Czech passport and his American affidavit in lieu of passport, which "he had hidden inside a lady's stocking." Horrified at the poet's displaying these two contradictory documents, Sternberg shouted at him to put the papers away. Fortunately, no one noticed, there were no further problems, and Sternberg put the poet on the train to the Spanish border.

In Perpignan, Mehring had to change trains for the border town, Cerbère; he went into a café to wait and sat nervously drinking coffee. He had tried to disguise himself by wearing a beret, but of course this failed, and the police swooped down on him. Although "he pleaded the toilet trick and flushed the precious Czech passport down the drain," he was arrested. Shipped to St. Cyprien, a "pesthole" of a French camp that was filthy, cold, and lacked sanitation, food, and water, Mehring immortalized it in a poem:

> *Our Prison camp. With what satanic gall*
> *This torture hole was planned! A stroke of a pen*
> *Dipped deep in hate can damn free living men*
> *To perish in a bottomless despair.*

We weep . . . we shriek . . . deliver us! Oh where
Are saint and Deity? No heart . . . no ear!
Four thousand Jews are slowly rotting here.

Fry heard of Mehring's arrest and hired an attorney. Eventually St. Cyprien's commandant gave Mehring a release order, and the little poet was set free. Back in Marseille, Mehring was more panicked than ever. When the French secret police tried to arrest him during the raid in which they took Breitscheid, Hilferding, and Wolff, Mehring hid under the covers in Fry's bed. The police leaned over and told him he must dress and come down to the lobby immediately. The orders to arrest him came "from your compatriots," they said, meaning direct from Berlin.

Miriam Davenport, alerted that Mehring was about to be arrested, rushed to the hotel. Upstairs, in Fry's room, she told Lena Fischman to call U.S. vice consul Bingham. Then she returned to the lobby and held the police off until Bingham showed up. There were six plain-clothesmen wearing "purple and green and blue suits with pointy-toed shoes, looking like pimps." In the fine tradition of resistance that characterized Fry and his staff, Davenport invented a title for herself, general secretary of the Centre, and told the police it was "absolutely impossible" for Mehring to be arrested.

I suddenly became conscious of the power and prestige of my country. . . . I proceeded to explain . . . the international renown of our desperately ill poet—and by then he really was ill—the great concern for his welfare of a good many influential men and women in the United States, not the least of whom was Mrs. Franklin Delano Roosevelt, wife of the President.

Finally, she warned them off their prey. "If they valued America's feelings of good will towards their suffering country," she said, "they would be well advised to leave Mr. Mehring in peace."

Davenport's arguments were supported by the arrival of the distinguished Hiram Bingham, whose "towering height and prematurely white hair made everyone else in the lobby look insignificant." The colorfully dressed officers gave up and left, believing that this brazen and talkative young woman spoke for the U.S. government.

Upstairs, a sympathetic physician was writing a certificate attesting to Mehring's ill health and inability to travel. Mehring, called "Baby" "because he was little and because he gave us so much trouble and he was always whining," remained in Fry's room for weeks, annoying Fry and everyone else, although no one had the heart to tell him off. Not until much later could Fry admit to a friend his feelings about some of the German refugees, including Mehring, describing them as "conceited . . . demanding and sometimes not even quite honest." Then he warned the friend to "never say this aloud. The poor devils have a hard enough time . . . there is quite enough prejudice against them already." (Much later, Fry was able to save one of the protégés in forced residence; he smuggled Wolff out after six months of running and hiding.)

In America, the ERC was fighting its own battles, and when Fry cabled the ERC about the arrests of Breitscheid, Hilferding, and Wolff, there was little the organization could do. Its function was to raise funds, lobby the State Department to issue more U.S. emergency visitors' visas, and find sponsors for refugees. Each day hundreds of letters were delivered to the ERC, each one pleading for a specific European refugee. The Committee answered every letter, passing names on to Fry. He, of course, was sending the organization names of people he had discovered in France who were not on his original lists.

Much of the Committee's time was spent complying with U.S. government requirements for emergency visitors' visas: It secured financial affidavits—including tax returns, salary information, and bank statements—from U.S. citizens who swore an oath that the refugees they were sponsoring would not become burdens on the government. American citizens also signed moral affidavits that these people would comply with standards of decency and morality set by the State Department. Cables flew back and forth daily between the ERC and Fry. But his relationship with the organization was about to grow cold, in part because of his independence, but more because of the U.S. State Department's negative attitude toward his work.

By this time, the fall of 1940, the State Department had grown unhappy with the President's Advisory Committee and had "announced severe curtailment of the emergency visa program." Assistant Secretary of State Long continued to advise President Roosevelt "that tighter [immigration] restrictions were necessary," reminding him that many refugees' "records" of political activism indicated they were "not of the desirable element." In his diary, Long quoted the American ambassador to Russia Laurence Steinhardt's views on Eastern European immigrants: "[They] are lawless, scheming, defiant—and in many ways unassimilable . . . the general type of intending immigrant was just the same as the criminal Jews who crowd our police court dockets in New York."

Eleanor Roosevelt, championing the cause of the refugees along with the President's Advisory Committee, kept the battle alive, but President Roosevelt, under pressure from both the State Department and the country's imminent entry into the war, abandoned the refugees. He left the issue of refugees to his Advisory Committee, the Justice Department, and the State Department, "to fight [it] out among themselves."

Knowing nothing of the political and ideological struggles at home over the refugee issue, Fry learned, in late September, that while he was in Spain after the Werfel expedition, the Vichy *préfecture* had lodged complaints against him and Frank Bohn with U.S. consul Hugh Fullerton. Vichy said it was not comfortable with Fry and Bohn's refugee work. Although no formal charges were filed, Fullerton cabled Vichy's concerns to the State Department in Washington.

A few days after Fry returned to Marseille, Fullerton asked Fry to come to see him. Fry had no premonition of trouble and was dismayed when he heard of the *préfecture*'s complaint and of Fullerton's cable to Washington. Fullerton did not tell Fry what he had written the State Department but showed him the Department's reply:

> This government cannot countenance the activities as reported of Dr. Bohn and Mr. Fry and other persons in their efforts in evading the laws of countries with which the United States maintains friendly relations.

It was at this meeting that Fry informed the consul that Mme. Delapré was a spy, according to information he had received from British intelligence. Fullerton ignored this and told Fry he thought the Nazis would win anyway.

Feeling betrayed by Fullerton and by his own government, Fry was demoralized. The State Department had accepted Vichy's and Fullerton's charges against him without even bothering to talk to him. Since his first day in Marseille, he had received nothing but coldness from his own consulate, no support or encouragement. After this incident, American representatives, including consulate "clerks, doormen, and secretaries" who had heard of him and his operation, treated him like a pariah. They insulted him, "slandering and libeling our organization and the Americans active in it." Fullerton tried for months to force Fry to leave Marseille and would be instrumental, later on, in reassigning the American official who was most helpful to Fry, Hiram Bingham.

It was true that Frank Bohn had acted in a cavalier, careless manner, calling Fry "comrade," talking loudly in rooms with open doors about their illegal refugee work. Fry, therefore, decided that perhaps if he completely disassociated himself from Bohn, then he might get back in his government's favor. When he learned that Fullerton had not informed the Vichy police that there was no official association between the two Americans, Fry was furious and gave up on U.S. support for his operation. Certain his phones were tapped by Vichy, he was careful about what he and the others in the office said over the telephone. He took other precautions. He tailored a letter to Eileen for the censors: "It appears . . . that the Prefecture had got the absurd idea that some member of my staff had been conducting persons illegally over the border. Actually no member of my staff had been near the border, or has been since."

On September 23, Fullerton, as the most senior representative of the U.S. government, told Fry to leave France at once, to close the Centre and return to New York. As Fry sat in the consul's office, he seemed to accept this and said he would leave as soon as the ERC could send a replacement. He did not see this as the end of the Centre Américain de Secours, however, because he intended to remain until this replacement arrived.

But Fry had no real intention of leaving. The day before his meeting with Fullerton, Fry and Eileen had spoken on the telephone about his return; he had originally planned to stay in France only four weeks. When she got off the phone, Eileen showed how well she understood her husband, as she wrote, "I am now writing to you because I think you may stay there long enough to get my letter." She knew Fry had found the job of a lifetime, doing critical work that allowed him to use all his skills and aptitudes. Furthermore, he was in charge and enjoyed a heady sense of authority, both within the operation and in Marseille itself. Fry felt brave, powerful, and competent, and Eileen knew he would not relinquish these new feelings easily.

Another problem for Fry now was losing his source for Czech passports. The Vichy police had registered charges against the YMCA's Donald Lowrie, who, with Czech consul Vladimir Vochoč, had helped German and Czech anti-Nazis escape and had provided Fry with Czech passports, in phony names, for his protégés. Fry now had to rely more on forged documents, which were always riskier.

At the end of September, as a result of the many letters he received from refugees in French camps, the "unspeakable" conditions in these camps became a concern of Fry's. The French interned foreigners to separate them from the general population, but the camps also served as holding pens for people they planned to turn over to the Germans. Fry informed the ERC and the State Department about these places in which Jews, political prisoners, stateless persons, and other refugees were forced to live without sufficient water, sanitation, and food. "The most diseased imagination could not conceive the conditions of life in them," he wrote. Internees suffered from fleas, lice, bedbugs, and diseases, including typhoid. "People who run concentration camps," commented Davenport, "are indifferent to the welfare of the people they're penning up, and they're a little bit sadistic."

Fry was determined to change the way Vichy ran its camps, by drawing America's attention to them. The United States, however, refused to intervene in what it viewed as an internal French affair and ignored Fry's emotional letters. He sent so much mail on this subject that, over time, U.S. officials dismissed his stream of complaints as "Fryana." "I am enclosing some fryana," wrote Hugh Fullerton, "which somebody up there may care to read and which were left with me the other day." The French government also ignored his letters, which "have long since been reposing in the Department of the Interior and the Red Cross at Vichy." Fry had no effect at all on the circumstances in which internees were housed, fed, or treated.

Thirty years later, Mary Jayne Gold went back to visit a French concentration camp. She saw a hill with graves—German, Polish, Spanish, American—and noticed that the stones were laid out in rows, as if representing the prisoners in their barracks. "It's a very simple monument . . . about the people who died here," she said.

IIIIIIIII

When I Was Baggage:
Michael Kaufman

Michael Kaufman, who became an author and *New York Times* reporter, does not remember being carried across the French-Spanish border when he was two, but he has lived all his life on the epic tale his parents, Adam and Paulina, told him of their family's escape. "My greatest story was when I was baggage, not a sentient being," says Kaufman.

In 1934, his father, Adam, a former communist revolutionary, fled from his native Lodz, Poland, to Czechoslovakia after he was arrested. Paulina joined him later. Then, when the Czechs politely informed Adam that the Polish government was seeking his extradition, Paulina purchased a passport for her husband from a cooperative cabdriver, and he used it to escape to France. Paulina followed.

Adam and Paulina were living in a tiny apartment in Paris when Michael was born on March 23, 1938. After war broke out in the autumn of the following year, Adam joined the French Army. Paulina and Michael remained behind. One of her neighbors was a White Russian who lived on the top floor of their building. He was a taxi driver and, the Kaufmans suspected, an anti-Semite. However, when the Germans started bombing the outskirts of Paris, the neighbor said to Paulina, "Madam, you cannot stay here. You and your child have to leave." The day after France fell, he presented himself, clicked his heels, and offered to drive her in his taxi to the station. "He may have been [anti-Semitic] but he was a very honorable and decent man in this moment . . . and drove us to the [Gare d'Austerlitz], where the trains left for Limoges."

Only a short time after Paulina and Michael left the apartment, the Germans came looking for them, she learned. The Kaufmans were "on their extermination list."

In Limoges, Paulina got Michael into an orphanage that housed the children of Spanish women and Republican volunteers from the Spanish Civil War. He remained there until his mother found a potato storage shed for them to live in.

Once the armistice with Germany was signed, Adam, like all soldiers, was given leave and joined his family in Limoges; they had kept in communication. One day a telegram arrived: If they could get to Marseille, visas were waiting for them at the U.S. consulate. Michael believes that "the Varian Fry operation was involved," as well as Eleanor Roosevelt, and the Jewish Labor Committee.

The Kaufmans immediately took a train to Marseille. To ensure that the trip would be as uneventful as possible, Adam wore his army uniform. It worked, and he was even saluted in the Marseille train station. On September 14, at the American consulate, the Kaufmans presented their precious telegram and received U.S. emergency visitors' visas, which were signed by Hiram Bingham. As they left the consulate, someone "took us in hand and put us in this hotel." It was probably Fry, according to Michael Kaufman.

The U.S. visas were only a start, and the family needed more papers in order to leave France. Since Michael had been born in France, he and his mother were given legal exit visas, rare and almost impossible to obtain. Adam, technically a soldier on leave, could not obtain one, and once again the family had to split up. Paulina and Michael took a train from Marseille to Portbou, arriving on September 24. Adam, following directions he had received either from Fry or from Vice Consul Bingham, had a different journey. He was told to take a train to Banyuls-sur-Mer, then sit in a certain café and look for a woman in a red dress. At the train station café, Adam and another refugee, an artist from Riga, Ephraim Schloss, both stood when they finally saw a woman wearing a red dress. They followed her out of the café and walked over the mountain, until they arrived at a small shed. It was the studio of the French artist Aristide Maillol, and the woman was his young model and muse, Dina Vierny. Fry had given her the red dress, Vierny has said. "Then I wore it and then Maillol did a painting of it."

At Maillol's studio, Kaufman and Schloss rested until the patrols were off duty, between two and three in the morning. Vierny then led them across the mountains, a rocky, uphill, and difficult climb that took two to three hours, to Portbou. "She walked people across the mountains. She walked my father across," said Michael Kaufman. Vierny had been working for Fry and Bohn as a guide for a short time; after Bohn left Marseille, she worked just for Fry. "For these two . . . I will bring the people out of France," said Vierny, who was then twenty. Within two months, she, too, was arrested. She met Fry only once, she recalled.

The Kaufmans were reunited in Barcelona. Adam was told to look for a legendary redheaded train porter named Kaplan. Kaplan was part of an unofficial group of Jews in Spain, formed after Hitler's rise to power, who worked together to help Jewish refugees trying to escape. "There was in the train station at Madrid an agent, a Jewish man, a redheaded porter . . . who was on the lookout and steering people," recalled Karel Sternberg. Kaplan may have worked for HICEM, the relief agency. "He knew when somebody seemed stranded or lost in Madrid," said Sternberg. From Spain, Adam, Paulina, and Michael Kaufman traveled to Lisbon, arriving there in late September. They sailed to America on the *Nea Hellas,* along with Feuchtwanger, Werfel, and Heinrich Mann, docking in New York Harbor on October 13, 1940.

CHAPTER FIVE

||||||||||||||||||||||||||

THE DOORS CLOSE

It is the refugees . . . who do NOT enjoy life here. . . . They are now cut off from funds and means of livelihood and most of them cannot get permission to leave France to start over again somewhere else.
Varian Fry

I N THE MIDDLE OF SEPTEMBER, Fry sent a refugee couple, David Schneider and his wife, off to Cerbère. He was certain they would manage their escape without a problem because they possessed every paper imaginable; their documentation was a refugee's dream. They had valid Polish passports that had been issued four or five years earlier, U.S. emergency visitors' visas, and Spanish and Portuguese transit visas. They even had French exit visas. Sometime during September, France had begun issuing them on a very limited basis only to certain Russians, Romanians, and Poles born in the non-German part of Poland. The Schneiders were from this area of Poland. Fry, certain the Schneiders' journey would go smoothly, could not have imagined what did happen. After the couple arrived in Cerbère, they went on to Portbou, where they intended to cross the border into Spain. Four times the Spanish border patrol refused them admission, and they were denied entry a fifth time at a border crossing at Bourg-Madame. Crushed, they returned to Marseille and went immediately to see Fry, "in a state bordering on despair."

He comforted them, but in the few days since they had left Marseille, Spain had again closed her borders to people from Germany or German-occupied countries. Then, within days, Spain reopened her borders. And, just as abruptly, she closed them again. This arbitrariness was typical of late 1940, when all European countries and their governments were in flux, panicked by the German onslaught. For Fry's protégés, the closing of the Spanish border—no matter how temporarily—was a disaster.* Fry tried to resolve each refugee's emigration problems by negotiating with the governing bureaucracies, but with constantly shifting policies he was often frustrated. And he often failed.

In the beginning of October, Portuguese consuls in France stopped issuing transit visas except to those refugees who could prove, by showing overseas visas and passage reservations, that they would definitely leave Portugal. This meant trouble in Spain, for Spain would not issue a transit visa to anyone without a Portuguese visa. At the same time, the end of September, "the Gestapo had commenced to tighten control of the French-Spanish border."

Added to this was the complication that many refugees traveling through Spain and Portugal held overseas visas, which purported to allow them to enter countries such as China, Thailand, and the Belgian Congo—not their real destinations. This deception was necessary to prove to Spain and Portugal that the refugees would not remain and become government wards. But the subterfuge was dealt a blow when Portugal stopped issuing transit visas to people holding Chinese, Thai, or Belgian Congolese visas. At this point, France, Spain, and Portugal had created a network of irrational, unreasonable immigration laws that seemed to almost completely stop all refugee movement out of Europe.

Fry did have one moment of happiness in the midst of the disasters of late September, when he realized the group he had escorted earlier that month *had* made it out. "We escaped but that was the last moment," said Golo Mann. "Three weeks later it would have been too late . . . [because] the Gestapo had sent their men to Madrid and then the frontier was closed for Germans. We did it just at the right moment."

---

*The Schneiders escaped eventually and David wrote to Fry in mid-1941 from Hollywood: "I am now eight months in this wonderful country. . . . There are many of your Marseilles children here."

Fry, with Hirschman's help, had to quickly find new routes across the Pyrenees. It was an urgent search. And when a journey begun had to be interrupted until it was deemed safe by Fry, or someone on his staff, the frustration was enormous. Not everyone could endure such tension, and suicide became the only way out for a number of refugees.

One of the victims of the closing of the Spanish border was the philosopher Walter Benjamin, described later by another philosopher, Hannah Arendt,* as "the outstanding literary critic of the twentieth century." Among the refugees, it was known that a young German couple, Lisa and Hans Fittko, were helping fellow émigrés cross the foothills into Spain. On September 23, Walter Benjamin was part of a small group of refugees who landed on Lisa Fittko's doorstep in Port Vendres, a tiny village on the sea near Banyuls-sur-Mer. That morning Fittko was awakened by Benjamin, whom she had known in Germany and in Paris. He asked for her help in guiding himself and a Frau Gurland and her son across the border, recalled Albert Hirschman.

Benjamin, perhaps the most noted scholar among the German refugee population in Marseille,† was born in Berlin in 1892. A student of philosophy and a writer, as a young man he had been deeply affected by the suicide of his friend the poet C. F. Heinle on August 8, 1914. Later, Benjamin earned a doctoral degree, became involved with Marxism, and sought work as a lecturer at the University of Frankfurt. Failing to achieve that position, he became a radio raconteur, then experimented with psychopharmacology, ingesting hashish, opium, and mescaline and writing about their effects on him. By 1933, he had emigrated to Paris and was publishing groundbreaking works of criticism and philosophy. Not only were his ideas original, but his prose style was also unique. His "prose rhythms . . . matched the flaneur's [idler's] recalcitrance," wrote émigré Anthony Heilbut. "[H]is formula for great prose called for breaking up a sentence's rhythm, shifting meter in the manner of a jazz improvisation."

Benjamin, rounded up along with other German exiles when Ger-

---

*Arendt, listed as Mme. Bluecher, was number 128.

†Harvard University recently purchased the rights to English translations of Benjamin's works. A monument to him, created by the Israeli artist Dani Karavan, was installed in Portbou on May 15, 1994, and inscribed with Benjamin's words: "It is more arduous to honor the memory of the nameless than that of the renowned. Historical construction is devoted to the memory of the nameless."

many invaded France, was imprisoned in a camp in the Nievre. When the exiles were released, Benjamin made his way south to Marseille. Sponsored by intellectuals in America, he received his U.S. emergency visitor's visa, and by September he was ready to escape.

Lisa Fittko had just learned about a new route across the Pyrenees from Mayor Azéma. He told her that Spanish police were watching the old route, "apparently on orders from the German Kundt Commission." The Kundt Commission was "a detachment of German officials and Gestapo agents . . . [that] combed French concentration camps in the unoccupied zone" searching for the Germans they wanted returned to Germany. When Benjamin asked Fittko to guide him that day in October, she warned him that the climb would be difficult. He acknowledged that he would have to climb slowly because of the steepness of the path as well as his heart trouble, but he wanted to try. "Not to go," said Benjamin, "that would be the real risk."

Fittko led Benjamin, who was carrying a heavy black briefcase that held a manuscript, and the two other refugees on an exploratory climb to gauge the difficulty of the path. In the evening, when the others returned to Banyuls-sur-Mer to sleep, Benjamin remained on the mountain because he had no desire to backtrack: "His goal was to cross the border so that he and his manuscript would not fall into the hands of the Gestapo. He had attained one-third of this goal." The following morning, the group rejoined Benjamin, who had slept on the mountain. After a day of strenuous climbing, with frequent stops so the philosopher could rest, they reached the summit. Fittko returned to Banyuls-sur-Mer while the little group continued on, crossing the Spanish border. That night, Benjamin stayed in a tiny hotel in Portbou. Fry heard that, for no apparent reason, at some point that day Spain again closed its borders. The Spanish police called on Benjamin and the others and informed them that they would have to go back to France, since Spain was closed to all those without legitimate French exit visas. But Walter Benjamin made a different choice.

That night, faced with returning to France, Benjamin took a lethal dose of morphine. He had been given the pills by a fellow German émigré, writer Arthur Koestler. Karel Sternberg believes that since Benjamin had the narcotic with him, suicide was something he had long been contemplating. "I don't think it was the immediate fear that he would be sent away," said Sternberg. "People who carry poison, it's not the first time the idea of suicide comes to them." In the morning, Benjamin's body was found, and the black briefcase was empty. Its contents have never been recovered. The day after Benjamin killed himself, Spain again opened its borders and the others in his group were allowed to leave the hotel and continue on through Spain; they eventually arrived safely in the United States.

Although he was only forty-eight when he died, Walter Benjamin made contributions to many fields, including the study of mass entertainment and popular culture. Fry was aware of Benjamin's credentials and importance within the refugee community. Reverberations from his suicide grew stronger each day because it was so unexpected, because Benjamin had appeared so composed and in control. He "was not one of the hysterics. He usually didn't have much fear," said Sternberg. "But he killed himself because he was afraid of being turned over to the Germans."

Sternberg recalled that during the summer of 1940, he was certain that "Hitler would take all of Europe. I didn't think there was a chance. But I was young, I was street smart, and I could get around on my own." His hopefulness was a rarity among the refugee population; many tended toward depression. The psyche of the refugee is explained by Arendt:

> [T]here is something wrong with our optimism. There are those odd optimists among us who . . . go home and turn on the gas or make use of a skyscraper in quite an unexpected way. They seem to prove that our proclaimed cheerfulness is based on a dangerous readiness for death. Brought up in the conviction that life is the highest good and death the greatest dismay, we became witnesses and victims of worse terrors than death—without having been able to discover a higher ideal than life.

Depression was not new to Fry, having seen its effects on his mother. "Now, it seemed, the refugees were really trapped," Fry wrote. "They were to be kept in France as cattle are kept in the pens of a slaughterhouse, and the Gestapo had only to come and get them."

Suicide became epidemic. Refugees were "overrun by this evil . . . [which seemed like] the end of the world," said Hirschman. Their despair was both "about what had happened and foreboding about what might happen." Marseille was "a city of doom" where everyone expected "that the Germans would take over at any time." Some of the refugees were older people who had been well-to-do and could not adapt to life without money. "That's one problem people had to adjust to, the idea of not being able to pay rent, that you had to go to beg someplace." They had lived through a decade of fascism, and sometimes the desire to end the struggle prevailed over the desire to continue it.

Refugees committed suicide before Fry arrived in France, after he arrived, and even years later.* "Another one of our clients, Benjamin Walter, committed suicide a few days ago," Fry wrote, "after going through the same procedure as Schneider," meaning the sudden closing of the Spanish border. Benjamin was the third suicide of those from his original list. The others were Czech expressionist novelist Ernst Weiss, who swallowed a lethal substance when Paris fell to the Germans, and German expressionist poet and playwright Walter Hasenclever, who poisoned himself in mid-August while he was interned at Les Milles, a former brick factory turned concentration camp.

Fry used these deaths to convince the Committee of the urgency of his work, and his need for more money. "Give me ten thousand dollars a month, and I can continue to do your job for you," he wrote. "It isn't much to ask to keep alive some of the most talented men and women in all Europe. Deprive me of it, and I warn you these same men and women will be slowly and painfully squeezed until, if they do not die of disease and starvation, many of them will take their own lives."

Willi Muenzenberg, an "able and well financed Comintern agent" who organized communist-front groups in Paris, had been found hanging from a tree. Poet, writer, and art critic Karl Einstein hanged himself at the frontier. Photographer George Reisner, who covered the antifascist Olympics during the Spanish Civil War, killed himself after "waiting for an American visa" for months. A few days after Reisner was buried, Fry received notice from the American consulate that the young man's U.S. emergency visitor's visa had been authorized.

But others, perhaps more hopeful by nature, maintained their sanity and focused on escape. Fry, hearing of Lisa Fittko's extraordinary

---

*Writer Stefan Zweig had escaped and was living in Brazil. In 1942, hearing of Hitler's triumphs, he and his wife killed themselves. Arthur Koestler and Nellie Mann committed suicide years after Fry helped them escape.

courage in guiding Benjamin across, attempted to commandeer her services as a guide. He met with Lisa and her husband, Hans, a "German Socialist of considerable underground experience," in a bistro in the Vieux-Port, the waterfront. Fry was accompanied by Bohn, who was planning to leave Marseille within days, and Hirschman, who would translate. The Fittkos were not comfortable with Fry and Bohn, whose American ways were alien to them; at first, they were reluctant to even talk with them. When Fry blundered by offering them money to take refugees across the border, the couple became outraged. Did the American think money could convince them to risk their lives? Hirschman soothed them and said that Fry was well-intentioned despite this mistake. The Fittkos calmed down. After further discussion, they agreed to "postpone their own plans for escape" and lead refugees across the foothills for Fry—for a while, at least.

By the end of September, they had established a residency in Banyuls-sur-Mer, and during a two-month period guided more than fifty of their fellow refugees across "those abrupt precipices, making the hazardous journey whenever it was required, without regard to storms, fog, or the bullets of the military police." Some of those they guided were Werner Wille, president of the German refugee group, Friedrich Wilhelm Wagner, and Heinrich Müller and his children, all protégés of Fry's.* The Fittkos' route was named the F Route by Fry, both to pay tribute to them and to keep their identities secret.

Banyuls-sur-Mer's Mayor Azéma, who had aided fleeing Spanish refugees during the Civil War years from 1936 to 1939, told the refugees how to dress for their excursions: They should wear espadrilles for safety on loose rocks, and should not carry baggage. Despite these instructions, the frightened émigrés were often afraid to part with their belongings, which were all they had from the past. One couple insisted on bringing a suitcase. Lotte, the wife, "didn't want to be separated from it," and her husband, Max, insisted that he carry it over the mountains. But Hans Fittko refused to take them with the luggage. "It has to do with safety," said Hans. "What's more valuable to you, your life or the rags in there?" He made his point, and the suitcase was left behind.

---

*Wille was number 1454, Wagner was number 1408, and Müller was number 918.

Fry's operation was succeeding in getting the refugees out, despite the many obstacles. Then, suddenly, at the end of September, he received news that he was being called back to New York. The leadership of the Committee all agreed that he should be brought home. In contriving to save as many lives as possible, he had overstepped his mandate and was working on his own in a way that was judged by the Committee as too unorthodox. Fry vacillated. If the ERC sent a replacement, he would have to accept the new man and return to New York; he wrote to the Committee that he would go only when a successor arrived, so that his leaving could be managed "without condemning dozens [of refugees] to severe privations and possibly [arrest and death].

"[S]ituation refugees desperate enough even with all the help and protection I can give them," he cabled. "[W]ill be infinitely worse if I leave before substitute arrives." But, despite what he wrote, Fry really did not want to leave Marseille. He pretended to the Committee, the American consul, and his wife that he would comply with the order to come home. He even lied to himself. He could not admit that he loved his position too much to leave it, that he intended to remain and finish what he had begun, that being in charge of this gratifying and meaningful work was all he cared about now.

Unbelievably, the frustration and obfuscation inherent in his work were once again ratcheted up as, in late September and early October, the French enacted a series of measures against foreigners and French Jews. Vichy's *Statut des Juifs* of October 3, 4, and 7 "spoke bluntly of race . . . was also more inclusive . . . [and] included in its definition those with only two grandparents 'of the Jewish race.' "

Now Vichy could intern anyone, French or foreign, considered dangerous to the public safety. It was under this law that the Jewish former prime minister of France, Léon Blum, was interned. Vichy also decreed that foreigners, both Jewish and non-Jewish, between the ages of eighteen and fifty-five were subject to arrest, imprisonment in camps, or forced residence. At this time, "[f]oreign Jews were already in detention . . . and before nine months were out French officials would be seizing Jewish property in the Unoccupied zone; before two years had passed, French police would be rounding up Jews for German deportation schedules." These laws were designed "to make the Jews vulnerable to deportation," according to historian Sarah Farmer. "The

French did not invent the final solution but facilitated the deportation of Jews. It was the French police who came to arrest and hand over Jews to the German authorities," she said. With the passage of the *Statut des Juifs,* Fry was under even more pressure to get the refugees out.

Why did France refuse to stand by the thousands of refugees who had sought shelter in the land of *liberté, égalité, fraternité?* Perhaps some thought that by following Germany's harsh anti-Jewish laws, France would ingratiate herself with her conqueror. But France had already veered to the right as unemployment grew during the thirties. With jobs scarce, émigrés from Germany and Eastern Europe were unwelcome, and France was interning foreign Jews well before the Nazis smashed the country in June 1940. Lastly, the Catholic Church in France was anti-Semitic. Vichy "enjoyed the blessing of the Church and the Church appreciated Vichy's efforts to protect France from communism and the Jews."

"It would be unreasonable, in a Christian state, to permit [the Jews] to exercise the functions of government and thus to submit the Catholics to their authority," wrote Léon Berard, then-ambassador from France to the Vatican. "Consequently it is legitimate to bar them from public functions."

Anti-Jewish laws were passed and obeyed in France in 1940 because France is an anti-Semitic country, according to Gys Landsberger, daughter-in-law of Georg Bernhard, on the Nazi's wanted list. A teacher of French, Landsberger said she always tells her students "that a French person is born anti-Semitic."

Vichy next curtailed the freedom of French citizens who happened to be Jewish, passing a law that forbade them from holding public office and working in the civil service, the armed services, the media, and education. "The laws were not applied in full immediately but they were on the books and gradually Jews were being weeded out from positions of public office and the media," wrote Mary Jayne Gold. French Jews had no recourse, no court of appeal, no say in their fates. All French citizens were forbidden to listen to English radio broadcasts or to speak favorably of General Charles de Gaulle. Fry saw, in the streets of Marseille, that certain stores were now posted *"Enterprise Française,"* or French-owned, to differentiate them from Jewish-owned. According to authors Gay Block and Malka Drucker:

No other occupied country cooperated more with Germany's efforts against the Jews in France. The French wrote their own anti-Semitic legislation, provided French police for deportation, and voluntarily deported Jews from the south of France. . . . When the Vichy government refused to allow Jews to hold civil service jobs and began its discriminatory legislation against French and foreign Jews in 1940–41, no group spoke out.

During this crisis, Fry received an impassioned cable from Karl Frank in New York. Frank had arranged for U.S. emergency visas for four Neu Beginnen members—Franz Boegler, Siegfried Pfeffer, Hans Tittle, and Fritz Lamm*—but they could not pick up their visas, since they were imprisoned at Le Vernet. Could Fry help them escape? Frank asked. Le Vernet was "a special punishment camp." Its inmates, stateless persons and those "considered politically dangerous," were "brutally beaten and punished, often with no reason," according to Frida Itor-Kahn, who was interned, along with her husband, pianist Erich Itor-Kahn,† at a different sort of camp where inmates were neglected but not beaten. An article on Vichy France described camp conditions:

> Food was scarce and generally spoiled; the drinking water was polluted; there were no latrines. Inmates were prevented from wading into the sea to wash away the lice, fleas, and excrement. Thousands succumbed to pneumonia, dysentery, typhus, gangrene, and starvation.

No matter what type of camp one was in, Frida Itor-Kahn wrote, internment was harrowing, especially for those refugees "without inner resources [who] were completely demoralized" by the experience. "No outsiders were allowed to visit the punishment camps," but they have been described by those who survived them, such as writer Arthur Koestler.‡

Fry had by now realized that he could not change the way the French ran their camps, but he resolved to help Frank's friends, despite Le Vernet's reputation. No one came up with an idea, however, until Hirschman and Davenport thought of Mary Jayne Gold. She had the

---

*Boegler was number 132, Pfeffer number 1021, and Lamm number 738.
†Erich Itor-Kahn and family were number 638.
‡Koestler, number 694, wrote about the camps in his book *Scum of the Earth*.

sophistication and beauty to charm Le Vernet's commandant into allowing Boegler, Pfeffer, Tittle, and Lamm to visit Marseille, under guard. After the men were safely out of the camp, Gold would have to figure out a way to get herself back to Marseille, Hirschman and Davenport said, with her virtue intact.

Fry invited Gold to meet with him, Hirschman, and Davenport at a café on the boulevard d'Athenes, across from the Hôtel Splendide. They sat at a tiny round table, nursing coffee laced with Armagnac. Gold would have to convince the commandant to release the four men, said Fry, then she would have to oversee their flight to Marseille. Once in Marseille, they would arrange their own escapes. Gold was reluctant, afraid she would fail and cause more trouble for these prisoners, but Hirschman convinced her, saying, "It's a matter of their lives." Fry and Davenport told her she was the only person alluring enough to disarm the commandant, and she finally agreed to do it. Hirschman suggested she present herself as an "old friend" of the prisoners' wives and tell the commandant their families "would like to see them come down to Marseille." Davenport even suggested that she wear her designer suit, the blue one with yellow piping, and "all your grandmother's diamonds" so she would appear to be what she was, a wealthy American.

At Le Vernet, Gold visited with the men briefly. Their "shaven heads" and "emaciated faces" were difficult to look at, she wrote, but the men smiled at her "as poor kids look at a Christmas tree." Two of them, Pfeffer and Tittle, had been imprisoned for more than a year. Since by the fall of 1940, "the Nazis had already visited Vernet" to select inmates to send back to Germany, these men were in immediate "danger of being deported."

"I didn't know how I would seduce [the commandant] or what it would cost me to sleep with him," Gold said in an interview years later, "but there were lives to save." Davenport always pointed out that no one expected Gold to sleep with the commandant. "We simply had in mind that she . . . looked innocent. She was beautiful and she had these great beautiful blue eyes." Gold succeeded in her mission using only her wits and her stylish Americanism, according to what she later said. The prisoners were allowed, under guard, to accompany her to Marseille, where they bribed the guards with a small fortune in francs, telling them to "go off and have fun." The guards, described by Gold as "underpaid and primitive voluptuaries," spent the money on drink and sex while the four prisoners made their way to the American consul to pick up the visas Karl Frank had arranged for them. Then they contacted Fry.

He and Hirschman met them at a café, where they talked intently about getting out of France. The "whores [in the café] were completely disconcerted by the . . . behavior" of these men, who ignored them. "No amount of caressing or come-on seemed to distract them." Finally, one of them rose, said, *"Je vais me sacrifier,"* and took a girl upstairs. It was Hirschman, always willing to do anything for the cause.

When Hirschman came back, he and Fry worked out an escape for the Neu Beginnen members. At this point, the Spanish border was closed, so Fry decided, against everything he knew, to get them on a ship. He paid for four places on the *Bouline,* an old yacht that had just been purchased by French Gaullists and was about to sail for Gibraltar, the British crown colony and free port on the southern coast of Spain. Although she already had a full load of French and Belgian officers, the "skipper . . . an old Marseille sea captain," agreed to add Boegler, Pfeffer, Tittle, and Lamm. The day before the ship was to sail, Fry learned that it might be a ruse, that the *Bouline* had been bought and sold before but had never actually left its moorings. Nevertheless, Fry and the four men remained hopeful, and a day later the ship sailed without a problem.

As gratified as he was that Frank's friends had escaped, Fry—who had recently been warned by the cooperative Vichy officer, Dubois, that the police were following him because they knew of his real mission—feared that when the Le Vernet guards sobered up, they would blame their prisoners' escape on him. After all, it was Gold who worked for him, who had engineered the men's release from Le Vernet. He waited anxiously for news, then heard that on its second day out, the *Bouline* encountered a vicious storm. The terrified passengers wanted to return to port, except, of course, the Neu Beginnen members. But the ship did turn back, and on its way to Marseille it was met by a French coast-guard ship that towed it into port at Toulon. There, the four men were discovered and rearrested. Fry knew he should not publicly ally himself with them, but he could not turn his back on Karl Frank's friends and hired a lawyer to plead their case. (At the trial, some months later, a court in Aix sentenced them to thirty days, and they were returned to Le Vernet. Tittle and Pfeffer escaped to Martinique, but Lamm and Boegler remained in prison. Eventually, all four escaped to America.)

In the midst of the Le Vernet escapes, Fry was called in again by U.S. consul Hugh Fullerton, who had a cable for him from the State Department: "Must request you return immediately . . . not only in view of our understanding but also of local developments." He continued the pretense that he was quite prepared to leave if he had to, but inwardly he was seething. Not only was his own organization in New York against him, but now the U.S. government itself. His common sense told him that the ERC had bowed to pressure from the State Department, which in turn had been influenced by foreign relations.

Unfortunately, this flare-up coincided with the arrival in America of several refugees whose escapes Fry had arranged: the Feuchtwangers, the Werfels, and the Manns. Their escape from the Nazis, and from France, received prominent attention in the press. Feuchtwanger told reporters about the Marseille operation's clandestine smuggling of refugees across the border, "of unidentified American friends who helped him steal out of France." Articles about the Werfels and the Manns said they were met at the dock "by Dr. Frank Kingdon, chairman of the Emergency Rescue Committee, which has helped many intellectuals in their flight from Europe." These news reports substantiated what the State Department believed to be the truth about Fry, that he had broken the laws of his host country by helping refugees escape illegally. "They gave us away. They told how they got out," said Davenport. "They should have kept their big traps shut." Rather than silencing the talkative émigrés, the ERC "spread" the story "because it helped them raise money." In France, however, the publicity only got Fry and his operation "in trouble."

After Fry received orders to return, he asked Eileen to request that his former boss at the Foreign Policy Association, William T. Stone, find out more about the State Department's position on him. Stone inquired and learned that Fry had been correct: The Vichy government had pressured the U.S. authorities "to get in touch with Mr. Fry's 'principals' to request his recall." But, Stone wrote to Eileen, that was all in the past. At this time—his letter to Eileen was dated October 15—no American official thought it urgent to recall her husband. A Mr. Pell at the State Department had "heard nothing more from the

Consul General at Marseilles and has made no further inquiry," wrote Stone. "As long as this situation prevails, he is quite willing to 'let sleeping dogs lie.' This seems to reflect the general attitude in the State Department." When Fry heard this, he was relieved; for the moment, it seemed, his problems with the U.S. government had abated.

October brought German refugees Hannah Arendt and her husband, Heinrich Blücher,* to Fry's doorstep. To Fry, both Arendt, who would become a renowned social philosopher, and Blücher were unknown quantities but Hirschman stepped in to vouch for them. "Blücher I'd known quite well," recalled Hirschman. "I probably spoke quite strongly about him." With the Centre's assistance, Arendt and Blücher were granted visas after several months. In January 1941, they took a train to Lisbon, then, after a three-month wait, sailed to the United States. Their tickets were "provided by HIAS," although engineer and philanthropist Charles Goodman (grandfather of 1960s civil rights martyr Andrew Goodman) "contributed money to bring Hannah Arendt here."

October 15 was Fry's birthday, and for the first time in weeks he let go, celebrating at a restaurant with members of the Centre's staff. At the table, decorated with "dinner-plate size" dahlias, his birthday gift from Davenport, Fry was in a "giddy and joyous" mood. He selected the wines—"nothing but great vintages"—and food for everyone. After dinner, a sated Fry took off his tie and collar, stretched out on the banquet, and rested his head on Davenport's lap and his feet on someone else's. The waiter, as well as his French friends, were "shocked and horrified," but Davenport thought it funny and didn't object, because she had "seen too many cuckoo American movie comedies." Fry loved behaving in a "completely unbuttoned" manner, said Davenport. A "master at dropping the drawing-room brick," he enjoyed rattling the bourgeoisie by acting unconventionally in public.

A week later, Fry pleaded with the Committee, which had just told him to come home, for more money because the intellectuals "are already flat broke, and the rest soon will be." At the moment, he wrote, the Centre was "keeping alive: [painter] Eugen Spiro, Walter Mehring, Hans Sahl, André Breton, writer-translator Franz Hessel and family, and dozens of others." He had even more refugees to worry

*Heinrich "Bluecher" was number 129.

about, he wrote, because Frank Bohn had spent his last money on the *Bouline* and now, heeding warnings from the American consul, had left for the United States after turning over his list of trade unionists and socialists to Fry. Fry begged the Committee to send a decent sum each month so he could do his work. Without this money, he wrote, his mission would fail.

Even in the face of dwindling funds, Fry began hiring more people. Gold introduced him to Danny Bénédite, a Socialist who had worked six years for the *préfecture* in Paris. Gold knew Bénédite's family and believed he was perfect for the Centre. "Danny would be just the man for the Committee. He had been dealing with refugees at the Service des Etrangers at the Prefecture of Police in Paris. . . . He had great moral courage and was as stubborn as a mule." Fry reacted emotionally at first to the suggestion that he hire a former policeman. "Préfecture de Police in Paris did you say?" exlaimed Fry. "I've had quite enough trouble with the cops without putting one of them in my office! No! Not on your life! Ridiculous!"

Even though Fry had initially been reluctant to hire Gold, he now trusted her and was eventually swayed by her vouching for Bénédite, and by several refugees who told him how easily and agreeably Bénédite had renewed their papers when he was at the *préfecture*. Then, near the end of October, Fry met the young Frenchman. Bénédite's attitudes jibed with his, so he hired him, and his wife, Théo. It turned out to be a wonderful decision, for Bénédite sorted out Fry's police problems, and later, when Hirschman left, he became Fry's second-in-command. After Bénédite had worked for him for a while, Fry wrote Eileen that he and the prefect in Marseille had had a "cordial talk" and that he was "on the best of terms with a number of his subordinates, and also with the Sûreté Nationale and many other official bodies." Fry and Bénédite became close friends.

Bénédite introduced Fry to another Frenchman, Jean Gemähling, who had been trying to escape from Pétain's France to join the Free French in London. Twenty-eight and a chemist by profession, Gemähling was "very fair, with blue eyes and high coloring." When he asked Fry for help in getting to London, Fry replied, "I can't do anything for you, but on the other hand, this is what I'm doing here, and are you interested?" Gemähling agreed to stay on in France, joining forces with Bénédite and Fry. "An ardent Gaullist and . . . good Catholic,"

Gemähling at first conducted interviews but eventually became part of the inner circle; much later, he went on to become a hero of the French Resistance, as did Bénédite.

Fry had also hired a physician, Marcel Verzeano (code name "Dr. Maurice" Rivière), to minister to the refugees' ailing minds and bodies as they experienced physical and emotional breakdowns. (When Hirschman left, Verzeano took over his job of setting up illegal escape routes.) For gaining entrée to upper-class French society, Fry employed Marcel Chaminade, who was "small, grey-haired, sort of mousy, correctly dressed" and "Catholic and conservative." Chaminade had connections in the government because he had worked in the French foreign service. Hirschman and Bénédite were wary of Chaminade's character, so he was never invited to join the inner circle; his function was mainly to guide Fry through the confusing layers of French diplomatic relations. When Fry later learned that Chaminade was writing for a "rabidly pro-German and anti-Semitic newspaper," he dismissed him. Also hired was another friend of Davenport's from Toulouse, musicologist and journalist Charles Wolff, a socialist who "had been protecting refugees in Paris in his little house."

Even with his larger staff, Fry still complained to Eileen: His work was "like trying to stay a flood—not even God can do it." But he had accomplished much in a short time. The 250 people for whom he had been responsible—he had saved them, an achievement that probably would have been impossible for anyone else. He had saved writers Heinrich and Golo Mann, Franz Werfel, Konrad Heiden, Lion Feuchtwanger, Arthur Koestler, and Hertha Pauli; mathematician Emil Gumbel; Nobel prizewinner Dr. Otto Meyerhof; and many others, including Egon Erwin Kisch, Leo Borochowitz, Hans Natonek, Conrad Reisner, Boris Nikolaewsky, Fritz Adler, Walther Victor, Leonard Prusak, Babette Gross, Baldur Olden, Franz Pfemfert, David Schneider, Friedrich Stampfer, Jacob Walcher, Milly Zirker, and Friderike Zweig.

By late autumn, France, no longer as chaotic as it was immediately after its capitulation to Germany, had "pulled itself together remarkably." As a result, the refugees still in Marseille had an even more difficult time trying to escape. When Hitler met with Marshal Pétain at Montoire on October 24, there were photographs of the historic conference in all the newspapers. Vichy tightened its regulations concerning refugees, and, hard to believe, the situation grew even grimmer. There were horror stories everywhere, Fry wrote Eileen. Art critic Paul Westheim was going blind "for lack of proper medical attention" in a French camp; chemical physicist Peter Pringsheim was imprisoned in a camp "unfit for hogs."* Men who had volunteered for the French Foreign Legion were being arrested because they were Jewish.

|||||||||

The Nobleman's Son:
Walter Meyerhof

The Fittkos took on an errand boy in the late autumn of 1940, Walter Meyerhof,† a young German émigré who was waiting for his U.S. visa to come through. Walter was born on April 29, 1922, in Kiel, Germany, the same year his father, Otto, an eminent biochemist, won the Nobel prize in physiology and medicine. As a child, Walter believed his father's award had bestowed nobility upon the family, that he was the son of a nobleman.

In 1929, Otto became the director of the physiology department at a research institute in Heidelberg, the Kaiser Wilhelm Institut. Otto and his wife, Hedwig, who were Jewish, "decided their children would adapt better to German culture if they were baptized into a Christian religion. They themselves left the Jewish religion, and had their three children baptized Lutheran." When Hitler became chancellor, Walter, then eleven, was "unaware that [he] was of Jewish origin." One day, in a quarrel with a Jewish classmate, Walter painted a swastika on the boy's desk. When he came home and told his parents what he had done, they revealed to him that they were Jewish. (He is still horrified at what he did.) Within a short time, Hitler saw to it that life changed for Walter and his family.

In 1936, Walter was sent by his parents to England to live with a family who took in Jewish children, and he remained there for two years. Meanwhile, in Germany, the Gestapo confiscated Otto's pass-

---

*Westheim was number 1708 and Pringsheim was number 1058.
†Walter Ernst Meyerhof was number 896.

port; he somehow reclaimed it and fled with his wife to Switzerland, then to Paris. The Meyerhof family reunited in Paris in December 1938, shortly after Kristallnacht. Otto became director of a research group in biochemistry at the Institut Rothschild, and Walter began his graduate studies in physics.

In September 1939, Walter was interned, released, then reinterned in May 1940, just before the fall of France. Internees in the camps, wrote Walter, were classified as *prestataires*—or laborers—the lowest rank in the French Army. Shortly after the Franco-German armistice, the first visits of the camps by Nazi authorities—the Kundt Commission—took place, with the Germans refraining from arresting anyone because, at this point, they still honored an agreement that had been made with French general Weygand not to arrest any French Army personnel. "At the time, the *prestataire* classification may have saved many lives of internees such as myself," recalled Walter.

On August 9, Walter was demobilized, and he met his parents in Marseille and they "went by train . . . to Banyuls-sur-Mer." Otto had a U.S. emergency visitor's visa plus a salary from his former position: "The French government continued to pay its employees after the armistice." He also had a research professorship waiting for him at the University of Pennsylvania. The Meyerhofs' sponsors, prestigious American institutions, had been unsuccessful in their attempts to secure the correct documents for the emigration of the Nobel laureate and his family. "Appeals for issuance of French exit visas to the Meyerhofs were made by both the Rockefeller Foundation and the University of Pennsylvania to the Secretary of State, to other officials of the State Department and finally by Mr. Orville Bullitt directly to his brother, Mr. William C. Bullitt, then the U.S. Ambassador to France, but all apparently to no effect," according to a speech given at Otto Meyerhof's memorial service years later. Walter, as a young man of eighteen, had to obtain his own U.S. visa, something his parents planned to do once they arrived in the United States.

Walter had applied for a U.S. quota immigrant visa in 1938. By all rights, he should have received it. "As all Consulate[s] have received authorisation to grant regular immigration visae to all Germans who have applied before July 1, 1939," Walter wrote, "my quo[t]a number is free." Then Lisa and Hans Fittko offered to take him across the border and he accepted because his Spanish and Portuguese transit visas were about to expire. In a summary of these extraordinary events, Walter recalled his feelings: "According to a barely readable note in my mother's 1940 calendar, it was on Friday, September 6, that we set out at noon, because then the border policemen . . . would all be at lunch. Waving good-bye to my parents was the saddest moment of my life; I thought I would never see them again."

Walter and the Fittkos walked for five hours until, as they approached what they thought was the last hill, police emerged from the woods and arrested them. In Cerbère, where they were jailed, Walter wrote to his parents on the "stiff French toilet paper" he "always carried with him," informing them of his arrest. The note was relayed to the Meyerhofs via a helpful customs officer, and aid was immediately sought from Mayor Azéma. The "mayor called the judge (both were socialists), and the judge set us free when our case came before him."

Walter remained in Banyuls-sur-Mer, living in a *pension* while his parents prepared to leave. Fry had arranged for them to be escorted across the Pyrenees into Spain by Dick Ball, one of his most dependable guides. At the beginning of October, the Meyerhofs said good-bye to their son and, led by Ball, set off for the Pyrenees. Walter recalled what his parents later told him:

> They went in a single file and were not permitted to talk. As they approached the border line they once had to hide in the bushes because [Ball] thought he heard somebody coming. After that everybody had to take off their shoes until they were in Spain. Then [Ball] showed them the way to the Spanish border and left them. . . . The Spanish border officers were extremely arrogant and generally returned people to France if they did not have a French exit visa. People without Spanish visas were jailed. On that Sunday, too, when my parents had to wait in line to be examined, everybody was returned to France.

As she waited, Mme. Meyerhof noticed John Hurley, a U.S. consul who was on his way to Spain and had also stopped at the Portbou border station. She asked him to help and he arranged for the border patrol officer to see the Meyerhofs. The officer repeatedly refused to allow them through. "Then suddenly he said they could pass." They went to Barcelona, then to Madrid and to Lisbon. "[T]here were no further difficulties." The Meyerhofs sailed to America on October 16 aboard the *Exaohorda*.

Before he left France, Otto had asked Fry to see to it that his son did not get arrested. Walter remained in Banyuls-sur-Mer, but whenever he visited Marseille, "it was always Fry who ensured he had a place to sleep." And it was to Fry that he turned for reassurance that he would, eventually, manage to escape.

Dozens of letters between Walter Meyerhof and Fry attest to the young man's anxiety and despair, as well as his patience and perseverance. Fry's letters demonstrate the lengths to which he went for his refugees, the endless bureaucratic obstructions he overcame to get his people out. In October, Walter was preoccupied with obtaining an identity card (which proved who he was and without which other papers were unobtainable) and a safe-conduct pass, which permitted him to travel within France. Fry sent Marcel Verzeano to Banyuls-sur-Mer to visit Walter and provide him with some confidence that the Centre was trying on his behalf. Eventually Walter's identity card was "found at the Consulate," but his safe conduct was refused. He applied once again to the Vichy government and also asked the local prefect to help him. "I am a German citizen, Jew, changed to be Protestant," wrote Walter. "I wish to be with my parents in the US." He was, of course, still waiting for a U.S. visa. When Walter heard that his case would go before Vichy on December 10, he asked Fry to write to the American embassy on his behalf. Fry did, requesting the embassy to "lend your special support to Mr. Walter Meyerhof's demand."

In early January, the determined young man obtained both a U.S. visa and a Portuguese transit visa and was waiting for his Spanish transit visa. At the end of the month, when he received a French exit visa, his papers were almost all in order. Then he heard that the Spanish transit visa had been denied. He immediately reapplied and, hopeful that his escape was imminent, asked Fry about a boat from Marseille to Lisbon. Fry told him that no boats between Marseille and Lisbon were "authorized to take passengers" but added that he was "telegraphing Dr. Joy" of the Unitarian Service Committee to enlist his help in obtaining Walter's Spanish transit visa.

By March, Walter finally received it and wrote to Fry, "I am really 'off.' In fact I am starting tomorrow and hope to arrive at Lisbon at the beginning of next week. A place on a boat is not yet booked. . . . I want to thank you most sincerely for the great assistance you have given me during these months of waiting, which now fortunately have come to an end."

But he was not free yet. Earlier, he had obtained an affidavit in lieu of passport, stamped and signed by U.S. vice consul Myles Standish, attesting to the young man's identity as a German national who had no passport. "I had thrown my German passport away on the flight between two internment camps," Walter recalled. When he presented this affidavit to Spanish border guards at Le Perthus in the Pyrenees, they "claimed that they had never seen such a document and that they had to call their headquarters in Madrid to find out whether they could let me into Spain." Walter waited for six hours before he was told he would not be admitted. Two weeks later, he finally was able to cross into Spain by posing as "secretary" to the head of the Unitarian Service Committee, Charles Joy. At that time, "no fuss was made about the affidavit," recalled Walter.

He boarded a freighter to America (a vessel that on a later crossing was sunk by German submarines), arriving safely in New York Harbor on May 16. Before he sailed, he again thanked Fry "for the great help and kindness you showed to me, always. Everything turned out so well for me in the end. . . . I have heard that you have some small troubles, and I hope that is nothing, and that we may meet soon in U.S.A."

In America, Walter became a physicist, married a woman who had escaped Germany on the last *kindertransport* (children's transport), and had a family. For many years, he gave little thought to Fry. "I had every intention of seeing him in the States, but . . . I had to concentrate on physics study and that's very absorbing," he said. "I didn't think about Fry anymore because I had to pass my exams. I'm sure that's how it happened with many people. You simply picked up your life and you didn't really think back."

Though he never saw Fry again, in 1996, through a series of coincidences, he was reminded once more of the man to whom he owed his life. Forty-five years after his escape from Europe, Walter Meyerhof created the Varian Fry Foundation. His purpose was to inform "young people in this country . . . about Fry . . . somebody who helps others against all odds."

CHAPTER SIX

||||||||||||||||||||||||||

RESPITE AT
AIR-BEL

Somehow, through a strange confluence of chance encounters and unlikely coincidences, I had been swept into a place where grief, consternation, disillusionment, and anger had become the gentle servants of justice.... Our little tribe of amateurs, relying solely on brute intellect and the leadership of [Fry], had been successfully outwitting Hitler's Gestapo.... This was intoxicating enough. Now, Air-Bel, a country refuge ... I was fully aware that life would probably never again offer me another such moment.

Miriam Davenport

THE WARM, SALTY WATERS of the Mediterranean slapped gently at the hulls of fishing boats tied to a dock off the rue Royale. A tall, slender figure in a pinstriped suit, a red and white silk handkerchief peeking out of his jacket pocket, hastened down the silent street toward the dock. It was Fry, and he was late for a meeting with Hirschman and three of his most important protégés: endangered editor and publisher Georg Bernhard; Klaus Dohrn, a young German Catholic who had been interrogated by the Nazi Kundt Commission; and Walter Mehring.

Since the French, Spanish, and Portuguese governments had recently initiated more restrictive policies that made escape even more difficult, no one, including Fry, could be certain of the border situation. He had been looking for sea routes since his arrival in France and had envisioned dozens of escape-by-ship scenarios. However, ship captains and other intermediaries were often unscrupulous and greedy, providing little service for the money they charged. Skippers inflated prices for a "gaunt hulk" and middlemen could be informants, so Fry did not trust them.

The resourceful guide Dick Ball now got word of a trawler whose captain was willing to ferry a small group of refugees to Gibraltar. The price was 225,000 francs, or about $4,500, a huge sum. Fry had a strong hunch the captain would steal the money without transporting anyone. And yet this was his only opportunity to save Georg Bernhard's life. "Hitler had a list of the ten most wanted people and my father-in-law was number three on that list," recalled Gys Landsberger, Bernhard's daughter-in-law.* Fry had seen the list courtesy of Dubois of the Vichy police, so although he feared he might lose the money, he yielded to the sheer desperation of his protégés rather than his own growing cynicism.

The trawler could also be used to transport some of the British prisoners of war. According to his prior arrangement with British intelligence, Fry spent some of the money the British were paying him to hire the ship. When the plan was set, Fry sent word to the Bernhards, Dohrn, Mehring, and the British soldiers to meet him in a shed on the pier, left of the lighthouse, at ten on Sunday night, October 27. They were to bring their belongings, and enough food and water for four days.

That night, the German émigrés and British soldiers gathered on the pier. Fry talked in low tones to his protégés, checked to make certain they had the correct papers, and reassured the terrified Mehring. Then he said good-bye and strode off to the Gare St.-Charles, where he took the night train to Tarascon, fifty miles northwest of Marseille. He wanted to be far from the city in order to be able to deny his involvement should an enemy stop the trawler and question its passengers.

The refugees and the soldiers huddled on the dock for three hours.

---

*Gys Landsberger's family fled Germany early because her father "had foresight and said Hitler would last and last." After the fall of France, the family was interned, and Gys's father was arrested and sent to Majdanek extermination camp in Poland. Gys's brother walked to Spain and joined the British Army. Gys's future husband, Herbert Landsberger, volunteered for the French Army and was sent to North Africa. She describes the willingness of the French Army to send Jewish volunteers to North Africa as "the only decent thing the French did." Had they remained in France, "the Germans would have killed them." When Landsberger was demobilized, he went to Marseille, and he and Gys were married. They lived underground in Marseille with his mother, Gertrud, and stepfather, Georg Bernhard.

Then Hirschman came to the shed and told the group there was a hitch. He was meeting Ball at a bistro in front of the Vieux-Port and would report back to them. He returned a short time later to tell them that the captain was asking for more money. Finally, at two A.M., he returned and sent everyone home because there would be no ship. No one was escaping that night. They slipped away, one at a time, to avoid attracting attention. Even Bernhard went quietly.

In Tarascon, Fry spent a nervous night. He wrote a long letter to Eileen saying the pressure was finally diminishing, "not because the situation is improving but because more and more of our charges are being re-interned—and I am at long last getting an occasional chance to breathe." Fry admitted that he had "reached a point in nervous exhaustion a few weeks ago when I actually was glad to have a few of the most insistent and most pestiferous 'clients' carried shrieking off." It was shocking for him to admit this, that the pressure was so intense he almost felt relieved when a protégé was arrested; that would mean one less person to worry about—although, at the same time, it meant one more loss, one more failure. In this letter to Eileen, Fry made clear that his work was an unending "nightmare of horror."

When he returned to Marseille the next day, he half expected to be picked up at the station by a police wagon, but to his relief he slipped out of the station and back to his hotel without being noticed. He was in his room changing when he heard a tap on the door. It was Mehring. The ship had not sailed; the captain had stolen the money. The refugees were downstairs, waiting for Fry to tell them what to do.

Fry asked the little poet to wait outside, then sat down and reached into his desk for a bottle of absinthe. In a recent letter, Eileen had questioned why he was still there. Even Eileen, who shared his values and beliefs and who had been an early volunteer for Harold Oram, the well-known supporter of antifascist causes, now concluded he was fighting a hopeless battle. Fry sat at his desk, asking himself the same question: If he could not get them out, why did he remain in Marseille? Fry's reflection lasted only a moment. He finished his drink, vowed to stop second-guessing himself, and went downstairs to deal with Mehring and the others. He would start over: If the boat scheme was doomed, he would concentrate on escapes by land.

Undermining Fry were the leaders of the Committee who kept calling him home. The ERC leadership was disorganized and divided, as bureaucratic organizations often become, so that some people on the Committee supported Fry, while others did not, and they switched sides often. Kingdon, Adams, and Hagen (Karl Frank) were "united in a desire to get you back," wrote Eileen. Suddenly, though, they changed their minds and appeared "reconciled to [Fry's] continued presence in France." Eileen was misinformed, however; perhaps, as Fry's wife, she was not told the truth by those running the Committee, for within the month, a journalist, Jay Allen, was appointed to take over Fry's position.

Allen's contract with the ERC was as vague and open-ended as Fry's. It acknowledged that Allen's journalism came first, before saving lives. He was to take over a "situation [that] . . . has greatly changed and it may be necessary to change ways and means of handling it." The one-month contract stated that he would receive the sum of $5,500, presumably to cover both refugee aid and his salary.

The Spanish border closed again at the very end of October. Fry and his inner circle of colleagues continued to do double duty. "I still begin at 8 in the morning and work until 11 at night and sometimes until one," he wrote. "I still see dozens of people every day." By day, he interviewed refugees and spoke with officials, while his staff conducted interviews, carried messages, and secured visas. By night, they met to plan escape routes. Crossing the Pyrenees was made more difficult in November because Vichy replaced the heroic Mayor Azéma with a government appointee, "some collaborationist official who isn't even from this region," as Lisa Fittko wrote, and Azéma was not seen again.

The inner circle was a seamless company of single-minded people with the same objectives, although their politics, methods, and behavior differed widely. Fry held them together with the force of his personality and character. They were loyal to one another. A bond of love developed, as it often does with people sharing a common goal, fighting a common enemy. Fry loved Hirschman deeply, then, when Hirschman left, transferred these feelings to Bénédite. Gold seemed unable to refuse when asked to contribute money and continued donating cash all the time she remained in Marseille. Each member of the inner circle gave fully of his or her resources of energy, time, and love to aid Fry.

Despite Gold's generosity, however, Fry found himself increasingly short of funds. The Centre Américain de Secours was "a deluxe relief bureau for a special type of client," he wrote, people whose prior lives had not prepared them for the humiliation of poverty. Unable to sell their work or gain employment, they were forced to rely on the kindness of strangers. If he did not receive more money from New York, at least ten thousand francs a month, he wrote to Eileen, his protégés would either go on relief or be interned. This would be devastating even for the toughest people and "few [refugees] are tough."

Because Fry's mail was censored, he could not tell Eileen that he also needed money to fund the Centre's underground operation, but he hoped she would read between the lines. Smuggling refugees across borders was expensive. He had to pay for guides, information, and safe accommodations. "Sooner or later" the Centre would have to close unless the ERC stepped up its fund-raising. Remind "those boobs in New York," he wrote, that this was "no romantic job . . . [but] a hard office job . . . it is going to go on; and get harder, until the war is over."

He asked Eileen to tell the Committee that, in addition to money, he needed a successor, a "good one." Fry had strong ideas about his replacement; it would have to be someone as dedicated as he. (In reality, he felt he was irreplaceable.)

He also needed visas. "They have got visas for all their 'friends,' and very few for the really valuable people—the novelists, poets, painters, historians, philosophers, scientists, doctors," he wrote. "They *must* do something also for these people, and quickly, for it gets more and more difficult to find a way out of France every day." The New York office had to understand, he wrote, that without the Centre, the Nazis might imprison many of the refugees he was trying to help. His operation was different from those of the Quakers and the local Jewish relief agency; the Quakers did not have adequate funds "nor the understanding to do the job as we do it; their task is mass relief, and they can't really tell an intellectual of genuine value from a faker." The Jewish agency also had limited resources, plus problems "too enormous to enable it to give anything but the barest subsistence allowance."

Fry chafed at the end of October as the United States issued no more than a handful of emergency visitors' visas. The State Department's official line was that it feared infiltration of the United States by Fifth Columnists posing as refugees. Could Eileen find out from the Committee if the government planned to issue more of these precious visas? Fry asked.

Charles Reuben Fry,
a lifetime employee of the
Children's Aid Society,
inspired his grandson, Varian,
to care deeply about people.

As a child,
Varian often visited his grandfather,
who was superintendent of the Children's
Summer Home at Bath Beach, Brooklyn.

Fry's love of nature,
especially birds, began early.
When he was ten, he rescued
a cedar waxwing from a cat.

Fry's parents, Lilian and Arthur, were supportive during his problematic
years at a succession of prep schools.

Fry in 1926.
That winter, he and fellow Harvard
freshman Lincoln Kirstein founded
the respected literary journal
The Hound & Horn.

During his junior year,
Fry fell in love with Eileen Hughes,
and they married shortly
after his graduation.

As editor of *The Living Age,* Fry traveled to Berlin in 1935, shortly before
the passage of Germany's Nuremberg Laws.

Five years later, he returned to Europe, where he set up an office for the Emergency Rescue Committee in the Hôtel Splendide, not far from Marseille's Vieux-Port.

"Good God!" Fry commented about his demeanor in Marseille.

In Marseille, Fry created a cover operation, the Centre Américain de Secours, and hired Europeans and a few Americans to aid his efforts to help refugees escape.

The hallway outside the office was always filled with refugees seeking relief from their desperate situation.

Albert Hirschman, *right,* and Fritz Heine were two of Fry's associates. Hirschman, nicknamed "Beamish" by Fry, was indispensable, developing escape routes and changing money on the black market.

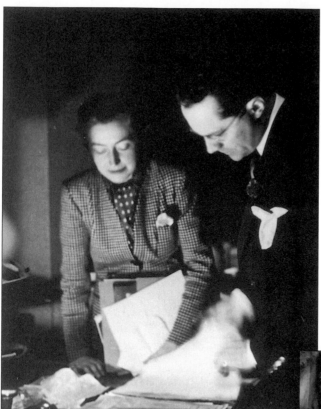

Miriam Davenport, an American art student, conducted interviews and discussed refugee cases with Fry.

Another American working for Fry, Mary Jayne Gold, charmed a French concentration camp commandant into releasing prisoners.

Secret nighttime meetings of Fry and his staff determined the refugees' fates.
From left, in the back: Marcel Verzeano, Frederic Drach, Paul Schmierer,
Jacques Weisslitz; in the front, Marcel Chaminade, Hans Sahl, Heinz Oppenheimer,
Daniel Bénédite. Bénédite became Fry's second in command after Hirschman,
threatened with arrest, fled France. Weisslitz died at the hands of the Nazis.

In the end, the final decisions were Fry's.

At Sunday gatherings of surrealists at the
Villa Air-Bel, Fry managed to forget, for
a time, the seriousness of his mission.

The father of surrealism, André Breton,
often walked in the Air-Bel gardens
with his daughter, Aube, then five.

At Air-Bel, Fry and Consuelo de Saint-Exupéry, wife of writer Antoine de Saint-Exupéry, hung paintings from the branches of a platane tree.

In his bedroom at the villa, Fry reviewed the papers of André Breton, his wife, Jacqueline Lamba, and Max Ernst.

Jean Gemähling, another of Fry's
lieutenants, shares an intimate meal
with Consuelo de Saint-Exupéry.

U.S. vice consul Hiram Bingham, the only
American official sympathetic to Fry, worked
with him on refugee escapes. As a result, the
United States removed him from his post
and prevented him from advancing in the
Foreign Service.

Many documents had to be forged, and Fry's master forger, Austrian cartoonist Bill Freier, was at his drawing board day and night. Eventually captured and sent to Auschwitz, Freier managed to survive the war.

When he was not creating false papers, Freier drew caricatures of his boss.

VARIAN MACKEY FRY

Bill

After Vichy expelled Fry on September 6, 1941, his friends saw him off
at the Cerbère train station. From left, Paul Schmierer, Helen Hessel, Daniel Bénédite,
Marcel Verzeano, Lucie Heymann, Jeanne Vialin, Charles Wolff, Ludwig Copperman,
and Annette Pouppos. Later, Wolff and Bénédite (and Jean Gemähling as well)
fought in the Resistance. Wolff, betrayed, was tortured to death by
the French milice (fascist militia) in August 1944.

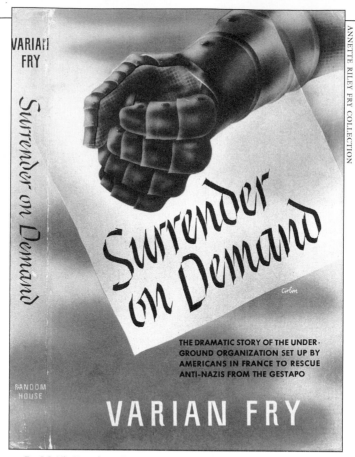

In 1945, Random House published *Surrender on Demand,*
Fry's memoir of his year in Marseille.

Fry married Annette Riley in 1950,
several years after his divorce from Eileen.

Original lithograph by Marc Chagall for inclusion in "Flight,"
the International Rescue Committee's portfolio collection. Fry worked for years
to obtain works of art for the collection, but some artists, including a few
whose lives he had saved, resisted contributing.

Fry's first honor came in 1963 when sculptor Jacques Lipchitz,
who stated that he owed his life to Fry, presented him with
the International Rescue Committee medal for
"contributions to the cause of freedom."

Fry, surrounded by Annette and their children, James, Sylvia, and Thomas,
received the Cross of Chevalier of the Legion of Honor, France's highest award,
in April 1967, five months before his death.

Fry had long relied on the intelligence and skill of Miriam Davenport, who now told him she was resigning the first week of November in order to be with her Yugoslavian fiancé. He would miss her input greatly. When she was no longer there to help cope with the influx of refugees, Fry's work would be even more overwhelming. Each day he received at least twenty-five letters, and every hour he took nearly a dozen telephone calls. "Sometimes the refugees walk right into my bedroom without knocking or announcing themselves," he wrote to Eileen. A few of the protégés, not the "most intelligent, the most polite and the most charming," were "insufferable." Davenport recalled that "the German refugees were being so forward and pushy and not giving him a moment's rest, that he was beginning to dislike Germans. He hated to say that. He hated to think it." She remembered that some German refugees shored her "Spanish clients to the back of the line." A few protégés' attitude was: "Why are you helping him? I'm more important." But, as Davenport explained, "We were dealing with desperate human beings."

One protégé, Wilhelm Herzog, took the room next door to Fry's so he "could stop me when I went out in the morning and see me again when I came back in the evening." Another, Margot Wolff, entered Fry's room before he was dressed.* A third literally popped up in front of Fry whenever he exited or entered the hotel lobby. "They await me in the salon, and spring at me when I come out of the elevator," he complained. "They catch me on the streets." As a result, he no longer wanted to live in the Splendide where some refugee interviews were done.

At the same time Fry was at his wit's end with the more intrusive refugees, three of the women on his staff happened to go house hunting: Davenport, Gold, and Danny Bénédite's wife, Théo. Gold and the Bénédites had talked about sharing a cottage, although the Bénédites had also promised to live with Victor Serge and his family. Davenport, who was leaving Marseille shortly, went along for fun, she recalled.

Serge, an old friend of Danny Bénédite's, was an activist and writer whose conversation was "like reading a Russian novel," according to Fry. An experienced émigré who had moved from country to country for years, Serge was a "founder of the Third International later exiled by Stalin to Siberia," a Trotskyist, and a member of the Comintern. He

*Wilhelm Herzog was number 1503 and Margot Wolff was 1467.

had lived for a time in Paris, then went to the south of France, where he soon heard of Fry and the Centre. At the Centre, he was interviewed by Davenport, who introduced the names of Serge, his son, Vlady, and companion Laurette Séjourné* at the nightly conference. Fry immediately approved helping them. "Yes," he said, "we'll give them money for room and board" and see about getting them out.

Jean Gemähling accompanied Gold, Davenport, and Théo Bénédite on their house-hunting expedition that day near the very end of October. They took a train from Marseille, and, after about half an hour, when it stopped in the suburb of La Pomme, Gemähling and the three women noticed an attractive café near the station. They got off the train and were walking toward the café when they passed "tall stone gate posts . . . carved with the name 'Air-Bel' " marking the entrance to an estate. They looked in and saw an elderly man raking leaves in front of a large, deserted farmhouse. Gold did not want to stop, thinking the house much too big, but Davenport insisted they at least inquire. M. Thumin, who turned out to be "an eccentric amateur ornithologist," stopped raking long enough to tell them the farmhouse was not for rent. When Gold showed him some American dollars, however, he agreed to show them around. At first, Gold and Bénédite judged the eighteen-room house oversized for what they needed, but Davenport talked them into it. She reasoned that since the house, Air-Bel, had almost the same name as her "flea-bag hotel, the Paradis Bel Air," it was meant to be. Also, since the Centre paid living expenses for certain "favorite clients," why not invite them to share the villa and contribute toward running the household? She suggested they rent the house, hire a cook and maid, and invite staff and protégés to live there.

Gold and Bénédite decided to take the house; Gold paid the rent and Bénédite, who was a French citizen, signed the lease. That same day, they hired a housekeeping staff: Mme. Nouget to cook, Rose to clean, and Marie, a fifteen-year-old Spanish refugee, to care for the Bénédites' young son. Then they returned to the office and excitedly told everyone about their wonderful new house only thirty minutes from Marseille.

Located "where the city ended and the real country began," Air-Bel

---

*Laurette Séjourné was number 1248.

had eighty-five acres and was a quarter-mile off the main road. The three-story "tumbledown chateau" was so spacious "that even twelve people and three servants don't get in one another's way." Downstairs was a breakfast room, kitchen, dining hall—used for eating, working, and listening to the radio—greenhouse, and a black-and-white tiled parlor, furnished with Louis Quinze chairs and tables and a grand piano adorned with elaborate antique candlesticks. Upstairs was a library, a master bedroom with a vast dressing room, and another capacious bedroom with elaborate furniture. All the bedrooms had fireplaces and marble mantels. The grounds had plane trees, acacias, and cedars of Lebanon, a formal garden, flower beds, and a lily pool with a fountain, although the fountain was "more like a stagnant pond." Air-Bel even boasted a garden, which eventually produced fresh fruits and vegetables, a welcome supplement to the inadequate wartime diet.

Fry was overjoyed at his first view of the villa, running from room to room, exclaiming over the frescoes of mythological scenes on the library's walls. "This was the only time, to my knowledge, that his classical knowledge served him during that year in Marseille," wrote Gold. "[I]n one of his antic moods," he rushed into each room, "opening each little bedside cabinet" to see the chamber pots.

Air-Bel provided "one of those magnificent views that only the Mediterranean area can boast," wrote Fry, "a view of pine trees and olive trees, dark green and light, of soft red-tiled roofs, of mist and the fascination of distance, and back of it all the rugged grey limestone mountains which surround the Marseille area like a great amphitheater." The terrace in front of the house was "flanked by two enormous plane trees cut in the French manner—arbitrarily truncated, gnarled and knotted." Beyond the garden was a meadow, and beyond that, "other fields, groups of Mediterranean pines, little houses with red-tiled roofs, the suddenly startling thrust of black cypress trees, and the grey and sage-green pepper-and-salt mountains just this side of the sky."

The rental began on November 1. Gold, Davenport, and the Bénédites moved in, but Gold was initially reluctant to have Fry join them. For the usually generous Gold, this was unusual but could be blamed on her probable assumption that the house would be for her and her friends, not for Fry and the staff of the Centre. Because even though Gold worked for him, "she didn't see any reason why he should be hanging around in her house," as Davenport recalled. "After all, she was paying the rent." But Gold capitulated when Davenport urged her to invite Fry to stay, since, as director of the Centre, he was more overworked and in need of relaxation than anyone. Fry spent that first weekend at Air-Bel in a second-floor bedroom, sleeping cozily under Miriam Davenport's old rabbit coat.

Davenport left Marseille on Monday, November 4, and two weeks later, Charlie Fawcett was gone, too. Davenport "had waited until the last minute in hopes of getting a return French visa" but had no luck. "Alas, my own dreams were frustrated by Vichy," Davenport wrote. "I left for Slovenia . . . and my return to France was firmly denied." When she left Air-Bel, Fry, and France, the young woman sensed that the experience had been "a moment of rare privilege."

Fawcett recalled that in his job as a doorman and messenger, he did not take part in the underground work but carried information from Fry to refugees and others. Once, the artist Henri Matisse, who was not on the run, invited Fawcett to dinner. "They say that Matisse never helped," said Fawcett. "But when they say that . . . I can tell that he had a barn which he used to hide refugees." Fry was not at all pleased on a day in mid-November when Dubois stopped by to warn him that his genial doorman was about to be arrested. When Fry called Fawcett in to hear the grim news, the young man remained unshaken and told Fry and Dubois he would leave the next day. "No," Dubois countered, "you leave tonight, because I'm coming at six o'clock tomorrow morning to arrest you."

It was Thursday, November 14, and Fry decided to take advantage of Fawcett's departure by asking him to smuggle out messages to the Committee. Even though the Committee didn't approve of Fry's illegal actions, he felt compelled to communicate to them about his operation's progress. His method for smuggling out sensitive material, such as this report to the Committee, had been learned from his European colleagues. He had his secretary type messages on thin sheets of paper, cut them into tiny strips, and insert the strips into condoms. These were put into emptied-out toothpaste tubes and then carried out of France, either by refugees or others. Fawcett smuggled out Fry's reports in condoms hidden in the third valve of his trumpet and in a plaster-of-paris model he had made.

Fawcett, although young, knew how to evade the police: "You could always tell which were the Germans because their suits were always pressed, the French never." But he worried that his tendency to blush and stutter when embarrassed or afraid might, if he were questioned, give him away. He went to a bar "to drink a little courage" shortly before he left and saw a woman there with her legs crossed and "a little bit of garter belt showing." This gave him an idea. He quickly drew a handful of pornographic pictures on scraps of paper torn from a menu, then placed them on top of the clothing in his suitcase. Now he had a legitimate reason to look and act embarrassed if his luggage was searched and he was questioned. At the border, a guard found the sexually explicit drawings in Fawcett's suitcase and said, "You can't take disgusting material like this into a Catholic country. We'll have to confiscate them." He let Fawcett go. Fawcett, crossing the border, noticed the guards passing the pictures around and heard them "roaring with laughter."

Fry had also asked Fawcett to deliver a verbal message about the British soldiers in Marseille to the British assistant chargé d'affaires in Barcelona. When Fawcett finally arrived in Barcelona, he went to the British embassy and delivered Fry's message. But as he left, he was spotted by the Spanish police. "What were you doing in there?" they yelled. They arrested him and took him back to occupied France, to Gestapo headquarters in a small town outside of Biarritz.

Fawcett waited on a bench, plotting his escape. When he saw a German officer emerge from a room and stride toward him, followed by a "cringing French civilian collaborator who was sort of hanging on trying to impress the Nazi," Fawcett knew he had found his way out. He jumped up and held the door open for them, then followed, carrying his belongings. Others watched as Fawcett walked behind the Gestapo officer and the civilian down a courtyard that seemed "a million miles long," trying to give the impression that he was carrying the officer's luggage. When the pair drove away, Fawcett ran. He boarded a train, exited on the other side, then hitched a ride on a truck. "The driver was carrying cabbages and told me to eat one. When I woke up, I was outside the railroad station in San Sebastian." He took a freight train to Madrid.

By December, he was safely in Lisbon with his suitcase, trumpet, and the plaster-of-paris head. "I met with Donald Darling," recalled

Fawcett, "the famous head of British intelligence." Fawcett did "little errands" for British intelligence and he may have become a liaison between British intelligence and Fry and his protégés, according to one expert.

While Fawcett was having his adventures, Fry had been visiting a reluctant refugee, artist Marc Chagall,* who lived in an old stone cottage in Gordes and refused to admit that he might be in danger. He was quite comfortable remaining in Gordes and working in his studio, which contained "a big kitchen table, a few wicker chairs, a cheap screen, a coal-stove, two easels and his pictures." Sometime later, Chagall's resistance to emigrating softened a bit after he visited Fry in Marseille to discuss the subject over wine and bouillabaisse. Fry and M. and Mme. Chagall were nearly finished eating when sirens sounded and the restaurant owner drew the blackout curtains; they completed their meal by candlelight. When the all-clear whistle sounded, they left the restaurant, but it was a false whistle because the air raid was still on. Fry put a protective arm around Chagall, another around Mme. Chagall, and the three of them walked quickly to the station at Noailles. They remained until the air raid was really over. The bombing, Fry speculated, may have been done by the British or by the Italians "eager to turn French opinion against Britain." Although, as Fry wrote, "It wasn't much, as bombings go," this brush with reality may have influenced Chagall, for he eventually decided to emigrate.

With Air-Bel available as a refuge and escape, Fry reduced his demanding schedule, cutting down on his hours and even taking off an occasional weekend. He befriended one refugee family, the Hessels, particularly their young son, Stephane, who was then twenty-three. Cultured and refined, from a literary, well-to-do background, Hessel was a perfect companion for Fry. The Hessels had followed the usual route of escape from Germany: to Paris after Kristallnacht in 1938, then to Marseille after the fall of France. Stephane's father, Franz, had been friends with Walter Benjamin, and together they had translated Proust into German. That autumn, Fry grew close to Stephane and his mother, Helen. She "helped Varian in all possible respects" while he "financially supported her." Whenever Fry had free time, he would contact Hessel at his hotel, the Moderne, and they would go off together, touring the south of France.

*Marc Chagall was number 210.

Hessel recalled that he "nursed" Fry through periods of depression and melancholy. "When he was tired and despondent because life was not easy for him, then I would come and cheer him up." Fry, frustrated "because he wanted to get people out and he couldn't," never had enough money or visas. During their excursions, they focused on art, sculpture, and architecture, particularly Romanesque churches. They grew close, talking about everything, including marriage. (Hessel was also married.) He recalled that Fry seemed unhappy with Eileen: "His first marriage was, I wouldn't say a failure, but something that he didn't speak of with great enthusiasm." He said that Fry "had the bearing of a husband who was not entirely satisfied."

In contrast, Gold recalled that Fry "longed for his wife . . . and hoped she would join him." Gold was certain that Fry had no "serious affairs during that year, [that] whatever he did it was with great discretion." Verzeano recalled that "Varian liked good looking women and occasionally had an affair of very short duration. That was true of all of us." Fry also made occasional visits to prostitutes, as he wrote Eileen. "I would like to have you back in bed very much for despite your suspicions I always sleep alone and don't like it. . . . I went to a cat house a few times with Otto [Hirschman] and DON'T like it . . . and have gone a few times alone even more forlornly since he left." He fantasized about having her in France: "[I]t would be wonderful to have you here, not only for your companionship in bed and out, but also for all the help you could be to our work."

Fry's relationship with Hessel was important to him, but it played no role in his letters to Eileen. The two men shared a private warmth and affection, a friendship of "very close companionship between two young men, not particularly homosexual, although there was a physical nearness, closeness, hugging of each other," recalled Hessel.

> It isn't something where we were physically close to the extent that we wanted to sleep together. But we were close enough to feel that we were not only soul mates, but we were also buddies.

Fry also had another companion, his poodle, Clovis. Fry brought Clovis to live at Air-Bel and described him as "a very sweet doggy" even though "he piddles everywhere." Because of Air-Bel, Clovis, and Stephane Hessel, Fry's life contained some pleasure in addition to grueling work. The refugee operation continued to be demanding—and rewarding—but now he had a private life that afforded him some enjoyment and relaxation. As winter began, Fry felt happier than he had ever been in his life.

‖‖‖‖‖‖‖‖
Not Degenerate Enough: Charlotte Brand

Fry's mandate was to help artists who had been labeled "degenerate" by the Germans. In most cases, their names were on his original list, provided by the Museum of Modern Art's Alfred Barr. Because she was an art student, Miriam Davenport helped Fry decide which artists should be added to his list. But as much as he wanted to, he could not save every artist. "We couldn't. That was not our mission," said Davenport. "A guy who goes over with a list of 200 names to be rescued and $3,000 taped to his leg can't help everyone."

One day, Charlotte Brand,* a German artist in her twenties, came to the Centre and was interviewed by Davenport. Brand had been a student at the Bauhaus but had grown tired of modern design and had gone to Rome to paint watercolors. By the time she arrived in Marseille, she had a portfolio of paintings that were "quite beautiful," according to Davenport.

Brand was hungry, homeless, and in danger because she "was probably Jewish," Davenport recalled. "It didn't count if you were raised Protestant or if, like Hirschman, you had been baptized a Protestant. It was racist. If you had a Jewish ancestor, that meant you had Jewish blood. That meant you were Jewish."

"I can certainly see to it that you have enough money to pay for a roof over your head and to keep you fed modestly," Davenport told Brand. "And I will see if there is any chance of our getting an American visitor's visa for you so that you can immigrate." With Fry's approval, she gave the young woman money from the Gold List. Brand had not been labeled as "degenerate." Recalled Davenport, "Her watercolors were not non-objective, so one could recognize them. They were flowers, buildings in Rome, Roman landscapes." When she

*Charlotte Brand was number 153.

suggested Brand leave her portfolio behind so her work could be shown to Fry, the young painter "looked a little brighter." That evening, during the conference on cases held in Fry's hotel room, Davenport brought up Charlotte Brand. "Here's this young artist who's gifted. She has had the best training. She was in the Bauhaus with Walter Gropius and she's been working in watercolors lately. We should do everything we can to get her a visa. We could put up a show of her work in your office, and ask Hiram Bingham to see it."

Fry looked at the portfolio and thought the paintings were wonderful. He told Davenport to go ahead with her plan. They stuck the paintings on the walls of Fry's office with thumbtacks, and Fry invited Bingham: "Come take a look and see if she's worth a visa." Within a day or two, the accommodating vice consul was there to see Brand's art. "This is very good," he said. "I think she deserves a visa. I'll see what I can do."

With Bingham's intervention and Fry's help, Brand got a visa, a first step in her eventually successful emigration. When she arrived in New York, her first stop was the Museum of Modern Art. To her disappointment, "they weren't the slightest bit interested in her. They wanted no part of her."

"Charlotte didn't last long. She finally did get a dealer in New York, but not soon enough to do her any good," recalled Davenport. Brand developed tuberculosis and went for a rest cure in White Sands, New Mexico. "But she didn't get better and she came back to New York, where she was in a nursing home. She died of cancer."

CHAPTER SEVEN

||||||||||||||||||||||||||

EXQUISITE CORPSE: THE SURREALISTS

Surrealism left no one that came in contact with it unaffected.
Martica Sawin

T HE INHABITANTS OF Air-Bel that first weekend were Fry,
Gold, Davenport, Gemähling, the Bénédites, young Gussie
Rosenberg, Marcel Verzeano, and journalist Charles Wolff. After
Davenport departed, Fry, with Gold's approval, invited two special
protégés and their families to join the household. Some weeks earlier,
the writer André Breton had asked Victor Serge whether "the young
ladies from the [Centre Américain de] Secours" could assist him financially. Breton, his wife, Jacqueline Lamba, and their five-year-old
daughter, Aube, came to live at Air-Bel, where they occupied a huge
third-floor bedroom. Serge took a second-floor room and nicknamed
Air-Bel the Chateau Espére-Visa (waiting for visas). These were the
only refugees who actually resided at Air-Bel, although the artists Max
Ernst and André Masson, and surrealist poet Benjamin Peret, stayed
there briefly.*

Among the Centre's staff, only Hirschman resisted the charms of

---

*Breton was number 168 and Lamba number 167, Ernst was 316, Masson was
858, and Peret was 1522.

the chateau. He "was doing the dirty work" and felt Fry should remain in town in case of an emergency. "I was against the Villa Air-Bel. I thought it would take too much of his time and of his energy," recalled Hirschman. "There was a certain amount of jealousy on my part [of] the other people that he got increasingly close to." However, for Fry, the need to relax and escape the pressures of his job outweighed Hirschman's misgivings. Davenport, on the other hand, loved Air-Bel but was there only that first weekend before leaving Marseille. "I still regret missing out on all that I had so successfully promoted," she said.

Air-Bel revived Fry, giving him "peace and quiet at last, after three months of the most grueling work I have ever done in my life." He had "almost drowned," he wrote his mother, "in a flood of anguished human beings in search of advice and help." The work was "like living in a crowd and being the center of it and the object of its attention . . . like a doctor . . . during an earthquake." The villa became his sanctuary during his remaining months in Marseille with its art, music, games, and laughter providing a respite from the grimness of the occupation. "It is too bad there is a war," Fry wrote his father, "because we could all live here in Marseille in surroundings that are not far from perfect." The Air-Bel experience was sublime, and Fry always remembered the glory days at the villa. "I have never in my life before lived in such a beautiful place; I wonder if I ever shall again," he wrote. "Of the hundreds of thousands of images which my year in France has left in my memory, the images of the chateau are the most precious." Mary Jayne Gold, too, never forgot, and named the St. Tropez villa where she lived, and died, after that magical place.

When Fry invited Breton to share the craggy antique splendor of the villa, he set in motion a revitalization of the surrealist movement, which was at risk of dying that autumn. At Air-Bel, Breton, the "father of surrealism," gathered to him the leading surrealists of the day, bringing new life and vitality to the movement—and to the house. "[A]n extraordinary presence . . . striking looking . . . [with] a marvelous voice," Breton had written the surrealist manifesto—*Manifeste du surrealisme*—in Paris in 1924. Although the term "surrealism" did not originate with him (the poet Guillaume Apollinaire first used it in 1917), his writings defined the movement, and he was the force that held it together in late 1940 by turning Air-Bel into a camp for adults. They often acted "like children: singing, playing and laughing," forgetting briefly that their lives were at risk, that this was the Chateau Espére-Visa and they did not know when, or if, they would escape.

Before the war, the visual, literary, and political movement known as surrealism had held regular meetings at headquarters in Paris, but after the occupation, the movement "fell apart and was never the same." Surrealists were in danger of arrest because their work had been defined by the Germans as "degenerate." Nevertheless, they continued to make art. Struggling to stay alive, and out of jail, the surrealists lived and worked in dozens of towns throughout France, trying to keep one step ahead of Vichy and the Germans: Breton had been in the French Army, Benjamin Péret was imprisoned for his pacifism, and Masson, whose wife was Jewish, lived in the occupied zone. Péret was accidentally released by the German occupying force, which had mistaken him for a German sympathizer, and he made his way south "hidden in a wagonload of straw." When France fell, most surrealists, realizing they were in danger, retreated south to Marseille and its environs, where they soon heard about the American who was helping people get away.

When Fry met Breton, the writer was straining to support his wife and child. After the French Army demobilized him in early summer, Breton had journeyed to Salon-de-Provence to join forces with Dr. Pierre Mabille, a writer who specialized in "anthropological subjects" but who was best known as "the Surrealists' physician." Breton had asked surrealist artist Kurt Seligmann,* who had already emigrated to New York, to help him find work there, perhaps giving lectures. Breton knew the U.S. State Department required him to be self-supporting before he could receive an emergency visa, and asked Seligmann to find American sponsors who would supply affidavits and other documents required for him to obtain such a visa. Seligmann secured all the necessary papers for his friend, with assistance from the ERC and Alfred Barr and his wife, Margaret Scolari Barr. By October, he had even arranged for Breton to give a lecture series in the United States. But it would be some time before Fry could smuggle the writer out of France.

Seligmann and the Barrs obtained affidavits and supporting documents for many other artists and writers, including Mabille, Masson,

---

*In 1962 Kurt Seligmann "slipped and fell on the ice, discharging a bullet into his skull."

Ernst, Jacques Lipchitz,* and Chagall. They also raised funds for the ERC, with Margaret Barr collaring friends at parties and importuning them to sign affidavits and contribute money.

The other permanent refugee resident at Air-Bel, Victor Serge, in contrast to Breton, was almost paranoid as a result of his many years as an exile. Always conscious of the danger around them—"prowlers—the *Surete,* the lodging-house patrol, the Gestapo . . . the Falangist police"—Serge was a critic of the United States and other nations that could have accepted refugees but did not. "[B]ecause of their reactionary or bureaucratic leanings," he wrote, these countries "have displayed neither humanity nor sense in their immigration policies." They grant visas in "a manner so criminally stingy that thousands upon thousands of real victims, all fine human beings, were left to the mercies of the Nazis."

While Serge provided a nuanced political background to the assembly at Air-Bel, and Breton an artistic sensibility, it was Fry who supported the artists and writers financially and reassured them emotionally, always projecting confidence and certainty that, one day, they would be free. "If it had not been for Varian Fry's American Relief Committee," wrote Serge, "a goodly number of refugees would have had no reasonable course open to them but to jump into the sea."

While they waited to escape, Breton and the many surrealists who came to visit him created an intimate, pleasurable world at Air-Bel that was based on the movement's philosophy: Surrealism is a "Noun, masculine" in which one expresses "verbally, in writing or by any other method, the real functioning of the mind." To the surrealists, words and visual images were expressions of subconscious fantasies and dreams.

Their opposition to authority and tradition put the surrealists in danger but at the same time gave them their strength. Fry fell under their influence, and from November through May, although he never strayed far from his strict work ethic, his interactions with these artists and writers enlivened his existence and validated the antiestablishment attitudes of his youth as well as his rebellious personality. Gemähling might have grimaced at some of his behavior, but his new friends applauded it. The surrealists believed the world would do better if it were

*Jacques Lipchitz was number 795.

upside down and inside out. How else should one live but freely, without any censorship at all?

No sooner was the villa filled with residents than the surrealists and other artists from Marseille and nearby towns rushed to see Breton. Because of Breton, Air-Bel became a cynosure for the most creative minds in France, with artists such as Hans Bellmer, Eugen Spiro, and Tristan Tzara gravitating from all over "to show their loyalty to Surrealism" and their opposition to the enemy.* Despite an uncertain future, the surrealists turned Air-Bel into a madcap party, removed from the reality of war.

Artist Wifredo Lam† was one of the first to arrive. A Cuban of "polyglot ancestry, both aesthetic and ethnic," Lam had emigrated to Spain, then to France. Not long after they met at Air-Bel, Breton asked him to illustrate "Fata Morgana," a new poem in which "love undergoes hermetic transmutation and ends as a sun, signifier of hope." Lam, who had previously not identified himself as a surrealist, created forty-five drawings in black ink on parchment for Breton, and thus was inaugurated into surrealism. The poet selected "the seven most lyrical" drawings, and he and Lam had five illustrated copies secretly printed in March 1941. ("Fata Morgana" was published officially later that year in Argentina.)

Breton spent most of his time writing but was also absorbed by nature, and after dinner on his first evening at the villa he opened a bottle of praying mantises onto the tablecloth. Soon they were "walking around like so many pets," with the poet particularly amused that the female mantis ate the male after copulating: "You see, they're making love and the female is eating her lover's head," he told the assembled group.

Another important surrealist, artist André Masson, had arrived in town and was living at the estate of the Countess Pastré, the arts benefactor who had been so helpful to Fawcett when he needed shelter for his truckload of refugees and Brits. As soon as his family was settled, Masson visited the Centre to see about emigration. Gemähling, who interviewed him, informed him that Breton was at the villa; Masson left immediately to see his fellow surrealist, and "the two Andrés met,

---

*Bellmer was number 82, Spiro was number 1284, Tzara was number 1379.
†Lam was number 998.

at Air-Bel." Masson became a regular guest at the picnics. It was an unusually warm, long autumn—"what the French call a St. Martin's summer"—and the group spent late afternoons and early evenings sitting for hours around a table on the lawn of Air-Bel. When the weather changed, they brought the celebration indoors. Sometimes they entertained themselves singing "old barrack-room songs," with Verzeano's "fine tenor voice" rising above the others. Other nights, Breton lectured about surrealism or read aloud "from the witty letters of [artist Marcel] Duchamp or [poet Benjamin] Peret."

Although Fry, Gold, and other staff members viewed Air-Bel as mystical and unforgettable, not all of Fry's associates felt that way. To Gemähling, the villa's unconventional inhabitants and weekend guests "were totally bizarre." As an example, he recalled how Jacqueline Lamba Breton went shopping adorned with "bracelets around her ankle and a fake bird pinned into her hair." Tall and beautiful, eccentrically dressed, she must have looked "like a conqueror" to the local villagers at the market, said Gemähling.

But Fry was enthralled by the surrealists' uninhibited behavior. As hard as he worked during the week, on Sundays he played. He was more than an observer as Breton and the other artists "basked and frolicked madly in each other's daily company." He shared fully, even dancing with the others to a shortwave radio that brought them "forbidden . . . decadent music" from Boston, according to Gold. Fry was "a great joker," she said, always looking for relief from the bleakness around them.

Never again in his life would Fry be so free of the dictates of convention or so unconsciously creative, for the surrealists' games were often the genesis of colorful and inventive works of art. Fry made art and exhibited art. He even climbed trees to adorn them with art. In one photo taken at Air-Bel, "the decorous Fry and Consuelo de St.-Exupery," the wife of writer Antoine de Saint-Exupery, are "perched in the spreading branches of a venerable *platane*." Taken by photographer André Gomes who, with his wife, Henriette, had joined the salon, it was one of a series of pictures of Air-Bel that "capture the spirit of solidarity that sustained the group and the humor with which they met" reality. That winter, even the reserved Gemähling loosened up and, when he did, fell passionately in love, most likely with Consuelo.

The salon at Air-Bel included German chemist Helena Benitez, the wife of Wifredo Lam, surrealist artists Victor Brauner and Jacques Hérold, and the wives, companions, and lovers who accompanied the surrealists. With few exceptions, however, the surrealists "rigorously excluded women"—unless they were making food or making babies. The exceptions were Breton's "scandalously beautiful wife" Jacqueline Lamba, Benitez, and Péret's lover, the Spanish painter Remedios Varo, who had met Péret in 1936 while he was fighting for the Republicans in the Spanish Civil War.*

During the long winter months, the residents and their guests at Air-Bel played a series of surrealist games, including Verité, a no-holds-barred truth or consequences; a complex, demanding version of charades; and Exquisite Corpse, the most popular and well-known game, named from a sentence created the first time the game was played: "The exquisite corpse will drink the new wine." Players of Exquisite Corpse contributed nouns, verbs, and other words to create a communal sentence without knowing what anyone else's word was. When Breton read the resulting sentence aloud—"The oyster from Senegal will eat the tricolor high tide," for example—it was greeted by shouts and exclamations from the surrealists, who always saw profound meaning in these collective works. Fry and his colleagues, however, saw in the absurd sentences "surprise and hilarity" rather than profundity. A second version of Exquisite Corpse began that winter when Benitez was absent from the villa on her birthday. The group decided to create for her a communal work of art, which they did on a single sheet of paper, with tiny drawings by each artist present. The members of the salon also made collages and created a colorful new tarot deck, unlike traditional tarot cards. They named the new cards Jeu de Marseille to "memorialize . . . that tense and uncertain interval" at Air-Bel.

As autumn faded, however, not even the games were enough to distract Fry and the others from the "bitter cold" winter that was setting in. The biting winds and snow were nearly intolerable because of the lack of fuel and warm clothing. There was no central heating at Air-Bel and little firewood. One Gomes photograph of that period shows Lam and Hérold sharing a single winter coat. The gloomy weather mirrored

---

*Brauner was number 160, Jacques Hérold (whose original name was Hérold Blumer) was number 130, and Varo (her real name was Remei Lissaraga Varo) was number 1118.

the melancholy felt by the surrealists and the other refugees, who were unprepared for the freezing temperatures. Restrictions on food and other commodities annoyed Fry and, although he recognized that this complaint was trivial, he could not help lamenting the loss of those delicacies he associated with life in France. "I too am Alka-Seltzerized when after dinner gasses rise," he wrote, a sarcastic reference to the aftereffects of bad food.

Shortages, aggravated by restrictions imposed by Vichy in order to supply food for the German occupying force, caused everyone to lose weight. Fry, who weighed 175 pounds when he arrived in Marseille—an average weight for his five-feet-ten-inch frame—was twenty pounds lighter now. Meals consisted of "stewed carrots, rutabagas, turnip greens in lieu of spinach, sparse rations of bread, and 'coffee' made from acorns." Bread was strictly doled out, and, since almost everyone ate the entire share in the morning, they had no bread left for the evening. The cook finally purchased a scale and distributed bread rations fairly, then locked what remained in a cupboard. But the villa's residents were sometimes hungry enough that they "would take the door . . . off its hinges and raid the bread supply of the next day." What little bread there was was stale and eaten, of course, without butter or jam.

Because of shortages, Fry ate his minuscule sugar rations "like candy" to make up for the lack of carbohydrates in his diet. Meat was so scarce that Fry considered an occasional "slice of an old horse" a treat. At Air-Bel, he and the others jokingly put a copy of a book, *Le Boeuf Clandestin*, "in lieu of meat" in the pantry. Instead of coffee, they drank Postum, made from grain, and they had it black since there was no milk. Butter and oil were practically unavailable so that cooking became problematic, and fresh fruit was rare.

"You hear that in little out of the way places there is butter to be had, or milk, or even jam made with real sugar, but it's so difficult to travel," Fry wrote to his father. "Instead you stay home . . . and dream about beefsteaks, mashed potatoes with butter, and ice cream." To supplement their meager diet, Fry and Bénédite "hunt[ed] snails on the garden wall," ate goldfish out of the villa's pond, and, when they could, purchased food on the black market. Eventually, even wine and cigarettes grew short, and clothing was no longer available, except for children's. The "High Life Tailor" on the Canebière, Marseille's main thoroughfare, for example, had nothing to sell, in a "city totally devoid of 'high life.' " For Fry, the final blow came when the management of the genteel Hôtel Beauvau, where he was staying for the duration of the winter—it was warmer than Air-Bel—informed him that he should no longer leave his shoes outside the door for polishing. If he did, they would probably be stolen. This was the end of French civilization as Fry had known it.

Still, he had his friendships with André Breton, André Masson, Wifredo Lam, and the others at the Air-Bel salon. And within a short time, he would get to know three of the greatest artists of the twentieth century—Jacques Lipchitz, Marc Chagall, and Max Ernst—and save their lives.

Saving Ernst, Losing Straus

When Fry first met Max Ernst in December 1940, the artist was famous for his talent but also known for having abandoned his first wife, Louise Straus, and their son, Ulrich. After serving in the German Army during World War I, Ernst left his family and his country in 1922 and settled in Paris. In time, he became identified as a French, rather than a German, artist.

In a prescient early painting, "Europe after the Rain I," Ernst expressed his conviction that "Europe was threatened by a calamity that could be likened to a great flood tide of filth," that the entire world was being "poisoned" by the Nazi onslaught. His works, featured in Hitler's show of "degenerate art" under the label "Insult to German Womanhood," made him one of the artists most wanted by the Gestapo.

In France, however, Ernst was free to paint and to pursue women, none of whom seemed able or inclined to resist him. For a while, he lived in a ménage à trois with the poet Paul Eluard and his wife, Gala Diakonova (who would later marry Salvador Dalí). He then seduced and married a seventeen-year-old, Marie-Berthe. His relationships were "with beautiful and tempestuous women" who were attracted to his "reserve and cool, astonishing white-blond looks." In 1937, he fell deeply in love with Leonora Carrington, a British artist and great beauty who had "[a]labaster skin, wavy black hair, and big, brown eyes." They lived together in a village, St.-Martin-d'Ardèche.

When war broke out in 1939, Ernst was imprisoned "as an enemy alien" and spent time at several camps, under poor conditions, including Les Milles. Desperate to escape from France, Ernst wrote to his son Ulrich, now grown and called Jimmy, and employed at the Museum of Modern Art. "I'm being detained here. You can help me (in my liberation) through your excellent connections. Do something," implored Ernst. "Ask important people." Jimmy Ernst immediately went to his boss, Alfred Barr, who promised to help. "The Emergency Rescue Committee is working on problems like this through Frances Perkins and Immigration," Barr told the young man. "I am sure they'll do their best to get your father without the need for all those affidavits."

For months, Ernst was in and out of French concentration camps, escaping, then being recaptured. In May 1940, while they were interned together, Ernst and surrealist Hans Bellmer collaborated on several paintings. Ernst was finally released when it was discovered that he was legally married to Marie-Berthe, a French citizen. He headed immediately for Marseille and Fry. He was anxious to emigrate, afraid "that the Gestapo was after him." Fry helped Ernst obtain the documents he needed, which in some ways was easier than usual because of the well-known artist's support in the United States. Ernst was in great danger, however, despite his fame. He was "a German citizen who refused to return to Germany after the Nazi regime came to power," was outspoken about his "dislike of all totalitarian forms of government," and had the added difficulty of a former wife (Louise Straus) who was Jewish.

Ernst's arrival at Air-Bel was an event. Even among the attractive, unique surrealists, Ernst was "the most extraordinary person you've ever seen," according to Mary Jayne Gold. Handsome and white-haired, with "bright, bright blue eyes," he was wearing a dramatic and flattering white sheepskin coat. At their first meeting, he stared at Gold and then told her that she reminded him of a woman with whom one of his girlfriends had run off. Gold assured him that a predilection for other women was "not in [her] taste."

Ernst had brought along many of his paintings, which he hung inside the villa, and outside, on trees. Fry and the others immediately put on an exhibit that attracted a large crowd. Ernst still longed for artist Leonora Carrington, who, after her lover was interned, "had fled to Spain, suffered a breakdown, and been committed . . . to a sanatorium." But he was ready for his next romantic entanglement, the American heiress Peggy Guggenheim. She was then in France, buying art and ignoring the Germans. Kay Sage, Yves Tanguy's American wife, had asked Guggenheim to pay passage to the United States for the Bretons, Ernst, and Dr. Mabille. Guggenheim agreed and decided to go to Marseille to meet with Fry and see for herself what was being done to get these artists out. Her arrival thrilled several of the artists who had sought her financial support, especially Victor Brauner. Brauner, "in constant fear of being picked up and interned as a foreigner and a Jew," had corresponded with Guggenheim, asking her for help.

As soon as they met, Fry asked Guggenheim to contribute money to the Centre, since she "was an American, had money, and was committed to art and artists." He also hinted that she might take his place for a short time so he could make a quick trip to New York to talk directly with the leaders of the Emergency Rescue Committee about the refugee situation. Guggenheim refused to replace Fry, even temporarily, however, saying that she knew nothing of the underground or of the Centre's business. A good American, she had gone to her consulate when she first arrived in Marseille. There, she had been advised to "stay away from any involvement with the Emergency Rescue Committee." Guggenheim, afraid to do anything risky, heeded the advice but did make a generous contribution to Fry's Centre and also agreed to pay passage for Breton and Ernst. Then she left Marseille to see about storing her newly acquired paintings.

A short time later, she returned to Marseille and was met at the station by Brauner, who was "in terrible shape." The U.S. Romanian quota was filled, so he had been unable to get a regular U.S. visa, and he did not have enough connections in the United States to arrange for an emergency visitor's visa. Guggenheim promised she would intercede, "but aside from giving him some money, making inquiries at the American consulate, and involving Varian Fry, she had very little power to do anything." She and Brauner enjoyed a brief romantic fling, but after she met Ernst at Air-Bel, where she had gone to select some of his works for her collection, she found herself "seduced by the painter as well as his art." Ernst soon replaced Brauner in Guggenheim's affections, and she decided to take him with her to America.*

On April 2, Ernst invited Fry, Guggenheim, and Brauner to celebrate his fiftieth birthday at a black-market restaurant at the Vieux-Port, where they dined on seafood. Ernst and Guggenheim flirted madly throughout dinner, oblivious to Brauner and Fry. Guggenheim even arranged to stay for a short time at Air-Bel in order to be closer to Ernst. One night, she was in her room, Mary Jayne Gold recounted, when she heard a knock at her door. Assuming it was Ernst, she threw the door open, only to be leaped on and licked by two poodles, Fry's Clovis and Gold's Dagobert. The dogs then "jumped up on the bed" and went to sleep next to the disappointed Guggenheim.

Fry had just secured Ernst's U.S. emergency visitor's visa, with the help of the Committee in New York, but it expired before the artist was issued a French exit visa; Fry had to shepherd him through the whole process again. On April 7, the Museum of Modern Art cabled Fry that Ernst's passage had been purchased. As a result, the State Department renewed the artist's visa.

Unfortunately, Fry could not help Ernst's first wife, Louise Straus, who was also in Marseille and in great danger. After Ernst left her, many years earlier, she had made her own way, developing a career as a journalist and art and theater critic. She, too, had left Germany and had lived peacefully in France for years with her son. After he emigrated to the United States, she remained in France. At the beginning of the war, she was interned at Gurs as an enemy alien, then released. Along with everyone else, she went south in order to find a way out of France, knowing it would be difficult because, in addition to being Jewish, she was linked to Ernst, the "degenerate" artist. She, too, was on the Gestapo's wanted list.

Fry, working on behalf of Straus, was informed by the U.S. consulate that she could receive a visa if she had a definite sailing date. But she did not. And, within a short time, the State Department enacted new policies for issuing visas, so Fry had to resubmit her visa applica-

---

*Ernst and Guggenheim eventually married, but the marriage was short-lived and they divorced in 1946.

tion. In New York, Ulrich Ernst suggested to Alfred Barr that perhaps his parents' German divorce was not valid in France. If that were the case, he reasoned, his mother could escape along with his father, as his wife. Fry, informed of Ulrich's idea, urged the committee to contact Eleanor Roosevelt about a U.S. visa for Straus. But the response, when it came, "evidently on specific instructions from Eleanor Roosevelt," stated that Straus "could not get by with posing as Ernst's wife. . . . [I]t would jeopardize not only her departure but [Fry's] entire operation."

Since this idea did not work, Ernst "immediately offered to remarry her, but Lou [Straus], in front of the Consul, rejected the idea." Fry urged Straus to accept, reminding her of the danger she was in, but she was too proud and angry to consider remarrying her former husband. "But Max," said Louise Straus, "you know that this is nonsense. We have led separate lives for a long time now. . . . A life for a marriage license?"

Fry told Ernst he had to leave immediately without waiting for a French exit visa, which might never come, so Ernst escaped Marseille on May 1 without the document. At the French border, he was searched, then admonished by an inspector: "You know your papers are not in order, don't you?" Ernst took a chance and let the official look at his paintings. It was a good move. The inspector, obviously impressed, said that Ernst must return to France, but he simultaneously gestured toward the train to Madrid, indicating that the artist should board it. "Petrified lest a misstep land him once again in an internment camp," Ernst boarded the train going to Spain. "A few moments later [it] crossed the Spanish border, and he was free."

From Spain, Ernst traveled to Lisbon for a rendezvous with Guggenheim and her ever-growing entourage, which now included her ex-husband, Laurence Veil, his wife, Kay Boyle, and assorted offspring. Fry cabled the Unitarian Service Committee to help Guggenheim and company if possible. Several weeks later, on July 13, Ernst and the others left Lisbon on a Clipper to New York. After a short but frightening internment at Ellis Island, where American authorities questioned Ernst's traveling on German papers, since he had lived for years in France, the artist was released into the custody of his son. In France, Fry was still trying to get a visa for Straus. Anna Caples Frank, a founding member of the ERC, said Straus would be added to "the list of people whose visas had not been actually issued although recommended by the State Department." The visa never came through, however, and Straus remained trapped in France. She was later interned at Drancy, the notorious French camp from which the Germans selected prisoners for shipment east. "In November, Marseille was occupied by the Germans. Mrs. Ernst thus became one of the many refugee victims who were no longer able to leave." One day, Louise Straus was among a group of women "put on Transport for shipment to Auschwitz."

CHAPTER EIGHT

||||||||||||||||||||||||

TROUBLEMAKER: WINTER '40–'41

This job is like death—irreversible. We have started something here
we can't stop. We have allowed hundreds of people to become depen-
dent on us. We can't stop now, say we are bored, and go home!

Varian Fry

I N THE MIDDLE of November, Fry packed a bag and told
Hirschman that he was taking a trip to Vichy, the provisional
capital of unoccupied France. One reason for the trip was "[t]o obtain
the release of . . . protégés in the concentration camps," and he took
Bénédite's detailed reports on the inhumane conditions in Vichy's
camps with him, hoping to "shame the French government" into freeing some refugees. He also intended to visit the U.S. embassy to find
out more about his own situation. No, Fry said, when Hirschman tried
to talk him out of it. He had to take affairs into his own hands and see
for himself why his letters were being ignored by American officials.
Fry left on November 13, accompanied by Marcel Chaminade, who
would ease his way with Vichy bureaucrats.

On Friday, November 15, 1940, Fry went to the U.S. embassy hoping to meet with Freeman Matthews, the U.S. chargé d'affaires,
naively believing that by a face-to-face talk, he could clear up the U.S.
government's misconceptions about him. But he was not able to see
Matthews and was instead invited into the office of the third secretary
of the embassy, a Mr. McArthur. Even though McArthur was "cold" to

him, Fry nevertheless asked for the embassy's support. McArthur rebuffed him: "We can't do anything for you, Mr. Fry. You don't seem to realize that the *Sûreté* has a dossier on you."

Fry pointed out that the Sûreté Nationale likely had dossiers on every American then in France, forcing McArthur to concede the point. Fry insisted he be allowed to see Matthews, and McArthur promised to get Fry an appointment. Fry returned to his hotel to wait.

Two days later, having heard nothing from the embassy, he wrote to Matthews that he was "shocked and pained that the embassy could do nothing whatever for me." He believed that this rejection resulted from the complaint that had been made against him in September by the Marseille *préfecture*. In any case, since the September contretemps was over, he wrote, it should not influence his standing with the State Department. The embassy had treated him as if he were "guilty of some illegal activities" and had denied him, an American citizen, his right to a hearing.

Fry also complained to the chargé about the attitudes of the staff at the U.S. consulate in Marseille. He had learned from friends, he wrote, that two clerks and the doorman had gossiped to others, saying that the Vichy government was about to expel him. Fry insisted that his operation in Marseille had always been within legal bounds—providing advice on immigration, helping with paperwork, and distributing living allowances. "No member of my staff ever has or ever will assist anyone to leave France illegally," he claimed.

For two weeks, Fry remained in Vichy, waiting for but never meeting with Matthews, spending his time distributing copies of Bénédite's report on the camps to everyone he met. As the days passed, he grew more and more angry. "Meanwhile, the Chargé saw American Red Cross workers, American Ambulance drivers, American expatriots on their way to the States," he wrote. "But he was too busy to see me." By the time Fry received an appointment, set for a much later date, he was already on his way back to Marseille. His own embassy's officials had let him down utterly. He could no longer wait—he had work to do. "I guess they were afraid Vichy would accuse them of helping political refugees if they had anything to do with me."

Back in Marseille, Fry went directly from the train station to his office. He could barely contain himself as he recounted to his staff what had happened. Fry, who always had a short temper, was outraged after being left to cool his heels for weeks in Vichy. He refused to accept "a purely negative attitude on the part of our Foreign Service" and expected "diplomatic support" and "consent and approval" from the American government in order to facilitate his refugee work.

Of course, Fry had lied to Matthews. He *had* broken the laws of France and intended to keep on breaking them, but he believed that saving lives justified lying—and he expected the State Department to back him in this subterfuge. "The continued liberty and perhaps in some instances the very lives of scores of writers, artists and scientists depend upon the continued existence of my Committee and its good standing in the eyes of the French authorities." But his single-minded dedication to his refugees did not take into account U.S. foreign policy at a time when America was more concerned with maintaining good relations with Vichy than with the fate of the mainly Jewish refugees.

He followed up his expedition in Vichy by sending a furious letter to a U.S. vice consul in Marseille, Lee Randall. While Fry was away, Randall had talked about him with a British officer, Captain Fitch, at Fort St.-Jean. In a discussion between the two men about escape attempts by British officers and enlisted men, Fitch had mentioned that he saw the sympathetic Fry often. Randall warned Fitch to stay away from Fry, telling him that "all such organizations, including Fry's, were under surveillance by the French authorities." When Fry expressed indignation at Randall's warning to the British officer, Randall defended himself. This was a time, Randall wrote, of "the wildest sort of rumors" about the "German authorities demanding the return of many of these refugees." The United States was therefore "concerned with Mr. Fry's well being" and its own "position." This was not true, however, as U.S. officials in Marseille, with the exception of Bingham and Standish, were not at all concerned about Fry, except as he interfered with American foreign policy and position.

Fry remained furious at Randall for his indiscretion with Fitch, his condemnation of the Centre's work, and his endangering Fry's relationship with the British. Fry also became increasingly aware that he was rapidly becoming an object of derision among most U.S. officials. Fry suffered deeply from this rejection by his own government and for a long time refused to take any responsibility for the situation. Later, he acknowledged that he was to blame somewhat because U.S. officials "were offended" that he did not "court" Vichy and U.S. representatives when he first arrived in France. "[T]his had a good deal to do with the attitude they ultimately took toward me."

Even if he did come to fault himself a bit, Fry never forgave the State Department for disowning him. From 1940 on, Fry was a voluble critic of the State Department, never missing an opportunity to express his condemnation of its lack of concern about the escalating violence against Europe's Jews. The Department, he wrote, is "America's open scandal. Everybody talks about, but nobody does anything about, this extraordinary situation."

Some weeks earlier, Fry had received a shocking letter from the ERC that he had done his best to ignore even though it affected him enormously. Mildred Adams, the ERC's secretary, had informed Fry that he was officially terminated and a successor was on the way. "[The Committee's] contract with you did not extend in any eventuality beyond October 31 and they are not willing to push the thing further," she wrote. The successor, journalist Jay Allen, "will take over your office at Marseille, and will make necessary changes to fit changed conditions. . . . He must use his judgment as you have used yours." The final indignity, to Fry, was that Adams ordered him to meet Allen's Clipper when it arrived in Lisbon and that Allen would be hand-delivering his termination letter. (Fry did not meet Allen's Clipper.) The irony that he was being replaced was not lost on Fry, for he had just written to his mother about "these unfortunate people," many of whom would be either "on soup lines (or in internment camps)" if it were not for his efforts.

Regardless of this notification, Fry kept on in the office as if nothing had happened, while Hirschman was on the street establishing relationships with consuls from Brazil, Cuba, Chile, the Dominican Republic, Venezuela, and Panama. Sometime after he returned from Vichy, Fry finally received an answer to his request for help from the embassy on behalf of refugees interned in French camps. U.S. chargé d'affaires Matthews wrote that, "[f]or obvious reasons," America "could not . . . obtain individual exit visas for the many thousand refugees who wish to leave France, much as we sympathize with the desire of these poor unfortunates to find a haven overseas."

Fry decided that if he could not get his protégés to America because of the lack of U.S. visas and the negative attitude of the State Department, he would help them emigrate to other countries. He also recognized that providing relief was an important part of his work, and that his responsibility was "to receive, encourage and reassure with almost maternal solicitude those who looked to the Centre for help." His protégés, for the most part, appreciated his help, although there was a handful who were never satisfied; a few even blamed him for their problems.

At the end of November, he lost his forger, Bill Freier, because of a turn of events precipitated by the request of a refugee named Bachrich who asked Freier to forge an exit visa for him. Freier told Bachrich—whose name he says he will never forget—that it was impossible because these documents were numbered, and the numbers were in the possession of Vichy border guards. A short time after he turned Bachrich down, two policemen showed up at the little forger's hotel room. "We know everything," they said, pointing to a metal box where he hid his forgery supplies. "Show it to us."

Sixty years after this betrayal, Freier (who, after the war, changed his name back to Bil Spira) speculates it may have been Frédéric Drach who betrayed him to the police, since Drach—who taught him how to forge—was "the only one who knew about the metal box." The police took Freier and his fiancée, Mina, on a bus to the police station. Since the old Marseille buses had an outside platform, Freier was able to get rid of some illegal materials by throwing them off the deck of the moving bus. Mina, released the next day, was walking back to her hotel when she saw the two arresting officers having drinks with Drach. She went immediately to see Fry and told him what had happened. He hired a lawyer to plead Freier's case, but the forger remained imprisoned for months. When he was finally freed, he asked Fry to hide him. Fry found Freier and Mina a deserted *maison close* (bordello), where they lived for days in a room with a mirrored ceiling. Freier, the consummate forger, would not himself use forged papers because, he recalled, "it was so obvious to me that the papers were false. Also, I was afraid that if the police stopped me, I couldn't control my emotions and would get all red." Despite his precautions, Freier was arrested again and interned at Le Vernet, then shipped to Auschwitz. (For many years, Fry believed that he died there, but in fact the intrepid artist survived. "Fry was a hero to save so many people," says Freier today. "He had been in Germany before and he knew what he was working against.")

That winter, more and more refugees sought Fry's help. Bénédite

and Hirschman reported to him that the number of people interviewed at the Centre had increased from fifty a day in November to
one hundred by December. Even when the office was closed, a couple
of dozen refugees would show up in hopes of seeing Fry. Fry also had
to husband his financial resources because, by the end of December, he
was supporting more than twice as many protégés than a month earlier.

Desperate with his old concerns, Fry wrote directly to U.S. secretary
of state Cordell Hull. Vichy had imprisoned thousands of the "new
stateless" in concentration camps, he wrote. They were "without hope
of release because they have no government to represent them." Fry
boldly suggested the United States issue a "new" U.S. passport that
would provide limited diplomatic protection to its holders, granting
"honorary citizenship and real national passports" to "especially distinguished" refugees. Such a deed, wrote Fry, "would shine as one of
the greatest acts of human kindness in modern history." Hull turned
Fry down.

Nevertheless, while Fry was living the problem in Marseille, the
U.S. government was quietly acknowledging its existence. Shortly
after the letter to Hull, the ERC's director in New York, Frank Kingdon, heard from U.S. assistant secretary of state Adolf A. Berle, Jr.
Berle admitted that he did not have "the same information . . . or
more accurately, not in as definite form" as the Committee had, but allowed that it was "true that constantly greater pressure will be imposed
on these unhappy exiles to get out of France."

It was also in December that Fry tried to process his own papers so
that he could return home if he had to. He had neither the required
French nor Spanish documents he needed. He applied for a Spanish
transit visa and waited for some time while "the Spanish in their de-
lightfully Spanish way" considered his application. To his surprise,
Spain twice denied his application. Always the joker, he wrote to
Eileen, "Really, travel in Europe *is* difficult these days!"

Smuggling refugees out became more difficult because now it was
almost completely reliant on forged or faked documents. And with
Freier in jail, Fry had no forger. Then the Germans raided the office of
the Lithuanian consul and took the names of those refugees to whom
he had sold phony passports; this meant there was one less consulate
from whom Fry could purchase passports.

Every few days, despite believing that the arrival of his replacement was imminent, Fry penned an update to the Committee in New York, either long cables or typewritten reports that were smuggled out. Fry told New York that Georg Bernhard was "still in hiding in France, where he is wanted by the Gestapo. We do not know whether he will be able to get out or not," that some refugees (such as Breitscheid and Hilferding) were unwilling to commit illegal actions, that the leader of the Italian Socialist Party, Giuseppe Modigliani, "won't even use the French passport which was given to him quite legally by the French Government," and that the "prominent . . . and endangered" former Prussian minister of finance, Otto Klepper, was still waiting for his U.S. emergency visitor's visa. Fry complained that many of those on the first list, such as H. W. Katz, Eugen Spiro,* and "distinguished Rumanian historian and philosopher" Valeriu Marcu were still waiting for their promised U.S. visas.

More than ever, he was the only protection keeping his protégés from "starvation or internment—which most of them consider the worst alternative." His operating expenses were "sky-rocketing." It cost him about twenty-five hundred francs—fifty dollars—to pay for food, guides, and documents for each refugee who escaped via Spain and Lisbon, and he again asked the Committee for more money. Fry tried hard to improve his relationship with the organization in New York, perhaps believing this might stave off his being replaced, playing up his now cozy relationship with several French authorities, including the new prefect in Marseille, as well as the Sûreté, the bishop, "and a number of very important French private citizens." But it did not work.

One day, he received a letter from Frank Kingdon suggesting that he save money by cutting his staff down to one or two. Fry blew up: He barely had enough staff members now to do what had to be done for his more than five hundred protégés, such as spending endless hours sorting out their "trouble with the authorities." In direct rebellion against Kingdon's suggestion, he instead beefed up the staff, hiring several new people. Soon he had fifteen men and women interviewing, typing, writing letters, bookkeeping, visiting consulates, and distributing allowances. Fry and several staff members spent long hours at consulates trying to help refugees renew their visas, since by

*Katz was number 666 and Spiro was number 1284.

now many protégés "had sunk into a mood of depression and could make little personal effort" on their own. Fry kept in contact with other organizations in Marseille and created a new "volunteer council of technical advisors [which] aided [the Centre] with information concerning the importance and leanings of political and intellectual refugees."

Some artists on his original list were not easy to locate and talk to: "Picasso . . . is in Paris, where he cannot send or receive letters . . . Raoul Dufy is gravely ill in a nursing home in Montpellier," Fry wrote. Matisse was in Nice, and Chagall lived "in one of the most inaccessible towns in southern France."

The ERC wanted Fry's operation to be neat, simple, and orderly, but he knew it to be dirty, messy, and frayed at the edges. Hurt by the Committee's disapproval and rejection, angry at this Jay Allen who was to take his place, Fry sent the organization a divorce letter: "This office is not your office: it is an independent committee consisting of various American citizens residing in France." He received funding from a variety of sources in France, including at least one American, Mary Jayne Gold. "If . . . my name is mud in your eyes," he wrote, "please let me know and I shall sever all connections with you, however remote"—a strange communication, since he had already been told he was to be removed from his position.

Of all the calamitous experiences and events that had occurred so far, Fry never expected the disaster that was about to befall him. Up to now, he had not personally been in danger, but that was about to change as Vichy announced that Marshal Pétain was planning to visit Marseille. One Monday morning in early December, Fry and Lena Fischman were upstairs at Air-Bel working on correspondence, when Fry heard cars pull up. Fry went to the window. Not many ordinary citizens had cars or gas at that time, so he expected to see police and he did, one police car and one *panier à salade* (police wagon). Before he went downstairs, he regretfully, and "with real pain," burned his address book; he could not allow names, addresses, and "records of all my illegal financial transactions" to fall into Vichy's hands. He also hid one false passport he happened to have at the time by throwing it on top of a freestanding closet. Then he walked down the stairs just as a commissioner and three plainclothes officers of the Sûreté entered the villa's parlor.

Fry was glad that Hirschman was not in Marseille that day. The young man had taken off immediately for the Pyrenees in search of new escape routes when he had heard that Marshal Pétain was about to visit the city. "I always make it a practice to clear out when the head of a fascist state comes to town," Hirschman told Fry. "I know from long experience what happens." Now, with the police at Air-Bel, Fry was about to find out. The officers and the residents of the villa—Victor Serge, the Bretons, and Mary Jayne Gold—stood there tensely while Fry "object[ed] in precise and controlled French, his voice scarcely audible," to the intrusion of the Sûreté. This was the voice he used when he was trying to control his emotions, according to Gold. One officer thrust a paper at him, and although he saw that it gave them permission "to search the premises," he refused to agree to this. "We protest and reserve all rights," Fry said in the same low, controlled voice, insisting that the house was private property and the police had no right to search it.

The police responded that they were there because of reported suspicious activities at the villa. Fry, afraid this related to the refugee work, was relieved when it turned out that nearby villagers had complained to the police that the villa was full of bizarre strangers, especially the exotic Jacqueline Lamba Breton. Furthermore, on the previous night, Mme. Breton's sister had arrived at the villa carrying a heavy suitcase. Fry, aware that a bombing had occurred years earlier on a nearby rail line during a visit by the Prince of Wales or "some other celebrity," surmised that the police visit had to do with Pétain's traveling on that same rail line.

Fry and the group took the questioning in stride, even when the police, after making "snide remarks about [Mme. Breton's sister's] valise," searched the house for contraband and evidence of illegal activities. They confiscated Serge's typewriter and gun, which they found upstairs. At some point, Gold noticed Fry "emptying the contents of his pockets into a green-tiled stove in the far corner of the room"; whatever he put into the stove, burned. Fry watched the police rifle through his personal correspondence and grew indignant when they took it, including letters from his wife and mother. He said nothing, however, relieved that no one had looked on top of the closet or noticed that the ashes in the stove were still warm. The police took his briefcase and the typewriters on which he conducted Centre business.

When one officer noticed Breton's drawing of a Gallic cock, entitled "Pétain Est Un Con" (Pétain is an asshole), he became quite upset and denounced it as "Revolutionary propaganda." Fry hid a smile as Breton explained the word was *putain* (prostitute), not Pétain. A Marc Chagall painting of a flying cow resting against a wall fortunately drew no attention; Mary Jayne Gold's boyfriend, "Killer," unbeknownst to Fry, had hidden stolen postal orders worth forty thousand francs behind it.

When Gemähling and Bénédite came home for lunch, they tried to run as soon as they saw the police vehicles but were tackled by officers, brought inside, and searched. Then, saying they had "nothing against" Fry, the police invited him along as a witness and loaded everyone in the house (Serge, Breton, Gold, Bénédite, and Gemähling)—except for the servants, and children and their mothers—into the police wagon.

The arrest had occurred "so suddenly and unexpectedly that I still find it difficult to believe that it happened at all," Fry said later. In the wagon, Fry whispered to his friends that he hoped no one was carrying any incriminating papers. Serge, an old hand at fascist roundups, said sotto voce to Gemähling, "Are you sure you don't have anything compromising in your pockets?" The young Frenchman blushed and quickly tore into little pieces his lists of people in the Resistance; some scraps he chewed and swallowed, while others he threw out the window. At the police station, Fry was locked up with the rest of the group, despite his insistence that they all be released. Then he demanded to know the charges. The police said only that they had no authority to make decisions about Fry and his group and placed them in cells with other prisoners, some of whom turned out to be Fry's protégés.

"Varian and I acted self-assured," wrote Gold. "We knew that we belonged to a still great and neutral country and it was most unlikely that we would disappear permanently behind a barbed-wire fence. For the rest of them, anything could happen." To Fry's astonishment, even though he was an American citizen and director of an established relief agency, he was held incommunicado and refused permission to contact either a lawyer or the American embassy. At eleven P.M., after being held all afternoon, they were transferred to a ship, the SS *Sinaia*, since Vichy had run out of holding cells for the many people it had rounded up that day. As Fry went aboard, he was struck by a coincidence and said, "I crossed the Atlantic on this boat," as indeed he had, on a trip to Greece during one summer vacation while he was a Harvard undergraduate.

A moment later, this incidental piece of his past lost all meaning as he realized the trouble they were in. They had been arrested without formal charges or a hearing and were now imprisoned on a ship without being allowed to talk to their consulate. They were fed dry bread, beans, and frozen beef, and for sleeping there were burlap bags filled with straw. "I am an American citizen," said Fry, outraged. "I demand to be allowed to communicate with my Consul." But his demands were ignored until the second day. Then, after he and the others had been held for nearly twenty-four hours, the ship's captain allowed him to send a note to the American consulate. Vice Consul Bingham promptly arrived, bringing with him ham sandwiches for his friends. He "had to fight with the police to get on the boat." His presence was some comfort to Fry, but even Bingham could not find out on what charges the group was held. Nor could he convince the police to release them.

Fry, incensed at Vichy's fascist tactics, was also furious that the consular representative of the United States, Hugh Fullerton, had not secured his group's release. Despite this, he remained outwardly "calm and determined," Gemähling recalled. While they were on the *Sinaia*, Kingdon of the ERC sent "the stupidest telegram"—in Fry's words— to the U.S. consulate, saying that he had called Fry home and requesting the consul to urge him to return. Of course, this was of no help to the prisoners. Kingdon should have issued "a vigorous categoric demand for the maximum diplomatic and consular intervention," according to Fry. When he learned of Kingdon's undermining message, he felt betrayed again: ". . . what props I had were whisked out from under me."

On the *Sinaia*, Fry heard rumors that the police had rounded up thousands of people that day in Marseille. They had picked up "anybody suspicious . . . anybody foreign," because of Pétain's visit. The *Sinaia* itself held six hundred prisoners. This explanation satisfied his need to know why he had been arrested, but he still fumed at the unfairness of the imprisonment and the conditions they had to endure. However, at night, everyone, Fry included, made the best of it and sang together to pass the time. Bénédite knew sailors' songs and popular songs, Gemähling recalled. By day three, he said, Fry was taking his imprisonment in stride, "rolling with the punches." They were all very hungry, though. Finally Fry and Gold, as the only Americans, demanded to see the captain and were invited to his cabin and treated to beer.

After Pétain left Marseille, the police released all of the prisoners except Bénédite, "for some unknown reason." Fry was relieved to see Verzeano on the quay to greet them, and to hear that nothing at the Centre had been disturbed. Back at the office, Fry asked Lena Fischman to have Officer Dubois arrange Bénédite's release. Dubois went to the *Sinaia*, flashed his badge, and Bénédite was freed.

For the next few days, Fry felt deeply the impact of being searched and arrested without a warrant or an explanation. It had been "one of the most surprising and shocking experiences of my life," he wrote Eileen. But even as his frustration and anger built toward the French, Fry continued to write comforting letters to his mother and to his father, giving them a false view of his life, reserving the truth for Eileen. He told her that many of the French were anti-Semitic and that they treated the refugees callously, especially those who were Jewish. However, he wrote to his mother that he attributed France's poor treatment of foreigners to "carelessness rather than cussedness." He lied to her: "I know no people pleasanter to live among than the French. They certainly deserve their reputation of being the most civilized people in the world." He blamed only the Germans for the state of affairs in Marseille, excusing the evils of the Vichy regime by describing France as "exhausted." The average citizen opposed the actions of French leaders but did not have the strength to stop them, he wrote, adding that France had "made a tremendous effort, and it suffered the greatest defeat in its history."

> Remember that, whatever the government is forced to do, and however dishonorable the decisions it takes . . . the French people remain what they always have been: highly civilized, deeply wedded to the conception of individual liberty and definitely opposed to the notion of the police state.

Even after four uncomfortable nights on the *Sinaia*, always protective of his mother, Fry described his arrest as "drole."

Pétain's visit to Marseille marked the beginning of the end for many refugees. During the roundup, the Sûreté arrested thousands of people, who were either under suspicion for some reason or named in *préfecture* files. After this, "people began to disappear." One example was "Julian Cain, former director of the Bibliothèque Nationale, [who] was arrested on February 12, 1941, and sent to Buchenwald."

Each day brought a new tragedy: In December, Largo Caballero, former premier of Republican Spain, was "turned over by the Vichy government of France to the Spanish government for trial and probable execution." Caballero's arrest meant that Spanish refugees were now under the same threat of imprisonment and death as those from other countries. Then a young German art student named Niemeyer was arrested by the Gestapo. An "Aryan" who had a U.S. visa and a scholarship to the New School for Social Research, he lacked only an exit visa. Fry had told him to wait, and above all to avoid confronting the Germans. But the impatient young man ignored this advice and went directly to the Gestapo office in Aix-en-Provence to demand the document. It can be assumed the Gestapo arrested him, because Niemeyer was never heard from again. When he heard about this, Fry thought: The gloves are off. Berlin was more and more involved in refugee cases and he, too, must step up his efforts.

When Hirschman returned from his brief foray to Toulouse, Fry warned him that the police were looking for him and he would have to leave France immediately. Hirschman had never applied for a visa, believing he would remain in France, but as it happened he had one. Earlier, before he was reassigned, Vice Consul Bingham, who knew Hirschman only under his nom de plume, Albert Hermant, told the startled young man that a visa had come for an Albert Otto Hirschman. Did he know this Hirschman? Hearing this exciting news, Hirschman responded, "I will tell you a secret. That's me, you know." The visa had come about as the result of efforts by a University of California at Berkeley professor with whom Hirschman had worked in Paris in 1938. The professor had applied to the Rockefeller Foundation for both a visa and a fellowship for Hirschman, and they had been granted. "It was a total surprise to me," recalled Hirschman.

"It's interesting to me and I believe you," said Bingham, hearing that Hermant and Hirschman were one and the same. But, to obtain the visa, Hirschman needed documentation to prove his identity. He had left a birth certificate and identity papers in a hotel room in Paris and paid one of the couriers who went "back and forth between the occupied and unoccupied zones" to fetch it. When the courier returned to Marseille with his papers, Hirschman showed them to Bingham and received his visa. When he heard from Fry that Spain was refusing to grant transit visas, the resourceful young German took a train to Toulouse and successfully applied for a transit visa there. He knew "from living in authoritarian countries with bureaucracies . . . they are not all that well organized . . . and you must find your way through the various meshes of the net."

With his papers in order, on December 20 Hirschman said goodbye to Fry and set off for the Fittkos in Banyuls-sur-Mer. Years later, he recalled the couple's "meticulousness." They insisted he leave his rucksack behind and substitute for it a particular type of native bag "so that I would look more like a French worker who goes up the hill to gather firs and other wood." Guided by Hans Fittko, Hirschman crossed into Spain in less than three hours. He made his way through Spain to Portugal, where he was "spirited" onto a ship by a representative of the Rockefeller Foundation and soon arrived safely in New York.

The morning after Hirschman's departure, Fry woke up feeling as if he had lost his best friend. For four months, the two had shared a close relationship, strengthened by the desperate urgency of their work. "My closest friend was Hirschman," Fry wrote. "For a while after he left I felt so depressed that I thought I'd quit, too." Eventually, his practical side took over and he continued his work. But he remained lonely: "I have loads of acquaintances but not one intimate friend." Not until he and Danny Bénédite developed a real bond later on would he feel less alone.

Fry divided Hirschman's work and assigned it to his three lieutenants, Bénédite, Gemähling, and Verzeano. Verzeano became the expert on land routes, and beginning in late December escorted groups of refugees to Banyuls-sur-Mer, where he would "meet Hans Fittko in a back street very early in the morning, about 4 or 5 o'clock." Fry consulted with Verzeano on both sea and land routes. In late December, despite the tightening of borders, Fry maintained his confidence; and to those who said it was time to give up, that nothing could be done for the refugees, he responded, "You're wrong." After all, Portuguese boats were still running and "people are still coming over, though far fewer than were coming a few months ago."

Fry put Gemähling in charge of acquiring passports for protégés who had none, or who had to assume new identities, mainly men who had fought in the International Brigade during the Spanish Civil War. For this, Gemähling used passports of people who were dead, or of those who for some reason could not use their own. Some of these documents had "names already scratched off [and] stains on them." And he maintained a network of contacts who sold stolen passports. "At that point in Marseille, around the police headquarters and the consulates," recalled Gemähling, "there were people who were just there looking to buy and sell papers." People would walk up and say to him, "I have a passport to sell." Or, "Do you need a passport or a visa?" When Gemähling heard of an available passport, he would buy it with cash on the spot. Prices for documents varied widely, anywhere from twenty-five hundred to twelve thousand francs; a Danish passport and a false Portuguese transit visa, for example, cost six thousand francs apiece.

Even in the midst of the chaos, Fry kept meticulous records. Bénédite, a careful record keeper, became Fry's money changer, accountant, and bookkeeper. The day after Hirschman left, Fry handed Bénédite a strongbox with three envelopes: one with 580 francs for petty cash; a second containing 345,000 francs to be used for "legal" costs, such as stipends to refugees, office expenses, and salaries; and a third with 89,000 francs "for occult uses (secret bookkeeping)," costs associated with illegal escapes. Bénédite doled money out from the strongbox to pay for Centre expenses and for refugees' allowances.

One night, Fry and his three lieutenants had dinner at La Daurade restaurant. It was a fruitful evening, Gemähling recalled, because the owner introduced them all to the local mafia. This expanded Gemähling's underground network, thus aiding him in the black market and in arranging escapes. "Some [of the criminals] helped us in some cases," he recalled, "but others didn't come through."

Fry trusted his lieutenants completely, as he believed in all of his staff with one exception: Marcel Chaminade. Hired by Fry to deal with Vichy officials, Chaminade turned out to be a Pétainist. He was a founder of the *Revue Universelle*, which published an article by Marshal Pétain called "Individualism and Nation" in January 1941. Chaminade was also known for "his campaigns in extreme right and Catholic papers." When Fry learned all this, he talked it over with Bénédite, Gemähling, and Verzeano and decided not to take any action. "If we throw him out right now," said Fry, "we'll have an enemy." He instead assigned Chaminade simple tasks and never again spoke in front of him about politics, protégés, or other confidential business.

It was an ordinary mid-December day when Fry received a message that threatened to change his life: to "meet a friend" at the bar of the Hôtel Splendide. It was Jay Allen, a fellow American whose arrival he had long been dreading, although it had been many weeks since he received the letter informing him that he was to be replaced by the journalist.

At the Splendide bar with Allen that day was Margaret Palmer, who had previously worked at the Carnegie Institute of Art; Fry described her as "a woman of more than middle years." He sat down at the table, trying to remain civil. Allen handed Fry a letter: "This will introduce Jay Allen. . . . Will you tell him all the details of everything. . . . He is the replacement for which you have battered at us for the last month. . . . He will take over your office at Marseille. . . . We hope that you will give him full benefit of your experience and your advice. After that, he must use his judgment as you have used yours." Here was his termination notice, hand-delivered by his replacement. What a thoughtless touch from the heartless bunch in New York! Fry thought.

Allen, whose journey from New York to Marseille had taken him six weeks because of stops along the way, said he intended to run the Centre on a part-time basis; some of the time he would do his newspaper work and travel in order to network with other organizations. Palmer would be his alter ego, remaining in the Centre and performing the day-to-day administrative work. Fry was doubtful that Palmer, with "her somewhat advanced age and her obviously delicate health," could keep up with the demands of the job, as he wrote to Eileen, "especially as it has always been a little too much even for husky healthy me." But that day he said nothing.

After a few exhausting hours with Allen and Palmer, Fry went off to cable Kingdon that the "replacements" were unqualified. How he determined that in such a short time is unknown, but it is typical Fry. Certain that he knew better than anyone how to run the Centre, he poured out his righteous anger at Kingdon. Having "devoted six months" of his life "to creating an organization which is known all over Free France as the one hope of the refugees," he wrote, "I do not wish to see the organization dropped."

When Palmer immediately became ill and spent two weeks in bed, Fry dismissed her as a sickly old woman. He wrote Eileen that Palmer had "a disturbing preoccupation with her insides," wryly acknowledging it was not unlike his own preoccupation. She spoke incessantly "about what she can and cannot eat, her intestinal flora, and her latest evacuation (unformed)." Fry was certain that she did not have the stamina to run an operation that he, in the "prime of life," found difficult.

Allen was another matter, and Fry took him seriously. At first he acted, pretending that Allen was to take over for him and explaining the operation to his "replacement." Outwardly he was calm, but to Eileen he wrote that "the Friend"—his sarcastic term for Allen—was "dictatorial and stupid," "incapable of listening to anyone," and "utterly uninformed about what we are doing and apparently quite uninterested in learning." During their ensuing battle for control, Fry "fought like a steer . . . because I and everybody else who saw him . . . said they thought he would wreck everything in two weeks. I really couldn't allow that to happen without putting up a fight, could I?"

For days after Allen's arrival, Fry was busy writing to the Committee and asking his colleagues at the Centre to write New York on his behalf. New York "could not realize the delicacy of [Fry's] position, operating in the twilight zone between legality and illegality with his fine network of contacts," Gold wrote to the ERC. "Nor could they appreciate the loyalty and confidence he inspired in his staff. No outsider could have held it together. . . ." Lena Fischman sent a cable: "This message sent [at the] request [of] clients staff please contact Ingrid [Warburg] explain Fry's leaving this point disastrous [to the] work welfare very lives [of the refugees]."

Colleagues from other refugee-aid groups knew the extent of Fry's commitment and also tried to help. "The situation in Marseille is terrible," wrote the Unitarian Service Committee's Charles Joy. "That is why Fry says he can't leave before three to four months." Joy rejected the notion that Allen could run the Centre part-time: The "job requires just about time and a half instead. If you are going on with the work, I believe it is of desperate importance to have as quickly a full-time man at Marseille to replace Mr. Fry." Joy also wrote that the "British soldiers helped by Fry urge he be allowed to remain."

Fry no longer had a job waiting for him in New York, as Eileen had recently informed him; the Foreign Policy Association was not holding his position. Since he had no work to go back to and he was not in any danger, he told the Committee that he should be allowed to remain in Marseille.

Allen's presence added to his determination. Before, Fry had vacillated about giving up this job. It was "ten times more interesting . . . ten times more important and at least five times more instructive" than anything he had done before. To Eileen, he had paraded the friendships forged with the well-known intellectuals of Europe: "I have met more famous people in the last three months than in all the rest of my life put together." He loved the work because it required him to use all of his strengths "for the first time in my life." In January, he wrote: "That is probably why I like it so much, why I flourish so under it, why I am so well and happy, sleep so soundly. . . . [T]he important thing is that I have created the job, and the office myself, and that I have twelve employees (and volunteers) and over two hundred fifty clients more or less dependent on my continued presence here." There were still times, however, that he fantasized about giving up all the stress and frustration and returning to the relative ease of a life at home.

Now that Allen had arrived, however, "Varian the contrarian" wanted to do the opposite of what he was supposed to do and demanded he be allowed to stay. The Committee stood by Allen, though, and rejected Fry. The ERC's members were "embarrassed because [of] Washington and local pressure," they wrote, and felt that Fry's "staff expenditures [were] overlarge considering emigration results." Fry was devastated. He could not believe that his months of hard work and sacrifice were so unappreciated. To Eileen, he described the ERC membership as "blithering, slobbering idiots" who were "incapable of catching on to the simplest idea."

The Committee's secretary in New York, Mildred Adams, believed Fry had "an indispensability complex." She was "the villain" in the whole contretemps, according to Eileen. "She has sent unauthorized cables . . . [and] certainly sides with Jay. . . . [She] is a dishonest woman." His wife urged Fry to remain confident and strong, because with the support of Kingdon's assistant, Ingrid Warburg, and fund-raiser Harold Oram, both of whom felt he should remain in France, he would eventually prevail. Eileen's soothing logic worked, and Fry eventually calmed down.

Near the end of December, while completely ignoring Allen, Fry expanded his operation by traveling outside Marseille to seek out people from his original list. A few days before Christmas, Fry went to Nice to see the historian Valeriu Marcu; Marcu's name had been placed on the list by émigré writer Hermann Kesten. The air was cold but the sun was shining as Fry walked up the stairs of the Gare St.-Charles. Inside the old station, he met his energetic young lieutenant, Verzeano, and they stood on the platform, waiting for Margaret Palmer, whom Fry had agreed to take along. He had some idea that if he brought her with him, she would see for herself how difficult his job was and give up and go home.

When Fry and his companions emerged from the station at Nice, they found Valeriu Marcu waiting for them. They went back to his apartment, where Marcu's wife, Eva, had prepared a feast of "unbelievable things: cheese and sausage and real coffee." Marcu, a Romanian Jew, had emigrated from Germany to Austria, and finally to France. He and his wife had lived in Nice since 1933, where their daughter, Monica, nicknamed Miki, was born on the last day of the year. Eva, who was German, had lost her father to the Nazis. In the beginning, she recalled, she had liked living in Nice. "After Miki was born, we had peace of mind and there were still very many friends." That changed, though, Eva said, as one friend after another was taken away, either interned or sent back to Germany. Eva had avoided internment, because Miki was only seven and, according to French law, mothers with children under twelve were exempt. Eva had heard that in Gurs, where most of her friends were interned, Nazi women were left alone while German Jewish women were tormented. "The French wouldn't touch a Nazi woman because the Germans ruled in France," she recalled. "But the Jews were seen as . . . dangerous enemies who had to be put into camps so they wouldn't spy or betray France to the Germans." By 1940, the Marcus were desperate to emigrate but could not, because Valeriu had no passport.

Eva, who remembers Fry as her family's savior, had been afraid of arrest for a long time. "The Germans were so terrifically victorious all over. . . . Always, the terror came always closer and closer," she said. "It was a feeling—when is it going to stop before we even feared for our bodies?" Fry, upset by the Marcus' plight, assigned Verzeano the task of helping the family get papers so they could escape. Verzeano, who was Romanian, said he would try to secure documents for them in a nearby town where he knew a Romanian consul.

Verzeano left the apartment to go on his mission, and Fry, for the first time since he had arrived in France, went to visit with a few people who he believed to be in danger but who had not come to him for help in escaping. These were the greatest names he had approached so far: André Gide, André Malraux, and Henri Matisse. First, he traveled to Cabris, in the mountains near Cannes, to the home of future Nobel prizewinner, writer André Gide. Cordial and friendly, Gide offered Fry tea and biscuits but declined to leave his beloved France. His books were not on the " 'Otto List,' the official Nazi index of condemned literature," so he did not feel at risk, he said. Another cultural icon, artist Henri Matisse, also refused Fry's advice to flee France.*

Fry then returned to the Marcus' apartment where he found that the Romanian consul had rewarded Verzeano with a passport for the historian, handwritten on parchment. Fry glanced at the document, then handed it to the Marcus, who looked up in horror after they read it: Miki's name had been omitted. Luckily, there was another guest present that day who would solve the problem, writer André Malraux. Malraux, who had arrived while Fry was out seeing Gide, looked at the passport and said, "Nothing to it. No problem. Let me see a little bit." He studied the paper for a while, then wrote a few words on another piece of paper. He finally wrote something on the parchment passport. To Eva Marcu's joy, Malraux "had imitated the handwriting of the consul and written in the name of our child."†

Fry brought up the subject of Malraux's own emigration, but the writer said that he "had just escaped from a prisoner-of-war

---

*Gide, Matisse, and Malraux remained in France through the war. Another who refused to go, Theodore Wolff, formerly "the much-feared editor of the *Berliner Tageblatt*," had a sadder ending. Wolff did not want to "abandon his books and pictures and apartment on the promenade des Anglais" even though he was wanted by the Gestapo. Fry tried to help him and asked the Committee to arrange a loan to clear up his debts. But Wolff hesitated too long, and was arrested. He died three years later in the Jewish Hospital in Berlin from "ill treatment in the concentration camps at Dachau and Oranienburg."

†Miki accompanied her parents when they emigrated later on, and because Malraux's forgery was "so right, nobody noticed," said Eva Marcu.

camp . . . was writing his memoirs [and] did not wish to leave France." Fry was still able to aid him, although somewhat indirectly. Malraux had asked Random House, his American publisher, "to act as receiver for all sums due him from non-French sources and to forward them to him." Because of U.S. limits on the amount of money that could be sent out of the country, Random House could only pay Malraux seventy-five dollars a month, which was inadequate. A plan was worked out between Malraux, Fry, Eileen, and Robert Haas, a director of Random House. The publisher would pay to "Mrs. Fry, the wife of Varian Fry . . . certain sums in cash." Then Eileen and Fry, using channels set up between the Marseille operation and New York, managed to get that money to Malraux in France.

Before he left the Marcus, Fry was informed of the arrest of German industrialist Fritz Thyssen; an early supporter of Hitler's, he had changed his allegiance and was now opposed to the dictator. Fry, wanting to help, traveled to Cannes, where the Thyssens had been staying. Arriving at their hotel, the Montfleury, on "a cold and slushy Christmas Eve," he learned from the hotel manager that several days earlier, on Friday, December 20, five plainclothes Vichy police had shown up at seven in the morning and "demanded Mr. and Mrs. Thyssen." Since the manager refused to disturb his guests that early, the police were forced to wait. Four hours later, when the Thyssens came downstairs, they were "ordered to pack their luggage and were carried off before lunch." When Fry pressed the manager for more information, the man became belligerent: "Why don't you go back where you came from, anyway, and leave us French alone?" he shouted. "If we want to collaborate with the Germans we will . . . and nothing you pigs of Americans say will influence us the slightest. Now get out!" He refused to tell Fry where the Thyssens were being held but did say the couple "had been arrested in order to deliver them over to the Germans." Without a word, Fry walked out of the hotel to go back to Marseille. He wrote a report on the Thyssens' arrest and, in hopes that the news would be publicized, mailed it before he boarded the train to a reporter in Vichy, a Mr. Archambault of *The New York Times*.

Fry had spent Christmas in Cannes and Nice. On New Year's Day, a gray, chilly Wednesday, he made a "quick trip to Vichy" to ensure that a report he had obtained on "Gestapo activities in the free zone" would arrive safely in New York. Although the Germans were not supposed to be in unoccupied France, they were there, riding "around with swastikas on the cars, kidnapping whomever they wanted." When Fry first arrived in Marseille, members of the German Armistice Commission had been quartered in the Hôtel Splendide, frightening the people who lined up to see him. He heard often of the activities of the Kundt Commission, who hunted in the camps of southern France for refugees wanted by the Gestapo. Fry had even heard from Charlie Fawcett before he left France that the Germans knew about him. "Sure we know all about Fry," they said, according to Fawcett's friends who had a cousin in the German Army. "We know he's trying to get our political enemies out of France. We aren't worrying. We're confident he won't succeed." To Fry, that the Germans were in the south of France was terrifying proof that Berlin was paying ever closer attention to the refugees.

This information on the Germans was too hot to put in the regular mail, so the only way to get it to New York was by diplomatic pouch. At the American embassy in Vichy, Fry found everyone on holiday except a doorman, but, desperate to get the report sent, he thought he would try his luck anyway. He introduced himself and politely asked that the report be included in the next diplomatic mail to New York. "I cannot promise," the doorman said, "but I will try." Fry added his calling card to the material, with this note: "I would be very grateful if you would send this to New York in the pouch. . . . [I]f you can't do that please *do not send it back to me* but keep it here." Fry placed the report inside an envelope engraved "The Foreign Service of the United States of America" that was provided him by the doorman.

Hoping for the best, he returned to Marseille. To Fry's dismay, however, he soon received back in the regular mail both the report and his note, as well as a nasty letter from the embassy informing him that, first, he could not transmit private correspondence by diplomatic pouch, and second, he should "return immediately all envelopes of the foreign service" in his "possession." The pettiness of this, and also the embassy's refusal to send his report to the United States, was added to his list of grievances against the government.

In the office, Fry found a memo from Jay Allen, which made his mood even worse. Allen wrote that as he was now "in charge," Fry should keep him informed him about Centre business in a "brief *memo daily,* no matter how cryptic." And Allen wanted to be kept "advised of all expenditures." Apoplectic with fury, Fry vented his feelings to Eileen as usual. Allen was "bullying" him into leaving, he wrote, "without ever stopping to consider the consequences." To his credit, however, Fry kept the feud out of the office.

During January, Fry moved the Centre from the rue Grignan to a new space, "four large, light rooms" on the boulevard Garibaldi. Ruth Sender Stern, then age ten, recalls visiting Fry in the new office with her father, Benedikt Sender.* She walked up a "not very clean staircase," into "a small, shabby, not clean office." Many people sat or stood around, some waiting, others doing "office work on an old typewriter." The space was jammed with people, and she recalled feeling "very crowded and pushed in." Her father told her, "This is a wonderful man who is trying to get people out."

Fry was also trying to clear his name with Vichy. Apparently his dossier at the *préfecture* included this note:

> At the present moment, Mr. Fry's activities are embarrassing to the French government as he insists on occupying himself with Jewish refugees undesirable not only from the French point of view but from the German as well.

Fry had Bénédite compose a formal letter to the French government in which he denied any illegal or secret activities: "Not only that the Center has no secret activity whatsoever, but it is prepared to submit its initiatives and the whole of its activities to the control of the French authorities." Fry wanted to work "closely" with the French government, Bénédite wrote, adding that the Centre was not "a Jewish or a pro-Jewish body" but helped all refugees, from all countries. Fry's operation was an open book, ready for inspection by the government of France.

Of course, this belied the truth: Fry's entire operation was built on deception. Each night, he had to burn most of the Centre's papers, which consisted of records of escapes and other illegal activities. The Centre's books listed incoming and outgoing money while covering up secret funds used for clandestine purposes—although by the beginning of January, these funds were drying up. Fry, by now receiving

*Benedikt Sender was number 1254.

more money from Mary Jayne Gold than from the group in New York, demanded the ERC honor its commitment to his rescue operation. If it continued to expect him to carry out "complicated and expensive commissions," such as saving lives, he wrote, it had "to share a part of the burden."

Under Fry's direction, Bénédite wrote a secret financial report detailing the "large sums" spent on "visas, passports and secret passage across the frontier." He described stipends paid by Fry to the Fittkos and others who guided the protégés across the border, as well as fees to lawyers, and payment for expensive roundabout cables sent through Switzerland. Fry's greatest expense, of course, was information: "to know what was in the air concerning extraditions and the handing over of persons to the Germans." Informants—who were not always honest—were, nevertheless, expensive. Needless to say, the secret financial report was not shared with Jay Allen. Nor did Allen know anything of Fry's ongoing deal with British intelligence, one of his most successful operations, which by mid-January was progressing as planned, with the British embassy "pleased" with his work. Allen was privy only to details of the cover operation, the providing of money and food to the refugees.

As the battle for control continued, the barbs flew back and forth. Allen accused Fry of being "so deeply involved emotionally" that he was using the pretext of not having an exit visa to support his claim that he could not leave. Fry's friend and supporter Charles Joy wrote to the ERC, charging Allen with being irresponsible and urging that he return home.

Meanwhile, Allen pressured Committee chairman Kingdon to oust Fry immediately. All of Fry's requests for money must go through Allen, he wrote Kingdon, "or I resign from here with considerable éclat." Fry calmly withstood Allen's attacks until the moment he learned that Allen had accused him of communist leanings. "Inform Kingdon confidentially," Allen cabled his wife, "Varian [is a] fine boy deeply involved work but tied up all sorts of splinter groups. Living with Victor Serge [and] backing Spanish POUM Trotskyites." When he heard about this, Fry could barely hang on to his self-control. Being called a communist or communist sympathizer was something he could not tolerate. By the end of the month, the enmity between them had grown to "major proportions" and was out in the open; Fry urged

Kingdon to send Allen home. Finally, Fry told Allen to leave. Margaret Palmer, with her "poor health" and "advanced age," should go also, he said.

In New York, Kingdon reacted characteristically to the heated messages from Fry and Allen. Trying to make peace, he did and said little, except to cable that the salary of "whatever director [was] chosen" for the Marseille operation would be reduced by one-half its present amount. In the midst of this, Lena Fischman, Fry's "excellent, if somewhat flashy and Jewish secretary," announced she was leaving, and Fry replaced her with another efficient woman, Lucie Heymann. At this point, with associates leaving and new ones being hired, Fry was the only stable element in his organization, the only one who had been there from the beginning.

Allen now started to waver, and it seemed to Fry as if he was about to win, that Allen was ready to give up and go home. Rather than being buoyed by the thought of victory over his opponent, however, Fry found himself "lonely and homesick . . . and unhappy." He wrote Eileen that he had no friends and, when he received a letter from her and a copy of *The New York Times,* his homesickness grew: "I wish I could leave right away, but how can I abandon all these people?" He was vacillating again. It was as if once Allen seemed ready to leave, the prize was no longer as desirable to Fry. He even tried unsuccessfully to convince Charles Joy to take his job.

One morning in early February, perhaps leaning more toward leaving than staying, Fry went to the U.S. consulate to renew his passport. Standing in a vice consul's office, he was shocked to learn that it could not be renewed unless he agreed to leave at once. It seems that the embassy, which "was cold (as ice)," had instructed the consul in Marseille to turn down his request for a renewal. Paranoid, Fry wrote to Eileen that he was certain that, when he arrived in New York, his passport would be "taken up, not to be returned." He was desolate. He was now an American in wartime France, with no papers. Was he any different from his protégés?

Even Allen sympathized with Fry. "Embassy and Consulate animosity to Varian is 80 percent due to disapproval of his work rather than methods and personality," wrote Allen, "and confiscation of his passport sets an awful precedent." At this point, the two men had a lengthy discussion about the future of the Centre, and Allen agreed to leave. Fry was the victor, but it was bittersweet, since in his mind he had won something he should never have had to fight for.

Allen left Marseille for good in the late winter, traveling to the northern, occupied part of France, where he was arrested by the Germans for crossing the demarcation line without permission.* Although Fry was pleased the Centre was back to the way it was, he stated that "it was an uncomfortable feeling to have one of our band in the hands of the Germans." To Eileen, however, he admitted different feelings: "Wasn't it perfect what happened to my 'successor'? Idiot!"

> I was kinda pleased, secretly: it was too perfect an end for a boasting, blustering fool not to give observers the moral satisfaction of seeing someone reap his just rewards.

||||||||

Martyrs: Breitscheid and Hilferding

Rudolf Breitscheid and Rudolf Hilferding had been in *résidence forcée* in Arles since the Sûreté placed them there in September. Prior to this, Breitscheid, Mrs. Breitscheid, Hilferding, and Breitscheid's secretary, Erika Bierman (daughter of the former chancellor of the Reich, Hermann Müller), had been living in Marseille. Rosa Hilferding had remained in Paris. Breitscheid and Hilferding had always been a priority for Fry because of their positions on the Gestapo's wanted list and because neither man perceived that he was in danger.

During the fall of 1940, Breitscheid and Hilferding possessed not only U.S. emergency visitors' visas but Spanish and Portuguese transit visas; they still refused to cross the French-Spanish border illegally. "They consider[ed] themselves to be persons of international reputation who would be recognized in Spain," wrote Fry and Bedrich "Fritz" Heine (formerly a secretary to the two men) in a detailed report on these two former leaders of the German Reichstag. They refused to disguise themselves and considered escaping illegally to be

---

*At the end of the summer, Allen was exchanged for a German journalist.

"incompatible with their position as statesmen. . . ." Exasperated, Fry and Heine wrote: "Haven't they grasped it yet?—that we didn't choose an 'illegal' method, it was forced on us by the lawlessness of the National Socialists!" Breitscheid and Hilferding maintained that Hitler would not "dare" to extradite them. Fry noted that this attitude was impossible to understand "after eight years of Nazi terror."

After their placement in *résidence forcée,* they did make more of an effort to escape, but compared to the efforts of other refugees, Breitscheid and Hilferding seemed relaxed. Fry waited. At the end of January 1941, the two former state leaders, based on information they had obtained on their own, asked the Vichy police about French exit visas. They were assured at the Arles police station that applying for these documents would not jeopardize them in any way. They applied, Vichy approved the exit visas, and the two men and their wives planned to sail in February to Martinique on the *Wyoming.* However, when they learned that there were no cabins available and they would have to sleep in a "between-decks dormitory," the Breitscheids canceled and decided to wait for a later boat. Hilferding, for once, did not go along and made a reservation for the February 4 sailing.

According to Walter Mehring, who was also wanted for deportation by the Germans, Breitscheid tried to convince Hilferding to change his mind and wait for a ship with better accommodations. But it was really too late, for on January 31 they learned that their exit visas had been rescinded and were now invalid. None of the police could explain this. Breitscheid and Hilferding were told only of "orders from Vichy" by a police officer in Arles, who "remained as kind as before and assured them repeatedly that they were under his personal protection and had nothing to fear. He repeated his former declarations that even in the case of the occupation of the Free Zone of France by the Germans, they would be taken care of and placed in security. He gave them his word of honour on this."

Meanwhile, Fry was learning that the rumored Nazi extradition lists were more than rumors: "I am convinced of the authenticity of the lists. . . . I studied [them] very carefully . . . and found that no one whose name was on any one of them ever received an exit visa legally." The people on the lists were being hunted down by the Gestapo. "[S]everal people whose names were on the lists as early as February, 1941, were subsequently deported."

Among the names were Breitscheid's and Hilferding's. Just before eleven at night on February 8, there was a "loud knock" on the Breitscheids' door, recalled Mrs. Breitscheid. Breitscheid was told to pack "a few necessaries immediately." His wife was ordered to remain in the house, although she argued that she wanted to accompany her husband. Breitscheid packed, gave his wife his money, and the couple went downstairs to the lobby of their hotel to wait for Hilferding, who had also been told to pack. Hilferding joined them and they walked to the local police station, where a number of officials waited. An hour or so later, cars arrived. They "bore Paris license numbers" and were Sûreté vehicles. The Sûreté official told them he knew no details, and when questioned as to whether the men were to be handed over to the Germans, he responded "that such was not the case."

Hilferding and the Breitscheids were transported to Vichy. Along the way, Breitscheid lost all desire to resist. "My husband said there was no hope left, if I took all facts into consideration," wrote Mrs. Breitscheid later. "The only goal now was surrender (to the Germans). But I still clung to the hope that [Vichy] could not sink as low as that."

In Vichy, the Sûreté took Breitscheid and Hilferding into custody and placed Mrs. Breitscheid in a hotel. She spent the rest of the day trying unsuccessfully to see her husband, and also applying for emergency help at the American embassy. "There (it was Sunday evening, already past eight) were only two servants, who simply gave me a pad of paper on which I wrote the necessary facts."

The next day was more of the same. She was desperate, but at the American embassy, once again saw only a functionary. "The servant explained to me the secretary wanted me to know that unfortunately nothing could be done. The Germans had the right, he had said, to demand extradition. The French could only yield to this demand. I stressed that this meant death for both men."

The two former German statesmen "were very badly treated by the Sûreté." Isolated from each other, stripped of their personal belongings and anything with which they might have committed suicide, they slept on straw and were not permitted to wash or to shave. "At 7 in the evening Breitscheid and Hilferding were told that they were to be extradited. They were very surprised but took the news with great courage. They were told that the German Government had asked for their extradition on December 17th 1940 and that since that date they had repeated the request for their extradition three times."

Mrs. Breitscheid was allowed to see her husband at five in the morning on Monday, February 10. She spoke with him and was reassured by his courageous demeanor. Then, at eleven, she was watching outside the Sûreté as two cars pulled up. Her husband "was placed in one and Hilferding in the other. They were driven to the frontier" and delivered over to the German occupation forces at Moulins.

Fry came to his office on Monday morning, February 10, and heard the news. That afternoon, the anti-Nazi attorney, Alfred Apfel, whom Fry had first met in Berlin in 1935, came to see him. They discussed the likelihood that Breitscheid and Hilferding would be turned over to the Gestapo and murdered, and "tried to guess who would be next."

> A shadow passed over his face, and I could see the color draining out of it. . . . "I think I'm having a heart attack," he said. I jumped up and caught him just in time to prevent him from falling on the floor. Within half an hour he was dead.

After his arrest, Hilferding's wife, Rosa, heard that her husband had killed himself but was unsure of the details and wrote to Fry months later seeking information. "You can imagine that it would mean all for me," she wrote, "could I ascertain that my husband committed suicide soon after his extradition, for I cannot bear the idea of his sufferings during weeks and months." Fry could not help her, however, and it would be some time before the exact date and manner of Hilferding's death was known: He committed suicide in his cell in La Santé prison in Paris, not long after he was imprisoned there by the Germans. Years later, Fry wrote about Hilferding, "I was there in France, trying until the last minute to save the man's life. . . ."

Breitscheid was deported to Germany and spent three years in concentration camps. He was an inmate at Buchenwald on August 24, 1944, when the U.S. Eighth Air Force conducted a bombing mission of an armament works, a radio factory, and SS offices at the concentration camp. Decades after the war, Fry, who had heard that Breitscheid died during this air attack, tried to confirm it with the Air Force. He was informed that the targets were successfully hit but that some bombs had "spilled over into adjacent areas," including several barracks in the camp. Since two barracks were "destroyed, three gutted, and two severely damaged," and about 360 prisoners of the concentration camp died in the bombing, it is fair to assume that Breitscheid was among them.

Several years after his death, a plaza around the Gedachtais Kirche (Church of Remembrance) in Berlin was named Breitscheid Platz in honor of Rudolf Breitscheid.

CHAPTER NINE

||||||||||||||||||||||||||||

SPRING RENEWAL

By the end of 1940 it was clear that our work had borne fruit. Universal aid and sympathy in our efforts proved that we were on the right track.

Danny Bénédite

F RY HAD HIS Centre back now that Jay Allen was gone, and he began to regret his many gripes to the ERC. "I wouldn't have [complained] if they had ever bothered to let me know what their difficulties were," he wrote Eileen. Fry had left the United States "before it began to be difficult to get visitors' visas . . . when people were still talking of 'danger visas,' which were supposed to be granted *quickly.*" He never understood, really, that in the months since he had left, government policy had changed so radically that every single emergency visa represented many hours of work and struggle on the part of the ERC in New York. Eileen had been working with the ERC for some time. She told Fry "how little" he understood State Department policy. "Any way of stopping the imports [refugees]," she wrote, "is what they are looking for, plus every form of appeasement [of the Nazis]." Visas were being held up, Eileen wrote, in "a maddening delay."

Actually, the work in Marseille was going better now than it had for some time. None of his protégés had been arrested in a while, and the United States had opened previously closed immigration quotas.

"Until January only those of our clients who were French, Russian, Belgian, Dutch, Italian, or Spanish were able to obtain emigration visas," wrote Bénédite, but "[a]fter the first of the year visas were issued also to Germans, Austrians, and Poles, who made up 95 percent of our protégés."*

But Fry soon received a disturbing message from his wife. She had heard from Clarence Pickett at the State Department that Eleanor Roosevelt was questioning whether Fry "should try to continue to carry out some service [in France] or to return to this country." From information provided to Pickett by "one of our [consulate] workers who is in Marseille," Pickett suggested that Fry return to America since he would probably "be disappointed in what he could accomplish by staying on."

Since he disagreed so strongly with this assessment, Fry chose not to pay attention to it, concentrating instead on informing the State Department that some consulates were not following its directives. Examples were the consulates in Lyon and Nice, Fry wrote, who informed everyone quotas were closed even though they were not. As proof, he offered evidence that the U.S. consul in Marseille was still issuing visas under the German-Austrian quota. But the consul in Lyon who had thirty German-Austrian quota numbers and could have issued thirty U.S. visas, issued none. He was too busy moving and "packing silver and linen," Fry wrote. When Fry heard that the consulate in Lyon had actually closed the German-Austrian quotas, claiming to be "understaffed," he insisted Ingrid Warburg at the ERC "pressure" the State Department to make changes at that consulate immediately and to make certain that U.S. officials were, at the very least, issuing the visas they should. He also asked her to urge the State Department to issue more visas.

When Warburg contacted the State Department, the Visa Division chief, Avra M. Warren, lied. "[T]here is no delay in the obtaining of numbers for qualified visa applicants born in Germany," he wrote, "and possibly only a short wait for persons born in Poland." There was no mention of visas for Austrians. By April, however, the Department finally admitted the "situation in Lyon" needed improvement and ac-

---

*U.S. immigration quotas for these last groups remained very small in 1941, however, and throughout the war.

knowledged that "certain administrative steps have been taken" there "to facilitat[e] the expeditious handling of the work at that office."

When he could not secure U.S. visas for his protégés, Fry often turned to the Brazilian consulate for visas, but suddenly those, too, became difficult to obtain. The Brazilians now refused visas to anyone using them only as a means of getting to the United States. The consul said he would, however, discuss this restriction with his superiors in Rio if he was requested to by the U.S. government. As hard as Fry tried, he was unable to get the State Department to act in the Brazil situation. According to U.S. policy, stated Avra M. Warren, American embassies could not "intervene with the representatives of another country in regard to the desire of aliens to obtain visas for entry into such country."

Nor would the State Department modify its policy regarding the lengthy and time-consuming "biographies" that visa applicants were forced to compile. The biographies were necessary, according to Warren, to ensure that "the applicants are admissible under our immigration laws and . . . are coming to the United States for a legitimate purpose." The Department, hysterical about Fifth Columnists infiltrating America, claimed that a detailed listing of a refugee's accomplishments revealed the truth about his political attitude. The Department also insisted that biographies weeded out refugees who might not be able to earn a living once they arrived in the United States. To Fry, this was ridiculous because biographies showed achievements of the past rather than future possibilities. As it turned out, he was correct, for there were many accomplished refugees who never rose to the level of achievement in America that they had enjoyed in Europe. Hans Sahl, for example, a respected novelist and poet in Germany, lived for fifty years "virtually unknown" in the United States. It was not until he visited his country of birth decades later that he achieved acclaim, winning the Goethe Prize. Another famed German writer, Heinrich Mann, known for several brilliant works, was, for ten years after he emigrated until his death in 1950, "an unemployed screenwriter living humiliatingly off his brother's charity." The ERC, too, agreed with the policy of requiring biographies and urged Fry to obtain "full biography moral affidavits and references" for each protégé.

Quite without warning, at the end of January, France suddenly began to issue exit visas once more. France's decision to issue exit visas came after the Gestapo had reviewed "the political and intellectual refugees in France and had decided which of them they wanted and which they would allow to slip through their net," according to Fry, based on recommendations of the Kundt Commission.

This made U.S. emergency visitors' visas more viable, so Fry expanded his staff again. Jacques Weisslitz, a Frenchman from Alsace, and Paul Schmierer, an Austrian physician who was unable to practice in France after the passage of the anti-Jewish laws, became Fry's main interviewers and part of his inner circle. Karel Sternberg, a "one-man operation" for the International Relief Agency, came to the office, too, using a desk near Schmierer and Weisslitz to work on his own refugee cases.

For some, the availability of French exit visas meant hope. One protégé, Ernst Langendorf, obtained all the necessary visas—American, French, Spanish, and Portuguese ("considered something phenomenal," especially since he had once been interned at Le Vernet and Les Milles)—and emigrated legally.

In truth, Vichy's previous refusal to hand out visas was at odds with its own stated policy of freeing itself of Jews and foreigners. Despite French anti-Semitism—both institutional and popular—evident before, during, and after 1940 and 1941, Vichy could not stop playing bureaucrat long enough to get rid of Jews and foreigners. "Vichy's formalities presented an obstacle at least as formidable as the others" in preventing the refugees from leaving France and created a bureaucratic nightmare for the mostly Jewish refugees who were trying to emigrate.

> Officials could hold up the quest for documents at any point along the line. Since so many foreign Jews were either stateless or came from countries considered belligerents, the local prefectures could not issue visas without consulting the Ministry of the Interior at Vichy . . . the transit of dossiers back and forth slowed things down further. . . . Here was an arrangement tailor-made for bureaucratic obstruction and for the fullest indulgence of antisemitic impulses or tyrannical dispositions.

No matter how great Fry's efforts, whether he escorted his protégés himself or supervised their escape attempts, there were many incidences of failure. Three of his most endangered protégés, for example, Georg Bernhard, Arthur Wolff, and Berthold Jacob, were wanted men and could not travel under their own names; applying for the official documents they and their wives required to emigrate would have attracted unwanted attention. In the worst cases, such applications led directly to arrests and deaths. Bernhard "was Number 3 on the extradition list that the Gestapo had presented to the French government." Wolff, "one of the first to lose his German citizenship," was the high-profile antifascist attorney sent to *résidence forcée* along with Breitscheid and Hilferding. His escape was nearly impossible to arrange if mountain climbing was involved, since he was handicapped by a paralyzed leg and needed crutches to walk. The third man, Jacob, a journalist and pacifist, was an "outspoken anti-Nazi long before Hitler came to power."

At the end of February, Fry found hiding places for the three men and their wives, while he figured out how to help them escape. "Mr. and Mrs. Wolff went to live in the room behind the packing boxes." Then Portuguese and Spanish transit visas were obtained for them through Gemähling's connection, "a man in the Vieux-Port" who claimed to buy these papers from consulate employees. (According to Lisa Fittko, these papers turned out to be forgeries. She left her secure hideout in Banyuls-sur-Mer to go to Marseille to warn Fry that these crude documents would do nothing for his endangered refugees but guarantee their arrest.) Gemähling had another acquaintance, an underworld character who promised to drive the Wolffs and Bernhards across the border in a diplomatic car—most likely "borrowed" from someone at the Spanish consulate in Vichy.

Because Wolff was afraid to travel by train for fear his crutches would make him conspicuous, Fry took him by another car—a "gangster's limousine" that was also acquired through Gemähling's network in Marseille—to Les Baux, a town built during the Middle Ages on a peak of Les Alpilles, a low mountain range. From there, the Wolffs would travel by train to Tarascon. Meanwhile, Gemähling would put the Bernhards on a train from Marseille to Tarascon. The diplomatic car would pick up the two couples in a nearby town, Ax-les-Thermes, and drive them across the border.

When he and the Wolffs arrived in Les Baux, Fry spent his time calming the nervous lawyer before returning to Marseille. Some days later, Fry heard that the diplomatic car turned out to be a hoax. There was no car at all, and as a result the Wolffs' and Bernhards' only alternative had been to walk across the Pyrenees to get to Spain. Fry was stunned by reports that they would have had to climb for ten hours to negotiate a snowy seventeen-hundred-foot mountain pass. Since this was an obvious impossibility for all of them, especially Wolff, they returned to Toulouse.

It was Marcel Verzeano who came up with a new escape route. His contact, Garcia, a member of the Spanish underground, promised that, because of expertise acquired running guns during the Spanish Civil War, he and his associates could successfully smuggle the Bernhards and the Wolffs across the border. The trip from Toulouse to Lisbon, Garcia promised, would be made "almost entirely by auto . . . even across the frontiers." Garcia added that, if they had to, his men would carry Arthur Wolff across the border. It sounded good to Fry and he sent the Wolffs and the Bernhards out again, with Garcia. This expedition failed, too, because, in the end, Wolff had to be carried and not enough men could be found. The Bernhards made it to Spain on their own but "ran into all sorts of trouble at the border crossing; so they fled back to France." Fry then sent them to the Fittkos who, having been at this for a while, had developed more sophisticated methods and with the aid of "a *resistance* group whose dependability" they had tested often, somehow got the Bernhards directly through to Lisbon. (Fry had not earlier sent the Wolffs and the Bernhards to the Fittkos because he did not believe they were physically able to walk across the border.)

Verzeano and Bénédite went to check on Garcia to find out why the mission with the Wolffs had failed. For Fry's two young lieutenants, the trip was "the beginning of disaster." Their guide took them over the wrong trail, and they were confronted by French border guards. Cornered by "guns on one side and fences on the other," Verzeano and Bénédite were searched and questioned but ultimately released. Verzeano speculated that the guards, who "had a love for France," believed them to be two young Frenchmen who were going off to fight with the British, "so they let us go."

The Wolffs, of course, were still in France and remained there for some time, enduring "an odyssey of experiences punctuated by fits of nerves and threats of suicide, going from one hideout to another— from Toulouse to Lyon to Aix-les-Bains." Fry turned their difficult case over to Verzeano, who brought them to the Fittkos in early March to see if, by some miracle, they could find a way out for the couple as they had for the Bernhards. The Fittkos thought of taking Wolff by mule across the foothills and even by dinghy "around the cape to Spain." But nothing came of it. Finally, Verzeano got them Danish passports, Cuban immigration visas, and even French exit visas, and the Wolffs escaped. (They finally sailed from Lisbon to Cuba on a Spanish ship, the *Magallanes*.)

Now, of the endangered trio, the Jacobs were only ones left in France. Fry bought them Venezuelan visas under false names, then persuaded a contact in British intelligence to purchase Portuguese and Spanish transit visas for them. They, too, went to see the Fittkos,* who somehow got them into Spain. However, when the Jacobs tried to leave Spain for Portugal, they were arrested at the border and jailed in Madrid's Model Prison. Fry heard of their arrest and asked the Unitarians to "overturn heaven and earth" to help them. The Unitarians "persuaded an influential Spanish businessman to get them released from prison and bring them to Portugal in his limousine—without visas." The Jacobs lived in hiding in Lisbon for months, "waiting for overseas visas, which never arrived."

Fry's certainty that a refugee was safe once he arrived in Portugal was shattered by what happened next. In Lisbon, Berthold Jacob was on his way back to his hotel one night from the Unitarian office, where he had gone to inquire about his pending U.S. visa, when he disappeared. His wife never saw or heard from him again.

Even though certain papers were of little use to some endangered refugees, such as Bernhard and Jacob, others, such as André Breton, would have benefited had they been able to obtain papers to emigrate. As a result, when the news came that France was again making exit visas available, Fry's entire operation changed. One night in February, after he had moved back into Air-Bel, he told Breton and Serge that transport by ship from Marseille to Martinique, in the West Indies— faster, cheaper, and more direct than traveling through Spain and

---

*The Fittkos ended their work of guiding refugees across the border shortly after they helped the Bernhards and the Jacobs. They emigrated to Cuba in the autumn of 1941; Hans died there and Lisa later emigrated to the United States.

Portugal—would soon be possible. And since Martinique was French, the only stopover between Marseille and New York would require no additional papers.

During the early spring of 1941, Fry had much to do; as always, he had to obtain documents for his protégés, make ship reservations, pay for their passages, and continue to submit visa applications. There was even a handful of people who got away that spring by train because they had all their documents. H. W. Katz recalled that he had French military papers and a U.S. visa. As a result, he and his wife and child were able to cross the border in style. "Lena Fis[c]hman will arrange for you to travel in a sleeper car from here to Madrid and then on to Lisbon," Fry told Katz. He asked the writer to take along another refugee couple, Siegfried Kracauer and his wife, and pass them off as "older relatives." Katz agreed and left with the Kracauers on March 1, 1941, thus eliminating from the Centre's rolls "one of our oldest and most perennial pests, Siegfried Kracauer." In Madrid, they apparently met the famous red-haired porter who helped them secure tickets for the night train to Lisbon. From there, on April 1, they sailed to America on the *Guine,* along with some two hundred other refugees.

But the Katzes and the Kracauers were fortunate exceptions, and the ERC informed Fry that "[i]mmigration visas for people who do not come under the category of the Emerescue visas [those on Fry's original list] need references not of big names but people willing [to] supply affidavits etc." Immigration visas were now, more than ever, "very closely defined," and each application had to go through the ERC, and Washington, "containing full biography [and] moral affidavit [and] references."

Somehow, the paperwork got done, and during March and April a steady stream of weary travelers left Marseille on vessels described by Fry as the nearest thing to "rescue ship[s]." While "passages were . . . available to those who could pay most for them," Fry paid for those protégés who had no money; Mehring was one of the first protégés to travel this route, and dozens followed.

Publishers Kurt and Helen Wolff* were on Fry's original list and although they sought his help a few times, they were among his most

---

*The Wolffs were numbers 1472 and 1473.

self-reliant clients. Kurt and Helen had met in Germany but left shortly after Hitler took over. Kurt "had been publishing a lot of avant-garde writers—leftist and so-called degenerates—many of whom were Jewish." (Helen was Catholic and Kurt was half Jewish.) They married in France in 1933 and lived in Nice. When the war began, they sent their son to live in a convent, which they thought would be safe; both Kurt and Helen were interned for a time.

Eventually, they, too, ended up in the south of France, along with everyone else. They successfully sought an American sponsor to attest to their reliability, and Fry "helped them to obtain their exit papers." Wolff retrieved gold bars he had managed to save, which were being held for him by a friend, a French citizen. He cashed the gold at the bank for dollars, "the most valuable currency at that moment," and purchased transportation for his family from Marseille to Lisbon, and from Lisbon to the United States. The Wolffs sailed on the *Serpa Pinto* in mid-March. After a three-day unscheduled stop in Bermuda, during which they and the ship's 640 other passengers "were questioned and their belongings examined," they were allowed to sail on, docking at Staten Island on March 30, 1941.

Max Ophuls, who had first contacted Fry in September, had been a successful stage and film director in Germany. He emigrated to France after the Nazi takeover in 1933. There, he directed a number of critically acclaimed films, and as a result of his fame he was granted French citizenship. After the war began, Ophuls created anti-Nazi broadcasts for the French ministry of propaganda. In the fall of 1940, he and his wife, Hilde, and son, Hans Marcel, were "in immediate and grave danger." By December, due to the efforts of the Centre and the ERC, affidavits of support were in hand and the New York Committee was trying to facilitate U.S. emergency visitors' visas for the Ophuls. By March, the family had their visas, and although Ophuls and his wife had received ship passage, their son had not. Ophuls "asks me to collect the funds necessary to pay for the ticket of his son [Hans Marcel], who is fourteen years old," a friend of the Ophuls family wrote to the ERC.

These efforts were successful, and the family was among those who sailed to freedom in the spring. Thirty years later, Marcel Ophuls made *The Sorrow and the Pity,* a monumental film depicting Vichy France as it was. "Vichy France had not been a valiant, patriotic effort to protect

French interests in the teeth of the Nazi beast," according to the film. "[O]n the contrary, collaboration, anti-Semitism, and fascist ideology were at the heart of its enterprise."

Because of Germany's escalation in its war efforts by the early summer of 1940, "points of departure from western Europe had narrowed almost to Lisbon and the British ports." While some refugees did sail from Spain or through Casablanca, "the vast bulk of emigration had been from Lisbon." But since Lisbon had waiting lists of one year for ships departing from its port, many of Fry's protégés left Europe via Martinique, and he "soon came to think of [it] as the chief route of evacuation for those who were ready and able to go," wrote Bénédite. "[A] few hundred refugees were able to take advantage of this avenue of escape before it closed in late May."

On February 18, fifteen protégés sailed for Martinique. Fry was overjoyed and wrote, "[T]he curtain has been lifted quite a way." His wonderful friendship with the surrealists was ending, however, as many of them planned to leave Marseille by ship, with the Centre paying for their passages.

On Tuesday, March 25, Fry went to the pier where the *Capitaine Paul Lemerle,* a converted freighter, was docked, to see off some of his favorite protégés—the Bretons, Victor Serge, Wifredo Lam, and Helena Benitez. Fortunate for Fry, whose purse was considerably leaner than Peggy Guggenheim's, the heiress had bought tickets for the Bretons. "She paid for the voyage, took care of us, and gave us some money until André found work in New York," recalled Jacqueline Breton. But it was Fry who had arranged for the Bretons' emigration as Aube Breton Elléouët, who was five at the time, remembers: "My father always said . . . that we owe so much to Varian Fry. . . . He had a very, very big admiration and esteem for [him]."

Fry also said good-bye that day to Dyno Loewenstein,* who was aboard with his mother. Loewenstein and his parents, active Social Democrats, had escaped Germany in 1933 and lived in Paris until his father's death in 1939. After the fall of France, Loewenstein was *prestataire* in the French Army, then worked for Fry in Marseille for a

---

*Loewenstein was number 804.

short time. When Fry waved good-bye to his young friend, he could not have imagined that only a few months later, Loewenstein would be back in Europe as an operative for the U.S. Office of Strategic Services. (OSS was the United States' intelligence-gathering agency during World War II.) "Dyno in those days was very adventurous," recalled his widow, Tilde. "The whole thing appealed to him that they could get people out and away from the Nazis." Loewenstein infiltrated both Italy and Yugoslavia during the war, said Tilde, and "rescued the mayor of Vienna."

Victor Serge's departure was hard won. Earlier, he had been denied help by the ERC in New York, and Fry had to fight the objections of those on the Committee who did not want their resources spent on this revolutionary writer. Serge and his son were "suddenly" granted transit visas through Martinique and were free to leave France. Traveling with at least forty of his political comrades, Serge had mixed emotions about leaving Europe for an uncertain future: "I feel no joy at going," he wrote. "I would a thousand times rather have stayed. . . . Europe, with its . . . invaded nations, its gutted France—how one clings to it." Despite everything he had experienced, he remained optimistic: "I have a faint inkling of what is really essential: that we have not lost after all, that we have lost only for the moment."

The wonderful moment of Fry's farewell to his surrealist friends aboard the *Capitaine Paul Lemerle* was spoiled by guards with pistols and violent tempers who kept the passengers and their visitors separated. The ship finally steamed from the port, carrying the surrealists and some three hundred others. Helena Benitez wrote that she leaned against the ship's railing, watching Europe slipping away, dropping red roses overboard, one at a time. Fry watched until the ship disappeared from view.

A week later, he was again on the pier, this time to say farewell to André Masson and his family, who were sailing on the *Carimare*. During the winter, the Centre had supported the artist and his family, and Fry had seen them often when they came from their place in Montredon to Air-Bel for the games and parties. He had worked cooperatively with Alfred Barr to obtain a U.S. visa for Masson, whom Barr described as "one of the most distinguished French painters of the middle generation"; Masson had works in collections and museums all over the world. "He is in danger now because of the nature of his painting," wrote Barr, "which Hitler and Hitler's obedient servants in France would consider radical."

Months earlier, in January, U.S. visas for the Massons had come through, and they were also granted Portuguese transit visas. At Fry's suggestion, the artist went to the Portuguese consulate to pick up the transit visas but was told he was in error; they were not there. When he heard this, Fry asked HICEM and the Unitarian Service Committee in Lisbon to help "the famous painter, André Masson." Masson eventually got all his papers and happily had his family's passage paid for by an American art patron.

As his sailing date approached, Fry helped Masson sort out his conflicted feelings. The artist loved France, but because he suffered battle fatigue after the First World War, he "had no taste" for fighting and did not join the Resistance. Reluctant to leave his country, Masson knew he had to because his wife, Rose, was Jewish. "When [Masson] heard on the radio the announcement of the Vichy government's racial laws, he literally vomited." When the Massons finally sailed, a relieved Fry cabled the Committee in New York: "Bretons Massons enroute Martinique."

Fry's pleasure at the surrealists' sailing would have been diminished had he known what it was like for passengers on these voyages. The vessels were like "convict ship[s]" and squeezed dozens of refugees into space designed to accommodate only a few people. "The dark, unventilated hold was turned into an improvised dormitory with straw pallets on a scaffolding. . . . On the deck were communal sanitary facilities, again crudely improvised and soon nauseatingly rank." During the voyage of the *Carimare*, Masson maintained a "detached, withdrawn attitude" even though his wife grew ill and his two sons soon ran wild "all over the ship."

Fry also knew little about conditions at refugee camps in Martinique. He was shocked when he found out that the Bretons were interned there and later asked Bénédite, "Did you know that André, Jacqueline, and Aube were interned in a concentration camp all the time they were at Martinique?" As a matter of fact, Fry discovered that many of his protégés were interned at Fort-de-France, in Martinique, some for months. The camp, a former leper colony, was even worse than the ship: inadequate food and terrible sleeping quarters. Among the refugees, Jews suffered particularly from insulting treatment by the guards. The Bretons and Massons were finally released and arrived in New York on December 18, 1941.

Because the lesser-known artists could not find sponsors in the United States, Fry was unable to help many of them. He had no success in arranging escapes for theatrical director Sylvain Itkine and artists Hans Bellmer,* Victor Brauner, and Jacques Hérold. Itkine, who had entertained at Air-Bel with his troupe of "far-left" actors, never escaped and in 1942 was "turned over to the Nazis by the local French authorities and sent to [his] death." Bellmer, whose father was "strict" and may have been a member of the Nazi party, created fetishistic dolls in the manner of Oskar Kokoschka. A year earlier, he had been interned at Les Milles along with Max Ernst, and the two had collaborated on "decalcomania," a painting style that originated with surrealist Oscar Dominguez.† Bellmer did not escape from France, but he did survive the war. Brauner and Hérold, both Romanian Jews, lived through the war, Hérold enduring "four years of alarm and poverty" and Brauner hiding his Jewishness in the Alpes-de-Haute-Provence. (Brauner, in whose paintings the subjects usually had their left eye missing or malformed, lost his own eye in a brawl with Dominguez.)‡

It was also possible to obtain visas for Mexico at this point, and Fry saw to it that Benjamin Péret and Remedios Varo received them. (They did not, however, escape France for some time. In October 1941, after Fry left France, desperate cables went back and forth across the Atlantic as negotiations were undertaken with Peggy Guggenheim and Helena Rubenstein to pay passage for Péret and Varo. "MRS. GUGGENHEIM MIGHT HELP . . . PERET[.] HE'S VERY SURREALIST," according to one cable. Finally, arrangements made, Péret and Varo sailed from Casablanca on November 20, 1941, aboard the *Serpa Pinto.*

As the last of the surrealists left his protection and either escaped or went into hiding, Fry received a note from Jacqueline Breton, who had just arrived in New York. "America is truly the Christmas tree of the

---

*Number 82, Jean Bellmer, may be the same person as Hans Bellmer.

†Dominguez, a Spanish painter who visited Air-Bel often, remained in France during the war and committed suicide in 1957.

‡Fry later took works by Brauner and Hérold to the United States in an unsuccessful attempt to gain supporters for their emigration.

world," she wrote. Fry was pleased: The senior surrealists—Ernst, Masson, and Breton—were safe.

Fry now turned his attention to Russian painter Marc Chagall and his wife, Bella.* Chagall was on Fry's original list but so far had ignored all of Fry's entreaties that he give up his studio in Gordes and move to Marseille. He remained oblivious that he was in danger and "didn't see any reason" why he should leave France. Many works in German museums by Chagall, a renowned modernist painter, were burned by the Nazis. But the painter had lived in France for so many years that he had no fears about being arrested.

Unaware of the repressive *Statut des Juifs* and believing America to be a cultural wasteland, Chagall had asked Fry at their first meeting, "Are there cows in America?" Fry replied that not only were there cows and pastoral settings, but an art community that would treasure Chagall. The artist and his wife, who was Jewish also, said they would think about emigration. Fry was concerned, even if the Chagalls were not, as Jews under Vichy were being increasingly limited.

By the end of 1940, a handful of Jews were allowed to remain in the army and as professors or other "specialists." Within a few months, however, French Jews had been "forced from public service and teaching." And in the spring of 1941, Chagall lost his citizenship under the anti-Semitic laws passed by Vichy. Chagall and his wife moved in late March to the Hôtel Moderne in Marseille. They had finally concluded that France was no longer safe. No sooner had they gone up to their room when a police wagon pulled up and Vichy officers ran into the hotel to arrest the famous artist. While her husband was being taken to jail, Bella Chagall called Fry. She told him of the arrest and frantically begged for help. Fry quickly called the *préfecture* and said to the officer in charge: "Do you know that Monsieur Chagall is one of the world's greatest living artists? If, by any chance, news of his arrest should leak out, the whole world would be shocked, Vichy would be gravely embarrassed and you would probably be severely reprimanded." He threatened to call *The New York Times* if the artist was not immediately freed. Thirty minutes later, Chagall was released and driven back to his hotel. A relieved Mrs. Chagall called to thank Fry.

*Marc and Bella Chagall were numbers 210 and 211.

At the beginning of April, Vichy signed an agreement with Germany to return *all* Germans and Austrians to their former countries. Foreign Jews were being arrested, and while native French Jews were still somewhat protected, that would not last long. The fate of Jews in France, foreign and native-born, was made horribly clear at an April 4 meeting between Vichy and German representatives in Paris, which "revealed that the Germans were now thinking in terms of 'last solutions,' the complete 'dejudaizing' of Europe." Soon, "Vichy's anti-Jewish program was in motion again. . . . New legislation narrowed Jewish access to the professions and intellectual posts. . . . Far graver, the French government now became involved in stripping Jews of their property in the Unoccupied Zone."

It seems that the Chagalls had waited too long to try to emigrate, and they were refused exit visas along with everyone else. Chagall's daughter, Ida, went to Vichy a dozen times to plead their case, but she was unsuccessful. Fry and the Centre were also helpless. "We can intervene in cases of foreigners, but we cannot very well intervene in a matter which concerns a Frenchman with his government."* Unless the Chagalls succeeded on their own, it seemed they would remain in France for the remainder of the war. Fry did buy passage tickets for them because a guaranteed passage was of great value in ensuring emigration, and he signed an affidavit certifying to Chagall's moral character and financial independence. By the time U.S. emergency visas finally arrived for the artist and his wife, he was eager to emigrate. The Chagalls were smuggled across the French-Spanish border on May 7, but before they left, Chagall gave Fry a parting gift, a drawing of a "lady goat in a fur piece holding a violin." They arrived in Lisbon on May 11 and sometime later sailed for New York, arriving there on June 23.

Fry wrote to Eileen, urging her to meet Chagall's ship. "Will you take care of the Chagalls when they arrive? We have become great friends, and I have promised Chagall that you will help him solve the problem of where to live," Fry wrote. "His tastes are very simple. All he wants is a small house somewhere with a big room in it where he can work. . . . He will not demand anything silly like a modern kitchen

---

*However, Chagall was not a Frenchman, since his naturalized citizenship had been rescinded.

or a bathroom . . . [or] a north light, or any other nonsense like that. . . . But he has a horror of New York and wants to get out of it as fast as possible, and into a quiet place. . . ."

In April, Fry advised writer Hans Sahl—who had been one of his first protégés and had worked at the Centre for months—to sail because, by now, Marseille had become too dangerous for him.* Sahl, carrying a "brand-new Danish passport" forged for him by one of Fry's associates, smuggled out key information for Fry, including "the list drawn up by the Germans at the Hôtel Splendide, the names of the persons who were to be surrendered to them." After being helped by the red-haired porter in Spain, Sahl arrived in Lisbon. "[I] walked, with my toothpaste tubes and shoe-polish cans full of secret notes, into spring in Portugal," he wrote, "where the almond trees were already in flower and where mountains of cake, tubs of whipped cream awaited me in the cafés . . . as well as my visa, which had at last arrived from Washington."

Ships were now almost the only way to get out. Fry paid for passages for scores of refugees, receiving blank tickets, which he distributed. Suddenly and to Fry's joy, the American consulate, for no clear reason, became more cooperative and helped by "minimizing delays in issuing visas and in arranging necessary interviews well in advance, so that prospective passengers could leave by the first available vessel." Fry was still hampered, however, by the shipping companies' refusal to reveal their dates of departure far enough in advance for the refugees to prepare. As a result, refugees without the necessary papers often had a very short time in which to secure them. In some cases, Fry just managed to obtain a refugee's U.S. visa only an hour or two before his ship was to sail, and handed him his tickets as he boarded.

Although they were the only alternative at this point, ships remained a dangerous method of transportation. Gemähling recalled, "It was extremely risky to put people on the boats and it was only good for people who were in very good health," he said. Refugees, already starving, sailed on vessels that carried almost no food. "You had to be young and strong to sail on an empty stomach."

---

*Sahl sailed to the United States on the Portuguese ship the *Guine,* along with Eva and Valeriu Marcu and their daughter. The *Guine,* carrying other protégés of Fry's, such as Georges Ascher (number 52), docked in New York on April 11, 1941.

Fry was as hungry as his protégés. "We are on the verge of a famine here," he wrote Eileen, asking her to send food. "We haven't had any bread at all for several days, and practically no meat: just Jerusalem ar-tichokes cooked in salted water . . . it isn't enough—we are developing signs of malnutrition like everybody else." Hunger made him cranky. "I am . . . cross . . . half the time," he wrote Eileen, "and after receiv-ing twenty five pests snap at the twenty sixth as though I were a dog snapping at something biting his leg."

One morning Fry received an alarming report that there were police offshore:

> The coast is closely watched by [patrols and planes and] coastal guard on horseback and on foot, and the surveillance of access roads to the harbors and beaches. . . . We cannot count on the authorities even if they are friendly; they are afraid of their shadow.

Nevertheless, ships continued to be the best available means of getting the refugees out.

Certain that Vichy would eventually close the ship routes, however, Fry was working on new escape routes with two Italian activists, Emilio Lussu and Colonel Randolfo Pacciardi. Ever since he had de-termined that political opponents of Hitler were among the most en-dangered refugees, he had included Italian antifascists in this group. Lussu was a "political refugee [and] expert on escaping" who had worked with Fry since the previous autumn; Fry had financed Lussu's smuggling of Italian antifascists into North Africa. Pacciardi, who had led the Garibaldi Brigade against Franco during the Spanish Civil War, was the "leader of the Italian republicans in exile."

Fry, along with these two men and some of his staff, believed North Africa to be a viable escape route. He had been getting the British pris-oners out this way for some time, recalled Verzeano. They traveled by ship from Marseille to Oran or Algiers, then on to Lisbon via Casablanca or Gibraltar. Since French territory was involved, Fry be-lieved it would prove easier to negotiate for his protégés than other routes. Instead, it turned out to be "much more delicate than we had at first imagined." Working through Pacciardi, he sent several refugees to North Africa, assuming that from there they could get to Lisbon or Gibraltar.

When one group was arrested not long after they arrived in Oran, Fry realized he had a leak in his operation. "[W]e do know that at the moment they were scheduled to leave, navy speed boats appeared with the police and it was 'each man for himself and let the devil take the hindmost,' " wrote Verzeano. Two men escaped and two were arrested. According to Verzeano, the leak originated with Gaullists who betrayed Fry to the French police. Despite this, the authorities had no real proof against Fry, so he was not arrested. Fry sent large sums of money to North Africa to free the two imprisoned refugees, but nothing was accomplished. The men were eventually released without Fry's intervention, and he, too, gave up North Africa as too difficult an escape route.

Although Garcia had failed him with the Bernhards and the Wolffs, Lussu now talked Fry into using him again. This time Garcia was successful, escorting several protégés into Portugal, including Lussu himself. His path into Spain became known as the Garcia Route.

Long after Vichy first began rounding up foreign Jews, on June 2 it passed another *Statut des Juifs*. This law defined who was Jewish—and it included native-born French citizens. If three grandparents were Jewish, then a person was Jewish, regardless of conversion to another religion. French Jews now had to list their assets and were not allowed to hold positions in certain professions. France now had more frequent border checks and patrols, a more organized police force, and strictly enforced and increasingly tyrannical laws. Fry, witnessing the new repressions, was driven harder and harder to save lives.

Fry found particularly daunting a formalization between France and Spain that all travelers crossing the border have their papers in order, including "Spanish visa, customs visa on entering Spain, authorization of the Bank of France to export dollars, French exit seal and the *'Entrada en Espana'* [Spanish transit visa] of the frontier stations." In Spain, there were more police on patrol and, as a result, even on the relaxed Portbou to Barcelona train, detectives inspected everything.

Visas, as Bénédite wrote, still could "only be had in chains," the issuance of one depending upon the issuance of another: Regulations were impossible, such as deadlines that could not be met or requirements that one must have documents from one government in order to receive papers from another. In addition, Fry had to keep various dangers in mind; for example, he almost never requested Spanish transit visas for the protégés most wanted by the Gestapo. He managed to arrange with the Panamanian consulate to stamp the passports of some refugees, but only if they agreed never to "set foot in Panama." He also obtained Danish and Czech passports, which then had to be "adapted" by a forger.

Fry, who had long been waiting for his own passport renewal, received an answer that made it clear he was still *persona non grata* with the State Department. "I regret to inform you," wrote U.S. Consul William Peck, "that I have now received a telegram from the Department of State instructing me that your passport may be validated only for immediate return to the United States."

Across the Atlantic, Eileen lobbied furiously for her husband, contacting Mrs. Roosevelt, Supreme Court Justice Felix Frankfurter, and others. Alfred Barr also weighed in for Fry by writing to congressional librarian Archibald MacLeish in hopes that MacLeish had influence with Adolf Berle at the State Department. Fry was doing "really heroic work," Barr wrote to MacLeish, and "it would be a real misfortune if [he] had to come home at this moment." He asked MacLeish to "get the low-down" from Adolf Berle about Fry's situation. Even the ERC director, Frank Kingdon, by now no great friend of Fry's, asked Berle to renew Fry's passport; his request was denied.

Fry continued going to the pier to see off protégés, as one by one they sailed for freedom. He was there on May 6 as Erhardt Konopka* and eighty other political refugees boarded the *Winnipeg*, a French freighter headed to Martinique. Fry grew anxious when he saw the ship's captain conferring with two Wehrmacht officers from the German-Italian Commission and watched in horror as several people were taken off the ship just before it sailed.

Konopka was a Protestant political refugee who had actively opposed the Nazis since 1923 as a member of the trade union and youth movements. After 1937, he continued anti-Nazi work in Holland, and then in France. After a stint in the French Foreign Legion and some time in Montauban, he met Fry, who enlisted Vice Consul Standish to help Konopka obtain a U.S. emergency visa; Konopka got his visa only moments before he boarded the *Winnipeg*.

---

*Konopka was number 604.

Of the *Winnipeg*'s 750 passengers, 300 were German and Austrian refugees. Also aboard were "40 French soldiers and 30 officers of the French Marines," according to a report by Konopka that detailed conditions aboard the crowded ship. French soldiers, naval officers, and some crew members were "German-oriented" . . . and often rude to the refugees, he wrote. Food was inadequate and the passengers slept jammed together in poorly ventilated barracks. These ships were not built to hold that many people, recalled Ruth Sender Stern, who traveled on a similar vessel, the *Mont Viso*. "A French banana company had decided to make money so they put bunks in the hold and took refugees," she said.

When the seas were rough, a few passengers fell and broke arms and legs. In port, only the French officers were allowed to disembark, and at Casablanca the refugees heard the town "was full of German soldiers in civilian clothes."

Two hours from Martinique, on the night of May 26, the *Winnipeg* was ordered to stop. According to Konopka, armed Dutch soldiers boarded the ship, arrested the French crew and officers, and interned them on the ship. Suddenly, the *Winnipeg* had become a Dutch ship. The refugees were told that "the Dutch had waited for us 3 days and nights. (We thank them for their patience!)" The *Winnipeg* now turned southward, with its terror-stricken passengers who were kept awake all night by the earsplitting noise of planes roaring overhead and alarms ringing. When the freighter made port at Trinidad, Fry's German and Austrian protégés were put ashore and trucked to a camp. "Food was brought in huge amounts. For the first time there was butter . . . soap . . . a shower room with 20 showers and toilets." Grateful for these creature comforts, the refugees, however, soon realized that the local residents assumed they were Nazis. The misconception was cleared up when the camp commander announced that Konopka and the other passengers were refugees. He also knew of the work of Fry and the ERC. "[H]e asked if we were political refugees," wrote Konopka. "When I said yes and said that the majority were union members, he was pleased & said he was a union member too. He shook my hand & wished us a good future."*

---

*Konopka and the *Winnipeg*'s other passengers were still in a camp in Trinidad when they heard that the *Evangeline* was to leave for New York on June 5.

Four days after the *Winnipeg* sailed, the *Mont Viso* set off from Marseille with another load of refugees, including Ruth Sender Stern and her parents. Stern's story is similar to Konopka's. Her ship was also stopped. "We were in Casablanca on the ship for seven weeks; then we were interned in Morocco." (Her parents had relatives in the United States. Stern speculated that they likely paid her family's passage and made arrangements for the family to sail from Morocco to the United States. They arrived in New York at the end of August.)

Believing that the protégés who had sailed were safe, Fry did not think of them at all. His problems now were with the Vichy police. They were paying too much attention to his boulevard Garibaldi office, prying and snooping, arresting some of his protégés. One after another, his protégés were either being ordered to leave Marseille, interned, or sent to *résidence forcée*. There were also unexplained disappearances. Fry "made numerous petitions . . . for modification of action of the police, for liberation of some prisoners, for indulgence for arrested persons provided with visas and ready to leave." The petitions were fruitless.

The next ship due to sail, the *Wyoming*, was supposed to leave on May 10. Fry was "besieged" each day by refugees who wanted to leave on it, some with tickets and some without. They needed "advice and favors often impossible to grant. Those who knew they were to sail came [to the office] . . . to be reassured . . . or to ask what might be packed in their baggage." The *Wyoming* finally sailed without mishap, carrying many of Fry's protégés, including physician Alfred Adler and his wife, Martha, physician and author Richard Berczeller and his family,* and chemical engineer and inventor Otto Reitlinger.†

Eileen, still trying to get her husband's passport renewed, had asked journalist Dorothy Thompson to plead with Eleanor Roosevelt to in-

---

"Telegrams & tickets arrived in droves" to pay for their passage and, in the early morning hours of June 5, the refugees boarded the ship. On Saturday, June 13, Konopka and the others arrived safely in America.

*Alfred Adler was number 12. Richard Berczeller was number 90; other Berczeller family members were numbers 88, 89, 91, and 1664.

†Reitlinger, number 1094, worked for the U.S. government during the forties, inventing a series of liquid fuels, called "Otto fuels," which were used in torpedoes, among other uses. He received many awards and honors, including the Distinguished Civilian Service Award in 1963, and is credited with saving the United States about $100 million in fuel costs during World War II.

tervene, but Mrs. Roosevelt obviously had problems with what she had heard about Fry. "Miss Thompson gave me your message and I am sorry to say that there is nothing I can do for your husband," Mrs. Roosevelt wrote to Eileen. "I think he will have to come home because he has done things which the government does not feel it can stand behind. I am sure they will issue him a passport to come home even though it means that someone else will have to be sent to take over the work which he is doing."

When Eileen communicated Mrs. Roosevelt's message to Fry, he was determined to go on, even though without a passport he could not travel outside France. He would leave only when a competent successor arrived. Meanwhile, focusing on the men, women, and children who still needed his help, he formed a *comité de patronage* (committee of patrons) comprised of influential French citizens who agreed to lend their names to his organization, thus establishing its legitimacy with the Vichy government. The *comité* included "three members of the *Conseil National*, the President of the French Red Cross and the acting President of the Departmental Commission of the *Bouches du Rhone*," as well as writers André Gide and Jean Giraudoux, artists Henri Matisse and Aristide Maillol, and cellist Pablo Casals.

But not even the support of this esteemed group of French citizens stopped the police from harassing Fry. They kept constant watch on him, and on his closest confidante, Danny Bénédite. One of Bénédite's responsibilities was arranging for the exchange of gold into paper money. For example, he had changed $1,100 in gold from a protégé, Arthur Wolff, who couldn't carry such a heavy item when he escaped, for three thousand dollars' worth of paper money. Whenever people gave gold to the Centre to be exchanged for paper, the transactions were carried out through an "intermediary," usually Dimitru, the colorful operator Fry and Bénédite had inherited from Hirschman. They were satisfied with his work, since he "had always been very decent in his relations with us, giving us a favorable rate of exchange and managing to keep us out of trouble." These exchanges continued through March, April, and May, until, as Bénédite put it, "a very regrettable incident occurred." One morning in May, Fry told Bénédite that he had a large amount of gold he needed to convert to paper as soon as possible. On May 18, Bénédite talked to Dimitru and within days, Dimitru had a buyer for the gold. Bénédite arranged to exchange the money in "two lots" and, after delivering the first $2,000 in gold to the "intermediary" without a problem, returned to get the rest of the money. But when he got back to Dimitru's hotel, Dimitru was standing on the street, a rather unusual place for him to be. Bénédite shook hands with him and Dimitru said, "You had better not come in now. There is something queer going on here. I'll see you later." Bénédite walked away, but within minutes he was surrounded by police, who searched him. When they found the gold, he was arrested. In jail, Bénédite claimed to be on his own.

> I . . . said . . . that I had received the $2000 in question from a grateful client who was leaving for Spain, and that I wished to exchange them at a more favorable rate than that given by the Bank of France, for the sake of the Committee; that I was acting thus without having consulted Mr. Fry nor anyone else belonging to the Committee.

Dimitru was a traitor and, as Fry and Bénédite later found out, an informer for Vichy; even more troubling, he was an agent for the Gestapo. "Marseille was such a confusing mass of interlocking combinations of all sorts—the gangsters with the police—the police with the Gestapo—the Gestapo with the gangsters," Fry wrote, "that I never knew whether I was talking to a friend or an enemy." Fry sent Gemähling to retrieve the two thousand dollars in gold from Dimitru, but the spy, of course, claimed the gold had been stolen. This made it clear that Dimitru had set Bénédite up not only to "denounce [him] to the authorities" but to also steal the money. Fry let it go; he did not want to risk any more arrests.

Fry implored the American consul to help free Bénédite. "I must have touched something very deep in him, because he did an extraordinary thing: he went [to the jail] and told them that as Danny was the employee of an American relief organization the consulate was following his case closely." Because of the consul's intervention, Bénédite was brought before a judge for a hearing and released on bail until trial. Fry went with Théo, Bénédite's wife, and Gemähling, to meet their friend when he got out of jail. When Bénédite emerged "dirty and unshaven . . . thin and pale," Fry broke down and cried: "I felt like an awful fool . . . but I couldn't help it." Bénédite was the person with whom he shared his daily life and work. "We . . . did almost everything, in fact, but sleep together," he wrote. "It was about as close a companionship as I have ever had with anybody."

Around the time of Bénédite's arrest, their best friend at the consulate, Hiram "Harry" Bingham,* was replaced because of the work he had done saving refugees and cooperating with Fry. The new vice consul was antiforeigner, anti-Jew, and anti-Fry. He "seemed to delight in making autocratic decisions and refusing as many visas as he possibly could." When Fry talked to him about Largo Caballero, who had been arrested back in December, the vice consul said, "If [Caballero] has any political views at all, we don't want him. We don't want any agitators in the United States. We've got too many already."

More than ever, the refugees felt "the air of fear, depression and hopelessness of the Marseille immigration." And suddenly "everything seemed to go to pieces at once." By the end of June, America had ceased issuing any visas at all; a short time later, they were issued again, but under even stricter, slower-moving regulations. When the U.S. emergency visitors' visa program ended a month later, "3,268 emergency visas had been authorized, but only 1,236 of these had actually been granted." Immigration into the United States slowed to a trickle, remaining that way throughout the war years.

*Bingham never recovered from his demotion and reassignment to more and more obscure locations. He finally quit altogether, and retired to his family home in Connecticut. "He was doing what he thought was the right thing to do. The loss of his career and the [dis]approval of his family would be the resulting punishment for listening to his conscience. . . . On April 26, 1941, in a telegram Secretary of State Cordell Hull sent to the American Consul in Marseilles, Harry was relieved of his post. It was emphatically stated in the telegram: 'This transfer not made at his request nor for his convenience.' . . . From there on in, Hiram Bingham IV would be repeatedly denied any further advancement in the Foreign Service."

▌▌▌▌▌▌▌▌▌

Toward World Peace:
Berthold Jacob

Journalist Berthold Jacob, one of Fry's most challenging cases, was a lifelong pacifist and activist who was murdered by the Nazis shortly before the end of the war. Jacob, whose real name was Bruno Salomon,* was an enemy of fascism, Nazism, and Hitler. In 1933, he fled Germany for Switzerland, where he wrote and published articles describing Germany's re-armament breaching the Versailles Treaty. Because he publicized Nazi Germany's perfidy, the Gestapo snatched him from Switzerland in 1935 and threw him into a German prison. This "was the first known kidnapping of a person in another country by the Gestapo," and Switzerland did not take it quietly, making a vehement case for Jacob's return. Hitler, rearming illegally, did not want to draw attention to Germany and therefore agreed to return Jacob to Switzerland. Nevertheless, he "foamed at the mouth about the incompetence of the Gestapo who weren't even able to execute a kidnapping smoothly."

When Jacob was released in Switzerland on September 18, 1935, the Gestapo warned him they would hold his father, a Berliner, to ensure Jacob's "good behavior." Jacob emigrated to France, where he "continued fighting for peace." He was interned when France fell, but escaped with his wife to Marseille, where he met Fry. After months of agonizing attempts, Fry finally managed to smuggle the Jacobs out of France to Lisbon and believed them to be safe at last.

Later on, while in Lisbon himself waiting to return to the United States, Fry heard that Jacob had disappeared. He wrote Bénédite immediately: "Rollin [Jacob's code name] was picked up the other day. . . . We are without news of him, and are trying to contact him through the lawyer. We are very worried, as he has no place to go, and may be sent home." Home, of course, meant Germany.

Fry tried desperately to learn Jacob's whereabouts. Even when he found out that Jacob had been returned to Germany, he, along with other refugee aid workers, continued to seek conclusive information.

*Bruno Salomon was number 1157 and his wife, Doris, was number 1158.

Several months later, Fry heard that the Commissioner for Refugee Questions in London had been asked to "do something for Rollin." Charles Joy had asked Sir Samuel Hoare, an old friend of his and Fry's, who was in Lisbon, to intervene. Hoare protested that he could not get involved, "because Rollin was a German subject," but was quickly corrected: "Rollin was no German subject but was a Jew." After some time, Joy, Fry, and the others were finally forced to conclude that Jacob had long since been sent back to Germany. But of course no one knew for certain, and it would be a long time before they did.

Years later, Fry searched out some old friends from the Marseille period to update his information. Inquiring about the fate of Berthold Jacob, he learned that he had died in a hospital in Berlin. Considering Jacob's "record, not only of pacifism, but also of espionage," Fry was skeptical that the Germans would allow him to die in a hospital and continued to try to discover the truth.

He also wanted to find out the fate of Mrs. Jacob. Had she "reached a haven" in some free nation? It was unlikely she was in America since the couple had been unable for so long to get U.S. visas.

> What . . . *bitter* irony: the United States Government refusing a visa to a man because he was known to have been an espionage agent acting against the German Reichswehr—and that just a few weeks before Pearl Harbor! Or did they perhaps refuse the visa because he had been a pacifist? . . . One will never know. But they never granted him a visa, when others were getting them fairly quickly, and he, like the others, had all the necessary supporting papers.

By the end of his investigation, Fry had uncovered the fact that even though "the Portuguese police were excessively concerned with Jacob's security and begged him never to go on the street during the day," it was they who had picked him up. They had then turned him over to the Spanish International Police, who held him at the Model Prison for delivery to the Reichswehr Security Forces. The Nazis transferred Jacob to Headquarters Prison at Alexanderplatz, in Berlin, where he survived for some time "under the most terrible circumstances." Ill with tuberculosis, he was tortured and systematically starved.

On January 5, 1943, the Germans arrested Jacob's father, David

Salomon, seventy-seven, and held him briefly in the same prison. The elder Salomon was then transferred to Auschwitz, where he was gassed on December 18, 1943. Somehow, Berthold Jacob lived on. On February 19, 1944, weighing less than eighty-five pounds, he was transferred to Berlin's "Jewish Hospital." (The last "Jewish doctor" at the hospital, "allegedly a Gestapo employee . . . committed suicide after the liberation.")

Jacob died seven days after he was admitted, on February 26, of "heart muscle weakness." He lies in the Berlin-Weissensee Cemetery, "a great pacifist, who by disclosing Hitler's . . . war machine tried to open the world's eyes and prevent World War II."

CHAPTER TEN

|||||||||||||||||||||||||||

THE END OF THE ADVENTURE

Dear Danny,
   . . . I left my heart in France, I guess.

Varian

O N A WARM, sunny day in June, Fry was asked to come to the U.S. consulate by Consul Fullerton. After a cool greeting, Fullerton bluntly told Fry that he had to leave France immediately. Repeating old news, Fullerton said that his "instructions" from the State Department were that Fry would not be issued a passport renewal until he agreed to return to the United States. But he added a new threat: Vichy was pressuring him to get rid of Fry, and if Fry did not leave France voluntarily, Vichy was going to arrest and expel him, he had been told by the chief of police, Maurice de Rodellec du Porzic. Fullerton admitted that, while he had agreed to pass on Du Porzic's threat, he had told the official that Fry "would not scare."

As Fry stood to leave, Fullerton suddenly asked, "Why do you have so many Jews on your staff?" Surprised, Fry answered that only about half his staff was Jewish.

"I think you make a mistake to have so many," said Fullerton. "The Department withdrew all the Jews on the Embassy and Consular staffs in France shortly after Pétain came to power. I think there's only one left, a clerk at the embassy." Fry left the consulate, walking slowly back to the boulevard Garibaldi. He should have been prepared for Fullerton's prejudice, but he was not. To Fry, the American seemed to be as heartless and anti-Semitic as Vichy and the Germans.

And Fullerton's biases had spread through the ranks at the consulate. Fry always remembered their effects on L, one of his protégés. L was born, before World War I, in Upper Silesia, which was then part of Germany. When he applied for a U.S. visa, L told an American vice consul that he was German. His papers, however, stated that the area of Germany he was from had since reverted to Poland. L was accused by the vice consul of making "a false statement before an American Consular office." The official said that because of this, he intended to deny L's visa application. "Furthermore I am going to see that you never get one. You were born in Poland and you know it." Fry wrote, "L was crying when he told me this. The worst of it is that his kids now have to stay in France, too. God knows what will become of them."

After he received Du Porzic's threat of impending arrest, Fry wrote to New York, asking Kingdon to intercede on his behalf. In a last-minute attempt to mend fences, he blamed Fullerton for being "the principal source of [his] misunderstandings . . . with the Embassy and the State Department." Fry saw himself as a "pawn" in the diplomatic game among the United States, Germany, and France. Vichy officials continuously "spread vague rumors of impending action" against him, making it difficult for him to do his job, he wrote. But he did not believe they would ever actually arrest him, because he was an American and such an act would create too much negative publicity.

Finally, Fry wrote, not supporting him was the same as cooperating with Germany. The United States should make his removal from France as "difficult and . . . embarrassing" for Vichy as possible. He also contradicted an assertion made by Fullerton that he was in danger: "I am not concerned for my safety; and I do not in the least mind resisting the pressure of the French authorities."

Fry now found himself harassed by constant police surveillance at his office and home. His phone was tapped: "One day I picked up the telephone and dialed a number, and when I got it I could hear a regular click, click, click in the receiver," he wrote. The police came often to Air-Bel, searching for subversive material. Still hoping to disguise the true nature of his work, Fry continued to lie, writing Du Porzic that he was in France representing prominent Americans such as

John D. Rockefeller, Jr., Henry Luce, Marshall Field, Edward M. Warburg, and Edsel Ford. As a matter of fact, he added, the committee that sent him to Marseille was made up of leading Americans in all fields, including Albert Einstein and Dorothy Thompson, "the most famous American journalist today." Fry used a deferential tone to Du Porzic, which he thought would win him favor: "I would be very honored to meet with you should you desire more information on my Committee. I am at your service. Please accept, Mr. Commissariat, my highest esteem." This letter was a mistake, for upon its receipt the police chief immediately summoned Fry to meet with him, and Fry's days in Marseille were numbered.

At the end of June, his trusted and loyal colleague Mary Jayne Gold left, carrying "secret messages wrapped in condoms and inserted into tubes of toothpaste and face cream." She delivered the messages to Donald Darling of British intelligence in Lisbon. Then she took the Clipper to New York, where she finally met Eileen Fry; the two quickly became friends.

By now, Fry had twenty-one people working for him. He was busy petitioning the Vichy police to free certain prisoners, especially those who had visas and were about to emigrate. Vichy not only ignored his requests but arrested more of his protégés, including several who were taken on the eve of their departures. "Some were sentenced to *résidence forcée* . . . others were sent to concentration camps or to labor battalions."

His joy a month earlier over the ship departures disappeared when he finally heard about the seizing of the *Winnipeg,* the French ordering of the *Mont Visa* and the *Wyoming* back to Casablanca, and the internment of all the passengers. He spent June and July working to free these people, appealing to officials and sending representatives and money to distant ports where the refugees were interned. He maintained contact with refugees in several concentration camps and kept lines of communication open with HICEM and "shipping agents, to find ways of resuming the abbreviated journeys via Lisbon, Cádiz, Seville, or Casablanca." His efforts to save these individuals were "feverish," made more so by frequent communiqués from "the distraught passengers, who imagined themselves abandoned and demanded priority among the next sailings."

Fry, faced with his own and his protégés' enormous problems, asked several prominent Americans to again plead his case for remaining in France. Burns Chalmers, secretary of education for the American Friends Service Committee and a friend of Eileen's, believed that Fry's "important work stands on its own merit," and he tried to speak about this to Undersecretary of State Sumner Welles. He had no success. New School president Alvin Johnson also urged the State Department to support Fry.

> His labors are a thorn in the side of the worst pro-Nazi element at Vichy. He is, nevertheless, apparently getting less than he has a right to expect . . . from some of our foreign service officials at Vichy. Unless matters improve rapidly . . . Mr. Fry will be forced to return, abandoning, among others, those protégés in whom we are interested and whose escape to this country would be a blow to Hitler and a gain for our national interest.

Not even a prominent educator such as Johnson could sway Assistant Secretary of State Berle, who responded with the standard State Department rhetoric on Fry: He "has got to get home as soon as he can . . . I should not be surprised to find that he . . . is now in considerable danger of arrest."

Pushing worries about his own fate aside, Fry had more urgent matters to attend to. Escape by ship, which had seemed so promising at the beginning of spring, had ended quickly. Vichy canceled all ship departures and Fry went back to smuggling refugees across the Pyrenees via the Garcia Route.

At this time, visas were more difficult than ever. "People with money and no political commitments got visas," wrote Victor Serge, "[while] a host of anti-Fascist fighters did not get them at all. Visas for practically every [nation] were habitually sold . . . and the Vichy officials conducted a trade in exit-permits."

The United States passed new visa regulations, whose "faint outlines" had appeared as early as April. Under a measure lobbied for by Breckinridge Long, the United States would now "centralize control of visas in the State Department," where "an expanded Visa Division would carry out initial processing of immigration applications." This regulation went into effect on July 1, 1941. "But before that date . . . the State Department stopped issuing visas to a large category of refugees. On June 5 instructions went to diplomatic and consular officers to withhold visas from all applicants who had [relatives living in] territory under the control of Germany, Italy, or Russia."

For the entire year Fry had been in Marseille, U.S. policy had prevented those refugees who might questionably endanger national security from entering the country. Now Long had succeeded in pushing through legislation that formalized this policy. The new exclusionary and very strict regulations that took effect on July 1 virtually ended the chances for emigration to the United States of almost all of Fry's protégés. People who had applied for visas were informed that their applications had been voided. This included refugees "who had received tentative consular approval" but did not yet have their actual visa in hand. They had to begin the documentation process all over again, on new forms, with new requirements. Finally, refugees who reapplied and were approved for visas had to obtain those visas from overseas consulates who had a right, under U.S. law, to refuse to hand over the documents. As a result, "[m]any fugitives from Nazism, almost on the point of escaping Europe, were turned back by the shift in [U.S.] policy."

Fry felt "helpless" in the face of the new policies but nevertheless tried to calm his panicking protégés. More than two hundred refugees who had spent months assembling their papers and "whose files lacked only one document" now had to seek visas to different countries. Only a handful of those "who had previously been promised visas were finally able to obtain them." Most "had to abandon all thought of emigration."

Fry's constant struggle over which people to help was made more difficult at this time by his knowledge that the majority of the refugees would not escape. He was haunted by the uncertain destinies of the people he failed to help; so many men, women, and children just faded away with their fates unknown. One such case was that of Charlotte Thormann,* who was wanted by the Gestapo because of her husband's politics. Werner Thormann, a leading anti-Nazi activist and political secretary to a former Reich official, emigrated in 1933 to Paris, where he worked for the French Information Service. When France fell, he obtained a passport under another name and escaped to New York, forced to leave Charlotte and their two sons behind. In France, Char-

*Charlotte Thormann was number 1676.

lotte and her younger boy lived in hiding, while the older son served in the French Army. From New York, Werner, who was described on Nazi-controlled German radio as the "worst German traitor," pleaded with Fry to help his family, who, he wrote, had "been interrogated six times by the Gestapo." Fry, working to get them visas since April, succeeded eventually, but they could not pick up the visas because their ship passages weren't confirmed. Werner, living "on the kindness of friends" in America, implored the ERC in New York to pay for his family's passage. This payment was critical because consulates issued visas only "when payment for transportation [had] been confirmed." (Months later, Charlotte Thormann and her sons received their visas and sailed from Lisbon on November 17, 1941.)

Even though emigration was now almost an impossibility, Fry still had some last-minute successes. After locating pianist Erich Itor-Kahn in a camp, Fry managed to smuggle him out. But the pianist's troubles were not over, for despite Fry's efforts Itor-Kahn and his wife, Frida, were unable to obtain U.S. visas, since his parents lived in the occupied zone of France. On July 21, only a day before their ship was to sail, the couple once again went to the consulate to beg for their visas. This time, the consul's secretary pointed out that since the pianist was not in contact with his parents, no one even knew if they were still alive. "The Consul found this reasonable and plausible, and he added the visas to our passports," wrote Frida Itor-Kahn. Papers in hand, they rushed from the consulate to the ship, which sailed a short time later. They reached New York on August 5, 1941.

Fry was now primarily concerned with helping the refugees who he knew would be trapped in France. He turned to Bénédite to develop arrangements for "a long stay in France for [his protégés] no matter what disillusionments or difficulties in making a living they might have to face." They would have to support themselves or they would be sent to camps. Together, Fry and Bénédite developed projects that allowed the refugees to earn incomes in light industry or agriculture, the best-known endeavor being a cooperative fruit-paste factory, Croque Fruits. Even though he went along on this with Fry, Bénédite believed that the German refugees would find it difficult to work in a factory or on a farm. Many were on their "third or fourth emigration . . . [and] belonged mostly to the intellectual professions, now closed everywhere to foreigners, particularly to Jews." They "led the lives of hunted creatures," sleeping in "dubious hotels," always "threatened by the police." He was not at all certain that they would accept work at any of the projects being set up for them.

On the Fourth of July, a Friday, Fry's staff joined him in celebrating the holiday and presented him with this message on a card: "To Varian M. Fry President, His staff is happy to share with him, a real national holiday . . . because today, those who had two countries and who have lost everything, have put their hope in you."

Fry, cheered by their good wishes and camaraderie, was nevertheless depressed, because at the same time that his operation had become almost ineffective his marriage also seemed to be disintegrating. During the last few months, he had corresponded with Eileen less frequently, writing only when he had time to spare, which was not often. In early July, he received a letter that ended a lengthy silence on both their parts; it was a response to an earlier letter in which he had told Eileen that "provocateurs" were trying to " 'frame' him, sending both girls and boys. . . . Needless to say, I don't touch the people sent."

Eileen wrote that the rumors of his being "framed on morals charges" were already familiar to her. These bizarre stories had reached her "in garbled form" and were "more disturbing" than any explanation he might offer. She was distressed by these strange tales, as well as by a "five weeks silence" on his part. She also criticized him for writing about his dislike of New York. "Why not stay in France since you like the standard of living so much?" she snapped. "A democracy is too good for you." Fry had hurt Eileen by not communicating, and she implored him not to wait another five weeks before writing. At any rate, she added, his letters were "not calculated to soothe and reassure hurt feelings and suspicions."

Kingdon, too, had sent him a painful letter, which Fry had to pick up at the consulate from Hugh Fullerton—and that made it seem even worse. Kingdon was ordering Fry home in a most definite way. This was a blow after the efforts Fry had made to have influential people write to the Committee, urging that he be allowed to remain.

Fry decided to give up. With the Committee, as well as Vichy and the State Department, giving him the same message, he "had no choice but to . . . withdraw as quickly as possible." Yet he still wrote Kingdon an anguished letter continuing an argument the two had been having all year. If Kingdon had told the State Department he should remain, he would have been able to stay on "indefinitely." Fry felt certain that it was only now, after his "friends" at the Emergency Rescue Committee had abandoned him, that the State Department and Vichy were really going to force him out. And, despite the Committee's rejection of him, Fry remained convinced that he would be allowed to work with them when he returned to the United States: "I can be useful to our work in New York. . . . I am looking forward very eagerly to seeing you and your collaborators." It did not seem to be a rational attitude.

Fry soon received a summons from Du Porzic, "the Breton gentleman, with the long title," who had been promoted from police chief to head of all police in Marseille and environs, the Bouches du Rhone district. He arrived punctually, but Du Porzic kept him waiting. When, after a long time, he was finally ushered in, the first words he heard were: "You have caused my good friend the Consul-General of the United States much annoyance." Du Porzic then told him he must leave France. Fry stalled, but finally agreed to go as soon as a successor arrived, most likely by mid-August.

On his way out of the office, Fry asked, "Why are you so eager for me to go?" The answer came quickly. *"Parce que vous avez trop protégé des juifs et des anti-Nazis."* ("Because you have protected Jews and anti-Nazis too much.") Fry walked back to his office, shaken by this encounter with a fascist. "In the new France, we do not need proof," Du Porzic had told him. "We believe that it is better to arrest a hundred innocent men than to let one criminal escape."

Everything had gone wrong for Fry. He felt he had to go on the run, to leave town immediately in order to avoid the police. "A day or so" after his meeting with Du Porzic, the U.S. consulate renewed his passport, "validated for one month, for westbound travel only, and with the Portuguese and Spanish transit visas and the French exit visa already in it." He packed a bag, took a train from Marseille, and then spent ten days traveling the Côte d'Azur, sight-seeing in Sanary-sur-Mer, St. Tropez, Cannes, Nice, and Monte Carlo. Members of his staff occasionally came to meet with him and he "tried to direct operations that way." More and more, however, the work and responsibility fell on Bénédite and Gemähling as Fry avoided Marseille.

Fry also used the time away to write to his wife. Trying to save his marriage, he told her he was depressed but loved her and was her "faithful and devoted dog . . . in spite of . . . occasional errings." He pleaded for a chance: "Please give me a couple of weeks more before you make up your mind to leave me." He would be home soon "to straighten things out. I'm sure they'll be all right, in spite of the year that has gone by."

Early on the morning of Friday, August 8, Fry returned to Marseille to review Centre business with Bénédite and the others. But he left Marseille again that evening, heading to Vichy, where he would try one last time to urge U.S. officials to "say a word in [his] favor" in hopes that Du Porzic would vacate his threat of expulsion. In Vichy, the American embassy refused to help him at all. He wrote later that he was denied aid by his own country because U.S. officials, too, disapproved of his protecting "Jews and anti-Nazis too much."

|||||||||
There Is No Way Out: Ylla

After Fry moved his office from the rue Grignan to the boulevard Garibaldi, he looked for a photographer to record the astounding events happening around him. He found Camilla Koffler,* who worked under the name Ylla. A native of Austria, Ylla had spent her childhood in Hungary, Romania, and Yugoslavia, studying sculpture at boarding school and then at the University of Belgrade. She went to Paris in 1931 and, after learning photography, decided to give up sculpture. Her first photo exhibit was a triumph, and in the midthirties she opened a studio for animal portraits. Three published collections of animal photos followed, and in 1938 she brought out her book *Animal Language* with a text by Julian Huxley. That same year, she applied at the American consulate in Paris for a U.S. visa. Ylla and Huxley were about to collaborate again, when France fell and Ylla, who was Jewish, fled to Montauban, where she remained in hiding.

When she heard of a committee in Marseille that was helping refugees emigrate, she contacted friends in New York, asking them to get in touch with the Committee on her behalf so she could obtain a

*Koffler was number 695.

U.S. emergency visitor's visa. They did so and gathered documentation for her visa application. Ylla knew she was wanted by the Gestapo and was, as the Museum of Modern Art's librarian Beaumont Newhall wrote, "in immediate danger of being put into a concentration camp, not only for her expressed anti-Fascist ideas but because she has no passport of citizenship and because she is Jewish."

A desperate Ylla wrote to her friends again: "The general uncertainty and nervousness, the growing financial need in my environment is very depressing and there is no way out. . . . It is more sad than ever before." And because of the war, she could no longer support herself. "In my profession, as in a thousand others, there is no possibility of work here, specially for a foreigner, as I am."

Fry and Ylla met to discuss both her visa and the photographs he wanted. They tried to work out a fair price, with Fry asking for more reasonable terms and Ylla protesting because of the high costs of processing. They quickly came to an agreement. "I am doing what I can to please you," she told Fry. "It is, after all, completely natural. The committee you are directing is one of the rare hopes that exists at the present time for many people."

Ylla photographed André and Jacqueline Breton on the grounds of Air-Bel, and took a picture of Jacqueline, alone, in the window of their bedroom, the room Fry took after the Bretons left. In February, Ylla photographed Fry and his colleagues in the boulevard Garibaldi office, pictures that are now in the Museum of Modern Art.

Still worried because she had not yet received a U.S. visa, Ylla wrote again to her friends. Having heard that "one has to wait for about nine years for a new immigration visa," she was afraid that her application for a regular visa would be canceled if she received the emergency visa. Yet she remained somewhat optimistic, even in her saddest moments: "[E]ven if one foresees logically the worst, in one's heart one always keeps the hope that the worst will not happen."

Fry arranged a commission for Ylla, recommending her to Richard Allen of the American Red Cross and suggesting that the "talented young photographer" take pictures of the Red Cross ship expected in Marseille with a shipment of flour and other food items for the starving French. Allen agreed, but Ylla was denied permission by the *préfecture* to photograph "the distribution of goods (food) which arrive by boat."

In April, Fry advised Ylla to hasten to the American consulate: "[B]ring all the documents in your possession. It is possible that the visa might be given to you at this occasion," he wrote. He paid for her passage on the *Winnipeg* but at the last minute learned that her name had inadvertently been omitted from the passenger list. "You have already seen Miss Koffler and advised her to return for her visa as soon as she had settled the formalities concerning her passage," Fry wrote Standish. He asked the vice consul to arrange the "remaining formalities for her visa" so she could sail. Perhaps it was the polite tone of his letter. Or perhaps it was a cable in support of Ylla sent by U.S. Camera, an American company that had promised to employ her. The visa came through, and when the *Winnipeg* sailed on May 6, Ylla was aboard.

Ylla remained forever grateful to Fry and his organization. In June 1941, safely in the United States, she attempted to return seven thousand francs that he had given her by sending a check to the Centre. Five years later, her letter and check were returned. She then donated the money to the International Rescue Committee. In the midforties, her studio on West Fifty-first Street in Manhattan was only three blocks from where Fry was living, and they ran into each other. To his delight, she came to his apartment and photographed his dogs, Clovis and Mrs. Clovis.

Between 1944 and 1954, Ylla published ten books, several of which are considered children's classics, including *The Sleepy Little Lion* and *Two Little Bears*. In 1954, she and her mother were in a plane crash off Martha's Vineyard. When the plane went down, Ylla treaded water while holding her mother out of the water until she became exhausted and had to let go. Her mother drowned. Ylla was rescued, but one year later, in India, while photographing a bullock-cart race, she fell out of the small truck in which she was riding. According to her godson, Pryor Dodge, she "hit her head and went into a coma," dying a short time later, on March 30, 1955. Since Ylla's death, nine books of her photographs have been published, and her works are in collections all over the world.

CHAPTER ELEVEN

||||||||||||||||||||||||||

EXPULSION

*I've always thought that what we did for the refugees in France re-
sembled the obligation of soldiers to bring back their wounded from
the battlefield, even at the risk of their own lives. Some may die. Some
will be crippled for life. Some will recover and be the better soldiers
for having had experience of battle. But one must bring them all
back. At least one must try.*

Albert Hirschman

N ow FRY BEGAN the longest journey he would make in
France on his own. From Vichy, he traveled to Sanary-sur-
Mer, where he was reunited with an old friend from Air-Bel, Consuelo
de Saint-Exupéry; he also visited a number of writers and artists as he
traveled the Côte d'Azur, including Matisse and Gide. Fry griped bitterly to Eileen in a series of complaining letters sent from the south of
France. He wrote of a new problem, a rumor spread by the police that
he was a communist "and nothing that anybody can say does anything
at all to change their minds." He attributed some of this to his living
with Victor Serge. "It was a very grave error for me to go and live in
the same house with Serge," a known Trotskyist.

As he wandered, Fry felt he could almost understand what it was
like to be *apatride*. As he had done all his life, he dealt with his powerful emotions by deriding and ridiculing the authority that had rejected
him: "The weight of [U.S.] stupidity is too great to bridge," he wrote.
"I hope my successor will fare better. . . . France is no place these days
for someone suspected, however wrongly, of being a communist." He
did glory, though, in being on the run from the police, describing his

last weeks in France as "nerve-wracking but exciting" as he "darted around the country with the idea that the police" were after him— "and that makes for excitement."

By August 19, he was in Cannes, staying at the Hôtel Majestic and drinking a lot. He described his imbibing as "seventh heaven," then listed in a letter to Eileen all the alcoholic beverages he consumed in a single day. The total was staggering. "I fear I have become an alcoholic," he joked. When he returned to New York, he and Eileen must "always have wine at meals," he wrote, because drinking "completely remove[d] the necessity for drugs." (Fry took sleeping pills and stimulants later in his life, although no one who knew him during the Marseille period mentions his using drugs then.)

At Fry's urging, Bénédite met up with him in Cannes, and they traveled together for a while. Fry offered to try to get affidavits for him and Gemähling, his two closest colleagues, in order that they might apply for U.S. visas. "We said no. Both of us did not want to leave at that moment," recalled Gemähling. "We were already organizing in the Resistance." In Nice, Fry was arrested for taking photographs of broken store windows and a sign forbidding entrance to "noncombatant Jews." No formal charges were issued and he was quickly released. They traveled to Monaco, and Fry loved that visitors there "could sense" they "were no longer in France. Vichy's propaganda was completely absent."

Bénédite returned to the Centre and Fry continued his travels, lunching in Toulouse one day, meeting with painter André Dunoyer de Segonzac* in St. Tropez, then moving on to the villages of St.-Paul and Vence.

Finally, however, he had to face whatever awaited him in Marseille and returned to town on August 26. He went directly home and prepared to leave his beloved France. He packed, wrote letters, and the next morning went to the office and talked with his staff about operating the Centre after he was gone.

By Friday, Fry began to relax. He "had been telephoning, walking about the town, and receiving visitors," but he had not been bothered

---

*De Segonzac was reported to be a collaborator, but Bénédite, who became a decorated hero of the Resistance, cleared him: Although "his behavior during the occupation was not particulary heroic," de Segonzac was not a collaborator.

by the police. Shortly before one P.M., however, two plainclothes detectives arrived at the boulevard Garibaldi office. In the building, they
saw Karel Sternberg and asked if he was Fry. "I was about the same age
and I didn't look French, I suppose," said Sternberg. The police continued upstairs, where they found Fry in the back room of the office.

"He was quite composed" when he saw the police, recalled Gemähling. "He had no reason to be frightened. He knew that they were after
him, though he didn't expect it that morning." The detectives were
"embarrassed but courteous" as they took him downstairs to their
waiting car. They informed him that he would be held at the jail until
he could be transported to the border. Fry was not officially under arrest since he had not been charged with a crime, but he was going to
be expelled from France against his will. "When he saw that the Emergency Rescue [Committee] would not send somebody to take his place
and when the police arrested him," said Gemähling, "he saw that he
couldn't do anything. He was not afraid but he was very sorry to leave
his job unfinished."

The police drove away with Fry and his secretary, Lucie Heymann,
whom they permitted to accompany him. At the jail, Heymann handed
her boss the food and newspapers she had brought along for him, then
returned to the office, where she called a police official, Roger Homo,
to beg for Fry's release. Homo could do little, he said, then "speculated about Mr. Fry's being either insane, a saint, or an anti-Nazi
'Bolshevik' agent." Fry "was possibly a saint, probably insane, but definitely not a 'Bolshevik' agent," Heymann replied.

In the meantime, Bénédite headed to Vichy to try to prevent Fry's
expulsion, and Verzeano and Paul Schmierer saw M. Fleury of the
Sûreté to find out what Vichy had in store for Fry. Fleury, who seemed
distressed, told them that Fry had been arrested on direct orders from
Du Porzic. He was not to be allowed visitors, added Fleury, but he
agreed to give Fry the food Verzeano and Schmierer had brought.

Later that day, an official from Du Porzic's staff told Heymann that
"Mr. Fry had behaved badly toward France" and had engaged in "secret activities." Heymann defended Fry, saying that his behavior reflected only "his anxiety to protect unfortunates persecuted by the
government." That night, Fry slept on a table in the jail, and in the
morning Heymann and Paul Schmierer's wife, Vala, arrived and gave
their "unshaven and smiling" colleague blankets and yet more food.

Fry was informed that he was not being expelled—which would have meant he could never return—but *refoulé*, or turned back. He would be escorted to the border "as soon as possible."

That afternoon, Fry's police escort, M. Garandel, arrived at the jail to take him back to his office and room so he could prepare to leave. At the Centre, Fry saw Bénédite, who had just returned from his fruitless sojourn to Vichy: No one there was interested in Fry's case. Garandel then took him to his apartment and gave him two hours to pack. When Fry complained that he had no transit visas, exit visa, or money, Garandel replied that that would be taken care of at the border. That night, Fry and his staff—the Bénédites, Gemähling, Verzeano, the Schmierers, Heymann, and Weisslitz—shared a farewell dinner under Garandel's watchful eye.

After dinner, Fry and his colleagues boarded a train for the border, riding in a special car reserved for the Sûreté Nationale. Heymann credited Garandel for allowing her and the others to "make Mr. Fry's departure worthy of the honor due him after his courageous campaign in France." The group arrived in Narbonne at one A.M. on Sunday, August 31, in the midst of a celebration commemorating the founding of Pétain's Legion. The scene, as Heymann described it, was "exciting," and she caught "a glimpse of the monument where the flame relayed from the Arc de Triomphe burned, guarded by the Legionnaires." Fry, however, focused on the flame as a fascist symbol "[i]n true Goebbels' fashion."

The group spent the night in Narbonne. In the morning, the excitement of the previous evening was gone, and faces were glum and somber. They all rode the train to Cerbère, but then Fry was not allowed to enter Spain without a Spanish transit visa, something he had feared would happen, since his papers were incomplete. They all had to return to Perpignan, where Garandel allowed Fry to stay in a hotel despite instructions from his superiors to put the American in the "Cooler." At this point, some of the staff returned to Marseille, but others remained. Fry again reviewed the Centre's future operation. Gemähling would be director, since he had never been in trouble with the police, Bénédite would manage operations "behind the scenes," and Verzeano would continue working on illegal escape routes. Fry had created, "inspired and energized the organization," but even without him, the Centre would survive.

Fry and his friends "spent a [few] half happy, half sad" days at Perpignan, waiting while the Vichy police secured his papers. During the week, almost every staff member came to say good-bye. They ate and drank well each day, most of the time without a guard, as "[o]ne way or another, [Garandel] managed to leave us alone, almost all the time." Fry later characterized the policeman as "a nice guy" and "a very decent sort of chap" who wanted to dissociate himself from fascist Frenchmen: "*Nous ne sommes pas de barbares nous Français,*" Garandel had told Fry. ("We are not the barbaric French.") When the sympathetic officer heard that the German Economic Commission was in Perpignan, he acted more as if he were Fry's protector and bodyguard than "a policeman preventing" his escape.

Within a few days, Fry had the papers he needed for his journey. On Saturday morning, September 6, he said farewell to his friends at the Cerbère train station. Fry noticed that the U.S. ambassador to Vichy, Admiral William Leahy,* was in the train station, too. Leahy, Mary Jayne Gold wrote, was the person who, "in a special gesture of friendship toward the Vichy government, refused to renew Fry's . . . passport." When his staff urged him to speak to Leahy, Fry "refused, feeling that in the circumstances, [he] might embarrass him by doing so." Fry and Leahy went through customs without acknowledging each other. Then Fry boarded the train, leaned out the window, and waved at the familiar faces looking up at him. They had worked together so closely, against such great danger. The bonds of love and loyalty between them would last a lifetime.

He pulled himself together as the dear faces faded from view. He and Leahy, in the same car, continued to ignore each other. On the way to Portbou, Fry read or looked out "at the lush green Catalan landscape." Changing trains at Portbou for the Barcelona train, Leahy and he again "stood side by side on the railway platform . . . and filed through the gate . . . all without saying a word to one another, or giving any sign" that they knew each other. "I was very proud of my self-control through this long voyage," Fry wrote. They also rode in the same train car to Barcelona.

At border checks, Fry found the guards so relaxed that he could easily have brought along reports and other documents he needed in

---

*In 1943, Leahy said, "The [atomic] bomb will never go off."

New York. No one searched his briefcase, and inspections of his luggage were cursory. The Spanish police noted the titles of his books to ensure he "was not importing propaganda," but otherwise he was left alone. In Barcelona, he left his luggage in his room at the Hotel Espana and walked out into the street. He found the city shockingly untouched by war: "Barcelona burns its street lights brazenly at night; Barcelona dances; Barcelona drinks milk and sugar in its coffee and eats cakes between meals."

The end of the adventure was bittersweet for Fry because, although he enjoyed being free of harassment, he suffered deeply from "melancholy nostalgia." In his Barcelona hotel room, with time on his hands for the first time in a year, he wrote long, reflective letters to Eileen and to Bénédite. He felt "[m]iserably depressed," obsessed with "the faces of a thousand" protégés. He missed the office and staff, Air-Bel, weekend trips with friends to the beautiful villages of southern France, and most of all his friend Bénédite. "Already I feel hundreds of miles away from you—and sad for it."

> We . . . have stood shoulder to shoulder with our eyes fixed on the same goal. . . . [T]he past year has wrapped cords about us which not even the violence of war can break.

Fry was so depressed that he even began to blame himself for his problems with the American embassy. He had been "too immersed in the details of the work," and as a result had ignored the government representatives to whom, as the director of an American agency, he should have paid attention. He berated himself for not socializing and entertaining, for not paying more courtesy calls. He criticized his behavior in Marseille, describing himself as a "bureaucrat" who enjoyed working in an office because he lacked "social graces" and was "shy [and] self-conscious in company." He even disapproved of his decision to begin work immediately upon arriving in France without first going to Vichy "to present myself to the Embassy and ask their blessing. I have been told that they were offended that I did not do so."

It was easy to castigate himself. Feelings of self-doubt took over when the confident Fry of the Centre Américain de Secours found himself with nothing to do. Another ingredient in the miserable stew brewing in Fry's psyche was the uncertain state of his marriage. He and Eileen had resumed their old fighting relationship and alternately sent sarcastic letters, then loving ones, during the early fall of 1941. He sent one letter that dealt specifically with their problems:

> If you will look in the "observations by Mr. Dooley" under the title "Women and marriage" . . . you will find a complete expla- nation of our differences and our difficulties. A man's first, last and only perennial love . . . is his job, and two weeks after the honeymoon is over it begins to come between him and his wife. Whereas a woman is romantic, and looks always for outward ex- pressions of her husband's continuing affection, a man is highly practical and distinctly unromantic: once married he takes his wife, and his affection for her for granted; what he thinks about is his job.

Eileen exploded. "Did you find [Mr. Dooley's] remarks on politics [and] art . . . as just as his remarks on women and marriage? Or per- haps you are better educated in those fields, and therefore less im- pressed by banalities!" Her sharpness was a reminder to her husband that he may be a hero in France, but in their house, she was still older, wiser, and better at sarcastic rejoinders. Eileen had her own insecurities and needs, however, and ended on a softer note: "I think I still love you, in spite of all you say and do to make me shudder! I shall know definitely when you've been home a week. How about you?" In an ear- lier letter, she admitted she was "quite frightened" and asked, "How do you think it will be when we are together again?"

In response, Fry wrote that he loved her and wanted to stay mar- ried. He begged for Eileen's understanding and sympathy because he was so miserable at leaving Marseille. "It is September 7, 1941, and I am again in Barcelona—for the fourth, and perhaps the last, time in my life." A year earlier, he had been there to see off Franz and Alma Wer- fel. "Now I am going to Lisbon and beyond, and I do not know if I shall ever see my beloved France again. Certainly I shall not see it again as long as this war lasts. Forgive me, then, if I am sad today." He con- tinued:

> It is not merely the sadness of parting from familiar sights and sounds. . . . It is also, and perhaps especially, the terrible let down that was sooner or later inevitable after such a strenuous and tur- bulent year. For I have just reached the end of the most intense

twelve months I have ever lived through. When I left New York on August fourth, 1940, I had no idea at all of what lay ahead of me. . . . Even during the first days and weeks in Marseille, I was far from realizing the true nature of the situation I faced. Today I think I understand as well as anyone else what is happening to France. And yet I still don't quite know what happened to me. . . . What I do know is that I have lived far more intensely in this last year . . . than I ever have before, and that the experience has changed me profoundly. . . . I do not think that I shall ever be quite the same person I was when I kissed you goodbye at the airport and went down the gangplank to the waiting Clipper. For the experiences of ten, fifteen and even twenty years have been pressed into one. Sometimes I feel as if I had lived my whole life (and one to which I have no right) since I first walked down the monumental stairway of the Gare St.-Charles at Marseille . . . Since that day I have had adventures—there is no other but this good Victorian word—of which I never dreamed. I have learned to live with people, and to work with them. I have developed or discovered within me powers of resourcefulness, of imagination and of courage which I never before knew I possessed. And I have fought a fight, against enormous odds, of which, in spite of the final defeat, I think I can always be proud. When I look back upon this year, the thing which impresses me most is the *growth* I have undergone. . . . I was transplanted 13 months ago, to a pot which I more than once had occasion to fear was too large, but I didn't die, in the end I think I very nearly filled it—not entirely, but nearly. At least I didn't die from the shock or the excuse of my own inadequacy. The knowledge of that fact has given me a new quality which I think I needed: self-confidence. . . . I don't know whether you will like the change or not. I rather suspect you won't. But it is there . . . to stay. It is the indelible work that a year spent in fighting my own little war has left on me.

Fry moved on to Lisbon, staying at the Hotel Tivoli. On October 1, when he went to the Pan American Airways offices to place his name on the waiting list for the October 18 Clipper, he learned that his round-trip ticket, purchased optimistically more than a year earlier, was out of date and no longer valid. He had to cable the ERC to pay five hundred twenty-five dollars for his ticket home. Forced to wait six weeks in Lisbon for a Clipper seat to New York, Fry used the time to improve the underground route from Marseille to Portugal. He knew, of course, that most of the refugees still in Marseille would not escape and would be interned in camps, or worse. Foreseeing the day when the Centre's doors would be padlocked by Vichy, Fry hoped the work could continue even without an office.

While in Lisbon, he also arranged transportation for those protégés who were still interned in North Africa, waiting to escape. HICEM was sending a rescue ship out from Lisbon, with stops in Casablanca, Havana, Veracruz, and New York, so Fry tried to get the stranded refugees on it. Before the ship sailed, however, Fry heard from his old colleague Emilio Lussu that it was not possible to travel on a ship from Casablanca to New York without French exit visas, so Fry passed this news on to Bénédite and Verzeano: "[T]he thing has broken down completely."

Verzeano was in Lisbon then and recalled working with Fry "for a while and with the Unitarian Service Committee as well to help the refugees who were there, waiting to leave for the U.S." One refugee, sculptor Bernard Reder,* turned up one day at Fry's hotel "in a deplorable state, both physically and nervously," telling an incredible story about Fry's trusted colleague Paul Schmierer. Reder said Schmierer had forced him to smuggle a subversive document across the border, which Reder had naively placed right on top of his belongings, where it was soon found by police. Reder, "hysterical by nature and after his experience practically mad," could not be believed, and Fry checked with the Centre. Schmierer denied the story; the papers he gave Reder had been unimportant and certainly not subversive. Then, Fry asked, why send them out with a refugee? He never received a satisfactory answer.

Although Fry was enjoying Portugal with its plentiful food and wine, he watched as every day the country fell "more and more under German influence." Spaniards were refused asylum unless they possessed "a valid Franco passport," and the Portuguese were rumored to have delivered to the Nazis without trial a German political refugee. Even American citizens had a hard time, unable to get transit visas

---

*Bernard Reder was number 1807.

"except in very exceptional cases." Fry's more traditional counterparts in France, who represented religious American aid organizations, were arrested, or nearly arrested. Donald Lowrie, the YMCA representative, "got out two jumps ahead of the cops." Robert Dexter of the Unitarian Service Committee could not obtain a French visa because of his "known connections" to the British. The Unitarians' Charles Joy "was on the very point of arrest when he left France."

In America, a rash of news stories stated that Ambassador Leahy had escorted Fry out of France. One New York story was headlined, "Leahy Takes Fry with Him into Spain." Officials in the United States assumed that Fry had leaked this false story to the press, and he now was in more disfavor with the government. The State Department did not want it to appear as if an American ambassador had aided the renegade Fry. "If anything unpleasant happens, if the Embassy is accused of harboring sympathies for the victims of Nazi oppression, listening sympathetically to the complaints of a Jew, or doing anything to protect the life of an American citizen who has been accused of being anti-Nazi," Fry complained to Eileen, "it is always that man Fry who is responsible." He criticized diplomats such as Leahy, who refused to acknowledge that the Nazis were engaged in a "new war on religion," and he continued to blast the State Department for its inhumane treatment of refugees.

About to go home, he found himself yearning for the early days of the operation, "the best days . . . when we were just learning our job and getting to know one another." It was like "the opening of a new term at boarding school," Fry wrote Bénédite. He had graduated, not at all pleased being "out in the world."

One morning, over coffee in a Lisbon café, Fry turned his mind to what he would do once back in New York. Eileen had told him of several possibilities: Harold Oram had suggested he make a fund-raising trip for the ERC, a publisher was willing to underwrite a book on his experiences in France, and Karl Frank and Ingrid Warburg had a new organization, the International Coordinating Council, which needed a director. Fry, however, wanted to continue refugee work, "which absorbs me completely." Overlooking his rejection by the ERC, he still intended to work for the organization when he returned. He planned to "straighten out a lot of misunderstandings, complete the organization (which still looks, from a distance, a little defective) and 'assure the liaison' between New York and Lisbon and New York and Marseille." He ignored a dozen warnings from Eileen and others that he would not be welcome back at the Committee.

As he indicated in a letter to Bénédite, his sense of failure over the refugees he had not helped was his strongest feeling now. Perhaps if he had not broken with the State Department, he could have stayed longer and saved more people. His thoughts lingered on the ones he had left behind, the protégés who "were demoralized and demanded impossibilities," those "whose claims for emigration were superior or particularly pressing," and the tragic men and women who could not be helped and so ended up hating him. He remembered friends and enemies, fascists and anti-Semites, the suicides, the deportees. Looking back, it was clear how "demoralized, nervous, even hysterical, and in no way predisposed to run the risks . . . required of them" the refugees had been. "Novices" at the illegal work, he and his staff had made so many errors. Bénédite wrote that they were "too trusting, even naive" in their choice of intermediaries, allowing themselves "to be 'taken in.'" They had not always chosen their "agents wisely."

Fry felt that he was responsible "for the many thousands who were not rescued," but he also placed blame on "the U.S. government . . . for the obstructionism of the State Department." Of the fifteen thousand refugees who contacted him during his thirteen months in France by his own estimate, he helped about two thousand to escape. When he arrived in August 1940, he knew the Nazis were barbarians and had some idea of Hitler's final solution from what he had been told in 1935 by Putzi Hanfstaengl. For the rest of his life, Fry would remember that, while he did everything he could, it was not enough, and many of those he did not help died at the hands of the Germans.

At the end of October, he renewed his passport. "The man in charge of American passports was the neatest, most exquisite thing I had ever seen in pants," he joked. When he booked passage to New York, he heard from Eileen about a fund-raising dinner planned for November 4 to honor his old enemy Jay Allen. According to Eileen, if Fry was not back by then, Allen would dedicate the dinner to Fry, saying: "This dinner should not be for me, but for VMF [Varian Mackey Fry]." But Fry felt distant from New York and fund-raising dinners. His letters to Bénédite expressed only a desire to remain in Europe. He did not want to return home. "I *prefer* the blackout, and would gladly trade even an occasional bombardment for what lies in wait for me in America. But I have to go home . . . to the hard geometry of New York." His memories of and longing for Marseille and Air-Bel dominated his emotions as the end of the adventure neared. He wrote to Bénédite:

> I left my heart in France, I guess. Somewhere between Les Baux and the Villa Air-Bel, in the moonlight and on a crisp winter night. . . . Someday, though, I shall be back in France. . . . Then we shall go arm in arm over the hills and into the valleys, singing the songs and drinking the wines, of your beautiful, your incomparable, country. Until then, Danny, good-bye. I love France, and I love you.

On Saturday, November 1, as his letter left Lisbon for Marseille, Fry boarded the Clipper and went airborne to New York. At the other end of his flight were Eileen, stability, and everything familiar.

|||||||||

Flight and Arrival: Jacques Lipchitz

> I felt very vividly all kind of disasters coming to the world . . . and I expressed it in some of my sculptures. . . . I made, for example, the sculpture "David and Goliath" in '33 . . . the year when Hitler came to power. It's a big Goliath with a swastika on his chest, strangled by a small David. . . . People were laughing at it, telling me how do you see that this little "David" will finally strangle Goliath. . . . But I said, It's a prayer. It's wishful thinking. I hope it will be like that.
>
> Jacques Lipchitz

Jacques Lipchitz was born Chaim Jacob Lipchitz on August 22, 1891, in a Russian village that is now part of Lithuania. He studied engineering, but after emigrating to France at the age of eighteen he turned to art, developing into a sculptor "of immense power and originality, who helped to create the basic grammar of modern art and then aspired to go beyond his own creation." After returning to Russia briefly to serve in the Russian Imperial Army from 1912 to 1913, he returned to Paris, where, influenced by Picasso and Braque, he created sculptures in the Cubist style.

When, in 1939, the Germans crashed through the smaller European nations and headed toward France, Lipchitz knew he was in danger because he was Jewish and had created art labeled "degenerate" by the Nazis, and later "banned" by Vichy for being antifascist. However, he remained in Paris even after the Germans began bombing the outskirts of the French capital. He recalled being distressed by events around him to such an extent that he "didn't have even the desire to act . . . didn't have . . . the energy . . . to fight." He "was under the influence of a German god of Valhalla . . . a little hunchback who doesn't have too much power but he . . . takes away the clear mind from his enemy and he can't act."

Finally, friends had to "force" the sculptor to leave Paris. "Look, Jacques," they said, "Hitler will be here tomorrow. We are going away from Paris and we will not go away without you." Lipchitz "woke up" from his stupor and, the next evening, when his friends arrived to pick up the sculptor and his wife, Russian poet Berthe Kitrosser, they gave their apartment key to a neighbor and left. Lipchitz took with him only two of his sculptures and a tiny pillbox that he had acquired days earlier from a physician friend. Lipchitz had asked this doctor to give him poison tablets, but the man had refused. "I am a physician," he said. "I don't help people die." But then he placed a box on the table and said, "If I were to help you, which I can't, this is what I would give you." Then, pretending someone outside was calling him, he left Lipchitz alone and the artist put the pills in his pocket. "I was certain I would perish and wanted to do it myself first."

When Lipchitz and his wife and friends left Paris, they went first to Vichy to see other friends, then continued on to another town, where they rented rooms. Lipchitz immediately began drawing, but alarmed by his brother's arrival and warning—"The Germans are behind us. They are coming"—he and the others left quickly. They drove toward Spain with, Lipchitz remembered, the Germans right behind them. Lipchitz recalled that "one night . . . somewhere over there in the Basque country," his friend was tired and wanted to stop. "My wife said, 'Look, it's only 12 o'clock. We can still go for a hour or two.' So we did. And this village was occupied the same night by the Germans. This is to tell you how close we were in front of them."

At this point, Lipchitz said to his wife, "Let's take the pills." But she replied, "Not yet." When they got to the Spanish border and found themselves stopped by the "wall of the Pyrenees in front of us," the artist became "quite desperate. I lost, a little bit, my courage." His friend secured some documents at a government office that allowed them into Spain. As they were driving, though, they noticed that the other "refugee cars," which were all "covered with mattresses against the . . . bombardment," were headed toward them; they were "not with us, but against us, and we were puzzled." Lipchitz and his friends discovered that France and Germany had signed an armistice, dividing France into two zones, and that the Spanish border had been closed that morning. "We turned our car and we went back, south, like the other cars." Lipchitz "was very, very sad" that Paris had fallen. He recalled that he believed the city "will be asleep for a while. I never doubted that the Allies will not be victorious . . . because it seems to me that it was impossible that Hitler becomes a conqueror." He began a sculpture, "Benediction," to honor Paris. "I wanted to sing Paris a kind of a lullaby, and I started to scratch, to scrape it and it came out . . . a woman playing the harp," said Lipchitz. "It is kind of a benediction to Paris which became prisoner and it went to sleep but will wake up one day."

After a long drive, Lipchitz and his wife ended up in Toulouse. They lived and worked in a rented studio, and Lipchitz spoke to art dealers about selling some of his drawings. "I didn't have any money. . . . In Toulouse I made a few portraits of friends . . . and a lot of drawings which were sold. And then one day I received a letter from the American Rescue Committee."

"What can we do for you?" Fry wrote to Lipchitz. "We are ready to do whatever we can." Convinced he would soon be captured—"Some people were arrested in the street . . . they were arresting Jews and taking them to concentration camps"—Lipchitz asked Fry to send his "last drawings to the Museum of Modern Art in New York." But Fry, who wrote that he had been "commissioned" to help Lipchitz, reassured the artist that not only would his drawings be sent but that he, too, would go to America.

Years later, Lipchitz admitted that he had some "strange ideas about

America" and believed it would be barren, with "only skyscrapers, no trees." Thinking he could not survive in such an environment, Lipchitz told Fry that he did not intend to leave. "I will not be able to live over there . . . I will die over there. Better to die here."

"He was concerned about starting all over again," recalled Lolya Lipchitz, the sculptor's daughter. "He knew no one; he didn't speak English." But Fry was not about to give up and suggested Lipchitz and his wife come to Marseille so they could meet and discuss the matter. Lipchitz agreed and, in Marseille, Fry urged him to emigrate. "He said, 'You have to pass a medical examination and then we'll make you a passport and then we'll bring you to America.' It was just like a dream. It was something so brisk, so quite impossible. . . . Everything was done nicely and generously." Fry arranged for them to pick up their U.S. emergency visas at the American consulate, according to Lolya Lipchitz.

But even though he had a visa, Lipchitz, still not ready to emigrate, returned to Toulouse. Just before he left Marseille, Fry reminded him, "When you are ready, you come here. We will send you to America." Once back in Toulouse, Lipchitz's old doubts took over and he refused to budge. Six months later, he again heard from Fry. "I received a . . . very severe letter from Varian Fry, who was a marvelous man," recalled Lipchitz. "He said, 'Well, if you don't come right now, you will lose your [visa] because people are . . . crazy to go to America and you have a [visa], you can do it.' "

Lipchitz's friends went to his studio and "threw [him] out." He must act on his "golden opportunity to be saved," they said, or he would "perish." They said that Hitler "will come, he will occupy the entire France, and then you will be caught." Lipchitz finally agreed and took a train to Marseille.

In addition to Fry's exhortations, Lipchitz was affected by "other influences from America at the time," according to Lolya Lipchitz. "The American Red Cross had donated flour to France. There were signs with American flags that said 'To the people of France from the people of America.' These were signs to my father that people here were good."

But Lipchitz said later that it was mainly Fry's persistence that saved him: "In some ways I owe him my life. . . . I did not want to go away from France. It was his severe and clairvoyant letters which helped me finally to do so. . . . And of what help he was once I decided to go to America!"

The warmth was mutual; as Fry wrote to Eileen, "Lipchitz is the best of the lot: polite, intelligent, and enormously grateful." On May 16, 1941, Fry gave the Lipchitzes money, and train tickets to Barcelona and Lisbon. In Lisbon, where they remained for a few weeks, they received an allowance for a room and ate their meals at a canteen run by a Jewish charity. They sailed to America on the *Nyassa*. "I was sick like a dog, and then we came to the harbor of New York," said Lipchitz. "I will never forget it. We were all on the deck. It was a little bit raining and here came the skyline of Manhattan. I can't explain . . . what kind of a feeling I had, like I came from death to life. . . . It's something I cannot forget and I cannot describe."

Just before he emigrated, Lipchitz made "Flight" and it was one of two sculptures that he carried across the Atlantic with him. After he arrived in America, in June 1941 he sculpted "The Arrival." In the context of the refugee emigration, Jacques Lipchitz never created two more important works.

PART TWO

||||||||||||||||||

AFTER MARSEILLE

CHAPTER TWELVE

IIIIIIIIIIIIIIIIIIIIIIIIIIII

GOING HOME

. . . when I go back to the United States I seem to be living in a black-
and-white movie. As soon as I cross the . . . border, I'm in color again.
Mike Eden in Marjorie Morningstar

ON NOVEMBER 2, 1941, when Fry climbed out of the huge Dixie Clipper and crossed the ramp into the waiting arms of his wife, Eileen immediately saw how much her husband had changed. They had discussed their relationship for the past few months, with Fry warning that he was different and Eileen expressing her fears: "I sometimes wonder whether you will ever come back, and if you do whether you'll be able to stand the monotony." Now that he had returned, it was not the expectation of monotony that was bothering him but an aversion to his former role as Eileen's "boy." He did not want to be bossed or mothered. Still, he left the airport arm in arm with his wife and they returned together to the apartment at 56 Irving Place, determined to try.

Two days later, Fry was an honored guest at a fund-raising luncheon given by Alvin Johnson and Frank Kingdon, at which several hundred guests were invited to hear Eleanor Roosevelt speak. After Mrs. Roosevelt canceled, Fry joked that perhaps she had been warned by the State Department not to associate herself in any way with "that man Fry."

A short time after he was back in New York, Fry walked into the

Forty-second Street offices of the Emergency Rescue Committee, still deluding himself that he would be greeted warmly. Instead, Kingdon and several others met him with reserve. Fry, the realist, knew Kingdon did not care for him, but the idealistic Fry thought it possible that things would be different when the two men were face-to-face. They were not. And while Fry pretended he did not want thanks for what he had done, he was deeply hurt that he had not been welcomed home as a returning hero at the ERC.

Only three weeks after his return, Fry found out just how antagonistic Kingdon, his assistant, Ingrid Warburg, the treasurer, David Seiferheld, and fund-raiser Harold Oram were toward him when he was forbidden from speaking on behalf of the ERC or portraying himself as its representative. Fry had displayed "attitudes," Kingdon wrote, that made his "continued cooperation with the committee inadvisable." Furthermore, the State Department would not grant visas to ERC clients if Fry was associated with the Committee. Fry's initial response to the State Department's ultimatum was to "fight it." But Kingdon insisted that opposing the Department was not possible. Fry could not quite believe this turn of events. By subterfuge and defiance of authority in Marseille, he had opposed, outwitted, and outmaneuvered the enemy. Now, in his own country, where questioning authority was a constitutional freedom, Kingdon was afraid to disagree with government policy. "Am I to assume from your letter that I may not continue to direct contributions to the E.R.C.," Fry asked Kingdon, "or to cooperate with the E.R.C. on cases?" He intended to continue the work of the Committee, despite Kingdon's attitude toward him, in no small part due to his needing the ERC as a base from which to raise money for refugees and to work on cases "which seem . . . particularly urgent or important."

Days later, Kingdon requested that Fry take a one-month leave of absence. Fry blamed his ouster on the fact that the State Department was "sore as a boil" at him and tried to maintain his fantasy that the ERC would come around. But with Bénédite he was honest, writing that Kingdon "will not hear of my having anything further to do with the committee."

Within a month, Japan attacked the U.S. naval base at Pearl Harbor, and America was catapulted into the war. This sneak attack added to Fry's sense of desolation about the war as Christmas approached.

"New York depresses me very much," he wrote. "It has been an extraordinary experience to come here from Lisbon overnight . . . and to find that my countrymen are only just beginning to wake up to the menace that hangs over all of us."

Fry and Eileen had not been able to repair their relationship, and the altercations that had begun in letters continued. Brooding, he wrote to Bénédite, "We are involved this Christmas season in a war on two fronts, against very powerful and very ruthless foes . . . how much of the world we know will there be left when it does end?"

Then Kingdon announced that the Committee would merge with the International Relief Association (IRA) to form a new organization, the International Rescue and Relief Committee.* Fry worked to stop the merger, characteristically insisting, "We *shall* succeed." But when Kingdon threatened to resign if board members did not go along with him, they agreed. Fry had lost. Later, Karel Sternberg arrived in New York and was welcomed into the IRRC; Fry kept his problems to himself and never complained about his treatment by the organization.

The loss to Fry of the ERC as a base, coupled with violent arguments with Eileen, took a toll on him, although he tried hard not to lose "heart or courage or determination." He found a job as assistant editor at the well-respected, liberal *New Republic,* but it could not replace what he missed. He had seen the world, saved lives, had an adventure; he had outsmarted German fascists, French dictators, and American bullies. The war had made him a leader, but now, back home, searching for something other than his ordinary job and everyday life that would thrill and challenge him the way Marseille had, he began the struggle that would occupy him for the rest of his life.

Hoping to use the Centre now as a base, Fry nevertheless told Bénédite to remove his name from the organization's letterhead. "Exercise the authority which rightfully is now yours for you are no

---

*The IRRC became the International Rescue Committee, "the largest non-sectarian refugee agency in the world." Karel Sternberg headed the organization for decades. According to the IRC's current president, Reynold Levy, "We claim Fry as one of our founding parents. The central features of his heroism are echoed in today's IRC advocacy. He pushed for policy changes in the U.S. and in Europe and expanded his own mandate. . . . Varian Fry's temperament and comportment are apparent in our staff today."

longer my deputy; you have really taken my place," he wrote. "It is folly to think of putting my name on . . . it will be a red rag to the bull to certain persons, and why stir up hostility unnecessarily? . . . Bury me decently and quietly. I shall live on, I trust, in your hearts and you in mine."

Under Bénédite's leadership, during the months after Fry's departure, the Centre helped hundreds to escape, including Fry's old friend, poet Benjamin Péret, sculptor Bernard Reder, and harpsichordist Wanda Landowska, "who was giving a series of concerts in the U.S.A., and for whom we were happy to be able to facilitate all things," as Bénédite wrote.

Then Bénédite wrote that Gemähling had been arrested after being betrayed by a double agent. In a café, this man had tried to sell him "military information about the defense of Marseille." When he demurred, the spy stuffed incriminating papers into Gemähling's pocket and ran from the café. "I ran out after him," recalled Gemähling, "but two policemen who were sitting outside jumped at me . . . and immediately picked up the envelope in my pocket. I understood that all had been arranged." He was held incommunicado at the military prison in Marseille for more than four months. Fry, worried about his sensitive young friend, tried unsuccessfully to get help for him from the IRRC and even implored writer Antoine de Saint-Exupéry (whose wife, Consuelo, Gemähling had been enamored of at Air-Bel), then in New York, to use his influence. Gemähling eventually escaped without anyone's help and spent the remainder of the war in the Resistance.

Fry continued to help refugees, but without a base in New York he could do little. He wrote often to Bénédite, expressing a sense of loss in his personal life and his refugee work. Feeling very much a failure, he also wrote to Théo Bénédite, telling her that he was no more a diplomat now than before; he still had difficulty getting along with others.

He longed more than ever for Bénédite and his other colleagues who loved and respected him: "I still feel as much as I ever did that my heart is in Marseille," he wrote to Bénédite. "I think of you constantly, wonder what you are all doing every hour of the day, and wish I could be with you." He continued to pretend to himself that his ouster from the ERC was caused by Kingdon's "jealous" feelings toward him. But since no one on the Committee tried to reinstate him, he eventually recognized that he was as disavowed by the Committee now as he had been in Europe. It was a stunning rejection.

Fry sought consolation with friends from Marseille, and just after New Year's 1942 he and Eileen visited the Bretons' "attractive studio apartment in Greenwich Village" and played surrealist games. They were joined by Consuelo de Saint-Exupéry "wearing a fantastic hat much like a tropical bird," and Ernst's former love, Leonora Carrington, accompanied by her new husband. "Speaking of marriages," wrote Fry, "Max has married Peggy Guggenheim!" But Breton seemed "like a fish out of water," and the games had lost much of their magic.

In the spring of 1942, Fry's dissonance with people in positions of authority ruined his chance for securing a government job, one that would have put an end to his growing sense of frustration. Once again, displaying ambivalence toward the government, furious at certain policies but admiring some leaders, such as FDR, he had applied to the Office of Coordinator of Information. Based on his "extensive and specialized experience" in France, he believed that he could not "fail to be of value" to his country. Apparently the officials who read his application agreed, writing that Fry was "probably the only qualified American expert on the means of moving the people around the continent of Europe despite regulations and occupations." Unfortunately former ERC treasurer David Seiferheld was contacted as a reference and he described Fry, according to a State Department official, as "intelligent but highly unstable [and] uncontrollable." Fry had "managed to irritate American officials to an extraordinary extent," and had "seriously embarrassed" the ERC. However, Seiferheld gave Fry credit for helping "a considerable number of people" to escape and for keeping his job and his "cover intact longer than . . . expected." Seiferheld suggested someone else for the job.

Still casting about for work, Fry applied in May to the Office of Facts and Figures. Although he was writing a book, he would "drop" it if he could be "useful in winning the war." Nothing came of this, and in December he applied to the Office of Foreign Relief and Rehabilitation. "If . . . I can be of service, I am always ready to drop what I am doing and answer any call which the government may make upon me." This, too, did not work out.

Fry saw that because of the war the country was different and wrote, "When I first got back it was still alarmingly isolationist, but I think it's changed. . . . The boys who thought we could sit at home and defend our own shores have had the wind taken out of their sails. . . . I think that has made a good many people realize for the first time that we can't live unto ourselves at all."

But still, no one seemed to care about the refugees. Even fewer U.S. visas were granted than before. "[T]he Department grants visas with record speed to Italian princes and the like but holds up those of refugees for months," wrote Fry, in despair over the bureaucratic "stupidity . . . cruelty, indifference and brutality." Aware that few people felt about refugees the way he did, it was not until his former secretary Lena Fischman visited the Visa Division in Washington that he received evidence of the government's inefficiency. Fischman told him that when she went to plead in person on behalf of the refugees, she witnessed refugee papers being processed so slowly that cases being worked on were months old.

They "complain that they are overworked and I believe them," Fischman told Fry. "Yet none of them miss their lunch hour and they close at 4 p.m. while refugees . . . [wait] in Europe and starve with panic." This confirmed what Fry had long believed. "People in Washington sit in great offices dealing with papers," he wrote. "It may be boring . . . but it doesn't tear their hearts out. It doesn't take their souls and twist them like towels until they can hear the fibres crack."

Now he had to become his own ERC and asked Walter Mehring, a screenwriter in Hollywood, "Do you know any people . . . who might give money?" Fry hoped to send funds to the Centre or other groups still operating in France for "small living allowances to keep [refugees] out of concentration camps."

By February 1942, obtaining visas had become "a question of wire-pulling" and only well-known refugees with influential American friends had a chance. Even cases supported by the Museum of Modern Art were on hold, but Fry did not abandon hope that "some day" artists Marcel Duchamp* and Jean Arp would emigrate.

Perhaps we can get to Archibald MacLeish. Perhaps the Attorney General, Francis Biddle, will take an interest. . . . Perhaps Mrs. Rockefeller will speak to her son, Nelson . . . and perhaps Nel-

---

*Duchamp emigrated that spring.

son Rockefeller will speak to Sumner Welles. Somehow, the thing will be done.

The number of visas issued diminished daily, Bénédite wrote. Still, the consulate was always "full of people waiting," although Bénédite feared that those who would never escape—"our orphans"—would "finish . . . in a lunatic asylum."

In 1942, the government censored Fry's mail, monitored his activities, and opened an FBI file on him. Still without his regular passport, he gave up a short-lived idea he had to become a foreign correspondent in Algiers. "I'm afraid that even if I could get a newspaper to send me the State Department would refuse me a passport. They don't like me at all." His friend, American Civil Liberties Union director Roger Baldwin, told Fry he "certainly" could file a civil liberties' case against the State Department for refusing to renew his passport. Instead, Fry continued attacking the Department for its visa policy and refusal to respond to the mass murder of Europe's Jews.

In his ongoing efforts to influence U.S. policies, Fry presented to Assistant Secretary of State Long a well-researched, thoughtful argument about the treatment of French civilians interned in camps. The Geneva Convention, which mandated humanitarian treatment of prisoners of war, should also apply to civilians who were interned, reasoned Fry. The so-called Tokio Draft Convention Proposal, created by the International Committee of the Red Cross, he explained, stated that hostile governments should "grant civil internees the benefits of the Geneva Convention." Long dismissed his careful argument and the United States continued its policy of not interfering in the treatment of civilians in French camps.

Fry next tried to send food to his friends in France and "to the anti-Fascist and Jewish refugees in the French concentration camps." Always imaginative, he also collected money for the Free French, the French government in exile under Charles de Gaulle, and applied for a license to allow him to send money to friends in the unoccupied zone. These efforts all failed.

For a few years after his return to New York, Fry maintained relations with many refugees and their families. "If I have been constant in my devotion to the refugees, it is because I believe very deeply in certain principles," he wrote, "not because I love any of the individuals among them." The daily urgent pleas were, in some way, "compensation," now that he was no longer part of the Committee.

While Fry was busy with this one-on-one work, the U.S. government's growing paranoia about America's possible infiltration by Fifth Columnists led to an investigation of organizations such as Fry's that had saved refugees. "The Report on Various Organizations and Individuals Engaged in Refugee Migration Activities" connected these refugee-aid agencies to Nazi spying and to communism. "A great danger in refugee operations," the report stated, "rests in the fact that the persons engaged in bringing these political and destitute refugees either do not know or do not care—and the record indicates the latter . . . whom they are bringing to the Western Hemisphere." The people who worked for these organizations were "tricky, deceitful, and absolutely unreliable."

Censorship of mail began after the United States' entry into the war; from the letters it intercepted, U.S. intelligence was convinced that Germany had "used the channels of refugee migration" for "infiltration" into America. The report claimed that "in return for permitting certain Jews to come to the United States . . . the Nazis demand that [the refugees] do espionage work or aid Nazi agents." It noted that "the Emergency Rescue Committee, Inc., still operates more or less independently under its own name" and named Fry as a "leading" member. Implicitly anti-Semitic, the report named a prototypical refugee "Joe Schmaltz" and his brother, "Isadore Schmaltz."

The report advised that the IRRC was "the focal point of Communistic activity in this hemisphere . . . the guiding light of a group of organizations consisting of those . . . already named and the UNITARIAN COMMITTEE, THE AMERICAN FRIENDS SERVICE COMMITTEE, and CENTRE AMÉRICAINE DE SECOURS." The report even concluded that the staff of the Centre was involved "in plans for a national revolution in France."

> Fry tells Bénédite that he has not received the propaganda material and thinks it was confiscated by the censors, so suggests that it be sent over by one of the next batch of refugees.

Most likely this "propaganda material" were newspaper summaries that Fry had requested from Charles Wolff so he could be kept up-to-date on events in Europe.

Even more than Fry, the émigrés he had saved were the subjects of intense surveillance by the U.S. government "born of concerns over Nazi infiltration and a fear that Germany might eventually establish a pro-soviet government." Franz Werfel and Lion Feuchtwanger were among those watched by the Office of Strategic Services (OSS), the FBI, the Immigration and Naturalization Service, and the State Department. Recalling the enormity of these men's struggles to escape to the freedom of America, the irony of their surveillance is immeasurable. Feuchtwanger's "dossier ran 1,000 pages," and the file on Werfel "continued for nine years after his death." As Feuchtwanger lay dying of cancer, in 1958, he was questioned roughly by immigration agents, then denied citizenship.

Fry, knowing nothing of this, continued his ambivalent relationship with the government. On July 1, 1942, he met with John C. Hughes of the OSS and tried to sell him Wolff's summaries. Fry could no longer afford the sixty dollars a month he had been paying Wolff. Would U.S. intelligence be interested? Apparently it was. "[Allen] Dulles and I are inclined to have Fry go ahead with this and underwrite the expense involved," wrote Hughes. But within a month, the OSS decided the news in the summaries was not worth the expense and ended the arrangement.

Fry still kept in touch with a number of former protégés and tried to discover the fates of others. Many, he learned, were lost because their documents had taken too long to arrive, such as Misczyslav Bortenstein,* a Polish general whose U.S. transit visa "arrived too late to save him," and Austrian Social Democrats Karl Brodek and Mr. and Mrs. Hermann Bieber, who had expired U.S. emergency visas, which "red tape prevented . . . from being renewed." All were deported.

Fry's forger, Bill Freier, wrote that while interned at Le Vernet, he had been given a twenty-four-hour leave to marry Mina, but when his child was born, he was not allowed to visit his family, "because the birth of an internee's child '*n'est pas un cas grave*'" ("It is not important"). Freier begged Fry to help him obtain visas for his family.

Nothing was as important to Fry as this refugee work, not his editorial job or his marriage. During this period, many émigrés had a hard time earning a living in the United States and Fry tried to find jobs for

*Bortenstein was number 144.

some, including his former colleague Heinz Ernst "Oppie" Oppenheimer, who had kept the books early in the operation. A production
engineer in Germany, Oppie was still "seeking a way to make himself
useful" in the United States but had not, so far, succeeded. Dyno
Loewenstein, a German who had worked at the Centre for a short
time, supported himself and his mother on seventy-eight dollars a
month, "not enough to live decently" in New York City. The artist
Charlotte Brand also had "no job and no money."

Once an award-winning novelist and biographer, and chief literary
critic for a major newspaper, Hans Natonek had come to New York
with Fry's help, but in early 1941 was forced to live on a tiny weekly
stipend from the National Refugee Service. Unable to work as a writer
or a teacher because his English was "not perfect," he asked Fry for a
reference to the Office of War Information. "I am passing through a
very hard time trying to train as a machinist, because I have to do
something to make a living," wrote Natonek. "To put it cautiously I
believe that, in my fiftieth year and after a lifetime of literary and political activities, I'll hardly be able to do so good a job as a machinist as
I would probably do as a writer." Fry contacted the National Broadcasting Company on his behalf but was informed that the government
"oppose[d] the use of any but American citizens in the preparation of
the shortwave broadcasts, or any other broadcasting."

Unable to help refugees in America, Fry continued working on people who were trapped in France. He and Eileen privately supported a
handful with their salaries. He told Anna Gruss, now the Centre's secretary, to pay protégé Rachel Schmetterling* 220 francs a week, instead of 100. "Don't fail to bill me for all of this," he wrote. "It can't
be charged to the Committee, for these people are in no sense the sort
of people the Committee was founded to help." That is, they were not
intellectuals. When he heard that Rachel's husband, Moritz, had been
interned, Fry told Gruss he would send up to ten thousand francs to
secure his release. "Let me know how much you spend and I shall see
that you get it back." Eight months later, however, Moritz Schmetterling was deported to Germany. Fry had to break the news to the
Schmetterlings' son, who was then in the United States. The boy
was desperate to find out about his mother. "If she hasn't gone east,

*Rachel Schmetterling was number 1208.

[he] would like that $50 I have been holding for his father to be given to his mother," Fry wrote Gruss, ending his letter, "Yours in gloom."

In April 1942, Fry advised a woman trying to obtain a visa for her former husband, E. A. Rheinhardt,* to refrain from using language at the State Department hearing that might imply he had communist sympathies. "Avoid . . . the use of the words anti-Nazi and anti-Fascist," Fry counseled, since most members of the Visa Applications Committee considered these terms "to be synonymous with Communists." He suggested Mrs. Rheinhardt use "Democratic" instead and "point out that Rheinhardt is a political refugee from Nazism." If her husband was a Jew, she should not mention that fact, because of the "anti-Semitism in the inter-departmental committee."

By June, Fry was ready to "beat the world and tear out handfuls of hair." Regardless of "*repeated* interventions" on behalf of Bill Freier, he had not been able to obtain a visa for him. "I have ranted and raved, written letters and made telephone calls and even gone up to the office and made speeches about it, but nothing happens." When Fry learned that Freier had been put on the last convoy east from Le Vernet, he grieved for years, believing that his little forger had died. Only decades later did he learn that Freier had miraculously survived Auschwitz.

In early summer, Fry received news he had been dreading: The Centre Américain de Secours had been raided at dawn on June 2 by the Sûreté Nationale and was closed down permanently. Bénédite protested to the Sûreté, who had a warrant to search not only the office but also the homes of those connected with the Centre, that there was no evidence of subversive activities on anyone's part. He was ignored and arrested along with other staff members and the few refugees who had the misfortune to show up. The police confiscated seven typewriters and all of the Centre's files. At Sûreté headquarters, the staff and refugees were questioned for hours about connections with the communist party. Eventually they were released, but the Sûreté kept the files, the office was sealed, and the business of the Centre was ended.

The American embassy at Vichy investigated the closing of the Centre and relayed its findings to the State Department. Assistant Secretary of State Berle sent Kingdon a copy of the embassy's report, but Kingdon did not bother informing Fry. During June, Berle and King-

---

*Rheinhardt was number 997.

don communicated often, with Berle conceding that "the Kingdon outfit" had "done some very useful work in saving refugees who would otherwise never have got out." Other than the organization's "well-intentioned but not very discreet representative, Varian Fry," wrote Berle, its work had been "constructive" and he requested the State Department to fund its continuance. He recommended "trying to help [the Centre's staff], if we can. They may save a few poor devils before the curtain goes down."

Fry and Bénédite knew nothing about this correspondence and assumed the worst, that the embassy had agreed with the Sûreté that the Centre was a communist front. Fry contacted an acquaintance at the State Department to find out what was going on. He was informed that Berle was supporting the Centre now that it was represented by Kingdon rather than Fry. But it was too late. Fry placed his trust in the other agencies still operating in France, hoping they would turn from providing relief to saving lives.

For four months after the raid, Bénédite and other Centre staff, despite having no office, "continued to help the most deserving of our cases." But in October, Bénédite wrote to the organization in New York with news that the Sûreté's arrests had led to a trial and several convictions. During the trial, "the Centre Américain de Secours was very much in the [spotlight]," Bénédite wrote, and "was considered as a 'centre de liaison' to the enemies of the [Vichy] regime." Severe sentences of "hard labor for life" were handed down to staff members, and to Karel Sternberg in absentia. Bénédite formally closed down operations, passing on open cases to the Service Social d'Aide aux Émigrants. Sadly, there were not many people left who could be helped. "[A] good number of clients have been sent to Germany," wrote Bénédite. Others were scrambling to hide from the police.

A month later, on November 8, 1942, U.S. and British troops invaded North Africa, and Vichy and the United States broke off diplomatic relations. An earlier report by Bénédite, written just before the raid, noted that since Fry's departure from France, nearly three hundred refugees had been helped to escape. Bénédite estimated the total number of refugees who escaped because of Fry and his staff at "1,500 persons who have emigrated toward the New World."

Bénédite wrote a farewell letter to the Committee before he left to join the *maquis*, the underground arm of the Resistance. He informed the Americans "that we have carried on the job as far as it was humanly possible to be done" and noted that material seized by the Sûreté in the June raid would not be returned. As a result, with a few exceptions, the Centre's thousands of files—filled with pleading letters, impressive biographies, and endless visa applications—were forever lost to history.

CHAPTER THIRTEEN

||||||||||||||||||||||||||

SURRENDER ON DEMAND

This is the story of the most intense experience of my life. I have been told that I can't tell it now; that I can never tell it. But I think I can tell it now, and what's more I think I must.

Varian Fry

D ESPITE THE CLOSING of the Centre and Fry's ouster from the ERC, what he had accomplished was not completely ignored. In November 1942, he was invited to join the sponsoring committee of the Common Council for American Unity, which honored at a dinner twenty-eight émigré Nobel prizewinners, including Otto Meyerhof, Walter's father. In December, a Philadelphia radio broadcaster, Isabella Manning Houston, produced a documentary about Fry ("Mr. X") and an "underground railroad."

It wasn't long . . . before the Gestapo realized that their victims were giving them the slip. Who was responsible? What about that American Relief Office? Tap the wires, search the mail, check up on the man in charge! But the "man in charge" smiled as he said to me: "They thought they were so clever. But they'd forgotten that the little gendarme who patrolled the beat was still a Frenchman, in spite of Vichy. He met me on the street the day the Nazis searched my office, and warned me, 'Be careful what you say on your phone.' "

The program inspired the president of the Laundry Workers' International Union to suggest that Fry be nominated for the 1942 Nobel prize "as the man who has done the most for humanity" during that year.

Nearly twelve months after the United States entered the war, Fry continued to try to change the State Department's visa policy. A valid overseas visa from the United States, he wrote, "has prevented a good many refugees from being deported during these last terrible months." The least America could do, according to Fry, was prevent the deportation of refugees to Germany by making U.S. visas easily available. "The question of what Vichy will do if the United States should decide to take in the remaining refugees," he argued, "should not prevent the United States from making up its own mind to offer them haven." Fry disagreed with the State Department's "public charge clause," which kept out people who might become financially dependent on the government. And he supported doing away with the rules against admitting people with criminal records if those "crimes" had been anti-Nazi or antifascist.

Fry was certainly only one of many who had difficulty with the State Department. In September 1942, the State Department announced that the American Red Cross would now handle all private relief operations in France, since independent humanitarian relief agencies could not be trusted, especially during a war. Despite the Unitarian Service Committee's huge effort under way in Europe at this time, Long, citing the break in relations between America and Vichy, refused to allow the Unitarians to continue their operation.

In 1942, Fry began a book about his experiences in France but found the writing difficult. He had not kept a journal, for it might have been used against his protégés, and his memory was less than perfect; he also had writer's block, caused, he thought, by his obsession with his experience. He could not differentiate "what is important" from "what is not." Finally, after a year of struggling, although he had completed a considerable portion of it, he put the manuscript aside. His difficulty in completing the book at that time likely had to do with depression.

It is all very well to tell oneself that even in a war like this books . . . must still be written and read. But it is another thing really to achieve the kind of deep concentration that one needs to do good work. I find it almost impossible, for I can never get out of my mind the terrible events of the Southwest Pacific and the Russian front.

Fry and Eileen finally separated in 1942 because, after years of "always quarreling and making up," their relationship had become "intolerable." Initially he said it was a mutual separation but later claimed that "*he* left *her*" because she was "too bossy." He was not "ecstatically happy" in his bachelor apartment, but "less unhappy" than he had been. The couple remained friends and saw each other often.

To somehow recapture the Marseille days, Fry wanted to become an officer in the U.S. Armed Services stationed in France. An attempt to join the OSS had failed. "The OSS held me at arms' length, but it asked me for all the details I could give it about the underground railroad," Fry wrote. "And, since I didn't suppose it was interested in bringing refugees out of Europe, I may have jumped to the conclusion that it wanted to use [it] to send 'Operatives' into Europe." While waiting to hear from the Army, Fry became an air-raid warden, patrolling the streets near his East Forty-ninth Street apartment.

By the end of the year, Fry began to drift away from refugee work. While he was emotionally "still living and reliving that tense full year in Marseilles," he now began to focus on trivia, such as acquiring perfectly fitted custom-made suits and shoes and maintaining a list of friends to whom he had lent books. He was at loose ends, separated from his wife, and dissatisfied with his work. "I am still lost here. . . . My wife says that I am obsessed by [Marseille]. I think perhaps I am."

To overcome his sense of displacement, Fry wrote several articles about rescue work in France and about the French underground. But nothing helped. "The massacre of the Jews continues unabated . . . the pace has actually been increased steadily," he wrote to a former protégé. "It is criminal that we content ourselves with deploring these horrible events and take no active measures to stop them." His most important article, "The Massacre of the Jews: The Story of the Most Appalling Mass Murder in Human History," was published in *The New Republic* in December 1942. In it, Fry revealed how information about the mass extermination of the Jews had been smuggled into the United States, and that American officials had known about the Holocaust to come.

According to a report to the President by leaders of American
Jewish groups, nearly 2,000,000 European Jews have already
been slain since the war began, and the remaining 5,000,000
now living under Nazi control are scheduled to be destroyed as
soon as Hitler's blood butchers can get around to them. Of
the 275,000 Jews who were living in Germany and Austria at
the outbreak of the war, only 52,000 to 55,000 remain. The
170,000 Jews in Czechoslovakia have been reduced to 35,000.
The figures for Poland, where the Nazi program has been pushed
very rapidly, are uncertain. There were 3,300,000 Jews in Poland
at the beginning of the war. . . . By the beginning of the summer
of 1942, this number had already been reduced to 2,200,000,
and deportations and massacres since that time have been on an
ever increasing scale. In the ghetto of Warsaw, in which 550,000
Jews once dwelt, there are today fewer than 50,000. In the city of
Riga, Latvia, 8,000 Jews were killed in a single night. A week
later 16,000 more were led into a wood, stripped and machine-
gunned. It is not merely central and eastern Europe which are
being "purged," or rendered "Judenrein," as the Nazis like to
say. The Netherlands has already given up 60,000 of its 180,000
Jews. Of the 85,000 who once lived in Belgium only 8,000 remain today, while of the 340,000 Jews of France, more than
65,000 have been deported. Even Norway has begun to ship her
Jewish citizens eastward to the Nazi slaughter houses and starvation pens.

Unfortunately, just as in 1935, when Fry wrote about Hitler's extermination plan, this article attracted little attention.

But he never gave up. His activities seemed endless. During 1943,
Fry helped organize the American Labor Conference on International
Affairs, which researched political and economic issues for the Ameri-
can labor movement, and became its executive director and editor of
its quarterly publication. He was hired part-time as editor in chief of
Common Sense, a liberal monthly magazine.

In early 1943, he finally heard from the Army, ripping open the envelope excitedly only to find that he had been classified 4F because of
an ulcer of "psychogenic origin." Fry knew he had a duodenal ulcer
but had not realized this would keep him from serving.

To deal with the ulcer as well as his writer's block, Fry decided to undergo psychoanalysis. He underwent a "didactic" analysis, conducted in French, with a former protégé, Dr. André Glaz. "[T]he doctor found that Varian knew so much about Freud that he gave him the same kind of analysis an MD gets." (Two years later, symptoms of his ulcer abated and Fry wrote that he felt as if he were "starting life over again with a new personality.")

During the war years, Fry never passed up any chance to strike a blow against the government, particularly the State Department. But when he wanted to, he could get along with the Department. In May 1944, he and publisher Victor Ridder and his son, journalist Walter Ridder, met with Assistant Secretary of State Berle to discuss an organization they were planning. Comprised of German Social Democrats and American labor leaders, it would promote the principles of democracy in Germany. Berle told Fry and the others that the Department had no objection to such a group; the government "allowed free speech and free organization in this country, so long as it was consistent with the conduct of the war."

During the summer of 1944, Fry returned once more to his book about Marseille and took a room at Elk Lodge in the Adirondacks, where, in only a few weeks, he completed the manuscript. The book "will remind you of those days of waiting in Marseilles," he wrote Victor Serge, "and the strange contrasts between the events of which we were witnesses and the background in which they occurred."

The book's dedication indicated that he held no grudge against Kingdon or anyone else connected with the ERC:

> For Anna Caples and Paul Hagen [Karl Frank], who began it; for Frank Kingdon, who lent it his support; for Ingrid Warburg and Harold Oram, who made it possible; and for all those who, in Switzerland, France, Spain, Portugal and Africa, forgetful of self, and sometimes at risk of their lives, carried it out.

Fry showed his completed manuscript to an editor at Houghton Mifflin, Robert Linscott, who decided to publish it.

Waiting for the book to be published, Fry continued to agonize about the fate of his friends in France. Just before Christmas 1944, he at last heard from Gemähling and Bénédite. For two years, hoping that his colleagues from the Centre would miraculously survive the war, he had been tortured by what he imagined might be happening to them. There were times when he "hardly dared hope" they were alive. "It was as though I feared that if I hoped too deeply and too strongly for you, my hope could never come true," he wrote when he finally heard from them. "If I believed in a God I would say Thank God that you are both alive and well. Since I do not believe in a God I can't thank him; but I can still be very happy."

Fry grieved, however, for two other Marseille colleagues, Jacques Weisslitz and Charles Wolff, who had been murdered. Wolff spent two years "relaying information back and forth between the French and the Spanish Resistance." Betrayed by a fellow agent who was himself tortured, Wolff was arrested by "the Milice, known as the French Gestapette," in August 1944. They beat him until he was dead.

Jacques Weisslitz, an interviewer at the Centre, and his wife were French Jews who had been denied U.S. visas. In 1942, Fry had suggested to the Weisslitzes that they wait six months, then appeal. He heard nothing for two years until he received a cable from Danny Bénédite in late November 1944: "Jacques deported Germany." Fry hoped that Weisslitz had been deported to work in Germany, since he was a skilled diamond cutter, and he responded to Bénédite's cable with a query: "Was Jacques deported as a worker or Jew?"

"Jacques and wife deported as Jews," came the answer. Although he tried, Fry was unable to find out why Weisslitz and his wife had been denied visas and found out only that the denial came after the Weisslitzes had been fully investigated by the FBI and the State Department. After their deportation, the Weisslitzes were never heard from again.

In April 1945, when Random House* published *Surrender on Demand,* the IRRC celebrated with a party. Frank Kingdon, however, took some attention away from Fry by announcing his retirement. "The publication of our story brings to an end the first phase of the work of the Emergency Rescue Committee," he wrote, adding that he

---

*Robert Linscott took the manuscript with him when he moved to Random House.

was stepping down as director of the International Rescue and Relief Committee.

As for the book itself, first reactions came from Fry's protégés. Fry was "not only a noble man but also a good writer," said writer Hermann Kesten. "Who could dare to survive the holocaust of one or two world wars—who could enjoy the thought of belonging to that so-called human race—if it were not for the existence of such real human beings as you." Kesten remained bitter toward the State Department, "those who helped to kill for they were not willing to help those whose lives were in danger." Konrad Heiden and Lion Feuchtwanger wrote enthusiastic letters to Fry, praising his book. For another former protégé, Charlotte Feibel, *Surrender* revived memories of Fry's operation, "which after one year of desperation, sorrow, strain and uselessness had given me back my first taste of life again."

Surrender also received good reviews in the press. *Brentano's Book Parade* judged it "an authentic adventure story . . . told with verve, humor and good characterization." But the best comment of all, to Fry, was by Russell Maloney of *The New York Times* who described him as "a good man [who] had added to the sum total of the world's happiness."

One of Fry's purposes in writing the book had been to expose the State Department's role in refusing the refugees admission to the United States; while a few people got the message, the book, which did not sell well, had no effect on America's views about the State Department, the war, refugees, or Jews. One reviewer, writing in the Providence, Rhode Island, *Journal,* even accused Fry of "smuggling operations [that] violated the laws of both France and the United States." Trying to set the record straight, Fry responded: "My attempts to save the lives of . . . refugees who were trapped in France . . . did sometimes violate the laws of the Vichy government but they never violated the laws of the United States."

"While this trickery embarrassed the United States Government, harmed our relations with France and caused the U.S. Government to bring pressure on Mr. Fry to stop it," the reviewer wrote in response to Fry, "Mr. Fry probably is correct when he says he violated no United States law. On this point the review probably was in error though it would take a lawyer to figure out Mr. Fry's exact status. Surely he conspired to get refugees into the United States who wouldn't have been able to get there by ordinary, legal methods."

To Fry, this last sentence validated the most important aspect of his rescue work: He *had* forced the United States to admit refugees it would not otherwise have allowed in, people who would surely have been murdered by the Nazis. And, while he used "trickery" and devious methods to achieve his ends, he did not violate any U.S. statute. Nevertheless, not everyone viewed his actions his way, and after the publication of *Surrender on Demand* the State Department was once again angry at Fry. "Apparently I have done the unforgivable thing, which is to tell the truth about them."

Fry's politics underwent a fairly radical change during this period as he turned away from the liberal ideals of his youth and began to embrace a more conservative philosophy. Before Marseille, his politics were middle-of-the-road liberal, with "a neutral liberal position arising from a good Protestant background and an education in humanism," according to historian Laurent Jeanpierre. "His education both at school and at home gave him a belief in Western values, tradition, and humanist culture." But after Marseille, he changed. His closeness to Bénédite, reliance on an underground network, and intimate knowledge of antifascist struggles combined to enhance his education in defiance and deviance.

When, after the war, two schools of liberals emerged, one antifascist and the other anti-Soviet, Fry allied himself with the anti-Soviets. Fry and a group of other anticommunists split away from the American Liberal party, claiming that "the Party had become Communist-tainted," and founded the Liberal party. Fry broke with many of his friends as he became more and more conservative in his rigid opposition to the Soviet Union and the communist party.

Contemptuous of anyone who said anything positive about Soviet Russia, Fry was now squarely on the side of fanatic communist haters such as the House Committee on Un-American Activities and Senator Joseph McCarthy. But he never supported, or even tolerated, these extremists and was furious at the McCarthy hearings.

His new conservatism had a negative effect on his ability to earn a living. Until March 1945, Fry was a contributing editor to *The New Republic,* even though he had long disagreed with its editorial policy. After the magazine published an editorial chastising the United States and Britain for abuse of power but keeping silent about the Soviet Union's "more blatant abuses of power," Fry resigned in a characteristically dramatic manner. "Frankly, it nauseates me," he wrote. "I'm just a simple American, I guess, unaccustomed, as yet, to swallowing, hook, line and sinker, Moscow's peculiar version of events. After reading your editorial I felt as though I wanted to vomit." He no longer wanted his name associated with the magazine.

After this, Fry was forever on the outs with the liberal establishment. His new affiliation, the American Labor Conference on International Affairs, which he had helped establish in 1943, was accused of being "a coalition of the anti-Soviet Social Democrats and the most reactionary leaders of the AFL," according to Samuel Sillen, writing in *New Leader* magazine. Fry and others of like mind, wrote Sillen, have joined forces with the Social Democrats in an "effort to crush the Soviet Union and the anti-fascist movement." Shortly after this, while Fry was on a tour promoting his book, the lecture bureau dropped him. No one wanted to hear his message, that the United States would eventually have to go to war with Russia.

But Fry's politics, like his personality, were never simple and could not be pigeonholed. While he criticized his government in many areas, he remained "extremely patriotic," "loved America," and never blamed his country "for not recognizing him." Instead, "he faulted the State Department . . . for being a bunch of bigots and stuffed shirts." Fry respected Roosevelt and, when the president died, sent Mrs. Roosevelt a condolence letter. "Mr. Roosevelt is the only man I have ever voted for for President," Fry wrote. "We shall, of course, learn to get on without him, but it will be very hard." He also thanked Mrs. Roosevelt for helping save refugees and sent her a copy of his book. People at the State Department continued to mock and belittle him; in a memo, one official wrote dismissively, "Incidentally, if you have a little time for light reading, you will be interested in looking over Fry's book, 'Surrender on Demand' which has just been published by Random House. . . ."

In August 1945, Fry once again became involved with refugees, interned not in France but in upstate New York. One thousand of them, mostly Jews, had been accepted into the United States but immediately placed behind chain-link fence at a camp in Oswego, Fort Ontario, near the Canadian border. They could not receive visits, nor could they leave the camp. In addition, they were informed that there was little chance they would receive U.S. immigration visas. Fry, afraid that these people would be deported, urged the U.S. attorney general to find a way to "enable the refugees now interned at Fort Ontario to obtain immigration visas to enter the United States legally."

Fry also remained in touch with some friends from the Marseille days, and even passed along gossip. Breton and his wife had separated, and Jacqueline was living with Roberto Matta, "a South American painter . . . (a nice looking guy, about half André's age)," he wrote Bénédite. Max Ernst had left Peggy Guggenheim for a student, "the greenest young woman I have ever seen." Consuelo de Saint-Exupéry still did not know the fate of her husband, reportedly "shot down over France last summer [with] no record of anyone's ever finding his plane or body." Hirschman and Verzeano were in the U.S. Army, stationed in Italy. Fry sometimes saw Mary Jayne Gold and Miriam Davenport, who were now in New York and much improved from their younger, wilder selves, he wrote.

Fry and Eileen had been separated now for more than two years, and he remained a bachelor, his only roommates Clovis and Mrs. Clovis, because, unlike Fry, Clovis "couldn't wait." Usually content living with his dogs, books, and pictures, at other times he was lonely: "The shelves of my tiny kitchen are lined with empty bottles . . . and not one of them has been opened without an invocation to your memory," he wrote Bénédite. "But I have had no one to drink them with who has appreciated them as you would appreciate them, and no one to sing the songs that go with them."

But living alone at least gave Fry time to engage in various hobbies; with his part-time editorial positions at *Common Sense* and the AF of L's *Journal of International Affairs,* he was earning a good salary, about fifteen thousand dollars a year. He joined the Gourmet Society and again indulged himself with custom-made shoes and suits. He generally found something wrong with the finished products and engaged in lengthy, vituperative battles with cobblers and tailors.

It did not seem to matter, at this point, if he was battling a cobbler or the State Department; he seemed compelled to confront everyone, small and large. And, just as he was spending increasing amounts of money, ways to earn it began to fast disappear. His main sources of livelihood, the two magazines, folded for financial reasons at the beginning of 1946. Although he signed on in January to write for *The Saturday Review,* by May it was clear that once again Fry could not accept criticism from those above him, and the magazine politely dismissed him. He submitted ideas to *Collier's*, the *Chicago Daily News*, *Coronet*, and other publications, with no success. During the summer, he was for two weeks executive editor of *Tomorrow Magazine* until he had an argument with his boss. "You and I would not agree on fundamentals if we *even* tried," wrote the editor, Eileen J. Garrett, who then asked for his resignation. He refused to resign, demanded far more than the offered two weeks' severance pay, and ended by advising the editor how to run her magazine, giving an indication as to why he had only lasted for two weeks: "Your magazine has always had the reputation of being very poorly edited. . . . If you want to lift the magazine out of the class of unprofessional publications . . . select an editor in whom you can have confidence . . . and leave it to him."

As the years passed, Fry's political involvement diminished. He served on the board of the International League for the Rights of Man from 1945 on but found himself less and less interested. He had even lost touch with his refugees and heard from practically none of them. "I wonder if you know how much your annual letter means to me?" Fry wrote to one man who corresponded with him. "Of all the people I helped in France, you are the only one to write me regularly every year on the anniversary of his arrival in the United States."

By 1946, since freelance writing and editing were not working out and Fry needed an income, he decided to try a business venture. With loans from Eileen and a friend from Marseille, Max Ascoli, he purchased Cinemart International, a small sound-recording studio and production company that made educational films and television commercials. He quickly mastered the technical aspects of sound recording and motion-picture production, but was not as effective on the business side.

Lonely and eager to fall in love and marry again, Fry began giving Friday-afternoon cocktail parties to meet women. A friend from Harvard, Jim Hess, recalled: "He invited me and lots of other male friends under the condition that we had to bring a different girl each time because he wanted to meet girls."

Fry continued to maintain his closeness with Eileen, even after their separation, and, when she was stricken with breast cancer, he nursed her until the end. Eileen, who had been working for Albert Einstein at the Emergency Committee of Atomic Scientists at Princeton, ignored her symptoms until the disease progressed too far to be treatable. Even after the cancer metastasized to her lungs, she would sit "at an open window gasping for breath with her 'flu.' In reality, she wanted to die. Earlier she had contemplated suicide," according to Miriam Davenport. Davenport, who worked for Eileen at Princeton, believed that Eileen had never gotten over the breakup of her marriage to Fry.

Eileen's illness prompted a sympathetic yet confusing note from Einstein. "I feel very sorry that you have to suffer so badly. You are too unselfish for this world and should have somebody to protect you," he wrote. "I wish with all my heart that you may soon feel well and that you will take to heart this lesson the devil has taught you." Near the end, Eileen was admitted to a hospital and Fry read to her every day, until she died, on May 12, 1948. In his tribute to Eileen, Einstein said that her death left her survivors with "a happy memory, and that intangible but abiding influence which a person of her rare qualities leaves behind."

For Fry, the loss of Eileen and the end of his involvement with political causes meant a death of sorts for him, too. Although he joined the board of the American Civil Liberties Union in 1946 and continued on at the International League for the Rights of Man, his interactions with fellow board members were increasingly acrimonious. At decade's end, though, Fry's fortunes changed in one respect, at least. During the winter of 1948–49, he met a bright, attractive, funny woman, Annette Riley, sixteen years his junior, an antidote to his sadness. They would spend the next two decades together, Fry's last years, building a life and creating a family.

CHAPTER FOURTEEN

||||||||||||||||||||||||

THE
FINAL YEARS

I have made a good life for myself. In 1950 I married a very beautiful and charming young woman and we have since had three wonderful children.

Varian Fry

ANNETTE RILEY was attracted to Varian Fry when they met. She suspected that life with him might be exciting, for he appeared to have within him "at all times an utterly unpredictable enfant terrible." Fry reminded Annette of her father, Woodbridge Riley, the "acerbic and erudite" chairman of the philosophy department at Vassar College and a man who "didn't suffer fools gladly." Annette found Fry intriguing in part because he did exactly as he pleased, with no fear of recrimination. "Also, he was fun," she recalled, "and he adored me."

Annette had been raised in comfort near the Vassar campus, in Poughkeepsie, New York, where "at age four" she "was the mascot of the 1928 class." When she was nine, her father died and her mother, Laura Troth Riley, moved back to Philadelphia with her children.

Of course, as much as Varian Fry's behavior amused and dazzled the young Annette Riley, his ignoring of social conventions did not always serve him well. The first time Annette brought the attractive older man home to meet her family—he was forty-three to her twenty-seven—Mrs. Riley served her special creamed chicken and rice. Fry pronounced the rice soggy and told his future mother-in-law how to improve it. He always behaved as if "his way was the right way" and usually convinced Annette that it was. "I was married to him for seventeen years," she said. "I thought he was god." Later on, when she realized he was not always in the right, she, as her mother had done for her father, "would sometimes go to people and try to smooth things over."

Fry "was mad to get married, have children" . . . and even a rose-covered cottage. Although Annette came to believe that Fry "was too old for me and too eccentric," when she married him on November 11, 1950, she did not consider any of this. He "had dreams of making a lot of money" and envisioned himself as a country gentleman. For several years, early in their marriage, he struggled to make Cinemart profitable so he could achieve this goal.

Cinemart did not support the couple in the style to which Fry aspired. And he was dealt a severe blow in the fall of 1951, when the U.S. Army-Navy-Air Force Personnel Security Board turned down Cinemart's attempt to bid for a government contract to make training films. Erroneous information, most likely from his FBI file, that he had been a member of the communist party since 1937 and was a "close and sympathetic associate of communist party members," kept the government from awarding him the right to bid. The charge was laughable, since Fry was so anticommunist, but its effects on his business were not. Fry assailed FBI director J. Edgar Hoover with protestations that he was opposed to communism and always had been, but Hoover denied Fry's charge that his difficulties with the government were based on "information furnished" by the FBI. Fry enlisted several prominent people to write letters on his behalf, including socialist Norman Thomas, who had run for president several times, and ACLU chairman Roger Baldwin. Finally, "Fry was cleared to bid for documentary film work with the U.S. Army," according to Annette, but no bids were awarded, and the company remained unprofitable.

Fry lacked skills in sales and marketing, and was not good at hiring a staff, quite unlike in Marseille. He "was gullible about people . . . and assumed they had his best interests at heart," recalled Annette, and as a result the people he hired often did not work out. In 1952, Fry took on a business partner who, as Cinemart began to go under, wanted to buy Fry out. Fry refused "because he had now turned violently against the partner," and as a result the company ended up in bankruptcy.

With Cinemart gone, Fry earned his living freelancing for Fortune 500 companies, writing brochures and other materials, and his substantial fees supported him for the next decade. He also wrote for magazines, ghostwrote graduate dissertations, and began a long business relationship with Coca-Cola Export. He first served as editorial director in the New York City office, and then, "by mutual agreement," returned to writing freelance. Freelance work was good for Fry; he could not be a team player unless "he was running the team."

Fry enlisted Annette to do research as well as some of the writing on his Coca-Cola assignments. By this time, the couple had two children, Thomas Varian, born on January 4, 1952, and Sylvia Woodbridge (who later changed her middle name to Varian), born on May 6, 1953. Since Annette was occupied as Fry's assistant, they hired a full-time "nursemaid."

When Fry began teaching to supplement his writing income, he discovered how much he enjoyed it. "He loved to pontificate," said his wife, "and was a wonderful teacher." Beginning in 1952, he taught creative writing for the Adult Education Department at City College. Teaching and writing worked well for Fry because they gave him a sense of autonomy; during the 1950s, Fry appeared to have worked out his life.

One evening, in the early spring of 1951, at a gathering in Westport, Connecticut, the Frys, writer Mary McCarthy, and other guests engaged in a lively debate about the investigation of *New Yorker* writer A. J. Liebling, who was alleged to be a communist sympathizer. While the others were outraged, Fry, who "enjoyed provoking his liberal friends," disagreed. "On the contrary," he said; not only Liebling, but all *New Yorker* writers "should be investigated by Congress for their fellow-traveler connections." An argument ensued, enlivened by jokes and laughter, and Fry told the astonished group of "his pleasure at being investigated by the Army Personnel Security Board when he was applying for clearance to work on a documentary film."

Not long afterward, while attending a conference, the Frys ran into McCarthy. "I don't believe Mary McCarthy ever got embarrassed," recalled Annette, "but I do believe she felt a bit awkward seeing us that afternoon for she was on her way to skewer Varian in her speech at the conference." McCarthy, in the speech and in a book of her essays entitled *On the Contrary,* called Fry a "demi-intellectual." Annette found the label funny, and she and other friends teased Fry about it. "Varian," recalled his wife, "who also never seemed to suffer from embarrassment—was actually rather sheepish about the going-over [McCarthy] gave him." Eventually, he came to laugh at it also.

By 1953, when Fry had been on the national board of the ACLU for seven years, his rigid anticommunist stance created dissension between him and fellow board members. To Fry, the communist party was "first and foremost a conspiracy, and not a true political party at all" and he was upset that some ACLU board members would "never admit this." However, he continued to take his membership on the board seriously and rarely missed a meeting. He was devastated, therefore, when his term on the board elapsed, and he was replaced in October 1956. He protested that he had not been notified that his term was expiring or been asked if he wanted to run again. At the same time, characteristically, he instructed the board on how to improve its election process. But he resigned graciously. "[T]here are few things in this world I could more keenly regret leaving than the company of the men and women who have made up the ACLU Board," he wrote. "This is not only because there is no cause which is closer to my heart than the cause of liberty. However hackneyed it may sound, it is also because I have never once forgotten what a great and rare privilege it was for me to enjoy the company of such men and women, and to match, or at least attempt to match, my wits with theirs."

In 1955, memories of Marseille came flooding back as he helped a former refugee, Margot Wolff, prove her case for indemnification, possibly one of the earliest lawsuits by a refugee against Nazi Germany. Fry, at Wolff's request, gave a deposition on her behalf, describing the effects of the "surrender on demand" clause on endangered refugees. His operation in Marseille, he wrote, had helped a former deputy of the Reichstag, Walter Oettinghaus, to escape. Since Wolff was Oettinghaus's closest associate, "[h]er personal safety was endangered not only because of her collaboration . . . but also because she is Jewish and her apprehension by the Gestapo would undoubtedly have meant her transfer to an extermination camp." To back up his point, he told the story of Jacques Weisslitz and his wife. "Had they gone into hiding before the total occupation, they might still be alive today," Fry wrote. "If Miss Wolff had not gone into hiding, she might not be alive today."

Marseille seemed remote from Fry's life during the fifties, but the experience, as well as his love of France, never left him. He longed to live there. "I can think of few things that would make me happier than to join you and Coca Cola in Paris," Fry wrote to a Cola-Cola Export executive. "Unless possibly it should be to work in the Coca Cola branch . . . in my favorite city in the world—Marseille. . . . What should I do to make the dream come true?"

In the midfifties, Fry joined the board of directors of the American China Policy Association, a conservative organization, and although Annette was "horrified," her husband "was having fun," she said. "He enjoyed confrontation, tangling. He got a kick out of riling people."

Now that he had a family, Fry, eager to be a country gentleman, told his wife that "New York depressed him and he would kill himself if he had to live [there]." He also wanted to invite his father to live with them. His mother had died in 1951, and he believed his father was lonely. Ignoring Annette's protests, Fry purchased an enormous, old twelve-room house on Olmstead Lane in Ridgefield, Connecticut, which Annette dubbed "Fry's folly." During the fall of 1956, along with Arthur Fry and Annette's mother, the family moved in. (Arthur Fry and Laura Riley stayed with Annette and Fry for one year.)

A country house fit Fry's image of himself; he was a lifelong bird-watcher and an expert mycologist, and he loved gardening. He even bred canaries in the house on Olmstead Lane. They had a huge flower and vegetable garden in which Fry worked constantly, with roses as his main passion. According to family friend Kerstin Brown, Fry "was incredibly fussy. . . . For example, how many minutes had to go by after you picked the corn until it hit the boiling water? He could make you a little crazy."

In Ridgefield, the young family lived well beyond their income, but Arthur Fry paid rent, and if they found themselves in a tight spot Fry borrowed from him. Annette typed Fry's notes and drafts for his free-lance work but over time took on much of the writing herself. Her husband indulged his various interests, which now included a return to the classical languages he had studied at Harvard. "I would say to him, 'We have this assignment,' " recalled Annette, "and he would say, 'I have to relax sometime.' "

Family life in Ridgefield became as complicated as life in the city. Annette remembered a husband with wit and humor, but she also recalled being frightened by his moods. Because of her fears, Annette never argued with her husband: "There was an inner violence there that I recognized.

"I think what began to unravel Varian was the death of his father," said Annette. Arthur died on April 3, 1958, and Fry was so shaken, according to a neighbor, that for days he would not allow the undertaker to remove his father's body.* He became concerned with his mortality and even composed his own obituary. Fifty when his father died, Fry brooded for months, and "his behavior became more bizarre." The birth of a third child, James, on July 1, improved his mood. But Arthur's death marked the beginning of a decade of emotional storms caused by real-life events as well as Fry's increasingly disturbed mood swings.

While he had not previously been upset by a lack of appreciation for his refugee work, by the early sixties he had "turned back to his wartime experiences in search of the recognition he felt he deserved." He became "obsessional once again," as he had been when he was younger, before his psychoanalysis. The marriage became a "roller coaster," according to Annette, sometimes "unbelievably awful." On the other hand, Fry remained witty and still loved to laugh and joke. Kerstin Brown said he would "bark like a dog" for fun; although it threw people, it also made them laugh. Fry "could be quite caustic . . . and a little raunchy [and] eccentric," she said.

Jokes aside, life with Fry became more and more difficult for his family as his personality began to disintegrate. He gave up writing for all corporations, except Coca-Cola, and turned back to his "first love, the classics," and teaching. Annette supported this decision, because she felt he was happiest in a classroom. And when Fry felt loving toward her, he was expressive and generous. Each year, for example, he gave her a Tiffany charm. On their tenth anniversary, November 11, 1960, along with the charm was a card that said, "They've been the best ten years of *my* life, dear—by a margin so wide it's almost infinite. I have loved every one of them, and I love you for them."

In 1960, Fry taught Latin and ancient Greek at Ridgefield High School, was a substitute teacher in Latin and French at Wilton High School, also in Connecticut, and continued his creative-writing classes at City College. After yet another blowup with an employer,

*Annette Fry does not recall this.

Fry lost his last corporate client, Coca-Cola, and the "very lucrative source of income" it had given him. Teaching could not support the house on Olmstead Lane, and in 1962 the Frys were forced to move into a smaller, more affordable house. He was no longer "lord of the manor."

In the spring of 1963, Fry was honored by the International Rescue Committee at its thirtieth-anniversary luncheon. Fry and eleven others were acknowledged "for their contributions to the cause of freedom since the committee's founding in 1933." Sculptor Jacques Lipchitz presented his friend with an IRC medal, inscribed: "With Appreciation to Varian Fry—in the service of freedom—1933–1963." A few days later, Fry heard from an old friend and protégé, Hans Sahl, who was thrilled to read about Fry's honor because he had believed him to be dead. "[Y]ou can imagine how happy I was!" wrote Sahl. "Varian still alive!"

That year, Fry took courses at Fairfield University to obtain a Connecticut teaching certificate, was finishing required classes for a master's degree in history at Columbia University, and taught Latin for a few months at Greenwich Academy in Greenwich, Connecticut. He was also working on a book about the Trojan War that was never published due to the inevitable "difference of opinion" with his editor.

Whenever life became comfortable, Fry would find a way to shift the balance. At Greenwich Academy, after learning that another teacher had reviewed exam questions with students, he wrote an angry three-page letter to the headmistress. To the academy staff, this was standard practice, but to Fry, it was "cheating and he was very moralistic about it." At the end of the semester, Fry was not rehired.

Before he left, however, he had a positive impact on two colleagues, recalled teacher Joan Austin. When he heard of her struggle to "resist the urge" to smoke, he described Eileen's death from cancer and told the young teacher she "really must" stop. Austin heeded his advice: "I have always wondered if Mr. Fry saved my life with his words." She also recalled Fry's involvement with another teacher, whose Christian Science beliefs prevented her from consulting a doctor despite her serious ailment. Upset, Fry did "research into the writings of Mary Baker Eddy and found a quotation which seemed to indicate . . . that seeking professional help in this case would not violate the teachings of Christian Science." He told the teacher, said Austin, and tried to convince her to see a physician. Austin, who knew nothing of Fry's past, once saw him "rather diffidently" hand the school librarian a book that he had written. "I assumed it was some boring treatise about Latin and never asked him about it or bothered to read it," she recalled. "How I regret this. I wish I could have talked with him about his experiences or gotten some insight into why this man could do the right thing when so many looked the other way. He seemed an unlikely hero and yet . . . his willingness to stand up for his beliefs and his wish to help others is clear."

The caring side of Fry's personality existed alongside his self-righteousness. "He was constantly correcting me," recalled Annette. "In the middle of a sentence he would correct my pronunciation, and then I would lose track completely." Once, he infuriated Danny Bénédite's sister, Zabeth, by rehanging all the pictures in her apartment. On the other hand, the "good" teacher in Fry showed Annette how to write more clearly and "built me up in many ways."

A quarter century after Marseille, an opportunity presented itself that would allow him to return to the scene of his greatest moment. "He wanted to earn more money doing something he felt worthy of his talents, and that's what got him involved with another task for the International Rescue Committee," said Annette. He devised a fund-raising idea for the IRC, which excited him as nothing had in years. Despite its promise, however, the project almost destroyed him.

> I thought I had something quite good. . . . It was to ask Lipchitz and nine or ten other 'grand old men' of art, like Chagall, Max Ernst, Henry Moore, Miro, Picasso, each to do a lithograph on the subject of Aeneas fleeing from Troy—the classical prototype of the refugee.

The IRC and Fry agreed in late 1963 that he would seek out the artists and acquire lithographs from them for a project to "commemorate the victims of the Nazi onslaught of 25 years ago." The IRC would then raise funds by selling the lithographs in a "portfolio." To Charles Sternberg,* then the executive director of the IRC, Fry was perfect for this assignment. To Fry, the commission meant he could

---

*In Marseille, Fry knew him as Karel Sternberg.

once again see his beloved France and reconnect with people from Marseille. "He was eager," recalled Sternberg. "It was a return to the battleground."

Fry signed a contract on January 16, 1964, that agreed to pay him travel expenses plus an advance against a 10 percent commission on portfolio sales. Sternberg and another old friend, Joseph Buttinger, would oversee the project. Fry discussed the theme for the portfolio with Jacques Lipchitz, the only one of the rescued protégés with whom he had remained close. Lipchitz agreed that T. S. Eliot's reference to Aeneas, "the original displaced person," was perfect.

This project meant Fry would once again be central to a critical undertaking connected with refugee rescue. It began well, with Lipchitz's donation of a lithograph valued at fifteen thousand dollars, and during the early months Fry was "quite his normal self." He contacted former protégés: Ernst, Masson, Chagall, and others to whom he had not spoken in years.

While Fry was doing this, Annette was looking for work, too. During the summer of 1964, as Fry excitedly prepared to leave for Europe, she was hired by the Democratic Committee—for whom she had worked before—and took on a housekeeper to look after the children during the week.

Only days after he signed the contract, however, Fry complained to his former colleague Marcel Verzeano about his lack of financial stability. "[Y]our life sounds much like mine," wrote Fry, "except that you have 'security' and I have none. I am still on my own and I shall never draw any pension or retirement pay." Nevertheless, he spent the fall and early winter of 1964 in Europe, trying to get commitments from recalcitrant artists. He had little success with Picasso, Chagall, and Ernst for a variety of reasons, and since there was no more expense money to support him, he returned home shortly before Christmas.

"Varian came home . . . very enthused about everything" but was dismayed to learn from Annette, whose job with the Democratic Committee had ended, that they could no longer afford to live in Ridgefield. She urged him to move with her to New York City, where she could find work, and he agreed. In January 1965, she found an apartment on the Upper West Side of Manhattan and arranged for the move. Fry returned to Europe. Then, as if he had only just realized what had happened, he sent "hysterical letters." Annette had tricked him, he wrote, and "he would die if he had to live in New York."

Fry capitulated, however, when a family friend implied that Annette's mental health was in jeopardy, and she moved into the New York apartment with the two youngest children, Sylvia and Jimmy. Tom, the oldest, was allowed to live with friends in Ridgefield and finish out the school year at Ridgefield High School, where he was popular and successful. "He was brilliant and the girls adored him," said Annette.

Fry continued to be frustrated with the artists he contacted. One possible reason for their reluctance to cooperate is that many were pro-communist; Picasso, for example, had joined the communist party in 1944 and "remained a loyal member till the end of his long life." Some artists may have objected to dealing with the conservative, anticommunist Fry despite his role twenty-five years earlier in saving their lives.

In January, Fry met with Rose, André Masson's wife, who "remember[ed] with gratitude her flight with her husband to Martinique & US with an 'emergency' visa provided by IRC." She promised that her husband would donate a lithograph. Other artists, including Jean Dubuffet and Jean Arp, rebuffed him, however. "Fry is depressed," wrote Sternberg. "He seems distraught and looks for assurance that he has 'fulfilled his contract.' " Fry felt "rejected" by Picasso and wrote, "No one ever calls me back."

"To tell you the truth," he wrote to his friend Lipchitz, "this task . . . may end up ruining me, as it drags on and on and I have almost no income whatsoever." Broke, he implored Sternberg for funds, but Sternberg instead advised him to return to New York.

Then Sternberg wrote that musician Wanda Landowska's "lifelong companion," Denise Restout, was canceling an IRC fund-raising concert in the harpsichordist's name. He asked Fry for clarification: Had Landowska been helped by his operation in Marseille? Fry replied that Landowska had been on the "budget list" and had been supported for months. After the war, she would break "away from her other admirers after concerts to greet him," he added. Fry was "positive" the operation had secured Landowska's emergency visa and passage on a boat to Martinique; he had "probably bribed the 'right man' for her to get on the boat."

Although he had no income, Fry remained in Europe, and by March 1965 he had "honest promises" for lithographs from Miró, Ernst, Masson, Giacometti, and Kokoschka. That spring, there was talk of honoring Fry for his wartime heroism, and the IRC began discussing "getting [the French] Legion of Honor for Varian Fry." And a Dr. Henry Cooper wrote to the IRC that the Taft School should present him with its Award of Merit (though nothing came of this).

Fry returned from Europe in April and, while living with Tom in the Ridgefield house, finally acknowledged that New York City was the only practical solution to his financial problems. He rented out the house, and he and Tom joined the rest of the family in the West Side apartment. Annette was working for Democratic gubernatorial candidate Howard Samuels. In July, Fry wrote an article to commemorate the twenty-fifth anniversary of the Emergency Rescue Committee, which was published in the *New Leader.*

For the twenty years since Marseille, other than confrontations with employers and his obsessive need to be right, Fry's emotions had been relatively level, probably because of the stabilizing effect of his family. But after being away from his wife and children for months, having spent two unsuccessful years trying to convince unwilling or disinterested artists to contribute lithographs, the breakdown of his personality that had begun with the death of his father accelerated. He felt unappreciated, and this, added to his frustration with the portfolio project, made him increasingly bitter. The episode in his life that had previously given him great satisfaction now brought him unhappiness.

As time went on, he grew more and more troubled. Although most of the artists were cordial, and a few, such as Lipchitz, Masson, and Lam, had promised lithographs, others—including Chagall and Ernst—put him off, time after time. How could they, when he had helped save their lives? Persistent to the point of being intrusive, he continued "batting his head on a stone wall trying to get them to hurry up and do what he wanted them to do. . . . He was very upset by this . . . [and] very disappointed."

Picasso continued to resist Fry's efforts, too, even though Lipchitz had described him to Picasso as "a legendary hero . . . who saved a great many people." Fry, ready to give up, was encouraged by Lipchitz: "I see you are confused. . . . Take care of yourself and don't torment yourself uselessly." Four months later, Lipchitz comforted Fry again as Picasso remained elusive and Fry grew more disheartened: "Above all, don't let go!"

In the fall of 1965, Fry urged Sternberg to send him back to Europe. He was "extraordinarily frustrated" and wanted to return to "get some *money* out of the enormous amount of time I have invested in this project." But Sternberg turned him down and Fry remained in New York.

The disappointments continued. Poet André Breton refused to become involved for reasons that are unclear, saddening Fry greatly, since they had been so close at Air-Bel. Breton did not even answer a letter Fry sent him. In September, Fry wrote despairingly that Chagall, "the rat . . . has done nothing and promised nothing." Ernst had not come through, either. As of September 1965, Lipchitz was the only artist who had actually completed and printed a lithograph.*

Fry grew "more and more agitated, angry, irrational." He worked on the project from home, dwelling obsessively on the house and the children. "I remember coming home from work every day and he would be telling me all the things that are going wrong at home," said Annette. He even blamed his wife for raising their children in the pollution of New York City. "He really was getting mental at this point, and would say things like, 'Don't you know the polluted air in New York is going to kill your children? To make them live in New York is as bad as stabbing them in the chest in their sleep.' "

After one argument, Annette took Sylvia with her out of town to visit a friend. When she returned, Fry said, "If you ever do that again, I'll sue you for taking my child across the state line." But his nastiness went as quickly as it came. "Then he would be perfectly fine and cheerful and we would have a nice time." When he was calm, he spent time with his children, whom he loved dearly. In January, he introduced Jimmy, then seven, to the Museum of Modern Art, then took him for ice cream and chocolate sauce in the members' lounge.

In the spring of 1966, Fry taught Latin and history at an Episcopalian day school but had his usual difficulties with the school admin-

---

*"Flight," a portfolio of original works by eleven artists, was eventually assembled and sold for eighteen thousand dollars each to benefit the IRC. Fry secured five of these works. Among the artists who contributed, four—Chagall, Lam, Lipchitz, and Masson—owed him nothing less than their lives.

istration. In class, he played "The Vatican Rag," a radical song that mocked genuflecting. And he would not correct his students' year-end examinations unless he was paid extra. When the administration refused, Fry sued. At the end of the year, his contract was not renewed.

Fry returned to Europe in the summer of 1966, more than a year after his last trip, determined to bring the portfolio project to completion. He had a joyful reunion with his old colleague Jean Gemähling at the Chagall house in Gordes, where Fry had been invited to stay by Ida, Chagall's daughter. "Happy to connect again," Fry and Gemähling spent two weeks together in July. "It was like the past, like we were really friends," recalled Gemähling. Fry was ill, he added, but attributed his agitated behavior to sunstroke.

Meanwhile, in New York, Fry's marriage was falling apart. Annette had time to think about her husband's "final taunting complaints before he left for Europe" and concluded that she could not "take this" anymore. She sent Fry a letter suggesting they separate.

Fry, in Cannes to see Picasso, was living there with a young German student, Momme Thomsen, who served as his companion and driver. By this time, Fry felt ill much of the time; he suffered from migraines and high blood pressure, and was "pathologically sensitive to light." On September 14, Fry's demeanor was so alarming that Thomsen called a doctor, and Fry was rushed to the hospital. He had had a heart attack. Depressed at being ill, Fry was cheered nevertheless because one doctor refused to believe he was an American, since his French was too good. Fry asked Annette to tell the children about his interchange with the doctor, "one of the most up-bucking experiences of my life, not noted for up-bucking experiences, especially in recent years." And, he added, "I write you all this, I guess, to read aloud to the children—*something* for them to be proud of about their father. God knows, they haven't *much*!" Later he gave her advice for them: "*Tell* the kids: *reality* never hurts; being *protected* from reality wounds for life. Look at me!"

A day later, he received her letter about separating and became hysterical: "My first impulse was to throw myself off the balcony and end my nightmare." But he rejected suicide as "a cowardly act and . . . more traumatic to my children than even the consequences of their mother's decision" and chose another way to respond. From his hospital bed, Fry mailed copies of Annette's letter to everyone they knew. "It went to Blue Cross/Blue Shield saying please drop this traitorous woman from your rolls. It went to everybody . . . to Verzeano, to Miriam Davenport," recalled Annette. Most people were too embarrassed to respond, but Lipchitz wrote to Fry, "I don't think it's a good idea to wash your dirty linen in public." Tom and Sylvia, then fourteen and thirteen, also received the letter, Annette remembered. "I remember these kids were sitting at the kitchen table and both of them handing me the letter and saying, 'I don't want this.' "

Annette had expected her husband's response to be extreme and had written, "I'm really frightened writing this to you because I don't know what your reaction will be." Fry was then taking a laundry list of medications to control his emotions, according to Annette, including the tranquilizer Valium, Elavil (a mood elevator), and the sleeping pills Nembutol and Doriden. "Furious" at Annette, fearful he would lose his children, he was also "lonely" and broke. Sternberg advanced him some cash and he booked passage home on the *Queen Mary* for November 24. Before he sailed, he asked a friend to contact Annette to see "if he couldn't return to the apartment. He apparently was very anxious to get back with us."

Fry returned from Europe a quiet, chastened man. Despite Annette's request for a separation, the couple agreed to stay together for a while. They made the effort, but the marriage, trembling and fragile, would not survive. In December, Fry signed a contract with Scholastic to rewrite *Surrender on Demand* for a young audience. His publisher had instructed him to "develop each chapter so it ends on . . . a 'cliff hanger' " in order to make the book appealing to younger readers. But Fry found the revision a struggle: "I have only just begun to write the new book, and I find it is not easy."

This may have been due in part to his failing health. He believed he was suffering from angina pectoris, the "pain . . . which follows a coronary thrombosis." Fry wrote that doctors attributed his illness "to tension . . . due to trying too hard on an impossibly difficult job in too little time." He was now "virtually bedridden" with bursitis. Still determined, however, to complete the portfolio, he continued to implore the artists, with little success. Dejected, he wrote, "I started active work on the album of lithographs in September 1964. Here it is, February 1967, and what do I have to show so far for all my efforts? Signed lithographs by Lipchitz, Masson and Miró, and a proof of Max Ernst's lithograph." Fed up with Chagall's procrastination, Fry called him "that old charlatan."*

In mid-March, Fry learned he had been nominated a Chevalier de la Légion d'Honneur for his rescue work during World War II. "I am at last being decorated," wrote an exuberant Fry, who believed the award had been arranged by writer André Malraux. "I made it possible for him to communicate freely with General de Gaulle in 1941, when Malraux was in France and de Gaulle in London." Fry received the honor on April 12, 1967, at the French consulate in New York City. Mary Jayne Gold, whom he saw whenever she visited New York, was at the ceremony; Albert Hirschman and his wife were also present. Afterward, the Conseiller Culturel threw a "good party with lots of excellent champagne," but Fry proclaimed that "the party Mary Jayne gave . . . was even better." He was proud that his children saw him being honored:

> My two boys stood like sentries . . . and when it was over my daughter rushed up to me, threw her arms around m[e], whispered "Oh, Daddy, I'm so proud of you I can't stand it" and burst into tears on my shoulder. Then my two boys came up and proudly shook my hand.

Fry was becoming more and more agitated, according to Annette, and "he wasn't getting along with people." He wrote letters obsessively, even falling in love with one pen pal, a doctor in New England with whom he exchanged letters for months. He told everyone that he was in love and that he and Annette were "separating and divorcing, alas. There just doesn't seem to be anything left between us but tension."

"She is a doctor, and I think he wanted somebody to take care of him because he was obsessed with his health," said Annette, who finally learned of this long-distance love affair when her husband broke the news to her in June 1967. This woman was everything Annette was not, according to Fry. "You are just a suburban housewife," he said.

*Ernst did not do a lithograph for the portfolio, and while Chagall contributed one, he did not sign it. Charles Sternberg recalled an article that "touched on Chagall's generosity yet 'unnecessary stinginess.' This mix is not uncommon, though in Chagall's case it seems to be on the extreme side."

"She is sophisticated and cultured, full of life, full of excitement." Then he asked for a divorce. Lawyers drew up a separation agreement, but Annette and Fry continued to live together. (He visited his new love several times, but the relationship never developed.)

Fry informed his agent, Josephine Rogers, that nothing was coming of his book revision either. "I have not succeeded in finding a way of telling my enormously complicated story both clearly and interestingly. . . . [T]here were hundreds of characters. . . . It's worse than WAR AND PEACE!"

In July, he asked a friend, Caleb Gray, to collaborate on the book, since he would be teaching Latin at Joel Barlow High School, in Redding, Connecticut, in the fall and would not have much time to write. Gray agreed to "rough it out" for one-half the advance, about eighteen hundred dollars.*

Fry and his family spent the next few weeks in a relatively peaceful state although, on occasion, his paranoia became disruptive, such as when he insisted they "were being poisoned by methane gas coming through the drains" of the bathrooms. On Wednesday, August 23, he checked himself into New York University Medical Center to find out the cause of his "strange headaches, attacks of dizziness, ringing and voices in the ears." During the checkup, doctors found no evidence of an earlier heart attack. Nor did they come up with a diagnosis for the symptoms he was then experiencing, although two weeks later their cause would become tragically evident.

Fry still wanted a divorce, and on Sunday, August 27, Annette flew to El Paso, Texas, and obtained a Mexican divorce the next day in Juárez. Back in New York, she visited her husband in the hospital and found that he was no longer "the manic, cold person he had been all summer. . . . He asked me in a sweet way how I was doing. He said he was deeply depressed." Later that day, he called to ask her if he could live in the apartment with the family for a few days. Annette agreed, and on Wednesday, August 30, he came home. He had changed suddenly from an agitated man to a thoughtful, responsible husband and father and immediately took over handling family matters. The next day, he put nine-year-old Jimmy on a train to Norwalk, Connecticut,

---

*The revised version of *Surrender on Demand* was published under the title *Assignment: Rescue* in 1968.

where he was to visit friends, and Sylvia left for a weekend in Province-town. On Saturday, Fry took Tom, then fifteen, to Connecticut to help him move some things into a house in Easton that he had rented from sculptor Louise Bourgeois and her husband, Robert Goldwater, where he would live while he taught at Joel Barlow High School.

Back in New York by Sunday night, after Tom went out with friends, Fry and Annette found themselves alone. They talked "to-gether for a long time, holding hands." Fry cried, while Annette tried to comfort him. The next day he was "desolate" and could not "bear to have [her] out of his sight." They shopped for groceries for the Easton house and again talked for hours. "How did this all ever come about?" he asked sadly. By the time he had to leave, they were both near tears. Fry left finally and drove to Connecticut. When he arrived at the Easton house, he found that Bourgeois's son had removed Fry's things from the bedroom he intended to use and placed them in a smaller one. Fry, in his fragile state, was upset by this.

On Tuesday and Wednesday, September 5 and 6, Fry attended teacher orientation at Joel Barlow High School, and he taught classes on Thursday and Friday. Friday night, he had dinner with Kerstin Brown. "He was terribly depressed," she recalled, "but sorry for him-self in such a self-dramatizing way that it was funny as well as sad." Sat-urday morning, he called Annette. "He was so blue" that she invited him to spend the weekend in New York: "Come in here right away. . . . Spend the weekend with us. We'll have dinner." When he arrived at the apartment, he threw his arms around her, sobbing. They discussed "the misunderstandings of the past year" and Fry spent time with his children with "all his old warmth and gentleness." Sunday night, An-nette helped him load the car. She felt happy; they had plans to see a Mozart opera the following weekend, and it almost seemed possible that they might even renew their relationship now that Fry was being reasonable.

Monday, September 11, was Fry's third and final day of teaching. His last conversation that night was with his old Marseille colleague Marcel Verzeano. Fry had called him to verify some facts for the book. "He told me that he enjoyed his new position in teaching," remem-bered Verzeano, "that the job would allow him to keep in close touch with his family—which made him very happy. . . . His tone was confi-dent and optimistic."

When Fry did not show up for work on Wednesday, the school called Annette, who immediately telephoned the Connecticut State Police. She gave them her husband's address and asked them to see if he was all right. When they arrived at the house, they found Fry in bed. He lay there, dead, surrounded by scraps of papers and notes, facts and reminiscences about that singular year in Marseille, his glory days with him in his moment of death as they had lived in his heart all the years since.

AFTERWORD

Dear Mary Jayne,
Varian died peacefully the other night. Can you notify Danny and
others?

love, Annette

FRY'S OBITUARY in *The New York Times* said he "helped intellectuals flee Nazis. . . . Led group that got Lipchitz, Chagall,
Werfel and others out of Occupied France." His hometown paper, *The
Ridgefield Press,* described him as a "writer and teacher." Friends, former protégés, and family remembered Fry and the contributions he
made at a memorial service on Wednesday, November 8, 1967, two
months after his death from a cerebral hemorrhage.

Jacques Lipchitz said, "In some ways, I owe him my life." Lipchitz
had not wanted to emigrate, but Fry "helped me finally to do so. . . . I
mourn with you this marvelous man, lost a little in our difficult
world." Letters arrived from his Marseille colleagues. Fry "was that
rarest of all creatures . . . a Good Man," wrote Miriam Davenport.
Danny Bénédite wrote to Tom, Sylvia, and Jim about their father's
heroic resistance before there was a Resistance. He "arrived in France
at a time when there was terrible chaos, extreme depression, and
among the refugees he was coming to assist, terrifying panic," wrote
Bénédite. "In the midst of an ocean of cowardice, compromise and betrayal, he remained lucid and energetic, relying at times on his intrinsic
integrity and at times on his sense of humor. . . . A man other than

who he was would have succumbed to the first pressures from American authorities who found him to be an embarrassment, the first persecutions by the police, the first attempts on his life. . . . Fry remained in France until the last possible moment, stating that as long as one case remained, his mission would not be accomplished."

After her husband's death, Annette Fry grieved for the enigmatic and difficult man she had loved. "The saddest and most heartbreaking thing about Varian's death is that he had changed so in the final two weeks. Suddenly he had waked up from the strange sick life he had been living all summer." She was concerned that his death might be due to a mix of drugs and alcohol but "did not consider suicide" even though he had "talked of this off and on for years." The coroner gave the cause of death as a "cerebral vascular accident"—a stroke—which might explain the headaches and dizziness he had suffered during the summer.

During the last years of his life, before manic depression was a common diagnosis, no one gave a name to Fry's problems, but "he was always up and down," recalled Annette. Often, he "was enormously loving [and] spent a lot of time with [the children] with their homework and everything else under the sun." On the other hand, he sometimes threatened to hit his two older children, Tom and Sylvia. Fry's death devastated the children because they had no time to resolve their feelings toward him. Sylvia "adored him [but] was angry at him for some of this treatment. . . . It was the worst thing that could happen that he died at that time," said Annette.

Remembering with love someone who hurt you is difficult. Fry's sudden death, after years of irrational behavior, led to many family problems. When Tom, "depressed about the death of his father," became a heroin addict, Sylvia told Annette: "Tom is shooting up." But Annette, unprepared at forty-three to be a widow and sole support of three children, refused to believe her daughter until the day she found Tom's drug paraphernalia. Lost, Tom dropped out of the Bronx High School of Science, took part in the Rockefeller drug program, then "just ran away" to California. He began drinking. In June 1974, back in New York, he fell off a wall on Riverside Drive and hit his head. "No one was with him to explain" the exact circumstances of the accident. He remained in a coma until he died on September 11. He was twenty-two.

Today, having survived these tragedies, Annette Fry recalls her husband as a caring, warm, and often funny man who also "had a lot of neuroses," but whose sweetness just before his death moved her. "He was so horrified at what he had done. He had alienated his children and made me get a divorce. I sometimes think he died of a broken heart."

Fry's heart had suffered many blows and breaks along the way, beginning with his prescient—but largely ignored—1935 article informing Americans that the Jews of Europe were about to be annihilated. His magnificent work in France gratified but also hurt him. After the war, he would have appreciated an apology from the State Department. That apology did come, nearly fifty years later, along with other posthumous honors, which, one could argue, were all too late. Fry was made an honorary citizen of Israel for his rescue of Jews during the Holocaust. The U.S. Holocaust Memorial Council awarded him the Eisenhower Liberation Medal in 1991. Two years later, the U.S. Holocaust Memorial Museum paid tribute to him in its inaugural exhibit, "Assignment: Rescue, the Story of Varian Fry and the Emergency Rescue Committee."

Fry became the only American in the esteemed group of sixteen thousand men and women who saved Jews during World War II when, in 1996, he was named "Righteous Among the Nations" by Yad Vashem, Israel's Holocaust memorial. "When we honor someone like this, we always ask how many people in his place would have gone as far," said Mordecai Paldiel, director of the Department for the Righteous. According to one journalist, "Fry was different from most other 'righteous gentiles' because his own country was never occupied by Nazi Germany."

At the Yad Vashem ceremony, then-U.S. secretary of state Warren Christopher offered an apology for the State Department's treatment of Fry.* "We come to pay tribute to . . . Varian Fry, a remarkable man and a remarkable American," said Christopher. "Regretfully during his

---

*With the declassification of war-era papers, researchers have documented that in 1940–41, the Fry years in Marseille, the State Department knew what the Third Reich was up to. ". . . the Third Reich was killing people it deemed useless," reported U.S. vice consul Paul H. Dutko on October 16, 1940. In early 1941, Assistant Secretary of State Berle told Secretary of State Hull "of reports from the embassy in Berlin that Jews were being sent to 'unnamed concentration camps in Poland.' "

lifetime, his heroic actions never received the support they deserved from the United States government, including, I also regret to say, the State Department."

Both the 104th Congress, in pending legislation, and the New York State Assembly have honored Fry for his "contributions and efforts to assist others."

And Walter Meyerhof, now a professor emeritus of physics at Stanford University, has established the Varian Fry Foundation/IRC, a project of the International Rescue Committee, to disseminate information about Fry. "I feel sad that the man died unrecognized. . . . I feel I owe him a debt, so it is his memory I honor."

By the end of his life, the idealistic young hero who risked his life for others in Marseille had become "like a racehorse hitched to a wagon load of stones." But that was all right: He lived on past triumph, the time when he waged a life-and-death struggle against the greatest evil of the twentieth century.

Acknowledgments

The scope of this story was such that I required considerable assistance, and I was fortunate to receive it from a number of talented, generous people. I am thankful to translator Maria Barnett, and researchers Esther Ratner, Amy Raff, and Maria Waller. Drafts were critiqued by Anita Kassof, a curator of the original Fry exhibit at the U.S. Holocaust Memorial Museum, by Professor Albert Hirschman, a colleague of Fry, and by my friend, Jed Horne, city editor of *The Times-Picayune.*

I am most grateful to the John F. Kennedy Library for awarding me the Abba P. Schwartz Research Fellowship for 1999.

For providing detailed information and countless contacts, I am thankful to Walter Meyerhof, creator of the Varian Fry Foundation. I am greatly indebted to the generous and spirited Annette Fry for providing me with invaluable interviews, traveling to Harvard and Columbia on my behalf, and allowing me access to her notes, photographs, and memorabilia.

My gratitude to others who helped with translation, research, transcription, and other aspects of my work: Fernande Angiel, Sarah

Beaver, Malcolm Collins, Chantal Deravin-Jayet, Bill Epstein, Judith Fischetti, Joanne Jaworski, Donna Kaplan, Rabbi Jonathan Kliegler, Susan Mesina-Bromberg, Erica Pagerey, Diana Pollin, Robyn Pollins, Michelle Rawl, Judith Reichler, Bonnie Sgarro, librarians at the M. E. Grenander Department of Special Collections and Archives at SUNY Albany, the staff at Columbia University's Rare Book and Manuscript Library, the International Rescue Committee, the New York Radical Debutantes, and Dominique Troiano and Dennis Ambrose and the outstanding editorial staff at Random House.

Fry's family and friends were generous in answering my endless questions, as were historians and others familiar with some aspect of his life: Joan Austin, Stephanie Barron, Bruce Bassett, William Bingham, Arthur Brenner, Kerstin Brown, the late Linette Burton, John Crowley, Pryor Dodge, Virginia Dortsch, Charles Ebel, Carolyn Goodman Eisner, Sarah Farmer, Robert Fishback, James Fry, Jim Hess, Laurent Jeanpierre, Richard Kaplan, Arnold Kramish, Walter Langlois, Reynold Levy, Susan W. Morgenstein, Jay Parini, Kate Bandler Ransihoff, Jack Sanders, Pierre Sauvage, Martica Sawin, Sonya Turitz Schopick, Sylvia Fry Severino, John Spalek, Nancy Stern, Richard Venus, Teri Wehn-Damisch, Michelle Weston, David Wyman, and Constanze Zahn.

I am deeply grateful to the men and women who told me about their experiences during the war, including those too young to remember, who heard it from their parents: Martha Adler, Christine Reitlinger Angiel, Helene Bénédite, Peter Bénédite, Peter Berczeller, Frances Berczeller, Victor Bers, Claire Ehrmann, Aube Breton Elléouët, Margaret Enoch, John Ettinger, Sophie Freud, Lucy Frucht, Delphine Herold-Wright, Stephane Hessel, Michael Kaufman, Elizabeth Koenig, Gys Landsberger, Franz Leichter, Henry Leichter, Lolya Lipchitz, Elizabeth Wittlin Lipton, Tilde Loewenstein, Fern Malkine, Eva Marcu, Margrit Osner, Jeff Sippil, Ruth Sender Stern, Charles (Karel) Sternberg, Kurt Sonnenfeld, Robert Stowe, and Dina Vierny.

I owe much to Fry's extraordinary colleagues from the *Centre Americain* who shared with me their memories and impressions: the late Miriam Davenport Ebel, Charles Fawcett, Jean Gemähling, Professor Hirschman, Justus Rosenberg, the late Bil Spira (Bill Freier), and Dr. Marcel Verzeano.

I thank my literary agent Elizabeth Kaplan, who believed in this book from the beginning and, as always, advised me well, and with heart. And I cannot overstate my appreciation to my editor, Bob Loomis, whose knowledge and critical and editorial skills guided me.

My daughter, Sunshine Flint, brought Varian Fry to my attention and for that, as well as her love and encouragement, I am grateful. Above all, to my husband, Chris Collins, for love, support, and endless hours of work on this book—I can never thank you enough.

In memory of Penny Lebow.

Notes

AOH   Albert Otto Hirschman
ARF   Annette Riley Fry
DB   Danny Bénédite
EF   Eileen Fry
MDE   Miriam Davenport Ebel
VF   Varian Fry
WM   Walter Meyerhof

EFPR   Exiles Film Project Records, Beinecke Rare Book and Manuscript Library, Yale University
GEC   The German Emigré Collection, M. E. Grenander Department of Special Collections and Archives, State University of New York at Albany
NA   National Archives
SF   Sealed files. Excerpts from papers in Varian Fry's sealed file, Office of the Registrar, Harvard College, compiled by Annette Fry, May 17, 1999
VFP   Varian Fry Papers, Rare Book and Manuscript Library, Columbia University

PREFACE

CHAPTER ONE: **THE DIXIE CLIPPER**

3   *Dear Eileen, We*   VF to EF, August 5, 1940, VFP.

4   *Fry left behind*   EF to VF, August 5, 1940, VFP.

4   *His paternal grandfather*   ARF interview, May 5, 1998.

5   *"hand nailed to"*   Gold, *Crossroads Marseilles 1940,* xvi.

5   *"The enemy is"*   Serge, *Memoirs of a Revolutionary, 1901–1941,* 355.

5   (*It was at*)   VF to Anna Caples, April 27, 1945, VFP.

5   *When Frank first*   Laurent Jeanpierre interview, March 19, 1999.

6   *Frank had been*   Chester, *Covert Network: Progressives, the International Rescue Committee and the CIA,* biographical glossary, 243.

6   *Niebuhr, formerly a*   "Niebuhr, Reinhold," Encyclopædia Britannica Online.

6   **"Julia," described by Lillian*   Charles (Karel) Sternberg interview, September 16, 1998.

6   *Founded in 1934*   Sheets, ed., *Encyclopedia of Associations: An Associations Unlimited Reference,* vol. 1, 1330.

6   *"heartbroken rage"*   Serge, 356.

6   *Article Nineteen of*   Armistice Agreement Between the German High Command of the Armed Forces and French Plenipotentiaries, Compiegne, June 22, 1940.

6   *"'Germans' included Austrians"*   Wyman, *Paper Walls,* 137.

6   *This government, led*   MDE, *An Unsentimental Education,* ms., 8–9.

7   *Vichy's plans to*   Dr. Sarah Farmer at New School panel discussion, "Assignment: Rescue, Then and Now," January 30, 1998.

7   *"points of departure"*   Wyman, 152.

7   *wrote to Eleanor*   Gold, xiii.

7   *Niebuhr asked the*   Spinelli, *Die Dringlichkeit des Mitleids und die Einsamkeit, nein zu sagen* [*The Need for Compassion and the Loneliness of Saying "No"*], translated from the German by Maria Barnett, 174.

8   *Fry said he*   Ibid., 177.

8   *The ERC took*   Gold, xviii.

8   *"The President has"*   Eleanor Roosevelt to VF, July 8, 1940, VFP.

8   *"In the end"*   VF, notes to self for manuscript of *Surrender on Demand,* VFP.

8   *"I believed in"*   VF, notes to self for manuscript of *Surrender on Demand,* VFP.

9   *"1,000 German anti-Nazi[s] . . ."*   Frank Kingdon to Benjamin Huebsch, June 18, 1940, VFP.

9   *"nativistic nationalism"*   Wyman, 3.

9   *"fear of the"*   Ibid., 10.

9   *"persons likely to"*   Ibid., 3.

9   *"2 percent of"*   Barron with Eckmann, *Exiles & Emigres, The Flight of European Artists from Hitler,* 18.

9   *"the solidity of"*   Wyman, 209.

9   *a 1938 survey*   Ibid., 47.

9   *Of the roughly*   Anderson, ed., *Hitler's Exiles,* 1.

9   *United States was reluctant*   Ibid.

9   *"10,000 Jewish children"*   Ibid., "Chronology of Events," 15.

10   *And he did*   Wyman, 211.

10   *"The half-filled"*   Ibid.

10   *"But the value"*   Ibid., 212.

10   **"was not the"*   Ibid., 221–222.

10   *"On the eve"*   Rubenstein, *The Myth of Rescue,* 39.

10   *"endangered European labor"*   Wyman, 138.

11   *"Is there no"*   Eleanor Roosevelt quoted in Gold, xiv, from Muriel Gardiner and Joseph Buttinger, *Damit Wir Nicht Vergessen: Unsere Jahre 1934 bis 1947, in Wien, Paris und New York,* (Vienna: Wiener Volksbuchhandlung, 1978) 153–154 (translation by Anna Caples).

11   *"It is due"*   Karl Frank to Eleanor Roosevelt, quoted in Gold, xiv.

11   *"to delay and"*   Breckinridge Long memo to Adolf A. Berle, Jr., and James C. Dunn, quoted in Wyman, 173.

11   *"been very generous"*   Breckinridge Long diary entry for September 1940, quoted in Jacobs, "A Friend in Need," 394.

11   *"the President's Committee"*   Ibid.

11   *"very careful to"*   Ibid.

11   *"[i]mpossibility" of India*   Morse, *While Six Million Died,* 38–39.

11   *approval of fascism*   Ibid., 40–41.

11   *His views of*   Wyman in *Paper Walls* and Feingold, *The Politics of Rescue: The Roosevelt Administration and the Holocaust, 1938–1945.*

12   *When Long and*   Jacobs, "A Friend in Need," 397.

12   *He claimed to*   In reality, Bohn was financed through the Jewish Labor Committee via the German Labor Delegation and the Italian Emergency Rescue Committee. Ibid., 398–399.

12   *The contract gave*   VF contract letter with ERC, August 3, 1940, VFP.

13   *"France is in"*   VF to EF, August 12, 1940, VFP.

13   *"It's a Spanish"*   Ibid.

13   *"of drains and"*   VF, *Surrender on Demand,* 3.

13   *to find out*   Ibid., 4.

13   *"hard-looking, peroxide"*   MDE, *An Unsentimental Education,* 12.

13   *A guard yelled*   VF, *Surrender on Demand,* 4–5.

14   *That night, Fry*   Ibid., 5.

14   *"the world is"*   Werfel quoted in his *New York Times* obituary, August 27, 1945.

14   *"When the last"*   Ibid.

14   *"time of great"*   Werfel, *The Song of Bernadette,* 6.

14   *"made a career"*   VF to Lena Fischman Fagan, November 27, 1965, VFP.

14   *One of her*   Gold, 182.

14   *"one of the leading"*   VF, *Surrender on Demand,* 57.

14   *"wondrous history of"*   Werfel, 6.

15   *"You must save"*   VF, *Surrender on Demand,* 6.

15   *if a refugee*   AOH interviewed by Richard Kaplan, EFPR.

16   *"two emigrations from"*   Anderson, 2.

16   *Under the September*   Wyman, 28.

16   **"Of the refugees"*   Ibid. 137.

16   *German Jews were* Anderson, ed., Chronology of Events, 9–18.

16   *Fry and Bohn* VF, *Surrender on Demand,* 11.

17   *This anti-Semitism* Judt, "France Without Glory," 38.

17   *"spread all over"* "The Emergency Rescue Committee in France" (this report consists mainly of extracts from letters written to the New York office by the ERC representative in Marseille, between the end of September and the beginning of December 1940), VFP

17   *"American in Marseille"* Charles (Karel) Sternberg interview, September 16, 1998.

17   *"When you get"* MDE, *An Unsentimental Education,* 12.

18   *Born in Dresden* Hans Sahl, "On Varian Fry," Anderson, 154.

18   *"[W]ho should open"* Sahl, *The Few and the Many,* 305–307.

18   **Sahl was number 1155* Liste Complète des Clients du Centre Américain de Secours, 1940–1944, Andover-Harvard Theological Library, included some individuals who were not clients of the Centre; others who were saved and/or helped by Fry are not named.

18   *He consoled* Claire and Henry (Heinrich) Ehrmann in A Book of Tribute to Varian Fry.

19   *"The most difficult"* Zuckmayer, *Second Wind,* 277.

19   **Carl Zuckmayer married* Michelle (Michaela) Weston interview, June 3, 1999.

20   *On his fourth* VF, *Surrender on Demand,* 14.

20   *"I am afraid"* VF to EF, October 31, 1940, VFP.

20   *Some of the "great"* VF, *Surrender on Demand,* 156.

20   *enlarging his mandate* Jean Gemähling interview, March 20, 1999.

21   *"The people who"* MDE interview, May 16, 1998.

21   *"not strictly kosher"* MDE interview, May 15, 1998.

21   *"neither humanity nor"* Serge, 364.

21   *"Visas were granted"* Ibid., 364.

22   *"were among the"* Robert Neumann to P.E.N., November 11, 1939, Ullmann file, GEC.

22   *"only one . . ."* "Biographical sketch of Mr. Ludwig and Mrs. Irene Ullmann" by Dr. Ernst Lothar, Ullmann file.

22   *"the Hungarian border"* Ludwig Ullmann to "My dear sire," August 4, 1940, Ullmann file.

22   *In his letter* Ibid.

22   *"who would be"* Mildred Adams to Erwin Piscator, August 29, 1940, Ullmann file.

22   *"[A]s of today"* Ludwig Ullmann letter, October 17, 1940. Ullmann file.

22   *Ten months after* ERC memo, June 16, 1941, Ullmann file.

23   *"continue to help"* Adrienne Gessner-Lothar to Ingrid Warburg, July 9, 1941, Ullmann file.

23   *In Marseille, Fry* Danny Bénédite to Lotte Loeb, December 16, 1941, Ullmann file.

23   *"the appropriate American"* President's Advisory Committee to International Rescue and Relief Committee, May 12, 1942, Ullmann file.

23   *Six days later* Frank Kingdon to Centre Américain de Secours, May 18, 1942, VFP.

23   *The Ullmanns finally* "Report on Various Organizations and Individuals Engaged in Refugee Migration Activities," August 8, 1942, NA, Department of State Division of Communications and Records, (RG 59), General visa correspondence 1940–1945, files 811.111 refugees/2000–2149, box 159, folder 2055 ½, pp. 51, 57, NA.

CHAPTER TWO: AUGUST: ARRIVAL

24   *The only thing* AOH at New School panel discussion, "Assignment: Rescue, Then and Now," January 30, 1998.

24   *"France is now"* DB, Auxiliary Services Report, VFP.

24   *"about the worst"* AOH interviewed by Richard Kaplan, EFPR.

25   *"the old sort"* AOH at New School panel discussion, "Assignment: Rescue, Then and Now," January 30, 1998.

25   *"particular merit because"* Ibid.

25   *"anti-Nazi refugees who"* AOH interviewed by Richard Kaplan, EFPR.

25   *"tried to save"* AOH at New School panel discussion, "Assignment: Rescue, Then and Now," January 30, 1998.

25   *The French could* Marrus and Paxton, *Vichy France and the Jews,* 112.

25   *"continued at least"* Ibid., 70.

25   *Three organizations that* http://motlc.wiesenthal.com/text/x10/xr1019.html

26   *"the immigrant agreed"* Wyman, *Paper Walls,* 140.

26   *"did not have"* Wyman, 140.

26   *"had to assure"* Ibid.

26   *"coordinating efforts to"* Ibid., 138.

26   *"to check carefully"* Ibid., 145.

26   *"on the basis"* Ibid., 150.

26   *"certainly were not"* AOH interview, December 16, 1998.

27   *"facilitate the Gestapo's"* Wyman, 150.

27   *"secret sailings"* DB, Auxiliary Services Report, VFP.

27   *"guards on the"* Ibid., 3.

28   *Heinrich, a German* Claire Ehrmann interview, September 12, 1998.

28   *After escaping, he* Ibid.

28   *"the famous Gestapo"* VF to Henry (Heinrich) Ehrmann, August 31, 1943, VFP.

28   *"hit it off"* Claire and Henry (Heinrich) Ehrmann interviewed by Richard Kaplan, EFPR.

28   *"forced . . . off"* Claire Ehrmann interview, September 12, 1998.

28   *"pointed out . . ."* Ehrmanns interviewed by Richard Kaplan, EFPR.

28   *The Ehrmanns set* Ibid.

29   **The Ehrmanns made* Birth announcement of Michael Max Walter Ehrmann, June 23, 1942, VFP.

29   *"in French uniform"* Ehrmanns interviewed by Richard Kaplan, EFPR.

29   *"someone who knew"* AOH interview, March 10, 1998.

29   *After leaving his* MDE, *An Unsentimental Education,* ms., 21.
29   *"with large, innocent-looking"* Ibid.
29   *Fry immediately nicknamed* Ibid.
29   *"very likeable, very"* AOH interviewed by Richard Kaplan, EFPR.
30   *"this evil thing"* Ibid.
30   *"He was the"* VF to EF, February 9, 1941, VFP.
30   *"an ebullient Polish"* Gannett, "Books and Things," *New York Herald Tribune,* May 1, 1945, VFP.
30   *"a talent for"* Ibid.
30   *"organized the office"* VF to EF, April 21, 1941, VFP.
30   *"both the* Almanach" Gold, *Crossroads Marseilles 1940,* 167.
30   *did not aid communists* Ibid., 156.
31   *"in underground operations"* AOH interviewed by Richard Kaplan, EFPR.
31   *"rounded up a"* "The Emergency Rescue Committee in France," VFP.
31   *"the representative of"* Ibid.
31   *"tremendous catastrophe"* AOH interviewed by Richard Kaplan, EFPR.
32   *"refugees in distress"* VF, *Surrender on Demand,* 34.
32   *Fry found that* MDE interview, May 15, 1998.
32   *Fry furnished the* MDE, *An Unsentimental Education,* 20.
32   *"in those days"* Gold, 169.
32   *"visas to give"* Charles Fawcett interview, August 6, 1998.
32   *"You are certainly"* Ibid.
32   *"Usually Jews would"* Ibid.
33   *Pretending to be* Ibid.
33   *"One little Scottish"* Ibid.
33   *the Montredon estate* Sawin, *Surrealism in Exile and the Beginning of the New York School,* 121.
33   *"radical theatre director"* Ibid., 377.
33   *"doorman and bouncer"* Charles Fawcett interview, August 6, 1998.
34   *"I felt awful"* Ibid.
34   *Miriam Davenport was* MDE interview, May 15, 1998.
34   *One day, Walter* MDE, *An Unsentimental Education,* 17.
34   *Her first impression* Ibid., 17–23.
34   *Davenport told Fry* Ibid., 12.
34   *She also described* Ibid., 12–13.
35   *"Do you do typewriting?"* VF to MDE, August 27, 1940, VFP.
35   *"Varian and I"* MDE interview, May 15, 1998.
35   *Fry presided over* MDE, *An Unsentimental Education,* 23.
36   *"He wanted very"* AOH interview, February 16, 1998.
36   *"We always wondered"* Ibid.
36   *"An unlikely hero"* MDE interview, May 16, 1998.
36   *"wasn't the sort"* Ibid.
36   *"By the end"* MDE, *An Unsentimental Education,* 23.
36   *One night Fry* MDE interview, May 16, 1998.
37   *"Mickey Mouse"* Ibid.
37   *"there was always"* AOH interviewed by Richard Kaplan, EFPR.
37   *One day, Fry met* Charles Fawcett interview, August 6, 1998.

37   *"the only way"*   AOH interviewed by Richard Kaplan, EFPR.
38   *theirs "was a very"*   Ibid.
38   *Although Fry and Hirchman*   Ibid.
38   *Vochoč "was willing"*   Gold, 155.
38   *"I had to give"*   AOH interview, December 16, 1998.
38   *Young Bill Freier*   Bil Spira (Bill Freier) interview, August 1, 1998.
38   *"more free than"*   Ibid.
39   *"squint-eyed, dubious"*   VF, *Surrender on Demand*, 43.
39   *He "had a double"*   Bil Spira (Bill Freier) interview, August 1, 1998.
39   *"We would try"*   Ibid.
39   *He needed a spot*   AOH interviewed by Richard Kaplan, EFPR.
39   *"had been spent"*   Ibid.
39   *Le'on "Dick" Ball*   Charles Fawcett interview, August 6, 1998.
40   *Fry had Hirschman*   AOH interviewed by Richard Kaplan, EFPR.
40   *"clients who were"*   MDE, *An Unsentimental Education*, 21.
40   *"distraught . . . by the"*   AOH interviewed by Richard Kaplan, EFPR.
40   *"One of my major"*   VF to Lilian Mackey Fry, November 3, 1940, VFP.
40   *"There were innumerable"*   VF to EF, October 31, 1940, VFP.
40   *"had a very clear"*   Jean Gemähling interview, March 19, 1999.
41   *"ordinary refugees"*   MDE interview, May 15, 1998.
41   *"old Mensheviks"*   Ibid.
41   *"[R]are indeed were"*   Marcel Verzeano, Report on "The problem of emigration as it existed in September 1940," October 27, 1941, VFP.
41   *"clung [and] sat"*   Henry (Heinrich) Ehrmann interviewed by Richard Kaplan, EFPR.
42   *"Eden is admirable,"*   VF to Herman Wouk, March 14, 1955, VFP.
42   *I'll tell you*   Wouk, *Marjorie Morningstar,* 506.
42   *"For three years"*   Ibid, 510–511.
42   *In August 1940*   This story is from a February 1999 interview with "Bruno and Klara Barth," a German couple who emigrated to the United States and settled in the Northeast.
45   *"It was an"*   Henry Leichter interview, September 14, 1998.
45   *the Nea Hellas*   Franz Leichter interview, February 23, 1998.

CHAPTER THREE: **EARLY DAYS**

46   *for us it*   AOH interviewed by Richard Kaplan, EFPR.
47   *Christian practice and*   ARF interview, May 5, 1998, and ARF revised "chronology," January 2, 1999.
47   *"He would have"*   Ibid.
47   *He taught manual*   Ibid.
47   *"migration of children"*   ARF, *The Orphan Trains,* 19.
47   *"whole life was"*   VF, *The Children's Migration,* ms., 1, VFP.
47   *He spoke with*   ARF interview, May 5, 1998.
47   *Despite "a long"*   Ibid.

48   *those sisters, Laura*   Ibid.

48   *Two years later*   ARF memo to Esther Wojcicki and Walter Meyerhof, August 24, 1997.

48   *"She had 'nervous'"*   VF, *Tribute to the Memory of My Father Arthur Varian Fry,* delivered at the Memorial Service, in the Chapel at The Community Church, 40 East 35 Street, New York City, April 11, 1958, VFP.

48   *When she was*   ARF memo to Esther Wojcicki and Walter Meyerhof, August 24, 1997.

48   *In business, Arthur*   Ibid.

49   *"to bed and"*   VF, *Tribute to the Memory of My Father Arthur Varian Fry.*

49   *"[B]anal though the"*   VF note to himself, n.d., VFP.

49   *The Summer Home*   VF, *The Children's Summer Home,* ms., 1, VFP.

49   *"I try to"*   Charles Reuben Fry, quoted in VF, *The Children's Migration,* ms., 15, VFP.

49   *"He called every"*   VF, *Tribute to the Memory of My Father Arthur Varian Fry.*

50   *"My father never"*   Ibid.

50   *"I have sometimes"*   Ibid.

50   *He was a*   ARF interview, May 5, 1998.

50   *"tender-hearted" boy*   ARF interview, May 1, 2000.

50   *"looked somewhat disappointed"*   Ernest F. Keller, "Bird Surgery on a Waxwing," N.Y. Zoological Society Bulletin, May 1919, VFP.

51   *"sunshine into a"*   VF to Arthur Fry, n.d., VFP.

51   *Fry ended his*   ARF note to author, May 1999.

51   *"he had to"*   Ibid.

51   *"depths of melancholy"*   VF to Arthur Fry, n.d., VFP.

51   *"aggressive party"*   Ibid.

51   *"That was the"*   ARF note to author, January 15, 2001.

51   *managed to obtain*   ARF interview, October 13, 2000.

51   *In December 1924*   ARF interview, March 8, 1999.

52   *"The fundamental principle"*   Hotchkiss Students' Handbook, 1922–1923, 22.

52   *As a result*   ARF interview, March 8, 1999.

52   *"unalterably opposed to"*   Acting headmaster Walter Buell to Arthur Fry, December 15, 1924, SF.

52   *"defiance of power"*   Perry London, quoted in Peter Steinfels, "For the young, a lesson in the acts of the 'Righteous Gentiles,' who defied the Holocaust," *The New York Times,* May 12, 1990.

52   *"The headmaster explained"*   VF, *Tribute to the Memory of My Father Arthur Varian Fry.*

52   *"seems very unlikely"*   Teresa J. Oden, Hotchkiss archivist, to Annette Fry, November 1, 1993.

52   *According to Fry's*   ARF interview, May 5, 1999.

52   *Living up to*   VF, *Tribute to the Memory of My Father Arthur Varian Fry.*

52   *His retelling of*   ARF interview, May 5, 1999.

52   *"an appreciation of"*   Horace Taft to Riverdale headmaster Frank Hackett, October 5, 1922, SF.

52 *"fixed ideas as"* Arthur Fry to Horace Taft, May 15, 1925, SF.

53 *"Mrs. Fry has"* Ibid.

53 *"frankly confesse[d] an"* Riverdale headmaster Frank Hackett to Horace Taft, October 7, 1925, SF.

53 *"the more sophisticated"* Conversation between ARF and Ferdinand Thun, January 1994, recounted by ARF in note to author.

53 *"He had become"* Handwritten report by Riverdale headmaster Frank Hackett on VF's Harvard admission form, March 23, 1926, SF.

53 *His first sexual* ARF interview, May 5, 1999.

53 *"It was like"* Ibid.

54 *"Here is a"* Handwritten report by Riverdale headmaster Frank Hackett on VF's Harvard admission form, March 23, 1926, SF.

54 *"thoughtful, scholarly, shy"* Edward H. Warburg to Chester N. Greenough, Dean of Harvard College, August 24, 1926, SF.

54 *"a kink somewhere"* Ibid.

54 *With others, Kirstein* Kirstein, *Mosaic: Memoirs,* 107.

54 * *With George Balanchine* Hamovitch, ed., *The Hound & Horn Letters,* 6.

54 *"These two kids"* ARF interview, May 5, 1999.

55 *"thought the* Advocate" VF letter in *The Harvard Advocate,* no. 2, Christmas 1934, 93.

55 *"Varian's tart antagonism"* Kirstein, 103.

55 *"make a sensation"* VF letter in *The Harvard Advocate,* no. 2, Christmas 1934, 93.

55 *"A Harvard Miscellany,"* Kirstein, 104.

55 *"snatched a tag"* Ibid.

55 *magazine was "funded"* Hamovitch, 5.

55 *"The poem became"* Kirstein, 103.

55 *"[W]e felt that"* VF letter in *The Harvard Advocate,* no. 2, Christmas 1934, 93.

55 *"Such a man,"* M. F. Werner, review of *Mein Kampf* in *Hound & Horn,* winter issue 1933, quoted in Hamovitch, 4.

55 *"Varian established the"* Kirstein, 104.

55–56 *"assistant, curator, treasure"* *Boston Post,* November 11, 1930.

56 *"to hail the"* VF letter in *The Harvard Advocate,* no. 2, Christmas 1934, 93.

56 *"it wasn't a"* Kate Ransihoff interview, February 1999.

56 *"hot intellectuals for"* Ibid.

56 *Ten years later* Kirstein, 106.

56 *"fair classical scholar"* Ibid., 101.

56 *"He felt his"* Ibid.

56 *"that there is"* Definition of the New Humanism of the 1920s, *Oxford Companion to American Literature,* sixth edition, James D. Hart, ed. (Oxford University Press, 1995), 308.

56–57 *real "family quarrel,"* VF letter in *The Harvard Advocate,* no. 2, Christmas 1934, 93.

57 *"an extraordinarily brilliant"* Katharine Hayes Durand to Henry and Elizabeth Urrows, March 29, 1990.

57   *Katherine Durand recalled* Ibid.

57   *"It was to"* VF letter in *The Harvard Advocate,* no. 2, Christmas 1934, 93.

58   *He learned that* Riverdale headmaster Frank Hackett to Harvard Dean C. N. Greenough, April 1, 1927, SF.

58   *After too many* Arthur Fry to C. N. Greenough, April 26, 1927, SF.

58   *In April of* VF petition "To the Administrative Board of Harvard College," April 24, 1928, SF.

58   *He overplayed his* Pink form for Academic year 1927–1928, Office of the Registrar, Harvard College, SF.

58   *That summer, Fry* ARF interview, May 5, 1999.

58   *Fry, while driving* Summons from the "Commonwealth of Massachusetts" to appear November 25, 1928 "to give evidence . . . relative to the death of one James Carroll," SF.

58   *"was found not"* ARF note to author, January 15, 2001.

58   *"was incapacitated somewhat"* Dr. Paul H. Means to Assistant Dean L. C. Keyes, April 30, 1929, SF.

58   *"girl in trouble"* VF, *Tribute to the Memory of My Father Arthur Varian Fry.*

59   *Still the rebel* "Harvard's Faw Down and Go Boom Class Makes Whoopee," *Evening American,* June 10, 1929.

59   *"One told the"* Ibid.

59   *This was too* Dean A. C. Hanford to VF, June 12, 1929, SF.

59   *was an "able"* Professor William C. Greene to Dean A. C. Hanford, June 13, 1929, SF.

59   *"older and wiser"* EF to Dean A. C. Hanford, July 24, 1929, SF.

60   *He had lined* VF to Dean A. C. Hanford, July 24, 1929, SF.

60   *In the fall* Assistant Dean L. C. Keyes to VF, September 13, 1929, SF.

60   *a midnight soiree* Catering bill, November 18, 1929, SF.

60   *he was arrested* VF to EF, cable, April 13, 1930, SF.

60   *"wistfully whether two"* VF to EF, cable, April 14, 1930, signed "the yellow pussin," SF.

60   *"guilty of malicious"* VF to EF, cable, April 14, 1930, signed "Christian student," SF.

60   *"go straight [back]"* VF to EF, cable, April 19, 1930, signed "Obedient Puss," SF.

60   *Eileen was in* ARF note to author, January 15, 2001.

61   *Eileen Avery Hughes* EF obituary, *The New York Times,* May 13, 1948, 25.

61   *"bossed him around"* ARF interview, May 5, 1998.

61   *"foreign trade, European"* "Application for employment—Harvard Alumni Placement Service," July 17, 1931, SF.

61   *was "European representative"* Ibid.

61   *Several months earlier* "Couple to wed in college romance," *Boston Post,* November 11, 1930.

61   *they were married* News clipping, n.d., VFP.

62   *"lived in freezing"* Barr, "Rescuing Artists in World War II," ms., revised January 7, 1980, 4.

62   *"so poor they"* ARF revised "chronology," January 2, 1999.

62   *Then Fry got* Ibid.

62   *He and Joseph* "Idle Collegians March Today," *Washington Times,* May 3, 1933.

62   *he "felt shy."* ARF memo to Esther Wojcicki and Walter Meyerhof, August 24, 1997.

62   *"appropriate money to"* "Jobless Alumni Hit U.S. Chamber," *Washington Evening Star,* May 2, 1933.

62   *thirty graduate credits* Columbia University Office of the Registrar, "note . . . sent at the request of Mr. Varian Fry" listing courses taken in the Graduate Faculties of Columbia, June 12, 1967, SF.

62   *"material from the"* Notes by Quincy Howe for his talk at VF's Memorial Service, November 8, 1967.

63   *"Nothing so became"* Ibid.

63   *As the editor* VF, sworn deposition regarding early years in Germany, November 1954, VFP.

63   *"going to Berlin"* Barr, "Our Campaigns. Alfred H. Barr, Jr., and the Museum of Modern Art," 39.

63   *In Berlin, Fry* VF, sworn deposition regarding early years in Germany, November 1954, VFP.

63   *"saw the S.A."* VF, "The Massacre of the Jews," *The New Republic,* December 21, 1942.

63   *the first pogroms* Julie Goodyear, *American Rescuers: Varian Fry,* ms., 37.

63   *The next day* "Beaten Berlin Jew Dies, Dr. Kleinfeld Succumbs to Injuries," *The New York Times,* August 1, 1935.

64   **Upon his graduation* Information about Hanfstaengl is from his FBI file, no. 100-76954.

64   *"I only half"* VF, "The Massacre of the Jews."

64   *"Extermination was, I"* VF, "The Massacre of the Jews."

64   *"emergence of the"* VF to Reverend Robert A. Graham, March 16, 1967, VFP.

64   *"German people are"* VF radio talk quoted in *The Ridgewood News,* August 15, 1935.

65   *"sweet, shy young"* Sonya Turitz Schopick to author, October 11, 1998.

65   *Fry became editor* VF résumé, 1950.

65   *"alerted young readers"* ARF interview, January 6, 1999.

65   *In 1937, at* Ibid.

65   *"got a kick"* Ibid.

66   *At the beginning* List of special cases, brought by Charles Joy, VFP.

66   *"were displeasing to"* Bernard Kadin, biography of Paul Krantz, December 3, 1940, submitted to U.S. State Department, Krantz file, GEC.

66   *"If the German"* Ibid.

66   *"grave danger of"* Mildred Adams to Ives R. Simon, October 16, 1940, Krantz file.

66   *Elena Krantz contacted* Elena Krantz-Noth to Heinz Ernst Oppenheimer, November 18, 1940, Krantz file.

66   *"almost three months"* Elena Krantz-Noth to VF, January 15, 1941, Krantz file.

67   *By this time*   Series of memos between VF and Danny Bénédite, February to April 1941, Krantz file.

67   *"continue to carry"*   Ibid.

67   *On the Fourth*   Bernard Kadin to International Rescue and Relief Committee, June 16, 1942, Krantz file.

67   *"All is okay."*   Jacques Weisslitz to VF, June 3, 1941, Krantz file.

CHAPTER FOUR: **OVER THE MOUNTAINS**

68   *Nothing that's human*   Marta Feuchtwanger quoted in Burt A. Folkart, "Marta Feuchtwanger, Widow of Famous Novelist, Dies," *Los Angeles Times,* October 30, 1987.

68   *By September, more*   Panel discussion, afternoon session, *Colloque Varian Fry, Sauvetage et résistance à Marseille: Varian Fry et le Centre Américain de Secours,* March 19, 1999.

68   *"We had no"*   AOH interviewed by Richard Kaplan, EFPR.

69   *"close surveillance by"*   VF to *Auswartiges Amt* (Foreign office), Germany, July 21, 1967, VFP.

69   *the Gestapo, becoming*   VF, *Surrender on Demand,* 50.

69   *Breitscheid had been*   *Der Grosse Brockhaus,* 1953, F. A. Brockhaus, Wiesbaden, 318, VFP.

69   *Hilferding had been*   Ibid., 442.

69   *Bernhard was former*   Gys Landsberger interview, November 15, 1998.

69   *"I want to"*   Ibid.

69–70   *"Gussie is a"*   MDE, *An Unsentimental Education,* 10.

70   *"low-winged monoplane,"*   Gold, *Crossroads Marseilles 1940,* 37.

70   *before donating it*   VF, *Surrender on Demand,* 87.

70   *"Big, beautiful, and"*   MDE, *An Unsentimental Education,* 11.

70   *If Fry agreed*   Ibid., 27.

70   *Hirschman, always on*   Ibid.

70   *"[about seven thousand]"*   In 1940, one dollar equaled 49.19 francs. Exchange rate from "Foreign Exchange Rate Database," http://www.globalfindata.com/freeexc.htm.

70   (*Karel Sternberg, future*)   MDE interview, May 15, 1998.

70–71   *"rank-and-file"*   Gold, 204–205.

71   *"herself a little"*   AOH interviewed by Richard Kaplan, EFPR.

71   *"If we had"*   VF to DB, October 20, 1941, VFP.

71   *"I was not"*   MDE interview, May 15, 1998.

71   *"a little bit"*   AOH interviewed by Richard Kaplan, EFPR.

71   *"a Corsican businessman"*   VF, *Surrender on Demand,* 45.

72   *"turned out to"*   Lewis Gannett, review of *Surrender on Demand* in "Books and Things," *New York Herald-Tribune,* May 1, 1945, VFP.

72   Nea Hellas *passengers,*   Kurt Sonnenfeld interview, February 1999.

72   *"asked me to"*   Claire Ehrmann interview, September 12, 1998.

72   *Käthe Leichter*   Franz Leichter interview, February, 1999.

72	*Berczeller was a boy* Peter Berczeller interview, October 2, 1998.
72	a *"joint venture"* Kurt Sonnenfeld interview, February 1999.
73	*"During these six"* DB, Accessory Services Report, VFP.
73	*"pepper in the"* Interview of guide in *Marseilles-New York: L'Etat de Piège ou La Filière Marseillaise*, a film by Teri Wehn-Damisch.
73	(*He never quite*) MDE interview, May 15, 1998.
73	*"Early autumn tour"* Map of escape route drawn by Karl Frucht, n.d.
73–74	*"Leaving Banyuls-sur-Mer; go"* Ibid.
74	*"Some of them"* Lucy Frucht interview, June 29, 1998.
74	*"remained a haunting"* Gold, 176.
74	*"widely read" writer* Henry (Heinrich) Mann obituary, *The New York Times*, March 13, 1950, 21.
75	*"As he became"* Folkart, "Marta Feuchtwanger, Widow of Famous Novelist, Dies."
75	*"had to flee"* Feuchtwanger, "The Grandeur and Misery of Exile," 169.
75	*"the health resort"* Gold, 189.
75	*His rescue, he* William Bingham interview, November 19, 2000.
75	*"out of his"* AOH interviewed by Richard Kaplan, EFPR.
75	*"Bingham was a"* Mary Jayne Gold interviewed by Richard Kaplan, EFPR.
76	as *"Harry's friends"* Gold, 190.
76	*"most solidly grounded"* Simon, "Mann and 'SuperMann,' " *The New York Times Book Review*, April 12, 1998, 12.
76	*He lived in* Golo Mann interviewed by Richard Kaplan, EFPR.
76	*"some not very"* Ibid.
76	*Heinrich Mann was* Heinrich Mann obituary, *The New York Times*, March 13, 1950, 21.
76–77	*"As Fry rather"* Charles (Karel) Sternberg interview, September 16, 1998.
77	*Adler, born in* Ibid.
77	*"He was not"* Ibid.
77	*"the romantic excursion"* Golo Mann interviewed by Richard Kaplan, EFPR.
78	*Werfel, noting that* VF, *Surrender on Demand*, 64.
78	*"[S]he was always"* Golo Mann interviewed by Richard Kaplan, EFPR.
79	*"the head of"* VF, *Surrender on Demand*, 70.
79	*After the others* Ibid.
79	*In fact, said* Gold, 187.
79	*"would get them"* AOH to John Wheeler-Bennett, British Press Service, January 17, 1941, VFP.
79	*He also passed* VF, *Surrender on Demand*, 72–73.
79	*The next morning* Ibid., 73–74.
80	*"The problem for"* AOH to John Wheeler-Bennett, British Press Service, January 17, 1941, VFP.
80	*Hoare would give* Ibid.
80	*"should never involve"* Ibid.
80	*Although Hoare offered* Ibid.
80	*"by some Catalan"* Ibid.

81 *Although by the* Panel discussion, afternoon session, *Colloque Varian Fry, Sauvetage et résistance à Marseille: Varian Fry et le Centre Américain de Secours,* March 19, 1999.

81 *The others were* Gold, 202.

81 *"spread panic"* Ibid.

81 *"Nobody refused on"* AOH interviewed by Richard Kaplan, EFPR.

81 *"was particularly poignant"* AOH interviewed by Richard Kaplan, EFPR.

81 *"thin,"* Zuckmayer, *A Part of Myself: Portrait of an Epoch,* 231.

81–82 *"He looked rather"* Charles (Karel) Sternberg interview, September 16, 1998.

82 *"would have killed"* Ibid.

82 *"a miserable little"* Ibid.

82 *"felt his star"* Gold, 173.

82 *After Fry gave* Charles (Karel) Sternberg interview, September 16, 1998.

82 *"he had hidden"* Ibid.

82 *"he pleaded the"* Gold, *Crossroads Marseilles 1940,* 174.

82 *"pesthole of a"* MDE interview, May 1998.

82–83 *Our Prison camp.* Mehring, *No Road Back,* 57.

83 *Fry heard of* VF, *Surrender on Demand,* 49.

83 *"from your compatriots,"* Gold, 202.

83 *"purple and green"* MDE interview, May 16, 1998.

83 *I suddenly became* MDE, *An Unsentimental Education,* ms., 31–32.

83 *"If they valued"* Ibid.

83 *"towering height and"* Ibid.

84 *"because he was"* MDE interview, May 16, 1998.

84 *"conceited, grafting, demanding"* VF to Golo Mann, September 3, 1942, VFP.

84 *"announced severe curtailment"* Wyman, *Paper Walls,* 143.

84–85 *"that tighter [immigration]"* Ibid., 144.

85 *"not of the desirable"* Breckinridge Long, quoted in Ibid.,

85 *"[They] are lawless"* Breckinridge Long diary, 1941, Quoted in Ibid., 145.

85 *"to fight [it]"* Breckinridge Long diary, 1940, 184, cited in Ibid., 147.

85 *This government cannot* U.S. State Department cable, quoted in MDE, *An Unsentimental Education,* 33–34.

85 *It was at* MDE interview, May 16, 1998.

85 *Feeling betrayed by* VF to EF, October 31, 1940, VFP.

86 *"clerks, doormen, and"* Ibid.

86 *Fullerton tried for* MDE interview, May 16, 1998.

86 *"It appears . . . that"* VF to EF, October 31, 1940, VFP.

86 *On September 23,* MDE interview, May 16, 1998.

86 *"I am now"* EF to VF, September 22, 1940, CFP.

87 *The Vichy police* MDE, *An Unsentimental Education,* 34.

87 *"The most diseased"* "The Emergency Rescue Committee in France," VFP.

87 *"People who run"* MDE interview, May 15, 1998.

87 *"I am enclosing"* U.S. Consul Hugh Fullerton to U.S. Chargé d'Affaires H. Freeman Matthews, August 14, 1941, VFP.

87 *"have long since"* VF to EF, October 8, 1940, VFP.

87 *"It's a very"* Mary Jayne Gold, interviewed by Richard Kaplan, EFPR.

88 *"My greatest story"* Michael Kaufman interview, December 14, 1998.

89 *Fry had given* Dina Vierny interview, April 1999.

89 *Vierny had been* Ibid.

90 *"There was in"* Charles (Karel) Sternberg interview, September 16, 1998.

CHAPTER FIVE: THE DOORS CLOSE

91 *It is the* VF to Lilian Mackey Fry, November 3, 1940, VFP.

91 *Sometime during* VF, *Surrender on Demand*, 86.

91 *After the couple* VF to Mildred Adams, September 1940, VFP.

92 **"I am now"* David Schneider to VF, March 10, 1942, VFP.

92 *In the beginning* VF, *Surrender on Demand*, 85.

92 *"the Gestapo had"* Wyman, *Paper Walls*, 151.

92 *"We escaped but"* Golo Mann interviewed by Richard Kaplan, EFPR.

93 *"the outstanding literary"* Hannah Arendt, introduction in Walter Benjamin, *Illuminations*, 2.

93 *He asked for* AOH interview, June 17, 2000.

93 *Benjamin, perhaps the* Lloyd Spencer, "Walter Benjamin: Some Biographical Fragments," http://www.wbenjamin.org/biog.html.

93 *†Harvard University recently* Ibid.

93 *†A monument to him* *Lisa Fittko: But We, We Said, We Will Not Surrender,* a film by Constanze Zahn © 1998.

93 *†"It is more arduous"* Walter Benjamin, quoted in Ibid.

93 *"prose rhythms . . . matched"* Heilbut, *Exiled in Paradise*, 5.

93–94 *Benjamin, rounded up* Lloyd Spencer, "Walter Benjamin: Some Biographical Fragments," http://www.wbenjamin.org/ biog.html.

94 *"apparently on orders"* Fittko, *Escape Through the Pyrenees*, 104.

94 *"a detachment of"* Marrus and Paxton, *Vichy France and the Jews*, 69.

94 *"Not to go,"* Walter Benjamin, quoted in Fittko, *Escape Through the Pyrenees*, 104.

94 *"His goal was"* Ibid., 107.

94 *That night, faced* Jacobs, "A Friend in Need: The Jewish Labor Committee and Refugees from the German-Speaking Lands, 1933–1945," 402.

94 *"I don't think"* Charles (Karel) Sternberg interview, September 16, 1998.

95 *In the morning* Fittko, *Escape Through the Pyrenees*, 115.

95 *The day after* Golo Mann, interviewed by Richard Kaplan, EFPR.

95 *"was not one"* Charles (Karel) Sternberg interview, September 16, 1998.

95   *"Hitler would take"*   Ibid.

95   *[T]here is something*   Hannah Arendt, "We Refugees," in Anderson, *Hitler's Exiles: Personal Stories of the Flight from Nazi Germany to America,* 255.

95   *"Now, it seemed"*   VF, *Surrender on Demand,* 85.

95   *"overrun by this"*   AOH interviewed by Richard Kaplan, EFPR.

96   *"That's one problem"*   Charles (Karel) Sternberg interview, September 16, 1998.

96   **The writer Stefan*   "Zweig, Stefan," Encyclopædia Britannica Online.

96   **Arthur Koestler*   "Koestler, Arthur," Encyclopædia Britannica Online.

96   **Nellie Mann*   VF to Jean Gemähling, January 9, 1945, VFP.

96   *"Another one of"*   VF to Mildred Adams, September 1940, VFP.

96   *Benjamin was the*   "The Emergency Rescue Committee in France," VFP.

96   *The others were*   VF, *Surrender on Demand,* 31.

96   *"Give me ten"*   VF to ERC, "Some Notes on Money," October 22, 1940, VFP.

96   *"able and well"*   Abrams, "The Multinational Campaign for the Nobel Peace Prize for Carl von Ossietzky."

96   *had been found*   VF, *Surrender on Demand,* 31.

96   *Karl Einstein hanged*   VF, *Surrender on Demand,* 31.

96   *Photographer George Reisner*   VF, notes for first draft, *Surrender on Demand,* VFP.

97   *"German Socialist of"*   Gold, *Crossroads Marseilles 1940,* 256.

97   *"postpone their own"*   Lisa Fittko: *But We, We Said, We Will Not Surrender.*

97   *"those abrupt precipices"*   Maurice Verzeano report, "The problem of emigration . . ." October 27, 1941, VFP.

97   *Banyuls-sur-Mer's Mayor Azéma*   Fittko, *Escape Through the Pyrenees,* 122–123.

97   *"It has to"*   Ibid., 127.

98   *Then, suddenly, at*   VF cablegram to EF, October 1, 1940, VFP.

98   *"without condemning dozens"*   VF to ERC, October 1, 1940, VFP.

98   *"[S]ituation refugees desperate"*   VF to EF, October 12, 1940, VFP.

98   *"spoke bluntly of"*   Marrus and Paxton, 12.

98   *"[f]oreign Jews were"*   Ibid., 20.

98   *"to make the Jews"*   Dr. Sarah Farmer, New School panel discussion, "Assignment: Rescue, Then and Now," January 30, 1998.

99   *"enjoyed the blessing"*   Block and Drucker, *Rescuers: Portraits of Moral Courage in the Holocaust,* 112.

99   *"It would be"*   Léon Berard, ambassador to the Vatican, to Marshal Pétain, quoted in Ibid.

99   *"that a French"*   Gys Landsberger interview, November 15, 1998.

99   *"The laws were"*   Gold, 226.

99   *Fry saw, in*   Ibid.

100   *No other occupied*   Block and Drucker, 112.

100   *During this crisis*   VF, *Surrender on Demand,* 86.

100   *"special punishment camp"*   Lerner, "A Michelin Noir," 50.

100   *"considered politically dangerous"* Kahn, *Generation in Turmoil*, 195.

100   *Food was scarce* Lerner, 50–51.

100   *"without inner resources"* Kahn, 196.

100   *"No outsiders were"* Lerner, 50.

101   *Fry invited Gold* MDE interview, May 15, 1998.

101   *their "shaven heads"* Gold, 222.

101   *"the Nazis had"* Margo Pfeffer in A Book of Tribute to Varian Fry.

101   *"I didn't know"* Mary Jayne Gold, quoted in *Marseilles-New York: L'Etat de Piège ou La Filière Marseillaise*, a film by Teri Wehn-Damisch.

101   *"We simply had"* MDE interview, May 15, 1998.

101   *"go off and"* Gold, 227.

102   *The "whores"* [*in*] Ibid., 228.

102   *"Je vais me"* VF, *Surrender on Demand*, 89.

102   *"skipper . . . an old"* Ibid., 88.

102   *the police were* Ibid., 150.

102   *But the ship* DB, Accessory Services Report, VFP.

102–103 (*At the trial*) Ibid.

103   (*Eventually, all four*) Gold, 400.

103   *"Must request you"* The Foreign Service of the United States of America, American Consulate, Marseille, France, October 3, 1940: "Dear Mr. Fry, The American Embassy in Vichy has just telephoned the following telegram which has been received for you from . . . the Department of State: MUST REQUEST YOU RETURN IMMEDIATELY COMMA NOT ONLY IN VIEW OF OUR UNDERSTANDING BUT ALSO OF LOCAL DEVELOPMENTS WITH RESPECT TO WHICH YOU ARE FAMILIAR (Signed) Sincerely yours, Hugh S. Fullerton, American Consul," VFP.

103   *"of unidentified American"* *The New York Times,* October 6, 1940.

103   *"by Dr. Frank"* *The New York Times,* October 14, 1940.

103   *"They gave us"* MDE interview, May 16, 1998.

103   *"to get in"* William T. Stone to EF, October 15, 1940.

103–104 *A Mr. Pell* Ibid.

104   *"Blücher I'd known"* AOH interview, December 11, 2000.

104   *With the Centre's* Young-Bruehl, *Hannah Arendt: For Love of the World,* 158–159.

104   *"provided by HIAS"* Ibid.

104   *"contributed money to"* Carolyn Goodman Eisner interview, December 12, 2000.

104   *"dinner-plate size"* MDE interview, May 15 and 16, 1998.

104   *"shocked and horrified,"* Ibid.

104   *"completely unbuttoned" manner* Ibid.

104   *"are already flat"* "The Emergency Rescue Committee in France," VFP.

105   *Gold introduced him* MDE interview, May 15 and 16, 1998.

105   *"Danny would be"* Gold, 203.

105   *"Préfecture de Police"* MDE, *An Unsentimental Education,* 35–36.

105   *a "cordial talk"* VF to EF, October 31, 1940, VFP.

105   *"very fair, with"* Gold, 203.

105   *"I can't do"* Jean Gemähling interview, July 31, 1998.

106   *Fry had also*   MDE, *An Unsentimental Education*, 28.

106   *was "small, grey-haired"*   MDE interview, May 16, 1998.

106   *"Catholic and conservative"*   VF, *Surrender on Demand*, 102.

106   *"rabidly pro-German and"*   Ibid., 221.

106   *"had been protecting"*   MDE interview, May 15, 1998.

106   *"like trying to"*   VF to EF, October 27, 1941, VFP.

106   *But he had accomplished*   DB, Accessory Services Report, VFP.

106   *"pulled itself together"*   VF to Lilian Mackey Fry, November 3, 1940, VFP.

106   *When Hitler met*   Gold, 226.

107   *There were horror*   VF to EF, October 27, 1940, VFP.

107   *As a child*   WM interview, December 3, 1997.

107   *In 1929, Otto*   WM to author, August 29, 2000.

107   *"decided their children"*   WM to author, August 31, 2000.

107   *"unaware that [he]"*   Ibid.

107   *One day, in*   WM interview, December 11, 1996, Survivors of the Shoah Visual History Foundation, Menlo Park, CA, 23797.

108   *Otto became director*   WM to author, August 29, 2000.

108   *In September 1939*   WM interview, December 3, 1997.

108   *"At the time"*   WM to author, August 29, 2000.

108   *"went by train"*   WM, "An episode missing from *Escape Through the Pyrenees* by Lisa Fittko," revised December 9, 2000.

108   *"The French government"*   WM to author, September 4, 2000.

108   *"Appeals for issuance"*   Read by A. N. Richards at the Memorial Meeting for the late Professor Otto Meyerhof, December 6, 1951, copy provided to author.

108   *"As all Consulate[s]"*   WM, "Data concerning my immigration to U.S.A.," November 23, 1940, Meyerhof file, Deutsches Exil Archiv 1933–1945, Die Deutsche Bibliothek.

109   *"According to a"*   WM, "An episode missing from *Escape Through the Pyrenees* by Lisa Fittko."

109   *"stiff French toilet"*   Ibid.

109   *They went in*   WM quoted in Read by A. N. Richards at the Memorial Meeting for the late Professor Otto Meyerhof, December 6, 1951.

109   *Mme. Meyerhof noticed*   WM to author, September 4, 2000.

109   *"Then suddenly he"*   Ibid.

109   *"[T]here were no"*   Ibid.

109   *The Meyerhofs sailed*   Read by A. N. Richards at the Memorial Meeting for the late Professor Otto Meyerhof, December 6, 1951.

109–110 *Before he left*   Otto Meyerhof to VF, n.d., Meyerhof file.

110   *"it was always"*   Pfefferman, "The American Schindler."

110   *"found at the"*   WM to VF, November 10, 1940, Meyerhof file.

110   *"I am a"*   WM to VF, December 5, 1940, Meyerhof file.

110   *"lend your special"*   VF to U.S. Chargé d'Affaires H. Freeman Matthews, December 17, 1940, Meyerhof file.

110   *In early January*   WM to VF, January 30, 1941, Meyerhof file.

110   *"authorized to take"*   VF to WM, February 1, 1941, Meyerhof file.

110   *"I am really"*   WM to VF, March 26, 1941, Meyerhof file.

111   *"I had thrown"* WM interview, December 11, 1996, Survivors of the Shoah Visual History Foundation, Menlo Park, CA, 23797.
111   *"claimed that they"* WM to author, August 29, 2000.
111   *Two weeks later* WM interview, December 3, 1997.
111   *He boarded a* Ibid.
111   *"for the great"* WM to VF, April 28, 1941, Meyerhof file.
111   *"I had every"* WM interview, December 3, 1997.
111   *"young people in"* Ibid.

CHAPTER SIX: **RESPITE AT AIR-BEL**

112   *Our little tribe* MDE, *An Unsentimental Education,* 39.
112   *"gaunt hulk"* VF, *Surrender on Demand,* 104.
113   *The price was* In 1940, one dollar equaled 49.19 francs. Exchange rate from "Foreign Exchange Rate Database," http://www.globalfindata.com/freeexc.htm.
113   *"Hitler had a"* Gys Landsberger interview, November 15, 1998.
113   **Gys Landsberger's family* Ibid.
113   *According to his* VF, notes to self for manuscript of *Surrender on Demand,* VFP.
113   *That night, the* Jean Gemähling interview, July 31, 1998.
114   *Finally, at two A.M.* Ibid.
114   *"not because the"* VF to EF, October 27, 1940, VFP.
115   *"united in a"* EF to VF, October 19, 1940, VFP.
115   *"situation [that] . . . has"* Mildred Adams of the ERC, contract letter to Jay Allen, October 30, 1940, VFP.
115   *The one-month* Ibid.
115   *"I still begin"* VF to EF, October 27, 1940, VFP.
115   *"some collaborationist official"* Fittko, *Escape Through the Pyrenees,* 133.
115   *Gold seemed unable* MDE interview, March 21, 1999.
115–116 *"a deluxe relief"* VF to EF, October 31, 1940, VFP.
116   *"few [refugees] are"* Ibid.
116   *"Sooner or later"* Ibid.
116   *"those boobs in"* VF to EF, October 27, 1940, VFP.
116   *"no romantic job"* VF to EF, October 31, 1940, VFP.
116   *"They have got"* VF to EF, October 27, 1940, VFP.
116   *"nor the understanding"* Ibid.
116   *"too enormous to"* Ibid.
116   *Could Eileen find* VF to EF, October 31, 1940, VFP.
117   *"Sometimes the refugees"* Ibid.
117   *"the German refugees"* MDE interview, May 15, 1998.
117   *One protégé, Wilhelm* VF, notes to self for manuscript of *Surrender on Demand,* VFP.
117   *"They await me"* Ibid.
117   *"like reading a"* VF, *Surrender on Demand,* 115.

117   *"founder of the"* Sawin, *Surrealism in Exile and the Beginning of the New York School,* 119.
117   *a Trotskyist, and* Gold, *Crossroads Marseilles 1940,* 243.
118   *"Yes," he said* MDE interview, May 15, 1998.
118   *"tall stone gate"* MDE, *An Unsentimental Education,* 37–38.
118   *"an eccentric amateur"* Sawin, 119.
118   *"flea-bag hotel"* MDE to ARF, November 10–13, 1998.
118   *Gold and Bénédite* MDE, *An Unsentimental Education,* 37–38. Also in Gold, 242–243, and in VF, *Surrender on Demand,* 114–115.
118–119 *"where the city"* Gold, quoted in *Marseilles-New York: L'Etat de Piège ou La Filière Marseillaise,* a film by Teri Wehn-Damisch.
119   *"tumbledown chateau" was* Serge, *Memoirs of a Revolutionary,* 364.
119   *"that even twelve"* VF to Lilian Mackey Fry, November 3, 1940, VFP.
119   *"more like a"* Théo Bénédite to VF, March 12, 1942, VFP.
119   *fresh fruits and* MDE interview, May 16, 1998.
119   *"This was the"* Gold, 243.
119   *Air-Bel provided* VF to Arthur Fry, May 14, 1941, VFP.
120   *"she didn't see"* MDE interview, March 21, 1999.
120   *"had waited until"* VF, notes to self for manuscript of *Surrender on Demand,* VFP.
120   *"Alas, my own"* MDE to ARF, November 10–13, 1998.
120   *"a moment of"* MDE, *An Unsentimental Education,* 39.
120   *Fawcett recalled that* Charles Fawcett interview, August 6, 1998.
122   *liaison between British* Arnold Kramish interview, February 10, 2000.
122   *"a big kitchen"* VF to EF, March 26, 1941, VFP.
122   *Sometime later, Chagall's* VF, *Surrender on Demand,* 130.
122   *"eager to turn"* VF to EF, November 29, 1940, VFP.
122   *"It wasn't much,"* VF, *Surrender on Demand,* 130.
122   *"helped Varian in"* Stephane Hessel interview, March 20, 1999.
123   *he "nursed"* Ibid.
123   *"longed for his"* Gold, 336.
123   *"Varian liked good"* Maurice Verzeano interview, May 8, 2000.
123   *"I would like"* VF to EF, quoted in Gold, 336.
123   *"[I]t would be"* VF to EF, February 23, 1941, VFP.
123   *"very close"* Stephane Hessel interview, March 20, 1999.
123   *It isn't something* Ibid.
123   *"a very sweet"* VF to EF, February 9, 1941, VFP.
124   *Not Degenerate Enough:* Brand story from MDE interview, May 15 and 16, 1998.

CHAPTER SEVEN: **EXQUISITE CORPSE: THE SURREALISTS**

126   *Surrealism left no* Sawin, *Surrealism in Exile and the Beginning of the New York School,* xv.
126   *Serge took a* André Breton to Victor Serge, October 13, 1940, VFP.

126 *Chateau Espere-Visa* MDE, *An Unsentimental Education*, 39.
127 *"was doing the"* MDE interview, March 21, 1999.
127 *"I was against"* AOH interview, September 17, 1998.
127 *"I still regret"* MDE interview, March 21, 1999.
127 *"peace and quiet"* VF to Lilian Mackey Fry, November 3, 1940, VFP.
127 *had almost "drowned"* Ibid.
127 *"It is too"* VF to Arthur Fry, May 14, 1941, VFP.
127 *"I have never"* VF to DB, October 31, 1941, VFP.
127 *Mary Jayne Gold* MDE interview, May 15, 1998.
127 *"[A]n extraordinary presence"* Gold interviewed by Richard Kaplan, EFPR.
127 *Breton had written* "Two Private Eyes: One Vision, A Conversation between Daniel Filipacchi and David Sylvester," (Filipacchi's answers translated from the French by John Goodman), Weisberger, ed., *Surrealism: Two Private Eyes*, 19.
127 *Although the term* Aloff, "Dinners with André," *The New York Times Book Review*, October 3, 1999.
127–128 *"like children: singing"* André Breton, "Jeu de Marseille," VVV 3 1943, 89–90 (translated by Carole Frankel), quoted in Elizabeth Berman, "Moral Triage or Cultural Salvage? The Agendas of Varian Fry and the Emergency Rescue Committee," in Barron, *Exiles & Emigres, The Flight of European Artists From Hitler*, 106.
128 *Before the war* Sawin, ix.
128 *"fell apart and"* Ibid., ix–x.
128 *"hidden in a"* Ibid., 112.
128 *in "anthropological subjects"* Ibid., 19.
128 *Breton knew the* Ibid., 114–115.
128 **Kurt Seligmann in* Ibid., 419.
128 *the Barrs* Fermi, *Illustrious Immigrants*, 86.
129 *"prowlers—the Sûreté,"* Serge, *Memoirs of a Revolutionary*, 362.
129 *"[B]ecause of their"* Ibid., 363–364.
129 *"If it had"* Ibid., 362.
129 *"Noun, masculine" in* André Breton, *Manifeste du Surrealisme*, 1924: "Surrealism, Noun, masculine. Pure psychic automatism, but which one intends to express verbally, in writing or by any other method, the real functioning of the mind. Dictation by thought, in the absence of any control exercised by reason, and beyond any esthetic or moral preoccupations."
130 *"to show their"* Gold interviewed by Richard Kaplan, EFPR.
130 *"polyglot ancestry, both"* Glueck, "Lam's Demons at the Matisse."
130 *"love undergoes hermetic"* Sawin, 124.
130 *Lam, who had* Benitez, *My Life with Wifredo Lam: 1939–1950*, 38.
130 *("Fata Morgana" was)* Ibid., 50.
130 *"walking around like"* VF to EF, October 31, 1940, VFP.
130 *"You see, they're"* André Breton, quoted in Gold, interviewed by Richard Kaplan, EFPR.
130 *Another important surrealist* Jean Gemähling interview, July 31, 1998.

130–131 *"the two Andrés"* Ibid.
131 *"what the French"* Sawin, 120.
131 *"old barrack-room"* Gold, *Crossroads Marseilles 1940*, 245.
131 *"from the witty"* Sawin, 124.
131 *"were totally bizarre."* Jean Gemähling interview, April 9, 1998, Survivors of the Shoah Visual History Foundation Ozoir-la-Ferriere, France, 43104.
131 *"bracelets around her"* Jean Gemähling interview, July 31, 1998.
131 *"basked and frolicked"* Timothy Baum, "The Surrealist Revolution," in Weisberger, 31.
131 *"forbidden . . . decadent music"* Gold interviewed by Richard Kaplan, EFPR.
131 *"the decorous Fry"* Sawin, 120.
131 *"capture the spirit"* Ibid., 125.
131 *"fell passionately in"* VF, *Surrender on Demand*, 180.
132 *and Jacques Hérold* Delphine Hérold-Wright to author, April 4, 2001.
132 *"rigorously excluded women"* Aloff, "Dinners with André," *The New York Times Book Review*, October 3, 1999, 26.
132 *"scandalously beautiful wife"* Gold interviewed by Richard Kaplan, EFPR.
132 *"The exquisite corpse"* Jose Pierre, "The Exquisite Game," in Weisberger, 618.
132 *"The oyster from"* Jose Pierre, "To Be or Not To Be Surrealist," in Weisberger, 39.
132 *"surprise and hilarity"* Gold, 251.
132 *A second version* Sawin, 132.
132 *"memorialize . . . that tense"* Ibid.
132 *"bitter cold" winter* Ibid., 127.
133 *"I too am"* VF, notes for *Surrender on Demand*, VFP.
133 *"stewed carrots, rutabagas"* Sawin, 127.
133 *"would take the"* VF, notes for *Surrender on Demand*, VFP.
133 *What little bread* VF to Arthur Fry, May 14, 1941, VFP, CU.
133 *rations "like candy"* VF, notes for *Surrender on Demand*, VFP.
133 *"slice of an"* VF to Arthur Fry, May 14, 1941, VFP.
133 *At Air-Bel* VF, notes for *Surrender on Demand*, VFP.
133 *"You hear that"* VF to Arthur Fry, May 14, 1941, VFP.
133 *"hunt[ed] snails on"* VF, *Surrender on Demand*, 183.
133–134 *"High Life Tailor"* VF, notes for *Surrender on Demand*, VFP.
134 *genteel Hôtel Beauvau* Ibid.
134 *the artist was* Vivian Endicott Barnett, "Banned German Art: Reception and Institutional Support of Modern German Art in the United States, 1933–45," in Barron, *Exiles & Emigres, The Flight of European Artists from Hitler*, 281.
134 *"Europe was threatened"* Russell, "Max Ernst: Catalytic Figure in 20th Century Art, Dies."
134 *"Insult to German"* Weld, *Peggy, the Wayward Guggenheim*, 231.
134 *ménage à trois* Ibid., 225.
134 *"with beautiful and"* Ibid., 226.

134   *"reserve and cool"*   Ibid., 226.

135   *"[a]labaster skin, wavy"*   Peggy Guggenheim quoted in Weld, 227.

135   *"as an enemy"*   Sawin, 130.

135   *"I'm being detained"*   Max Ernst to Jimmy Ernst, October 27, 1941, quoted in Jimmy Ernst, *A Not-So-Still Life,* 170.

135   *"The Emergency Rescue"*   Alfred Barr, quoted in Ibid., 171.

135   *Ernst and surrealist*   Stephanie Barron, "European Artists in Exile: A reading between the lines," in Barron, 15.

135   *"that the Gestapo"*   Sawin, 130.

135   *"a German citizen"*   Alfred Barr to VF, quoted in Sawin, 141.

135   *"the most extraordinary"*   Gold interviewed by Richard Kaplan, EFPR.

135–136 *Ernst had brought*   VF, *Surrender on Demand,* 184.

136   *"had fled to"*   Sawin, 130.

136   *Kay Sage, Yves*   Weld, 214.

136   *"in constant fear"*   Ibid., 215.

136   *"was an American"*   Ibid.

136   *"stay away from"*   Ibid.

136   *"in terrible shape"*   Ibid., 217.

136   *"but aside from"*   Ibid.

137   *"seduced by the"*   Patrick Waldberg, Ernst's biographer, quoted in Weld, 219.

137   *Ernst soon replaced*   Sawin, 141.

137   *Ernst invited Fry*   Weld, 228.

137   *Guggenheim even arranged*   Gold interviewed by Richard Kaplan, EFPR.

137   *On April 7*   Museum of Modern Art to VF, April 7, 1941, VFP.

137   *in addition to being*   Sawin, 141.

137   *Fry, working on behalf*   Museum of Modern Art to VF, April 7, 1941, VFP.

138   *In New York*   Ernst, 171.

138   *"evidently, on specific"*   Sawin, 141.

138   *"offered to remarry"*   Ibid.

138   *"But Max," said*   Ernst, 199.

138   *Ernst escaped Marseille*   Weld, 233–234.

138   *Fry cabled the*   VF to Unitarian Service Committee, April 3, 1941, VFP.

138–139 *Straus would be*   Miss L. Loeb to VF, July 3, 1941, VFP.

139   *"Marseille was occupied"*   Charles (Karel) Sternberg to VF, August 11, 1966, VFP.

139   *"put on Transport"*   Ernst, postscript. Also in Berman, "Moral Triage or Cultural Salvage? The Agendas of Varian Fry and the Emergency Rescue Committee," in Barron, 109.

CHAPTER EIGHT: **TROUBLEMAKER: WINTER '40–'41**

140   *This job is*   "The Emergency Rescue Committee in France," VFP.

140   *"[t]o obtain the"*   VF, *Surrender on Demand*, 124.

140   *"shame the French"*   Ibid., 125.

141   *"We can't do"*   VF handwritten note to self, "Vichy, Nov. 1940," VFP.

141   *"shocked and pained"*   VF to U.S. Chargé d'Affaires H. Freeman Matthews, November 17, 1940, VFP.

141   *"guilty of some"*   Ibid.

141   *"No member of"*   Ibid.

141   *"Meanwhile, the Chargé"*   VF handwritten note to self, "Vichy, Nov. 1940," VFP.

141   *"I guess they"*   Ibid.

142   *"a purely negative"*   VF to U.S. Chargé d'Affaires H. Freeman Matthews, November 17, 1940, VFP.

142   *"The continued liberty"*   Ibid.

142   *While Fry was*   Enclosure number 2, by American vice consul Lee D. Randall, "regarding V. Fry," November 20, 1940, part of Dispatch number 56 from the embassy at Vichy, NA.

142   *"the wildest sort"*   Ibid.

142–143 *Later, he acknowledged*   VF to DB, September 22, 1941, VFP.

143   *"[T]his had a"*   Ibid.

143   *"America's open scandal"*   VF to DB, November 25, 1941, VFP.

143   *"[The Committee's] contract"*   Mildred Adams to VF, October 30, 1940, VFP.

143   *"these unfortunate people,"*   VF to Lilian Mackey Fry, November 3, 1940, VFP.

143   *"[f]or obvious reasons,"*   H. Freeman Matthews, quoted in VF, *Surrender on Demand*, 128.

144   *"to receive, encourage"*   DB, "Administrative Report, The Stages of the Committee's Development, Jan. to April 1941," Marseille, August 20, 1941, and Perpignan, September 3, 1941, VFP.

144   *"We know everything,"*   Bil Spira (Bill Freier) interview, August 1, 1998.

144   *"the only one"*   Ibid.

144   *he asked Fry*   Ibid.

145   *Even when the*   DB, "Administrative Report, The Stages of the Committee's Development, Jan. to April 1941," Marseille, August 20, 1941, and Perpignan, September 3, 1941, VFP.

145   *the "new stateless"*   VF to Secretary of State Cordell Hull, November 13, 1940, VFP.

145   *"would shine as"*   Ibid.

145   *"the same information"*   Assistant Secretary of State Adolf A. Berle to Frank Kingdon, December 4, 1941, VFP.

145   *"the Spanish in"*   VF to EF, December 8, 1940, VFP.

145   *Smuggling refugees out*   DB, "Administrative Report, The Stages of the Committee's Development, Jan. to April 1941," Marseille, August 20, 1941, and Perpignan, September 3, 1941, VFP.

146   *Fry penned an*   "The Emergency Rescue Committee in France," VFP.

146 *More than ever* Ibid.
146 *"a number of"* Ibid.
147 *"had sunk into"* DB, "Administrative Report, The Stages of the Committee's Development, Jan. to April 1941," Marseille, August 20, 1941, and Perpignan, September 3, 1941, VFP.
147 *"volunteer council of"* Ibid.
147 *Some artists on* "The Emergency Rescue Committee in France," VFP.
147 *"This office is"* VF to Emerescue, n.d., box 2, VFP.
147 *One Monday morning* VF, *Surrender on Demand,* 134.
147 *"with real pain"* Ibid.
147 *He also hid* Ibid., 137.
148 *"I always make"* Ibid., 133.
148 *"object[ed] in precise"* Gold, *Crossroads Marseilles 1940,* 265.
148 *aware that a* VF to EF, December 8, 1940, VFP.
148 *"some other celebrity,"* Ibid.
148 *"snide remarks about"* Gold interviewed by Richard Kaplan, EFPR.
148 *They confiscated Serge's* Gold, 266.
148 *"emptying the contents"* Ibid., 267.
149 *"Pétain Est Un Con"* Jean Gemähling interview, July 31, 1998.
149 *as "Revolutionary propaganda."* Weld, *Peggy, the Wayward Guggenheim,* 214. Also in VF, *Surrender on Demand,* 139.
149 *A Marc Chagall* Gold, 270.
149 *When Gemähling and* VF, *Surrender on Demand,* 140–141.
149 *"so suddenly and"* VF to EF, December 8, 1941, VFP.
149 *"Are you sure"* Jean Gemähling interview, July 31, 1998.
149 *"Varian and I"* Gold, 273.
150 *"I crossed the"* VF to EF, December 8, 1940, VFP.
150 *"I am an"* VF, *Surrender on Demand,* 143.
150 *"had to fight"* Jean Gemähling interview, July 31, 1998.
150 *"calm and determined,"* Ibid.
150 *"a vigorous categoric"* VF to EF, January 5, 1941, VFP.
150 *"anybody suspicious . . . anybody"* Gold interviewed by Richard Kaplan, EFPR.
150 *The Sinaia itself* VF, *Surrender on Demand,* 143.
151 *"rolling with the"* Jean Gemähling interview, July 31, 1998.
151 *They were all* Gold, 276.
151 *"for some unknown"* VF, *Surrender on Demand,* 148.
151 *Back at the* Ibid., 148–149.
151 *"one of the"* VF to EF, December 8, 1940, VFP.
151 *"carelessness rather than"* VF to Lilian Mackey Fry, November 8, 1940, VFP.
151 *"I know no"* Ibid.
151 *Remember that, whatever* Ibid.
152 *"people began to"* Sawin, *Surrealism in Exile and the Beginning of the New York School,* 127.
152 *"Julian Cain, former"* Ibid.
152 *"turned over by"* "Caballero Seized—Ex Spanish Premier Reported Sent to Spain by France," *The New York Times,* January 4, 1941.

152   *Caballero's arrest meant*   VF, *Surrender on Demand,* 156.
152   *a young German*   Ibid.
152   *"I will tell"*   AOH interviewed by Richard Kaplan, EFPR.
152   *"a total surprise"*   Ibid.
152   *"It's interesting to"*   Hiram Bingham, quoted in Ibid.
153   *"from living in"*   Ibid.
153   *on December 20*   Ibid.
153   *the couple's "meticulousness."*   AOH at Jewish Museum panel discussion in connection with Varian Fry exhibit, December 2, 1997.
153   *"spirited" onto a*   AOH interviewed by Richard Kaplan, EFPR.
153   *"My closest friend"*   VF to EF, February 9, 1941, VFP.
153   *"I have loads"*   VF to EF, January 5, 1941, VFP.
153   *"meet Hans Fittko"*   Marcel Verzeano at Jewish Museum panel discussion in connection with Varian Fry exhibit, December 2, 1997.
153   *"people are still"*   VF to Karl Frucht, December 30, 1941, VFP.
153–154 *Fry put Gemähling*   Jean Gemähling interview, March 20, 1999.
154   *Bénédite, a careful*   DB, "Confidential Financial Report," VFP.
154   *a fruitful evening*   Jean Gemähling interview, March 20, 1998.
154   *"his campaigns in"*   "American Rescue Center" to "the French Administration," January 14, 1941, VFP.
155   *"If we throw"*   Jean Gemähling interview, July 31, 1998.
155   *"a woman of"*   VF, *Surrender on Demand,* 154.
155   *"This will introduce"*   Mildred Adams to VF, October 30, 1940, VFP.
155   *Allen, whose journey*   VF, *Surrender on Demand,* 154.
155   *"her somewhat advanced"*   VF to EF, January 5, 1941, VFP.
155   *Fry went off*   VF cable to Frank Kingdon, n.d., VFP.
156   *"a disturbing preoccupation"*   VF to EF, January 5, 1941, VFP.
156   *that "the Friend"*   Ibid.
156   *"fought like a"*   VF to EF, April 21, 1941, VFP.
156   *"could not realize"*   Gold, 292.
156   *"This message sent"*   Lena Fischman to ERC in New York, n.d., VFP.
156   *"The situation in"*   Charles Joy to ERC in New York, December 20, 1940, VFP.
157   *"British soldiers helped"*   Charles Joy to Emerescue, New York, January 21, 1941, VFP.
157   *Fry no longer*   VF to ERC, January 24, 1941, VFP.
157   *Allen's presence added*   EF to VF, January 28, 1941, VFP.
157   *"ten times more"*   VF to EF, October 8, 1940, VFP.
157   *"I have met"*   VF to EF, October 31, 1940, VFP.
157   *"for the first"*   VF to EF, January 5, 1941, VFP.
157   *"Varian the contrarian"*   ARF interview, May 8, 1998.
157   *"embarrassed because [of]"*   ERC to VF, January 21, 1941, VFP.
157   *"blithering, slobbering idiots"*   VF to EF, January 5, 1941, VFP.
157   *"an indispensability complex"*   Ibid.
157   *"the villain" in*   EF to VF, January 28, 1941, VFP.
157–158 *His wife urged*   Ibid.
158   *"unbelievable things: cheese"*   VF, *Surrender on Demand,* 156.
158   *"After Miki was"*   Eva Marcu interview, June 16, 1998.

158   *"The French wouldn't"* Ibid.

158   *"The Germans were"* Ibid.

159   *The " 'Otto List' "* Gold, 296.

159   **Theodore Wolff* VF, *Surrender on Demand*, 157.

159   *"Nothing to it."* Eva Marcu interview, June 16, 1998.

159   **Miki accompanied her* Ibid.

159–160 *"had just escaped"* Gold, 296.

160   *Malraux had asked* Langlois, "Malraux, 1941–42: Under the Nazi Shadow in Southern France," *Columbia Library Columns*.

160   *the Montfleury, on* VF to Willibald Dilger, March 25, 1967, VFP.

160   *"a cold and"* VF, Confidential Memorandum on Mr. and Mrs. Fritz Thyssen, n.d., VFP.

160   *"Why don't you"* VF, *Surrender on Demand*, 162–163.

160   *"had been arrested"* VF, Confidential Memorandum on Mr. and Mrs. Fritz Thyssen, n.d., VFP.

160   *He wrote a* VF, *Surrender on Demand*, 163.

160   *"quick trip to"* VF, notes to self for manuscript of *Surrender on Demand*, VFP.

160   *"Gestapo activities in"* Ibid.

161   *riding "around with"* Gys Landsberger interview, November 15, 1998.

161   *When Fry first* MDE interview, May 16, 1998.

161   *Fry had even* Charles Fawcett interview, August 8, 1998.

161   *"Sure we know"* VF, *Surrender on Demand*, 93.

161   *At the American* VF, notes to self for manuscript of *Surrender on Demand*, VFP.

161   *"return immediately all"* Ibid.

161   *now "in charge"* Jay Allen to VF, January 8, 1941, VFP.

162   *"bullying" him into* VF to EF, January 5, 1941, VFP.

162   *"four large, light"* DB, "Administrative Report, The Stages of the Committee's Development, Jan. to April 1941," Marseille, August 20, 1941, and Perpignan, September 3, 1941, VFP.

162   *Ruth Sender Stern* Ruth Sender Stern interview, November 8, 1999.

162   *At the present* "Note from Marseille, dated Jan. 15, arrived Jan. 17, 1941," includes "Note in Mr. Fry's Dossier at Prefecture Bureau of Information at Ministere des affaires estrangeres Vichy to Prefet des Bouches du Rhone Marseille," note in VF's handwriting: "Jan 15?" VFP.

162   *Fry had Bénédite* "American Rescue Center" to "the French Administration," January 14, 1941, VFP.

163   *"complicated and expensive"* VF to EF, January 5, 1941, VFP.

163   *secret financial report* DB, "Confidential Financial Report," VFP.

163   *British embassy "pleased"* AOH to Wheeler-Bennett, January 17, 1941, VFP.

163   *"so deeply involved"* Jay Allen to Ruth Allen, January 16, 1941, VFP.

163   *Fry's friend and* Charles Joy to ERC, January 17, 1941, VFP.

163   *"or I resign"* Jay Allen to Mrs. Allen, excerpt for ERC, January 24, 1941, VFP.

163   *"Inform Kingdon confidentially,"* Jay Allen to Mrs. Allen, excerpt for ERC, January 28, 1941, VFP.

163   *to "major proportions"*   VF to Ingrid Warburg, January 29, 1941, VFP.

164   *her "poor health"*   VF, quoted in Joy cable to Warburg, January 30, 1941, VFP.

164   *"whatever director [was]"*   Kingdon to VF, February 1, 1941, VFP.

164   *"excellent, if somewhat"*   VF to EF, February 9, 1941, VFP.

164   *Lucie Heymann*   Marcel Verzeano interview, May 8, 2000.

164   *At this point*   VF to EF, February 9, 1941, VFP.

164   *"lonely and homesick"*   VF to EF, February 15, 1941, VFP.

164   *"cold (as ice),"*   VF to EF, February 9, 1941, VFP.

164   *"taken up, not"*   Ibid.

164   *"Embassy and Consulate"*   Jay Allen to Mrs. Allen, February 24, 1941, VFP.

165   *"it was an"*   VF, *Surrender on Demand*, 208.

165   *"Wasn't it perfect"*   VF to EF, March 26, 1941, VFP.

165   *I was kinda*   VF to EF, April 21, 1941, VFP.

165   *Rudolf Breitscheid and*   Five-page description of arrest of Breitscheid and Hilferding, February 14, 1941, VFP.

165   *Breitscheid and Hilferding*   VF to Miss Hedwig Wachenbein, German Labor Delegation, New York City, May 15, 1942, VFP.

165   *"They considered themselves"*   VF and Bedrich Heine, "Report on the Case of Breitscheid and Hilferding," summer 1941. Also AOH interviewed by Richard Kaplan, EFPR.

166   *"Haven't they grasped"*   Ibid.

166   *Hitler would not*   Breitscheid quoted in Report: "Hitler wouldn't dare to request our extradition!"

166   *Fry noted that*   Ibid.

166   *when they learned*   Ibid.

166   *Breitscheid and Hilferding*   Five-page description of arrest of Breitscheid and Hilferding, February 14, 1941, VFP.

166   *"I am convinced"*   VF to Henry (Heinrich) Ehrmann, September 10, 1943, VFP.

166   *"[S]everal people whose"*   Ibid.

167   *Among the names*   Firsthand story of arrest of Breitscheid from Mrs. Breitscheid's account, Arles, February 20, 1941, VFP.

168   *"was placed in"*   Five-page description of arrest of Breitscheid and Hilferding, February 14, 1941, VFP.

168   *and delivered over*   VF to *Encyclopædia Brittanica*, April 27, 1967, VFP.

168   *"tried to guess"*   VF, *Surrender on Demand*, 177.

168   *A shadow passed*   Ibid.

168   *"You can imagine"*   Rose Hilferding to VF, November 30, 1941, VFP.

168   *"I was there"*   VF to *Encyclopædia Brittanica*, April 27, 1967, VFP.

168   *inmate at Buchenwald*   Maurer Maurer, chief, Historical Studies Branch, USAF Historical Division, Department of the Air Force, to VF, March 22, 1967, VFP.

168   *"spilled over into"*   Ibid.

169   *360 prisoners of*   F. A. Brockhaus to VF, April 4, 1967, VFP.

169   *Several years after*   VF to German Information Center, February 28, 1967, VFP.

CHAPTER NINE: **SPRING RENEWAL**

170   *By the end*   DB, "Administrative Report, The Stages of the Committee's Development, Jan. to April 1941," Marseille, August 20, 1941, and Perpignan, September 3, 1941, VFP.

170   *"I wouldn't have"*   VF to EF, February 23, 1941, VFP.

170   *She told Fry*   EF to VF, July 8, 1941, VFP.

171   *"Until January only"*   DB, "Administrative Report, The Stages of the Committee's Development, Jan. to April 1941," Marseille, August 20, 1941, and Perpignan, September 3, 1941, VFP.

171   *"should try to"*   Clarence Picket to EF, March 4, 1941, VFP.

171   *Examples were the*   VF to EF, March 27, 1941, VFP. "[T]he clipping about the quotas being closed again is wrong. The German and Austrian quotas are both open at Marseille, though closed at Lyon and at Nice, allegedly because those consulates are understaffed but also in part at least because their staffs are lazy and indifferent if not actively hostile to 'aliens.' The consul at Lyon is indignant when on rare occasions he is obliged to receive a Jew."

171   *"packing silver and"*   VF cable to ERC, March 5, 1941, VFP.

171   *to be "understaffed,"*   VF to EF, March 27, 1941, VFP.

171   *he insisted Ingrid*   VF cable to ERC, March 5, 1941, VFP.

171   *"[T]here is no"*   Avra M. Warren, chief, Visa Division, to Ingrid Warburg, April 5, 1942, VFP.

172   *the Brazil situation*   Ibid.

172   *"intervene with the"*   Ibid.

172   *"the applicants are"*   Ibid.

172   *The Department, hysterical*   "Report on Various Organizations and Individuals Engaged in Refugee Migration Activities," August 8, 1942, NA, Department of State Division of Communication and Records, (RG 59), General visa correspondence, 1940–45, files 811.111 refugees/ 2000–2149, box 159, folder 2055 ½, pp. 51, 57, NA.

172   *"virtually unknown" in*   Susan W. Morgenstein interview, June 15, 1999.

172   *"an unemployed screenwriter"*   Simon, "Mann and 'Super Mann,' " 12.

172   *"full biography moral"*   ERC cable to VF, March 3, 1941, VFP.

172   *Quite without warning*   VF, *Surrender on Demand*, 186.

173   *"the political and"*   Ibid., 186.

173   *"one-man operation"*   Charles (Karel) Sternberg interview, September 2, 1998.

173   *"considered something phenomenal"*   DB, "Administrative Report, The Stages of the Committee's Development, Jan. to April 1941," Marseille, August 20, 1941, and Perpignan, September 3, 1941, VFP.

173   *"Vichy's formalities presented"*   Marrus and Paxton, *Vichy France and the Jews*, 162.

173   *Officials could hold*   Ibid., 163.

174   *"was Number 3"*   Lisa Fittko, *Escape Through the Pyrenees*, 148.

174   *"one of the"*   VF, *Surrender on Demand*, 191.

174   *"outspoken anti-Nazi"*   Ibid., 198.

174   *"Mr. and Mrs. Wolff"*   Ibid., 191.

174   *"a man in"*   Jean Gemähling interview, March 20, 1999.

174   (*According to Lisa*)   Fittko, *Escape Through the Pyrenees,* 150–152.

174   *There was no diplomatic*   VF, *Surrender on Demand,* 195.

175   *It was Marcel*   Verzeano writes that the Carlos route or line was really the Garcia line and that Fry erred in *Surrender on Demand.* Marcel Verzeano, note to author, February 17, 2001.

175   *"almost entirely by"*   DB, "Accessory Services Report," VFP.

175   *"ran into all"*   Fittko, *Escape Through the Pyrenees,* 148.

175   *"a resistance group"* Ibid., 154.

175   *"the beginning of"*   Marcel Verzeano, Jewish Museum panel discussion in connection with Varian Fry exhibit, December 2, 1997.

175   *"guns on one"*   Ibid.

175   *"an odyssey of"*   DB, "Accessory Services Report," VFP.

175   *"around the cape"*   Fittko, *Escape Through the Pyrenees,* 157.

175   *Finally, Verzeano got*   VF, *Surrender on Demand,* 234–235.

175   (*They finally sailed*)   DB, "Accessory Services Report," VFP.

175   *However, when the*   VF, *Surrender on Demand,* 200.

175   *"overturn heaven and"*   Ibid., 201.

175   *"persuaded an influential"*   Ibid., 235.

175   *Fry's certainty that*   Ibid.

175   *France was again*   DB, "Administrative Report, The Stages of the Committee's Development, Jan. to April 1941," Marseille, August 20, 1941, and Perpignan, September 3, 1941, VFP.

177   *"Lena Fis[c]hman will"*   H. W. Katz in A Book of Tribute to Varian Fry.

177   *"one of our"*   VF to EF, February 23, 1941, VFP.

177   *In Madrid, they*   H. W. Katz in A Book of Tribute to Varian Fry.

177   *"[i]mmigration visas for"*   ERC cable to VF, March 3, 1941, VFP.

177   *to "rescue ship[s]."*   VF, *Surrender on Demand,* 187.

177   *"passages were . . . available"*   DB, "Administrative Report, The Stages of the Committee's Development, Jan. to April 1941," Marseille, August 20, 1941, and Perpignan, September 3, 1941, VFP.

177–178 *Publishers Kurt and*   Kramer, "Profiles: Helen Wolff," *The New Yorker,* August 2, 1982, 51–54.

178   *Eventually, they, too*   Ibid.

178   *Max Ophuls, who*   Biography of Ophuls by Heinrich Schnitzler, December 3, 1940, Ophuls file, GEC.

178   *By December, due*   ERC to George Warren, December 18, 1940, Ophuls file.

178   *Ophuls "asks me"*   Richard Eisemann to Irmgard [*sic*] Warburg at ERC, March 11, 1941, Ophuls file.

178   *The Sorrow and the Pity*   Buruma, "The Vichy Syndrome," *Tikkun,* January–February 1995.

178–179 *"Vichy France had"*   Ibid.

179   *"points of departure"*   Wyman, *Paper Walls,* 152.

179   *"the vast bulk"*   Ibid.

179   *"soon came to"*   DB, "Administrative Report, The Stages of the Com-

mittee's Development, Jan. to April 1941," Marseille, August 20, 1941, and Perpignan, September 3, 1941, VFP.

179 *"[A] few hundred"* Wyman, 153.

179 *"[T]he curtain has"* VF to EF, February 23, 1941, VFP.

179 *"She paid for"* Jacqueline Breton, quoted in Weld, *Peggy, the Wayward Guggenheim*, 215.

179 *"My father always"* Aube Breton Elléouët to author, November 12, 1998.

179 *Loewenstein and his* Tilde Loewenstein interview, December 14, 1998.

180 *"Dyno in those"* Ibid.

180 *Victor Serge's departure* Sawin, *Surrealism in Exile and the Beginning of the New York School*, 129–130.

180 *"suddenly" granted transit* Serge, *Memoirs of a Revolutionary*, 366.

180 *"I feel no joy"* Ibid., 366.

180 *The wonderful moment* Sawin, 136.

180 *Helena Benitez wrote* Benitez, *My Life with Wifredo Lam: 1939–1950*, 50.

180 *"one of the most"* Biography of Masson, Masson file, GEC.

181 *U.S. visas for* DB to André Masson, January 14, 1941, Masson file

181 *were also granted* Jean Gemähling to André Masson, January 25, 1945 [*sic*], Masson file.

181 *"painter, André Masson"* VF to HICEM, February 25, 1941, Masson file.

181 *passage paid for* Sawin, 136.

181 *The artist loved* Jacques Baron, "Biography of Masson," in Weisberger, ed., *Surrealism: Two Private Eyes*, 872.

181 *"had no taste"* Sawin, 132.

181 *"When [Masson] heard"* Ibid.

181 *"Bretons Massons enroute"* VF to Emerescue, New York, April 4, 1941, Masson file.

181 *like "convict ship[s]"* Sawin, 136.

181 *"The dark, unventilated"* Ibid.

181 *"detached, withdrawn attitude"* Ibid., 136–137.

181 *"Did you know"* VF to DB, May 29, 1942, VFP.

181 *The camp, a* Sawin, 137.

182 *Bretons and Massons* Barron with Eckmann, *Exiles & Emigres: The Flight of European Artists From Hitler*, 395.

182 *"far-left" actors* Sawin, 120.

182 *"turned over to"* Ibid., 146.

182 *father was "strict"* Jacques Baron, "Biographies," in Weisberger, 856.

182 *created fetishistic dolls* Ibid.

182 *had been interned* Barron, "European Artists in Exile: A Reading Between the Lines," *Exiles & Emigres: The Flight of European Artists From Hitler*, 158.

182 *"decalcomania," a painting* Ibid., endnote 12, 163.

182 *Bellmer did not* Jacques Baron, "Biographies," *Surrealism: Two Private Eyes*, 856.

182 *†Dominguez, a Spanish* Ibid., 862.

182   ‡*Fry later took*   Elizabeth Berman, "Moral Triage or Cultural Salvage? The Agendas of Varian Fry and the Emergency Rescue Committee," in Barron with Eckmann, 108.

182   *"four years of"*   Jacques Baron, "Biographies," in Weisberger, 866.

182   *Brauner hiding his*   Ibid., 857.

182   *lost his own*   Fern Malkine interview, October 15, 1998.

182   *visas for Mexico*   Elizabeth Berman, "Moral Triage or Cultural Salvage? The Agendas of Varian Fry and the Emergency Rescue Committee," in Barron with Eckmann, 108.

182   *desperate cables went*   Lotte Loeb to Peggy Guggenheim, October 6, 1941, VFP.

182   *and Helena Rubenstein*   Secretary for Helena Rubenstein to ERC, October 7, 1941, VFP.

182   *Péret and Varo*   Lotte Loeb to André Breton, November 25, 1941, VFP.

182   *"MRS. GUGGENHEIM MIGHT"*   Unitarian to ERC, October 15, 1941, VFP.

182–183 *"America is truly"*   Jacqueline Breton to VF, June 24, 1941, VFP.

183   *"didn't see any"*   VF, *Surrender on Demand*, 229.

183   *"Are there cows"*   VF, Ibid., 130.

183   *or other "specialists."*   Marrus and Paxton, *Vichy France and the Jews*, 75.

183   *"forced from public"*   Ibid., 76.

183   *"Do you know"*   VF, *Surrender on Demand*, 207.

184   *At the beginning*   Gold, *Crossroads Marseilles 1940*, 333.

184   *Foreign Jews were*   VF, *Surrender on Demand*, 207.

184   *"revealed that the"*   Marrus and Paxton, 96.

184   *"Vichy's anti-Jewish"*   Ibid., 76.

184   *"We can intervene"*   "The Chagall Children's Problem" June 4, 1941, VFP.

184   *The Chagalls were*   Bohm-Duchen, *Chagall*, 238.

184   *a "lady goat"*   VF to EF, March 26, 1941, VFP.

184   *arrived in Lisbon*   Bohm-Duchen, 238.

184   *on June 23*   Ibid., chronology.

184   *"Will you take"*   VF to EF, March 26, 1941, VFP.

185   *"brand-new Danish"*   Sahl, "On Varian Fry," from *The Few and the Many*, quoted in Anderson, ed., *Hitler's Exiles: Personal Stories of the Flight from Nazi Germany to America*, 155–156.

185   *Ships were now*   DB, "Administrative Report, The Stages of the Committee's Development, Jan. to April 1941," Marseille, August 20, 1941, and Perpignan, September 3, 1941, VFP.

185   *"minimizing delays in"*   Ibid.

185   *"It was extremely"*   Jean Gemähling interview, July 31, 1998.

185   *"You had to"*   Ibid.

186   *"We are on"*   VF to EF, April 21, 1941, VFP.

186   *The coast is*   Louis de Costier to VF, April 24, 1942 (*sic*) VFP.

186   *"political refugee [and]"*   VF, *Surrender on Demand*, 59.

186   *"leader of the"*   Ibid., 109.

186   *He had been*   Marcel Verzeano interview, April 8, 2000.

186   *"much more delicate"*   Marcel Verzeano report: "The Problem of Emigration . . ." October 27, 1941, VFP, CU.

187   *"[W]e do know"* Ibid.
187   *His path into* VF, *Surrender on Demand,* 205, and Marcel Verzeano interview, February 17, 2001.
187   *Statut des Juifs* Marrus and Paxton, 92.
187   *French Jews now* VF, *Surrender on Demand,* 208.
187   *"Spanish visa, customs"* DB, "Accessory Services Report," VFP.
187   *"only be had"* Ibid.
187   *"set foot in"* Ibid.
188   *"I regret to"* William Peck to VF, May 5, 1941, VFP.
188   *Alfred Barr also* Alfred Barr, Jr., to Archibald MacLeish, May 9, 1941, VFP.
188   *"really heroic work,"* Ibid.
188   *two Wehrmacht officers* Erhardt Konopka, "Report on *Winnipeg* Trip," June 29, 1941, Konopka file, GEC.
188   *Konopka was a* misc. biographical notes, Konopka file.
188   *he met Fry* Ingrid Warburg to Whom It May Concern, June 19, 1941, Konopka file.
189   *"40 French soldiers"* Konopka, "Report on *Winnipeg* Trip."
189   *were "German-oriented."* Ibid.
189   *"A French banana"* Ruth Sender Stern interview, November 8, 1999.
189   *When the seas* Konopka "Report on *Winnipeg* trip."
189   *Two hours from* Ibid.
190   *"Telegrams & tickets"* Ibid.
190   *"were in Casablanca"* Ruth Sender Stern interview, November 8, 1999.
190   *"made numerous petitions"* DB, "Administrative Report, The Stages of the Committee's Development, Jan. to April 1941," Marseille, August 20, 1941, and Perpignan, September 3, 1941, VFP.
190   *"besieged" each day* Ibid.
190   *"advice and favors"* Ibid.
190   *Reitlinger, number 1094* Christine Reitlinger Angiel interview, December 25, 1998.
191   *"Miss Thompson gave"* Eleanor Roosevelt to EF, May 13, 1941, VFP.
191   *"three members of"* VF to Frank Kingdon, June 24, 1941, VFP.
191   *Through an "intermediary,"* DB, "Confidential Financial Report," VFP.
191   *"had always been"* Ibid.
191   *"a very regrettable"* Ibid.
192   *"You had better"* VF to AOH, November 30, 1941, VFP.
192   *I . . . said . . . that* DB, "Confidential Financial Report," VFP.
192   *Dimitru was a* VF, *Surrender on Demand,* 214.
192   *"Marseille was such"* VF to AOH, November 30, 1941, VFP.
192   *"denounce [him] to"* Ibid.
192   *"I must have"* VF, *Surrender on Demand,* 213.
192   *"dirty and unshaven"* Ibid., 214.
192–193 *"We . . . did almost"* Ibid., 212.
193   *Bingham never recovered* Bingham, "Uncle Harry's Secret."
193   *"seemed to delight"* VF, Ibid., 215.

193   *"If [Caballero] has"* VF, *Surrender on Demand*, 216.

193   *"the air of"* Hans Sahl to ERC, March 5, 1941.

193   *"everything seemed to"* VF, *Surrender on Demand*, 215.

193   *"3,268 emergency visas"* Wyman, 148–149.

194   *In 1933, he* "I, Kurt Geissler, at present in Nuremberg previously criminal-commissar, give the following sworn testimony before Dr. Robert M. W. Kempner, Office U.S. Chief Counsel," n.d., VFP.

194   *"was the first"* Ibid.

194   *Hitler, rearming illegally* Dr. Robert M. W. Kempner, letter, *An die ZEIT*, Hamburg, July 5, 1963, VFP.

194   *"foamed at the"* Ibid.

194   *they would hold* Untitled German document, n.d., 16, VFP.

194   *"continued fighting for"* Ibid.

194   *"Rollin [Jacob's code]"* VF to DB, September 30, 1941, VFP.

195   *"do something for"* Max Diamant to VF, November 20, 1941, VFP.

195   *"Rollin was no"* Ibid.

195   *"record, not only"* VF to Hilde Walter, April 17, 1967, VFP.

195   *"reached a haven"* Ibid.

195   *"What . . . bitter irony"* Ibid.

195   *"the Portuguese police"* Hilde Walter, quoted in VF to Kempner, June 5, 1967, VFP.

195   *They had then* VF to Hilde Walter, April 17, 1967, VFP.

195   *The Nazis transferred* Kempner to VF, June 6, 1967, VFP.

195   *"under the most"* Kempner, letter, *An die ZEIT*, Hamburg, July 5, 1963, VFP.

195   *Ill with tuberculosis* Ibid.

195–196 *On January 5, 1943* Untitled German document, n.d., 17, VFP.

196   *eighty-five pounds* Kempner, letter, *An die ZEIT*, Hamburg, July 5, 1963, VFP.

196   *(The last "Jewish")* Kempner to VF, June 9, 1967, VFP.

196   *"heart muscle weakness."* Untitled German document, n.d., 17, VFP.

196   *"a great pacifist,"* Ibid.

CHAPTER TEN: **THE END OF THE ADVENTURE**

197   *Dear Danny* VF to DB, October 3, 1941, VFP.

197   *"would not scare."* VF to AOH, November 30, 1941, VFP.

197   *"Why do you"* VF, notes to self for manuscript of *Surrender on Demand*, VFP.

198   *L was born,* Ibid.

198   *"the principal source"* VF to Frank Kingdon, June 24, 1941, VFP.

198   *"spread vague rumors"* Ibid.

198   *"difficult and . . . embarrassing"* Ibid.

198   *"I am not"* Ibid.

198   *"One day I"* VF, *Surrender on Demand*, 216.

199	*"the most famous"* VF to Du Porzic, June 25, 1941, VFP.
199	*"I would be"* Ibid.
199	*"secret messages wrapped"* Gold, *Crossroads Marseilles 1940*, 383.
199	*"Some were sentenced"* DB, "Administrative Report, The Stages of the Committee's Development, Jan. to April 1941," Marseille, August 20, 1941, and Perpignan, September 3, 1941, VFP.
199	*"shipping agents, to"* Ibid.
199	*"feverish"* Ibid.
200	*"important work stands"* Burns Chalmers to EF, July 8, 1941, VFP.
200	*His labors are* New School for Social Research President Alvin Johnson to Adolf A. Berle, Assistant Secretary of State, July 7, 1941, VFP.
200	*"has got to"* Adolf A. Berle to Alvin Johnson, July 8, 1941, VFP.
200	*back to smuggling* Gold, 376.
200	*the Garcia route* Marcel Verzeano writes that the Carlos line was in reality the Garcia line, note to author, February 17, 2000.
200	*"People with money"* Serge, *Memoirs of a Revolutionary*, 364.
200	*"faint outlines"* Wyman, *Paper Walls*, 192.
200	*"centralize control of"* Ibid., 193.
200	*"But before that"* Ibid., 194.
201	*"who had received"* Ibid., 196.
201	*"helpless"* VF to EF, June 23, 1941, VFP.
201	*"whose files lacked"* DB, "Administrative Report, The Stages of the Committee's Development, Jan. to April 1941," Marseille, August 20, 1941, and Perpignan, September 3, 1941, VFP.
201	*"who had previously"* Wyman, 196.
201	*"had to abandon"* DB, "Administrative Report, The Stages of the Committee's Development, Jan. to April 1941," Marseille, August 20, 1941, and Perpignan, September 3, 1941, VFP.
201	*One such case* "Mrs. Lotte Thormann, nee Forschner, born on October 20, 1891, in Schwalemberg, Lippe-Detmold, Germany," Thormann file, GEC.
202	*"worst German traitor,"* Werner Thormann to Ingrid Warburg, June 8, 1941, Thormann file.
202	*"been interrogated six"* Werner Thormann to Ingrid Warburg, May 27, 1941, and June 8, 1941, Thormann file.
202	*"on the kindness"* Werner Thormann to Ingrid Warburg, June 8, 1941, Thormann file.
202	*"when payment for"* Werner Thormann to Ingrid Warburg, August 21, 1941, Thormann file.
202	*After Fry left* Jean Gemähling to ERC, November 3, 1941, and Lotte Loeb to Werner Thormann, November 21, 1941, Thormann file.
202	*"The Consul found"* Kahn, *Generation in Turmoil*, 221–22.
202	*"a long stay"* DB, "Administrative Report, The Stages of the Committee's Development, Jan. to April 1941," Marseille, August 20, 1941, and Perpignan, September 3, 1941, VFP.
202	*They would have* Ibid.
202	*"third or fourth"* Ibid.
203	*"To Varian M. Fry"* Staff note to VF, July 4, 1941, VFP.

203 *"provocateurs" were trying* VF to EF, May 31, 1941, VFP.
203 *"framed on morals"* EF to VF, July 8, 1941, VFP.
203 *"not calculated to"* Ibid.
203 *"had no choice"* VF to EF, July 16, 1941, VFP.
204 *"indefinitely"* Ibid.
204 *"I can be"* VF to Frank Kingdon, July 15, 1941, VFP.
204 *"the Breton gentleman,"* VF to AOH, November 30, 1941, VFP.
204 *"You have caused"* VF, *Surrender on Demand,* 222.
204 *"Why are you"* VF to AOH, November 30, 1941, VFP.
204 *"In the new"* VF, *Surrender on Demand,* 223.
204 *"A day or so"* Ibid., 224.
204 *"tried to direct"* VF to AOH, November 30, 1941, VFP.
205 *"faithful and devoted"* VF to EF, August 5, 1941, VFP.
205 *"say a word"* VF to AOH, November 30, 1941, VFP.
205 *"Jews and anti-Nazis"* Ibid.
205 *He found Camilla* Pryor Dodge interview, April 14, 2000, and users.aol.com/pryordodge/ylla.html.
205 *Her first photo* Beaumont Newhall to ERC, December 31, 1940, Koffler file, GEC.
205 *When she heard* Ylla to "Dear Friends," August 28, 1940, Koffler file.
206 *"in immediate danger"* Beaumont Newhall to ERC, December 31, 1940, Koffler file.
206 *"The general uncertainty"* Ylla to "Dear Friends," September 8, 1940, Koffler file.
206 *"In my profession"* Ylla to art editor, *Vogue,* October 15, 1940, Koffler file.
206 *"I am doing"* Ylla to VF, March 12, 1941, Koffler file.
206 *Ylla photographed André* VF to Jean Gemähling, January 9, 1945, VFP.
206 *In February, Ylla* VF to EF, April 21, 1941, VFP, and VF to Ylla, February 1 and February 28, 1941, Koffler file.
206 *"one has to"* Ylla to "Dear Friends," September 13, 1940, Koffler file.
206 *"[E]ven if one"* Ylla to art editor, *Vogue,* October 15, 1940, Koffler file.
206 *"talented young photographer"* VF to Richard Allen, February 17, 1941, Koffler file.
206 *"the distribution of"* Ylla to VF, March 12, 1941, Koffler file.
207 *"[B]ring all the"* VF to Ylla, April 3, 1941, Koffler file.
207 *"You have already"* VF to Myles Standish, April 24, 1941, Koffler file.
207 *The visa came* Camilla Koffler to IRC, March 14, 1946, Koffler file.
207 *In June 1941,* Ibid.
207 *To his delight,* VF to Jean Gemähling, January 9, 1945, VFP.
207 *Between 1944 and 1954* Pryor Dodge interview, April 14, 2000.
207 *"hit her head"* Ibid.
207 *Since Ylla's death* users.aol.com/pryordodge/ylla.html.

CHAPTER ELEVEN: **EXPULSION**

208   *I've always thought*   AOH, quoted in epigraph to VF's *Surrender on Demand,* 1945.

208   *"and nothing that"*   VF to EF, August 14, 1941, VFP.

208   *"It was a"*   Ibid.

208   *"The weight of"*   Ibid.

209   *"nerve-wracking"*   Letter from VF to EF, October 1, 1941, VFP.

209   *"seventh heaven," then*   Letter from VF to EF, August 17, 1941, VFP.

209   (*Fry took sleeping*)   ARF interview, January 14, 1999.

209   *"We said no."*   Jean Gemähling interview, March 20, 1999.

209   *"non-combatant Jews."*   VF, *Surrender on Demand,* 225–226.

209   *"could sense" they*   Ibid.

209   *Bénédite returned to*   Letter from VF to AOH, November 30, 1941.

209   *"had been telephoning"*   Ibid.

209   **De Segonzac was*   VF, memo to Charles (Karel) Sternberg, June 21, 1965, VFP: "I found this, dated Hôtel Majestic, Cannes, Monday, August 19, 1941. 'So on Monday morning I left Sanary for Toulon, lunched there, and then took the "Micheline" along the coast to St. Tropes, where I stayed until Friday talking to Dunoyer de Segonzac the painter. (He is a member of the local Legion group and has the reputation of being a collaborationist). . . .'Contemporary documents are generally more reliable than memory. . . ."

209   **"his behavior during"*   DB, quoted in VF, memo to Charles (Karel) Sternberg, April 8, 1965, VFP. VF had dinner with DB on April 7, 1965, and took notes: "He insists that Segonzac was 'not what one could honestly call a collaborationiste.' He said that Segonzac's behavior during the occupation was not particularly heroic: he did not for instance join the Maquis. But then he was already 60 years old."

210   *"I was about"*   Charles (Karel) Sternberg interview, May 5, 1999.

210   *"He was quite"*   Jean Gemähling interview, March 20, 1998.

210   *"embarrassed but courteous"*   Lucie Heymann report about VF's arrest, n.d., VFP.

210   *"When he saw"*   Jean Gemähling interview, March 20, 1998.

210   *"speculated about Mr. Fry's"*   Lucie Heymann report.

210   *In the meantime*   "Account of the visit of MV [Marcel Verzeano] and PS [Paul Schmierer] to M. Fleury, Chief of Government Police of Marseille," n.d., VFP.

210   *"Mr. Fry had"*   Lucie Heymann report.

210   *That night, Fry*   Ibid.

210   *"unshaven and smiling"*   Ibid.

211   *Fry's police escort,*   Ibid.

211   *"make Mr. Fry's"*   Ibid.

211   *"exciting," and she*   Ibid.

211   *"[i]n true Goebbels'"*   VF, *Surrender on Demand,* 228.

211   *The group spent*   Lucie Heymann report.

211   *in the "Cooler."*   VF to AOH, November 30, 1941, VFP.

211 *"behind the scenes,"* DB, "Administrative Report, The Stages of the Committee's Development, Jan. to April 1941," Marseille, August 20, 1941, and Perpignan, September 3, 1941, VFP.

212 *"spent a [few]"* VF to AOH, November 30, 1941, VFP.

212 *"[o]ne way or"* Ibid.

212 *"a nice guy"* VF to DB, September 22, 1941, VFP.

212 *"a very decent"* VF to AOH, November 30, 1941, VFP.

212 "Nous ne sommes" Ibid.

212 *"a policeman preventing"* Ibid.

212 **"The [atomic] bomb"* "Admiral Leahy to President Harry S. Truman a few hours after Truman assumed the presidency on the death of Roosevelt, April 12, 1945. . . ." in Shafritz, *Words on War: Military Quotations from Ancient Times to the Present,* 287.

212 *"at the lush"* VF to DB, September 8, 1941, VFP.

212 *"in a special"* Gold, *Crossroads Marseilles 1940,* 306.

212 *"refused, feeling that"* VF to AOH, November 30, 1941, VFP.

212 *"stood side by"* VF to AOH, November 30, 1941, VFP.

213 *"was not importing"* VF to DB, September 30, 1941, VFP.

213 *"Barcelona burns its"* VF to DB, September 8, 1941, VFP.

213 *from "melancholy nostalgia."* Ibid.

213 *felt "[m]iserably depressed"* Ibid.

213 *"the faces of"* VF, *Surrender on Demand,* 232.

213 *"Already I feel"* VF to DB, September 8, 1941, VFP.

213 *We . . . have stood* Ibid.

213 *"too immersed in"* Letter from VF to DB, October 20, 1941, VFP.

213 *"bureaucrat" who enjoyed* Ibid.

213 *"to present myself"* Ibid.

214 *If you will* VF to EF, August 14, 1941, VFP.

214 *"Did you find"* EF to VF, September 7, 1941, VFP.

214 *"I think I"* Ibid.

214 *was "quite frightened"* EF to VF, August 22, 1941, VFP.

214 *"It is September"* VF to EF, September 7, 1941, VFP.

214 *"Now I am"* Ibid.

214–215 *It is not* Ibid.

215 *On October 1* VF to EF, October 1, 1941, VFP.

216 *Forced to wait* VF, *Surrender on Demand,* 234.

216 *Foreseeing the day* VF to EF, October 1, 1941, VFP.

216 *HICEM was sending* VF to DB, September 22, 1941, VFP.

216 *"[T]he thing has"* Ibid.

216 *"for a while"* Marcel Verzeano, note to author, August 26, 2000.

216 *"in a deplorable"* VF to DB, September 30, 1941, VFP.

216 *"hysterical by nature"* Ibid.

216 *"more and more"* VF to DB, September 22, 1941, VFP.

217 *"except in very"* Ibid.

217 *"got out two"* VF to DB, September 22, 1941, VFP.

217 *"Leahy Takes Fry"* Newspaper headline, quoted in EF to VF, September 7, 1941, VFP.

217 *"If anything unpleasant"* VF to EF, October 1, 1941, VFP.

217   *"new war on"*   Ibid.

217   *"the best days"*   VF to DB, September 22, 1941, VFP.

217   *Harold Oram had*   EF to VF, September 7, 1941, VFP.

217   *"which absorbs me"*   VF to EF, October 1, 1941, VFP.

218   *He ignored a*   EF to VF, September 7, 1941, VFP.

218   *"were demoralized and"*   DB, "Administrative Report, The Stages of the Committee's Development, Jan. to April 1941," Marseille, August 20, 1941, and Perpignan, September 3, 1941, VFP.

218   *"demoralized, nervous, even"*   DB, "Accessory Services Report," VFP.

218   *"Novices" at the*   Ibid.

218   *"too trusting, even"*   Ibid.

218   *"for the many"*   Sawin, *Surrealism in Exile and the Beginning of the New York School,* 143.

218   *fifteen thousand refugees*   "Resume of the Activity of the Center Rescue Service American Relief Center, Marseille," May 9, 1941, VFP.

218   *"The man in"*   VF, note to self, October 1941, Lisbon, VFP.

218   *"This dinner should"*   EF to VF, September 22, 1941, VFP.

218–219 *"I prefer the"*   VF to DB, October 31, 1941, VFP.

219   *I left my*   Ibid.

219   *I felt very*   All quotes, unless otherwise noted, are from an interview of Jacques Lipchitz by Bruce Bassett, Histor Systems, New York City (three hundred hours on film over a period of five years).

219   *Jacques Lipchitz was*   *Who's Who in America,* vol. 32, (1962–1963), 1873.

219–220 *"of immense power"*   Hilton Kramer, "Link to Heroic Period: Lipchitz, 'always a cubist,' was noted for the peculiar eloquence in his art," *The New York Times,* May 28, 1973.

220   *After returning to*   *Who's Who in America,* 1873.

222   *"He was concerned"*   Lolya Lipchitz interview, February 29, 2000.

222   *Fry arranged for*   Ibid.

222   *"In some ways"*   Jacques Lipchitz, remarks at memorial service for Varian Fry, November 8, 1967.

223   *"Lipchitz is the"*   VF to EF, July 16, 1941, VFP.

223   *Just before he*   Lolya Lipchitz interview, February 28, 2000.

CHAPTER TWELVE: **GOING HOME**

227   *. . . when I go*   Wouk, *Marjorie Morningstar,* 506.

227   *On November 2*   VF to DB, October 31, 1941, VFP.

227   *"I sometimes wonder"*   EF to VF, October 19, 1941, VFP.

227   *as Eileen's "boy."*   MDE interview, May 16, 1998.

227   *After Mrs. Roosevelt*   VF to DB, November 25, 1941, VFP.

228   *"attitudes," Kingdon wrote*   VF, Notes for letter to Frank Kingdon, January 1942, VFP.

228   *to "fight it."*   Ibid.

228   *"Am I to"*   Ibid.

228   *"which seem . . . particularly"* Ibid.
228   *"sore as a"* VF to DB, December 24, 1941, VFP.
228   *"will not hear"* VF to DB, January 20, 1942, VFP.
229   *"New York depresses"* VF to John Graham, November 10, 1941, VFP.
229   *"We are involved"* VF to DB, December 26, 1941, VFP.
229   *Then Kingdon announced* VF to DB, December 24, 1941, VFP.
229   *"the largest non-sectarian"* Leo Cherne, "A Note from Leo Cherne, Chairman Emeritus" in Dawson, *Flight: Refugees and the Quest for Freedom: The History of the International Rescue Committee, 1933–1993,* 9.
229   *"We claim Fry"* Reynold Levy interview, September 1998.
229   *"We* shall *succeed."* Ibid.
229   *"heart or courage"* Ibid.
229   *He found a* VF to Jean Gemähling, January 9, 1945.
229–230 *"Exercise the authority"* VF to DB, December 26, 1941, VFP.
230   *"It is folly"* VF to DB, October 2, 1941, VFP.
230   *"who was giving"* DB, "Activity Report/Refugees, Addenda to Administrative Report of Nov. 6, 1941," May 25, 1942, VFP.
230   *"military information about"* Gemähling interview, July 31, 1998.
230   *"I ran out"* Ibid.
230   *Gemähling was held* VF to Antoine de Saint-Exupéry, April 13, 1942, VFP.
230   *Fry, worried about* Ibid.
230   *"I still feel"* VF to DB, December 24, 1941, VFP.
230   *"jealous" feelings toward* VF to DB, May 12, 1942, VFP.
231   *"attractive studio apartment"* VF to DB, January 29, 1942, VFP.
231   *"like a fish"* Ibid.
231   *"extensive and specialized"* VF to Colonel Solberg, Office of Coordinator of Information, April 23, 1942, VFP.
231   *"probably the only"* "Memorandum for A.D., Concerning Varian Fry," April 30, 1942. Reproduced from the collections of the manuscript division, Library of Congress.
231   *"intelligent but highly"* Robert J. Ullmann to George K. Bowden, "Varian Fry and Chadbourne Gilpatrick," September 16, 1942, RG 226, E 136-A, box 3, folder 58-Fry, Varian, WASH-SI-OP-54, reproduced from the collections of the manuscript division, Library of Congress.
231   *"a considerable number"* Ibid.
231   *"drop" it if* VF to John R. Fleming, Deputy Director of Office of Facts and Figures, May 8, 1942, VFP.
231   *"If . . . I can"* VF to Herbert Lehman, Director of Foreign Relief and Rehabilitation, Department of State, December 22, 1942, VFP.
231   *This, too, did* Hiram Sibley, Foreign Relief and Rehabilitation, Department of State, to VF, January 28, 1943, VFP.
231–232 *"When I first"* VF to John Graham, June 22, 1942, VFP.
232   *"[T]he Department grants"* VF to DB, November 21, 1941, VFP.
232   *"stupidity . . . cruelty, indifference"* VF to DB, February 2, 1942, VFP.
232   *Lena Fischman visited* Lena Fischman Fagen to Lotte Loeb, October 27, 1941, VFP.
232   *"complain that they"* Ibid.

232   *"People in Washington"* VF, first draft, *Surrender on Demand*, VFP.

232   *"Do you know"* VF to Walter Mehring, February 10, 1942, VFP.

232–233 *"Perhaps we can get"* VF to DB, February 2, 1942, VFP.

232   **Duchamp emigrated that* VF, *Surrender on Demand*, 236.

233   *"full of people"* DB to VF, January 7, 1942, VFP.

233   *"our orphans"—would* Ibid.

233   *In 1942, the* VF's FBI file, #100-79262 and 94-46787; excerpts from "letter written by Max Diamant to VF, dated Lisbon 12/24/41, received 1/14/42"; Max Diamant to VF, "dated Lisbon Nov. 20, 1941, received Jan. 12, 1942"; and VF to Max Diamant, June 14, 1942, from files of U.S. National Censorship, stamped "Received, Office of the Chief, Passport Division, July 21, 1941, previous records 15021, 15829, 15890, disposal of original letter—released."

233   *"I'm afraid that"* VF to Albert Gerard, June 14, 1943, VFP.

233   *"certainly" could file* VF from Roger Baldwin, February 3, 1942, VFP.

233   *"grant civil internees"* VF to Breckinridge Long, December 4, 1941, VFP.

233   *Long dismissed his* Breckinridge Long to VF, January 29, 1941, VFP.

233   *"to the anti-Fascist"* VF to Chadbourne Gilpatric, National Headquarters of American Red Cross, May 19, 1942, VFP.

233–234 *"If I have"* VF to DB, October 7, 1942, VFP.

234   *"compensation," now that* VF to Théo Bénédite, May 19, 1942, VFP.

234   *"Report on Various"* "Report on Various Organizations and Individuals Engaged in Refugee Migration Activities, August 8, 1942," NA, Department of State Division of Communications and Records, (RG 59), General visa correspondence, 1940–45, files 811.111 refugees/ 2000–2149, box 159, folder 2055 ½, i.

234   *"A great danger"* Ibid., i–ii.

234   *"tricky, deceitful, and"* Ibid., vii.

234   *"used the channels"* Ibid., i.

234   *"the Emergency Rescue"* Ibid., 51.

234   *"Joe Schmaltz," and* Ibid., 1.

234   *"Fry tells Bénédite"* Ibid., 57.

235   *"born of concerns"* Smith, "Book Details U.S. Spying on Wartime Exiles from Germany," *The New York Times*, E 1.

235   *"dossier ran 1000"* Ibid.

235   *As Feuchtwanger lay* obituary, "Feuchtwanger, Novelist, Dead," *The New York Times*, December 23, 1958.

235   *he was questioned* Smith, "Book Details U.S. Spying on Wartime Exiles from Germany," *The New York Times*, E 1.

235   *"[Allen] Dulles and"* John C. Hughes, Coordinator of Information, OSS, to William Arthur Roseborough, July 3, 1942, VFP.

235   *But within a* F. L. Belin, OSS, memorandum, July 15, 1942, VFP.

235   *Misczyslav Bortenstein, a* VF to André Geraud, August 26, 1942, VFP.

235   *"red tape prevented"* Ibid.

235   *"because the birth"* Bill Freier to VF, March 19, 1943, VFP.

236   *"seeking a way"* VF to John S. Russell, June 3, 1942, VFP.

236   *"not enough to"* VF to DB, December 26, 1941, VFP.

236   *Unable to work*   Hans Natonek to VF, August 23, 1942, VFP.
236   *"oppose[d] the use"*   VF to Hans Natonek, March 4, 1942, VFP.
236   *"Don't fail to"*   VF to Anna Gruss, January 29, 1942, VFP.
236   *"Let me know"*   Ibid.
236–237 *"If she hasn't"*   VF to Anna Gruss, September 3, 1942, VFP.
237   *"Avoid . . . the use"*   VF to Mrs. Felice D'Antbourg Wohlmuth, April 13, 1942, VFP.
237   *"beat the world"*   VF to DB, June 1, 1942, VFP.
237   *"I have ranted"*   Ibid.
237   *Only decades later*   Bil Spira (Bill Freier) interview, August 1, 1998.
237   *The Centre Américain*   VF, *Surrender on Demand*, 236, and VF memorandum, September 25, 1942, VFP.
237   *The American embassy*   Ibid.
238   *"the Kingdon outfit"*   Assistant Secretary of State Adolf A. Berle, Jr., internal memorandum, August 10, 1942, VFP.
238   *"trying to help"*   Adolf A. Berle, Jr., memorandum re: "Possible Protection of Emergency Rescue Committee in Unoccupied France," August 18, 1942, VFP.
238   *He was informed*   Adolf A. Berle, Jr., to S. Barlow, November 2, 1942, VFP.
238   *Fry placed his*   VF memorandum, September 25, 1942, VFP.
238   *"continued to help"*   DB to IRC in New York, October 4, 1942, VFP.
238   *"the Centre Américain"*   Ibid.
238   *Bénédite formally closed*   Ibid.
238   *"1,500 persons who"*   DB, "Activity Report/Refugees, Addenda to Administrative Report of Nov. 6, 1941," May 25, 1942, VFP.
239   *"that we have"*   DB to IRC, October 4, 1942.
239   *were forever lost*   Charles (Karel) Sternberg interview, September 16, 1998.

CHAPTER THIRTEEN: *SURRENDER ON DEMAND*

240   *This is the*   VF, *Surrender on Demand*, 1997 edition, Boulder: Johnson Books, 241 (from original, unpublished foreword to 1945 edition).
240   *In November 1942*   Nicholas Kelley to VF, November 20, 1942, VFP.
240   *an "underground railroad"*   transcript of Isabella Manning Houston's broadcast, 2, VFP.
240   *"It wasn't long . . ."*   Ibid., 3.
241   *"as the man"*   Isadore Frankel, president, Laundry Workers International Union, to Isabella Manning Houston, December 23, 1942, VFP.
241   *"has prevented a"*   VF to Dr. Samuel McCrea Cavert, November 4, 1942, VFP.
241   *"The question of"*   Ibid.
241   *"public charge clause,"*   Defined in Fermi, *Illustrious Immigrants*, 26.

241   *American Red Cross*   Breckinridge Long to William Emerson, November 23, 1942, VFP.

241   *Long, citing the*   Ibid.

241   *"what is important"*   VF to DB, April 10, 1942, VFP.

241–242 *It is all*   VF, "Dear Werner," March 5, 1942, VFP.

242   *"always quarreling and"*   VF to Gemähling, January 9, 1945, VFP.

242   *"he left her"*   ARF memo to Esther Wojcicki and Walter Meyerhof, August 24, 1997.

242   *not "ecstatically happy"*   VF to DB, December 8, 1944, VFP.

242   *wanted to become*   VF to William C. Greene, September 24, 1942, VFP.

242   *An attempt to*   ARF interview, November 1, 2000.

242   *"The OSS held"*   VF to Marcel Verzeano, May 5, 1967, VFP.

242   *became an air-raid*   VF to Miss A. M. Hicks, Air Raid Warden, May 15, 1942, VFP.

242   *"still living and"*   VF to DB, April 10, 1942, VFP.

242   *focus on trivia*   VF to Whitehouse & Hardy, Inc., May 2, 1945, and VF to Jules C. Weiss and Co., January 10, 1946, VFP.

242   *"I am still"*   VF to DB, April 10, 1942, VFP.

242   *"The massacre of"*   VF to Heins Guradze, January 12, 1943, VFP

243   *According to a*   VF, "The Massacre of the Jews," *The New Republic,* December 21, 1942.

243   *During 1943, Fry*   VF to Jean Gemähling, January 9, 1945, VFP.

243   *became its executive*   VF to DB, December 8, 1944, VFP.

243   *of "psychogenic origin"*   VF to Gemähling, January 9, 1945, VFP.

244   *"[T]he doctor found"*   ARF memo to Esther Wojcicki and Walter Meyerhof, August 24, 1997.

244   *"starting life over"*   VF to Jean Gemähling, January 9, 1945, VFP.

244   *"allowed free speech"*   Assistant Secretary of State Adolf A. Berle, Jr., memorandum of conversation, May 3, 1944, NA.

244   *During the summer*   VF to Jean Gemähling, January 9, 1945, VFP.

244   *"will remind you"*   VF to Victor Serge, April 2, 1946, VFP.

244   *For Anna Caples*   VF, dedication to 1945 edition of *Surrender on Demand.*

244   *Fry showed his*   VF to Charles Joy, July 24, 1944, VFP.

244   *Just before Christmas*   DB radiogram to VF, November 22, 1944, VFP.

245   *"hardly dared hope"*   VF to Jean Gemähling, January 9, 1945, VFP.

245   *"It was as"*   Ibid.

245   *"relaying information back"*   Gold, *Crossroads Marseilles 1940,* 396.

245   *"the Milice, known"*   Ibid.

245   *wait six months,*   VF to Jacques Weisslitz, November 4, 1942, VFP.

245   *"Jacques deported Germany"*   DB to VF, November 22, 1944, VFP.

245   *"Was Jacques deported"*   VF to DB, n.d., VFP.

245   *"Jacques and wife"*   Théo Bénédite to VF, January 9, 1945, VFP.

245   *Fry was unable*   Representative Emily Taft Douglas, "Dear Mike," March 23, 1945, and VF to DB, April 5, 1945, VFP.

245–246 *"The publication of"*   Frank Kingdon, "Dear Friend," April 17, 1945, VFP.

246   *"not only a"*   Hermann Kesten to VF, April 28, 1945, VFP.

246   *Konrad Heiden and*   Konrad Heiden to VF, June 8, 1944, and Lion Feuchtwanger to VF, June 6, 1945, VFP.

246   *"which after one"*   Charlotte Feibel to VF, March 23, 1945, VFP.

246   *"an authentic adventure"*   *Bretano's Book Parade,* May 1945, VFP.

246   *"a good man"*   Russell Maloney, "Scarlet Pimpernel, Streamlined," *The New York Times,* April 22, 1945, VFP.

246   *"smuggling operations [that]"*   VF's response to a review of *Surrender on Demand,* July 22, 1945, VFP.

246   *"My attempts to"*   Ibid.

246   *"While this trickery"*   Reviewer's answer to VF's response, n.d., VFP.

247   *"Apparently I have"*   VF to Father H. A. Reinhold, June 22, 1945, VFP.

247   *"a neutral liberal"*   Laurent Jeanpierre interview, March 21, 1999.

247   *"the Party had"*   Ibid.

247   *founded the Liberal*   ARF interview, January 6, 1999.

247   *But he never*   Ibid.

247   *"more blatant abuses"*   VF to Bruce Bliven, March 30, 1945, VFP.

247–248 *"Frankly, it nauseates"*   Ibid.

248   *He no longer*   Ibid.

248   *"a coalition of"*   Samuel Sillen, "Resignations from Liberal Weeklies Show 2 Tendencies," *New Leader,* VFP.

248   *"effort to crush"*   Ibid.

248   *"extremely patriotic," "loved"*   ARF memo to Esther Wojcicki and Walter Meyerhof, August 24, 1997.

248   *"Mr. Roosevelt is"*   VF to Eleanor Roosevelt, April 26, 1945, VFP.

248   *"Incidentally, if you"*   John C. Hughes to David Shaw, May 2, 1945, NA.

249   *"enable the refugees"*   VF to Tom C. Clark, August 22, 1945, VFP.

249   *he also passed*   VF to DB, n.d., VFP.

249   *"a South American"*   Ibid.

249   *Clovis "couldn't wait."*   VF to Jean Gemähling, January 9, 1945, VFP.

249   *"The shelves of"*   VF to DB, n.d., VFP.

249   *But living alone*   ARF interview, January 6, 1999.

249   *He joined the*   Ibid.

249   *He generally found*   VF to Whitehouse & Hardy, Inc., May 2, 1945, and VF to Jules C. Weiss and Co., January 10, 1946, VFP.

249–250 *magazine politely dismissed*   *Saturday Review* to VF, March 26, 1946, VFP.

250   *"You and I"*   Eileen J. Garrett to VF, August 2, 1946, VFP.

250   *"Your magazine has"*   VF to Eileen J. Garrett, August 3, 1946, VFP.

250   *He served on*   ARF interview, January 6, 1999.

250   *"I wonder if you"*   VF to John Sheldon, October 4, 1945, VFP.

250   *"Of all the"*   Ibid.

250   *With loans from*   VF to Max Ascoli, May 7, 1946, VFP.

250   *he purchased Cinemart*   VF to Théo Bénédite, July 24, 1946, VFP.

250   *He quickly mastered*   ARF interview, January 6, 1999.

250   *"He invited me"*   Jim Hess interview, April 1, 1999.

250   *ignored her symptoms*   MDE interview, March 20, 1999.

251   *"at an open"* MDE note to ARF, n.d.
251   *Davenport, who worked* MDE interview, March 20, 1999.
251   *"I feel very"* Albert Einstein to EF, May 3, 1948, VFP.
251   *she died, on* ARF interview May 5, 1998, and EF obituary, *The New York Times,* May 13, 1948.
251   *"a happy memory"* Tribute to EF by Albert Einstein, May 13, 1948, VFP.

CHAPTER FOURTEEN: **THE FINAL YEARS**

252   *I have made* VF to Monsignor Paul Gerard Scolardi, n.d., VFP.
252   *"at all times"* ARF to Alice M. Greenwald, January 8, 1990, in note to author, October 31, 1998.
252   *"didn't suffer fools"* ARF note to author, December 20, 1999.
252   *"Also, he was"* ARF interviews (February 16, 1998, May 4, 1998, May 5, 1998, May 8, 1998, January 6, 1999, January 14, 1999, March 3, 1999, March 8, 1999, March 29, 1999, May 1, 2000, June 3, 2000).
252   *"was the mascot"* Ibid.
252–253 *Fry pronounced the* Ibid.
253   *"was mad to"* Ibid.
253   *he was dealt* Ibid.
253   *"close and sympathetic"* allegations against VF, quoted in Norman Thomas to Col. Victor W. Phelps, Army-Navy-Air Force Personnel Security Board, October 12, 1951, VFP.
253   *"information furnished" by* J. Edgar Hoover to VF, October 31, 1951, VFP.
253   *Fry enlisted several* Norman Thomas to VF, October 10, 1951, and Thomas to Col. Victor W. Phelps, October 12, 1951, VFP.
253   *and ACLU chairman* Roger Baldwin to Col. Victor W. Phelps, October 19, 1951, VFP.
253   *"Fry was cleared"* ARF to author, June 1993.
253   *"was gullible about"* ARF to author, n.d.
253   *"because he had"* ARF memo to Esther Wojcicki and Walter Meyerhof, August 24, 1997.
254   *earned his living* ARF to author, May 15, 1998.
254   *He also wrote* ARF to Joseph Stone and Tim Yohn (authors of *Prime Time and Misdemeanors*), October 20, 1994.
254   *"by mutual agreement,"* ARF, "Varian Fry Chronology, September 15, 1988, revised January 2, 1999."
254   *"he was running"* Ibid.
254   *had two children* Ibid.
254   *full-time "nursemaid"* VF to Senator Richard L. Neuberger, April 14, 1955, VFP.
254   *"He loved to"* ARF interviews.
254   *"On the contrary,"* ARF to author, July 5, 1997.

254   *"I don't believe"*   Ibid.

255   *"first and foremost"*   VF to Morris Ernst, April 3, 1953, VFP.

255   *"[T]here are few"*   VF to Walter Frank, January 8, 1956, VFP.

255   *"This is not"*   Ibid.

255   *"[h]er personal safety"*   Deposition, "Varian M. Fry, being duly sworn, deposes and says: I reside at 321 West 78th Street, New York . . . N.Y. I have been requested to give an expert opinion in the matter of *Miss Margot Wolff,* of New York, N.Y." 1955, VFP.

255   *"Had they gone"*   Ibid.

256   *"I can think"*   VF to Dr. Alexander Makinsky, October 27, 1955, VFP.

256   *joined the board*   ARF interviews.

256   *"horrified," her husband*   Ibid.

256   *"New York depressed"*   Ibid.

256   *dubbed "Fry's folly"*   Ibid.

256   *"was incredibly fussy"*   Kerstin Brown interview, May 1999.

256   *"I would say"*   ARF interviews.

257   *"There was an"*   Ibid.

257   *"I think what"*   Ibid.

257   *would not allow*   Richard Venus interview, May 1999.

257   *He became concerned*   VF to Alfred Kohlberg, American China Policy Association, April 15, 1958, VFP.

257   *"his behavior became"*   ARF interviews.

257   *"turned back to"*   Ibid.

257   *"bark like a"*   Kerstin Brown interview, May 1999.

257   *"first love, the"*   ARF to author, August 5, 1998.

257   *"They've been the"*   ARF to author, December 20, 1999.

258   *"very lucrative source"*   ARF interviews.

258   *"lord of the"*   Ibid.

258   *"for their contributions"*   "Committee and Club Honor Varian Fry For His Wartime Rescue of Refugees," *Wilton Bulletin,* May 22, 1963.

258   *"With Appreciation to"*   Ibid.

258   *"[Y]ou can imagine"*   Hans Sahl to VF, May 16, 1963, VFP.

258   *"difference of opinion"*   ARF interviews.

258   *"resist the urge"*   Joan Austin to author, September 21, 1998.

258   *"I have always"*   Ibid.

259   *"rather diffidently" hand*   Ibid.

259   *"He was constantly"*   ARF interviews.

259   *"He wanted to"*   ARF, memo, "Those consulting the Columbia University Fry Papers who have come across articles on Varian Fry by Donald Carroll and David Kerr," June 15, 1997.

259   *"I thought I"*   VF to DB, March 10, 1964, VFP.

259   *"commemorate the victims"*   Charles (Karel) Sternberg to M. N. Bulla, October 7, 1966, VFP, and IRC chronology of the Portfolio correspondence, "Art Portfolio 1964," "11/4/63—First offer of contract to Varian Fry, 1/16/64—Fry responds."

259   *selling the lithographs*   Charles (Karel) Sternberg interview, September 2, 1998.

259   *in a "portfolio"*   Ibid.

260   *"He was eager,"*   Ibid.

260   *Fry discussed the*   ARF interviews, and IRC chronology of the Portfolio correspondence, "2/24/64—Memo mentions for first time Aeneas theme."

260   *"the original displaced"*   Lieberman and Castleman, "Flight, a Suite of Eleven Original Lithographs and One Original Serigraph."

260   *It began well*   Charles (Karel) Sternberg interview, September 16, 1998, and IRC chronology of the Portfolio correspondence, "7/13/64—Letter thanking Lipchitz for his gift valued at $15,000.00."

260   *"quite his normal"*   ARF interviews.

260   *Annette was looking*   VF to Marcel Verzeano, January 19, 1964, VFP.

260   *"[Y]our life sounds"*   Ibid.

260   *"Varian came home"*   ARF interviews.

261   *sent "hysterical letters."*   Ibid.

261   *"He was brilliant"*   Ibid.

261   *joined the communist*   Encyclopædia Brittanica Online.

261   *"remember[ed] with gratitude"*   IRC chronology, "Art Project 1965," "Jan. 27—Fry meets with Mme. Masson who remembers with gratitude her flight with her husband to Martinique & US with an 'emergency' visa provided by IRC. She promises a litho from Masson."

261   *"Fry is depressed,"*   IRC chronology, "February . . . Fry is depressed. He seems distraught and looks for assurance that he has 'fulfilled his contract.' "

261   *"rejected" by Picasso*   VF to Jacques Lipchitz, March 1965, VFP.

261   *"To tell you"*   VF to Jacques Lipchitz, February 10, 1965, VFP.

261   *"lifelong companion," Denise*   IRC chronology, "March 15—Long correspondence regarding Wanda Landowska's 'lifelong companion,' Denise Restout's statement that the IRC never did anything for Landowska & therefore ruining chance of fund raising concert."

261   *"budget list" and*   VF to Charles (Karel) Sternberg, March 25, 1965, VFP.

261   *"away from her"*   Ibid.

261   *"positive" the operation*   VF to Charles (Karel) Sternberg, March 29, 1965, VFP.

262   *"honest promises" for*   IRC chronology, "March 23—From Sternberg—'We have honest promises from Lipchitz, Miro, Ernst, Masson, Giacometti, Kokoschka.' "

262   *"getting [the French]"*   IRC chronology, "March 18—Discussion of getting Legion of Honor for Varian Fry."

262   *Annette was working*   ARF interviews.

262   *Fry returned from*   ARF to author, August 5, 1998, and IRC chronology, "April—Fry back in US."

262   *In July, Fry*   VF to Charles (Karel) Sternberg, July 17, 1965, VFP.

262   *"turned back to"*   ARF to author, "Some thoughts on the puzzling VF personality," October 31, 1998.

262   *"batting his head"*   ARF interviews.

262   *"a legendary hero"*   Lipchitz to Picasso, "My Dear Pablo," n.d., VFP.

262–263 *"I see you are"*   Jacques Lipchitz to VF, March 5, 1965, VFP.

263   *"Above all, don't"*   Jacques Lipchitz to VF, July 17, 1965, VFP.
263   *"get some* money"   VF to Charles (Karel) Sternberg, October 31, 1965, VFP.
263   *Poet André Breton*   VF to Charles (Karel) Sternberg, November 14, 1965, VFP.
263   *Chagall, "the rat"*   VF to Lena Fischman Fagen, September 10, 1965, VFP.
263   *"Flight," a portfolio*   IRC brochure: "Flight, a suite of eleven original lithographs and one original serigraph, by Eugene Berman, Alexander Calder, Marc Chagall, Vieira da Silva, Adolph Gottlieb, Wifredo Lam, Jacques Lipchitz, Andre Masson, Joan Miro, Robert Motherwell, Edouard Pignon, Fritz Wotruba, International Rescue Committee, New York, 1971 . . . Each impression, except for the Chagall, is signed by the artist."
263   *"more and more"*   ARF interviews.
263   *"I remember coming"*   Ibid.
263   *"If you ever"*   Ibid.
263   *"Then he would"*   ARF interviews.
263   *he spent time*   Ibid.
263   *he introduced Jimmy*   VF to Charles (Karel) Sternberg, January 31, 1966, VFP.
263–264 *In the spring*   ARF interviews.
264   *"Happy to connect"*   Jean Gemähling interview, March 20, 1999.
264   *not "take this"*   ARF interviews.
264   *Fry felt ill*   Jean Gemähling interview, April 9, 1998, Survivors of the Shoah Visual History Foundation, Ozoir-la-Ferriere, France, 43104.
264   *"pathologically sensitive to"*   VF to Charles (Karel) Sternberg, August 30, 1966, VFP.
264   *to the hospital*   IRC chronology, "9/14—VF in hospital after mild heart attack."
264   *"the most up-bucking"*   VF to ARF, September 18, 1966, VFP.
264   *"Tell the kids"*   Ibid.
264   *"My first impulse"*   VF to Max Ernst, October 4, 1966, VFP.
265   *"to Blue Cross"*   ARF interviews.
265   *"I don't think"*   Jacques Lipchitz, quoted in ARF interviews.
265   *"I'm really frightened"*   ARF interviews.
265   *laundry list of*   ARF interviews, and VF to Charles (Karel) Sternberg, October 1, 1966, IRC chronology.
265   *"Furious" at Annette*   VF to Charles (Karel) Sternberg, October 1, 1966, IRC chronology.
265   *Sternberg advanced him*   VF to Charles (Karel) Sternberg, November 19, 1966, IRC chronology.
265   *"develop each chapter"*   VF to Marcel Verzeano, May 5, 1967, VFP.
265   *"I have only"*   Ibid.
265   *"pain . . . which follows"*   VF to ARF, September 18, 1966, VFP.
265   *"to tension . . . due"*   VF to Charles (Karel) Sternberg, January 31, 1967, IRC chronology.
265   *"virtually bedridden" with*   VF to Jacques Lipchitz, March 6, 1967, VFP.

265 *"I started active"* VF to Charles (Karel) Sternberg, February 20, 1967, VFP.

266 *"that old charlatan"* Ibid.

266 **"touched on Chagall's"* Charles (Karel) Sternberg, letter to the editor, *The New York Times Book Review,* November 26, 1978.

266 *"I am at last"* VF to Johannes Skancke Martens, April 7, 1967, VFP.

266 *"I made it"* Ibid.

266 *"good party with"* VF to Marcel Verzeano, May 5, 1967, VFP.

266 *My two boys* VF to AG "[most likely Anna Gruss]," July 14, 1967, VFP.

266 *"he wasn't getting"* ARF interviews.

266 *"separating and divorcing"* VF to Caleb Gray, July 15, 1967, VFP.

266 *"She is a"* ARF interviews and VF to "AG," July 14, 1967, VFP.

266 *"You are just"* ARF interviews.

267 *Lawyers drew up* Ibid.

267 *"I have not"* VF to Josephine Rogers, May 15, 1967, VFP.

267 *"rough it out"* VF to Caleb Gray, July 15, 1967, VFP.

267 *"were being poisoned"* ARF interviews.

267 *"strange headaches, attacks"* ARF, "Varian Fry Chronology, Sept. 15, 1988, revised Jan. 2, 1999," entry for August 23, 1967.

267 *"the manic, cold"* ARF, "Varian Fry Chronology, Sept. 15, 1988, revised Jan. 2, 1999," entry for Tuesday, August 29, and ARF interviews.

268 *"together for a"* Ibid., entry for Sunday, September 3.

268 *By the time* Ibid., entry for Monday, September 4, Labor Day.

268 *"He was terribly"* Kerstin Brown, quoted in Ibid., entry for Friday, September 8.

268 *Monday, September 11* Ibid., entry for Monday, September 11.

268 *"He told me"* Marcel Verzeano to Tom Fry, January 8, 1968, quoted in Ibid.

269 *When Fry did* ARF, "Varian Fry Chronology, Sept. 15, 1988, revised Jan. 2, 1999," entry for Wednesday, September 13.

AFTERWORD

270 *Dear Mary Jayne* ARF to Mary Jayne Gold, September 13, 1967.

270 *"helped intellectuals flee"* "Varian M. Fry, 59, Who Helped Intellectuals Flee Nazis, Is Dead," *The New York Times,* Thursday, September 13, 1967.

270 *"writer and teacher"* "Varian M. Fry, Dies at Age 59, Aided Refugees," *Ridgefield Press,* September 14, 1967, 1.

270 *Friends, former protégés* ARF interviews.

270 *"In some ways"* Jacques Lipchitz to ARF, September 22, 1967.

270 *"was that rarest"* MDE to Annette, Sylvia, Thomas and James Fry, November 2, 1967.

270 *"arrived in France"* DB to Thomas, Sylvia, and James Fry, September 19, 1967.

271 *"The saddest and"* ARF to DB, September 15, 1967.

271   *"did not consider"*   ARF to author, March 1, 2001.

271   *"talked of this"*   ARF to DB, September 15, 1967.

271   *"cerebral vascular accident"*   ARF interviews.

271   *"he was always"*   Ibid.

271   *"adored him [but]"*   Ibid.

271   *"Tom is shooting"*   Ibid.

271   *"just ran away"*   Ibid.

272   *"had a lot"*   Ibid.

272   *"He was so"*   Ibid.

272   *Fry became the*   "Israel Honors Wartime Savior," *Ridgefield Press,* August 4, 1994, and "Only US Righteous Gentile Honored," *The Jerusalem Post,* February 6, 1996.

272   *"When we honor"*   Mordecai Paldiel, director of Yad Vashem's Department for the Righteous, quoted in Robert Grabar, "Ridgefield Man Saved Thousands," A-1.

272   *"Fry was different"*   Grabar, A-1.

272   **With the declassification*   Stout, "U.S. Knew Early of Nazi Killings in Asylums, Official Documents Show," A 14. ". . . On October 16, 1940, Vice Consul Paul H. Dutko cabled that information to his superiors at the American Embassy in Berlin and the State Department in Washington. . . . Documents, including Mr. Dutko's cable . . . seem to show that high American officials knew, or should have known, about the killings by late 1940, if not before. . . . Among the earliest documents discovered . . . was a Feb. 23, 1940, memorandum to Secretary of State Cordell Hull from Assistant Secretary Adolf A. Berle, Jr. Mr. Berle told of reports from the embassy in Berlin that Jews were being sent to 'unnamed concentration camps' in Poland. 'I see no reason why we should not make our feelings known regarding a policy of seemingly calculated cruelty which is beginning to be apparent now,' Mr. Berle said. (It was not yet known that the camps would soon be extermination centers.) One of Mr. Berle's colleagues, Assistant Secretary Breckinridge Long, wrote that he was 'thoroughly in sympathy with the sentiment' in Mr. Berle's memorandum. But, he went on, 'this is a question entirely within the power of Germany,' and he warned against any action that might involve the United States in the war in Europe."

272   *"We come to"*   "Remarks by Secretary of State Warren Christopher following ceremony honoring American Varian Fry, Yad Vashem, Feb. 5, 1996," press release issued by Office of the spokesman, U.S. State Department, February 5, 1996.

273   *"contributions and efforts"*   New York State Assembly Resolution L 2733 introduced by Assemblyman John J. McEneny, 2000.

273   *"I feel sad"*   Walter Meyerhof interview, December 3, 1997.

273   *"like a racehorse"*   Jacques Lipchitz remarks at Memorial Service for VF, November 8, 1967, as recalled by Lucy Burchard in note to ARF.

Bibliography

BOOKS

Anderson, Mark M., ed. *Hitler's Exiles: Personal Stories of the Flight from Nazi Germany to America*. New York: The New Press, 1998.

Arnason, H. H. *Jacques Lipchitz: Sketches in Bronze*. New York: Frederick A. Praeger Publishers, 1969.

Barron, Stephanie, with Saline Eckmann. *Exiles & Emigrés, The Flight of European Artists from Hitler*. Los Angeles: Museum Association, Los Angeles County Museum of Art, 1997.

Benitez, Helena. *My Life with Wifredo Lam: 1939–1950*. Lausanne: Acatos Publisher, 1999.

Benjamin, Walter, ed. by Hannah Arendt. *Illuminations*. Translated by Harry Zahn. New York: Harcourt, Brace & World, 1968.

Berczeller, Richard. *Displaced Doctor*. New York: Odyssey Press, 1964.

Block, Gay, and Malka Drucker. *Rescuers: Portraits of Moral Courage in the Holocaust*. Preface by Cynthia Ozick. New York: Holmes & Meier Publishers, Inc., 1992.

Bohm-Duchen, Monica. *Chagall*. (Art and Ideas Series.) London: Phaidon Press Limited, 1998.

A Book of Tribute to Varian Fry. A collection of various authors issued by the U.S. Holocaust Memorial Council on the occasion of Fry's posthumous Eisenhower Liberation Medal, 1991.

Chester, Eric Thomas. *Covert Network: Progressives, the International Rescue Committee and the CIA*. New York: M. E. Sharpe, 1995.

Dawidowicz, Lucy S. *The War Against the Jews 1933–1945*. New York: Bantam, 1991.

Dawson, Mark. *Flight: Refugees and the Quest for Freedom: The History of the International Rescue Committee, 1933–1993*. New York: IRC, 1993.

Dortsch, Virginia M. *Peggy Guggenheim and Her Friends*. Milano: Berenice Art Books, 1994.

Enoch, Kurt. *Memoirs of Kurt Enoch*. Privately printed by his wife, Margaret M. Enoch, 1984.

Ernst, Jimmy. *A Not-So-Still Life: A Memoir*. New York: St. Martin's Press, 1984.

Farmer, Paul. *Vichy: Political Dilemma*. New York: Columbia University Press, 1955.

Feingold, Henry L. *The Politics of Rescue: The Roosevelt Administration and the Holocaust, 1938–1945*. New Brunswick, N.J.: Rutgers University Press, 1970.

Fermi, Laura. *Illustrious Immigrants: The Intellectual Migration from Europe 1930–1941*. Chicago: University of Chicago Press, 1968.

Feuchtwanger, Lion. *The Devil in France: My Encounter with Him in the Summer of 1940*. Translated by Elisabeth Abbott. New York: The Viking Press, 1941.

Fittko, Lisa. *Escape through the Pyrenees*. Translated by David Koblick. Evanston, Ill.: Northwestern University Press, 1991.

———. *Solidarity and Treason: Resistance and Exile, 1933–1940*. Translated by Roslyn Theobold. Evanston, Ill.: Northwestern University Press, 1993.

Foster, Norman. *Humanism and America*. New York: Farrar, Straus & Giroux, 1930.

Fry, Annette R. *The Orphan Trains*. New York: New Discovery Books, 1994.

Fry, Varian. *Bricks Without Mortar: The Story of International Cooperation*. New York: Foreign Policy Association, 1938.

———. *The Children's Migration*, unpublished memoir.

———. *The Children's Summer Home*, unpublished memoir.

———. *The Peace That Failed: How Europe Sowed the Seeds of War*. New York: Foreign Policy Association, 1939.

———. *Surrender on Demand*. New York: Random House. 1945.

Gardiner, Muriel. *Code Name "Mary"—Memoirs of an American Woman in the Austrian Underground*. New Haven: Yale University Press, 1983.

Gold, Mary Jayne. *Crossroads Marseilles 1940*. New York: Doubleday and Company, Inc., 1980.

Goodwin, Doris Kearns. *No Ordinary Time: Franklin and Eleanor Roosevelt: The Home Front in World War II*. New York: Simon & Schuster, 1994.

Greenbaum, Leonard. *The Hound and Horn: The History of a Literary Quarterly*. The Hague, Netherlands: Mouton & Company, Publishers, 1966.

Hamovitch, Mitzi Berger, ed. *The Hound & Horn Letters*. Foreword by Lincoln Kirstein. Athens: University of Georgia Press, 1982.

Heilbut, Anthony. *Exiled in Paradise: German Refugee Artists and Intellectuals in America from the 1930s to the Present*. New York: Viking Press, 1983.

Hirschman, Albert O. *A Propensity to Self-Subversion*. Cambridge, Mass.: Harvard University Press, 1995.

Hope, Henry R. *The Sculpture of Jacques Lipchitz*. New York: Museum of Modern Art, 1954.

Jackman, Jarrell C., and Carla M. Borden, eds. *The Muses Flee Hitler: Cultural Transfer and Adaptation, 1930–1945*. Washington, D.C.: Smithsonian Institution Press, 1983.

Kahn, Frida. *Generation in Turmoil*. Great Neck, N.Y.: Channel Press, Inc., 1960.

Katz, Ephraim. *The Film Encyclopedia: The Most Comprehensive Encyclopedia of World Cinema in a Single Volume*. New York: HarperCollins, 1994.

Kirstein, Lincoln. *Mosiac: Memoirs*. New York: Farrar, Straus & Giroux, 1994.

Koestler, Arthur. *Scum of the Earth*. London: Hutchinson, 1968.

Levenstein, Aron. *Escape to Freedom: The Story of the International Rescue Committee*. Westport, Conn.: Greenwood Press, 1983.

McCarthy, Mary. *On the Contrary*. New York: Farrar, Straus and Cudahy, 1961.

Marrus, Michael R., and Robert O. Paxton. *Vichy France and the Jews*. New York: Schocken Books, 1983.

Mehring, Walter. *No Road Back*. Translated by S. A. deWitt. New York: Samuel Curl, Inc., 1944.

Morse, Arthur D. *While Six Million Died: A Chronicle of American Apathy*. London: Secker & Warburg, 1968.

Parini, Jay. *Benjamin's Crossing*. New York: Henry Holt & Company, 1997.

Paxton, Robert O. *Vichy France: Old Guard and New Order, 1940–1944*. New York: Alfred A. Knopf, 1972.

Persico, Joseph E. *Piercing the Reich: The Penetration of Nazi Germany by American Secret Agents During World War II*. New York: The Viking Press, 1979.

Rubenstein, William. *The Myth of Rescue*. London: Routledge, 1997.

Ryan, Donna. *The Holocaust & the Jews of Marseilles: The Enforcement of Anti-Semitic Policies in Vichy France*. Urbana: University of Illinois Press, 1996.

Sahl, Hans. *The Few and the Many*. Translated by Richard and Clara Winston. New York: Harcourt, Brace & World, 1962.

———. *In Search of Myself*. New York: Putnam, 1994.

Sawin, Martica. *Surrealism in Exile and the Beginning of the New York School*. Cambridge, Mass.: The MIT Press, 1995.

Serge, Victor. *Memoirs of a Revolutionary, 1901–1941*. Translated by Peter Sedgwick. London: Oxford University Press, 1963.

Shafritz, Jay M. *Words on War: Military Quotations from Ancient Times to the Present*. New York: Prentice Hall, 1990.

Sheets, Tara E., ed. *Encyclopedia of Associations: An Associations Unlimited Reference*, vol. 1. Detroit: Gale Group, 2000.

Spinelli, Ingrid Warburg. *Die Dringlichkeit des Mitleids und die Einsamkeit, nein zu sagen*. [The Need for Compassion and the Loneliness of Saying "No."] Hamburg: Dolling und Galitz Verlag, 1990.

Stephan, Alexander. *"Communazis": FBI Surveillance of German Emigré Writers*. Translated by Jan van Heurck. New Haven and London: Yale University Press, 2000.

A Tribute to Jacques Lipchitz: Lipchitz in America: 1941–1973. New York: Marlborough Gallery, Inc., 1973.

Weisberger, Edward, ed. *Surrealism: Two Private Eyes*. New York: Guggenheim Museum Publications, 1999.

Weld, Jacqueline Bogard. *Peggy, the Wayward Guggenheim*. New York: Dutton, 1986.

Werfel, Franz. *The Song of Bernadette.* Translated by Ludwig Lewisohn. New York: The Viking Press, 1942.

Who's Who in America. Chicago: Marquis Publications, 1962–63, vol. 32.

Wouk, Herman. *Marjorie Morningstar.* Garden City, N.Y.: Doubleday & Company, 1955.

Wyman, David S. *The Abandonment of the Jews.* New York: Pantheon Books, 1984.

———. *Paper Walls: America and the Refugee Crisis, 1938–1941.* New York: Pantheon Books, 1985.

Young-Bruehl, Elisabeth. *Hannah Arendt: For Love of the World.* New Haven: Yale University Press, 1982.

Zuckmayer, Carl. *A Part of Myself: Portrait of an Epoch.* New York: Harcourt Brace Jovanovitch, 1966.

———. *Second Wind.* Translated by Elizabeth Reynolds Hapgood. New York: Doubleday, Doran and Company, 1940.

ARTICLES

Abrams, Irwin. "The Multinational Campaign for the Nobel Peace Prize for Carl von Ossietzky." Paper presented at the International Conference: "Peace Movements 1919–1939. A Comparative Study." Stadtschlaining, Austria, September 1991.

Barr, Margaret Scolari. "Our Campaigns. Alfred H. Barr, Jr., and the Museum of Modern Art: A Biographical Chronicle of the Years 1930–1944." *The New Criterion,* special issue, summer 1987.

———. "Rescuing Artists in World War II." Ms., revised January 1, 1980.

Bingham, Lucretia. "Uncle Harry's Secret." *Northeast Magazine, Hartford Courant,* May 14, 2000.

Boehmer, George. "Remains of Hitler Aide Put to Sea." *The New York Times,* August 31, 1999.

Brandon, Ruth. "Surreal Lives." *The New York Times Book Review,* October 3, 1999, p. 26.

Burton, Linette. "Varian Fry: A Many-Sided Man: Writer, Teacher, Naturalist." *Ridgefield Press,* February 22, 1962, second section, p. 1.

Buruma, Ian. "The Vichy Syndrome." *Tikkun,* January–February 1995, vol. 10, no. 1, p. 44 (10).

"Celebrating Varian Fry's WW II Works." *Observer,* February/March 1998, p. 1.

Cook, Blanche Wiesen. "Underground Railroad." *The Nation,* April 6, 1998, p. 32.

Ebel, Miriam Davenport. *An Unsentimental Education.* Unpublished memoir, 1997, revised 1999.

Deal, Renee. "Shining a Light on an Unsung Hero." *Country Almanac,* October 1, 1997.

Dumas, Alan. "American Schindler." *Rocky Mountain News,* April 27, 1998, section D, p. 6.

Farber, Murray. "A Hero Among Us." *Alumni News Fairfield University,* October 1, 1997, p. 12.

Feuchtwanger, Lion. "The Grandeur and Misery of Exile." *Das Wort,* 1938. Reprinted in Mark M. Anderson, ed., *Hitler's Exiles: Personal Stories of the Flight from Nazi Germany to America.* New York: The New Press, 1998.

Figgatt, Bonnie. "Holocaust Survivor Speaks to RHS Students." *Ridgefield Press,* December 1998.

Folkart, Burt A. "Marta Feuchtwanger, Widow of Famous Novelist, Dies." *Los Angeles Times,* October 30, 1987.

Frankel, Max. "Pimpernel of the Press." *The New York Times Magazine,* November 23, 1997.

Fry, Varian. "The Massacre of the Jews." *The New Republic,* December 21, 1942.

———. "Operation Emergency Rescue." *The New Leader,* 1965.

Gannett, Lewis. "Books and Things." (Review of *Surrender on Demand.*) *New York Herald-Tribune,* May 1, 1945.

Glueck, Grace. "Lam's Demons at the Matisse." *The New York Times,* June 4, 1982.

Goodyear, Julie. *American Rescuers: Varian Fry.* Ms. of unpublished thesis.

Graber, Robert. "Ridgefield Man Saved Thousands." *Danbury News Times,* August 7, 1994, section A, p. 1.

Hughes, Robert. "A Cultural Gift from Hitler." *Time,* March 24, 1997.

Isenberg, Barbara. "Fry's List: The Artists." *Los Angeles Times,* December 14, 1997, p. 9.

"Israel Honors Wartime Savior." *Ridgefield Press,* August 4, 1994.

"It's Not Too Late." Editorial, *Los Angeles Times,* February 7, 1996.

Jacobs, Jack. "A Friend in Need: The Jewish Labor Committee and Refugees from the German-Speaking Lands, 1933–1945." *YIVO Annual,* vol. 23, 1996. Edited by Deborah Dash Moore. Northwestern University Press and the YIVO Institute for Jewish Research.

Judt, Tony. "France Without Glory," *The New York Review of Books,* May 23, 1996, vol. 43, issue 9, start page 39.

Kassof, Anita. *Intent and Interpretation: The German Refugees of Article 19 of the Franco-German Armistice 1940–1941.* Master's thesis, University of Maryland, 1992.

Kazin, Alfred. "Homage to Varian Fry." *The New Republic,* February 9, 1998, p. 27.

Keller, Ernest F. "Bird Surgery on a Waxwing." *New York Zoological Society Bulletin,* May 1919.

Kerr, David. "An American Schindler?" *Daily Telegraph,* March 3, 1998.

Kramer, Jane. "Profiles: Helen Wolff." *The New Yorker,* August 2, 1982, p. 54.

Kramer, Hilton. "Link to Heroic Period: Lipchitz, 'always a cubist,' was noted for the peculiar eloquence in his art," *The New York Times,* May 28, 1973.

Langlois, Walter G. "Malraux, 1941–42: Under the Nazi Shadow in Southern France." *Columbia Library Columns,* vol. 20, no. 1, November 1970.

Lerner, Barbara. "A Michelin Noir." *Commentary,* vol. 101, issue 5, pp. 49–53, 1996. New York: American Jewish Committee.

Lieberman, William S., and Riva Castleman. Introduction to "Flight, a Suite of Eleven Original Lithographs and One Original Serigraph." International Rescue Committee, New York, 1971.

McCabe, Cynthia. "Wanted." From Jackman, *The Muses Flee Hitler.*

Maloney, Russell. "Scarlet Pimpernel, Streamlined," *The New York Times*, April 22, 1945.

Martineau, Janet I. "Assignment Rescue." *Saginaw News*, April 25, 1997, section C.

Meyerhof, Walter, "An Episode Missing from *Escape Through the Pyrenees* by Lisa Fittko." Unpublished manuscript.

Nelson, Cary. "The Aura of the Cause: Photographs from the Spanish Civil War." *The Antioch Review*, June 1, 1997.

"Only US Righteous Gentile Honored." *The Jerusalem Post*, February 6, 1996.

Pfefferman, Naomi. "The American Schindler." *The Jewish Journal*, February 28–March 6, 1997, p. 10.

Pridmore, Jay. "Paying Tribute." *Chicago Tribune Museum Review*, April 24, 1998.

Russell, John. "Max Ernst: Catalytic Figure in 20th Century Art Dies," *The New York Times*, April 2, 1976.

Sanders, Jack. "Assignment Rescue 2." *Ridgefield Press Dedication*, 1997.

Simon, John. "Mann and 'Super Mann,' " a review of *Letters of Heinrich and Thomas Mann, 1900–1949*." *The New York Times Book Review*, April 12, 1998, p. 12.

Smith, Dinitia. "Book Details U.S. Spying on Wartime Exiles from Germany." *The New York Times*, August 30, 2000, section E, p. 1.

Steinfels, Peter. "For the Young, a Lesson in the Acts of the 'Righteous Gentiles,' Who Defied the Holocaust." Beliefs column, *The New York Times*, May 12, 1990.

Stout, David. "U.S. Knew Early of Nazi Killings in Asylums, Official Documents Show." *The New York Times*, July 29, 1999, section A, p. 14.

Trueheart, Charles. "Smuggler of the Lost Souls." *Washington Post Foreign Service*, May 16, 2000.

Urrows, Henry & Elizabeth. "Varian Fry." *Harvard Magazine*, March/April 1990, pp. 43–46.

Zweig, Paul. "A Good Man in a Bad Time." *The New York Times*, October 24, 1982, section 7, p. 1.

DOCUMENTARIES AND FILMS

The Artists' Schindler. BBC-TV documentary, August 1997.

"Assignment: Rescue, the Story of Varian Fry and the Emergency Rescue Committee. Produced by the Varian Fry Foundation of the International Rescue Committee, 1997.

Das Letzte Visum (The Last Visa). A film by Karin Alles, 1988.

An Evening of Tribute to Varian Fry. Sponsored by the United States Holocaust Memorial Fund, April 10, 1991.

The Exiles. Produced by Richard Kaplan in association with WNET/New York, 1989. Distributed by Richard Kaplan Productions/WNET.

Lisa Fittko: But We, We Said, We Will Not Surrender. A film by Constanze Zahn, © 1998. English translation by Nick Grindell.

Marseilles-New York: L'Etat de Piège ou La Filière Marseillaise. Written and directed by Teri Wehn-Damisch, 1987.

Villa Air Bel: Varian Fry in Marseille, 1940/41. Directed by Jorg Bundschuh, 1987. Distributed by Exportfilm Bischoff GmbH.

ARCHIVAL COLLECTIONS

Deutsches Exil Archiv 1933–1945, Die Deutsche Bibliothek.

Exiles Film Project Records, Beinecke Rare Book and Manuscript Library, Yale University.

The German Emigre Collection, M. E. Grenander Department of Special Collections and Archives, SUNY Albany.

National Archives, Washington, D.C.: general records of the Department of State (RG59), files 840.48 Refugees and 811.111 Refugees.

Survivors of the Shoah Visual History Foundation

Varian Fry Papers, Rare Book and Manuscript Library, Columbia University, New York, N.Y.

Washington National Records Center, Suitland, Md.: Records of the Department of State visa division (RG59), files 811.111 Refugees.

Index

ABOUT THE AUTHOR

SHEILA ISENBERG is the author of *Women Who Love Men Who Kill* and co-author, with William M. Kunstler, of *My Life as a Radical Lawyer.* A former reporter, she teaches English at Marist College and lives in upstate New York with her husband.

ABOUT THE TYPE

This book was set in Galliard, a typeface designed by Matthew Carter for the Merganthaler Linotype Company in 1978. Galliard is based on the sixteenth-century typefaces of Robert Granjon.